THE DEFENDERS

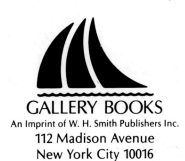

GALLERY BOOKS
An Imprint of W. H. Smith Publishers Inc.
112 Madison Avenue
New York City 10016

THE DEFENDERS

A COMPREHENSIVE GUIDE TO THE WARPLANES OF THE USA

© Aerospace Publishing 1990

First published in the United States in 1988 by Gallery Books,
an imprint of W.H. Smith Publishers, Inc.,
112 Madison Avenue, New York, New York 10016

This edition published in 1990

Gallery Books are available for bulk purchase for sales
promotions and premium use. For details write or telephone
the Manager of Special Sales, W.H. Smith Publishers, Inc.,
112 Madison Avenue, New York, New York 10016. (212) 532-6600

Printed in Italy

ISBN: 1-870318-10-2

ISBN: 0-8317-2181-2

Pictures were supplied by:

Robin Adshead, Agusta 177, Beech, Bell Helicopters, Boeing
Aerospace, Austin J. Brown, Philip Chinnery, Danish Air Force, David
Donald, Malcolm English, Peter R. Foster, (via) Rene J. Francillon,
Gates, General Dynamics, Grumman History Center, Grumman
Aerospace Corporation, Paul A. Jackson, A. J. Johnson, Jon Lake,
Robert L. Lawson Collection, Lockheed, Bob Munro, McDonnell
Douglas, R.J. Pickett, Lindsay Peacock, Stephen Piercey via Austin J.
Brown, Chris Pocock, John D. R. Rawlings, Terry Senior, Robbie Shaw,
US Air Force, US Army, US Marine Corps, US Navy, Roger P. Wasley.

Special thanks to TRH Pictures and Mike Hooks.

Production editor: Chris Marshall

Design: Brown Packaging

Title page: A line of USAF F-16s.

Opposite: A Grumman EA-6B.

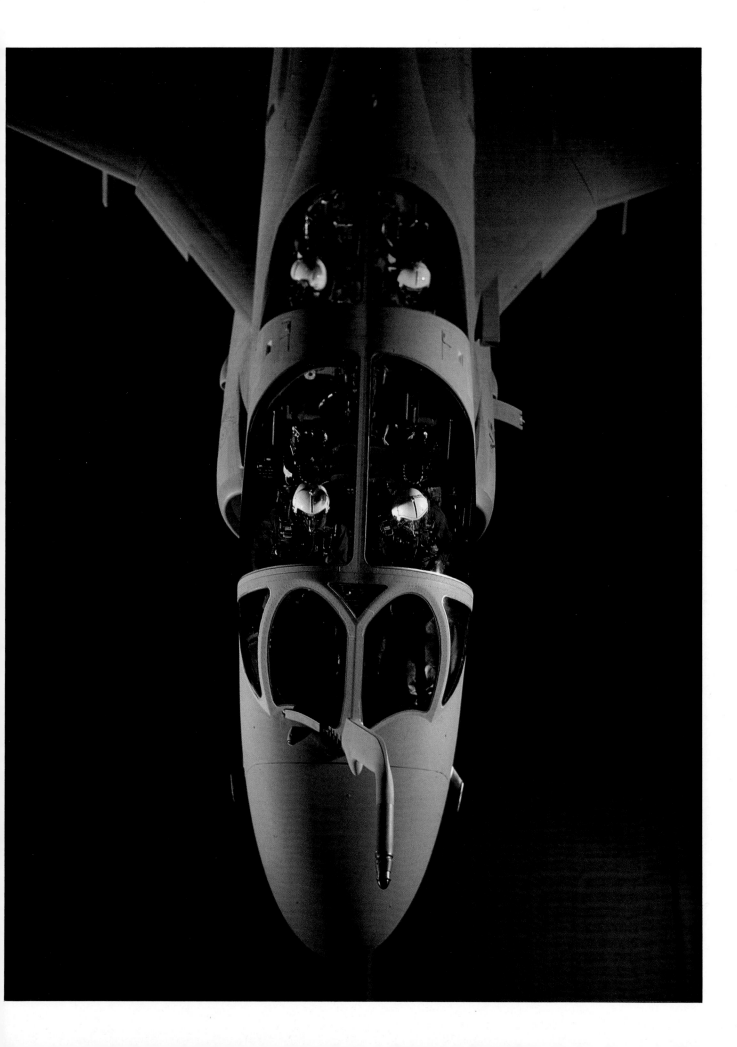

CONTENTS

AIRCRAFT BY ROLE

GLOSSARY

AABNCP Advanced Airborne National Command Post
AAFSS Advanced Aerial Fire–Support System
AAH Advanced Attack Helicopter
AAM Air-to-Air Missile
AAS Aeromedical Airlift Squadron
AB Air Base
ABCP AirBorne Command Post
ACCS Airborne Command and Control Squadron
ADF Air Defense Fighter
ADU Auxiliary Display Unit
AdvCap Advanced Capability
A&AEE Aeroplane and Armament Experimental Establishment
AEW Airborne Early Warning
AFB Air Force Base
AFCC Air Force Communications Command
AFRes Air Force Reserve
AFSATCOM Air Force Satellite Communications
AFTI Advanced Fighter Technology Integration
AFV Armoured Fighting Vehicle
AGM Air-to-Ground Missile
AH Attack Helicopter
AHIP Army Helicopter Improvement Program
AHRS Attitude and Heading Reference System
ALCM Air-Launched Cruise Missile
AMRAAM Advanced Medium-Range Air-to-Air Missile
AMSA Advanced Manned Strategic Aircraft
ANG Air National Guard
AOA Angle of Attack
APU Auxiliary Power Unit
ARBS Angle-Rate Bombing Set
ARIA Advanced Range Instrumentation Aircraft
ARM Anti-Radiation Missile
ARRS Aerospace Rescue and Recovery Service
ASARS Advanced Synthetic Aperture Radar System
ASD Aeronautical Systems Division
ASM Air-to-Surface Missile
ASPJ Airborne Self-Protection Jammer
ASRAAM Advanced Short-Range Air-to-Air Missile
ASV Anti-Surface Vessel
ASW Anti-Submarine Warfare
ATAF Allied Tactical Air Force
ATF Advanced Tactical Fighter
AUW All-Up Weight
AWACS Airborne Warning And Control System

CAF Canadian Armed Forces
CAG Canadian Air Group
CAP Combat Air Patrol
CFRP Carbonfiber Reinforced Plastic
CFT Conformal Fuel Tank
CILOP Conversion In Lieu Of Procurement
COD Carrier Onboard Delivery
COIN Counter Insurgency
Comint Communications intelligence
CONUS Continental United States (of America)
CORDS Coherent On Receive Doppler System
COSIRS Covert Survivable In-weather Reconnaissance and Strike
CRT Cathode Ray Tube

DARPA Defense Advanced Research Project Agency
DF Direction-Finding
DFE Derivative Fighter Engine
DoD Department of Defense
DT & E Development Test and Evaluation

ECCM Electronic Counter-Counter Measures
ECM Electronic CounterMeasures
EFIS Electronic Flight Information System
Elint Electronic intelligence
EO Electro-Optical
ERCS Emergency Rocket Communications System
ESM Electronic Support Measures/Electronic Surveillance Measures
EVS Electro-optical Viewing System
EW Electronic Warfare
EWO Electronic Warfare Officer
ExCap Expanded Capability

FAA Federal Aviation Administration
FAC Forward Air Controller

FCS Facility Checking Squadron
FLIR Forward-Looking Infra-Red
FM Frequency Modulation

HARM High-speed Anti-Radiation Missile
HDU Hose-Drum Unit
HUD Head-Up Display

ICap Improved Capability
IDS InterDictor/Strike
IFA International Fighter Aircraft
IFF Identification, Friend or Foe
IFR Instrument Flight Rules
II Image-Intensifying
ILS Instrument Landing System
INS Inertial Navigation System
IOC Initial Operational Capability
IR Infra-Red
IRD Infra-Red Detection Set

JASDF Japanese Air Self-Defense Force
JMSDF Japanese Maritime Self-Defence Force
JTIDS Joint Tactical Information Distribution System

LABS Low Altitude Bombing System
LANTIRN Low-Altitude Navigation and Targeting Infra-Red for Night
LARA Light Armed Reconnaissance Airplane
LGB Laser-Guided Bomb
LID Lift-Improvement Device
LLLTV Low-Light-Level TV
LORAN Long Range Aid to Navigation

MAC Military Airlift Command
MAD Magnetic Anomaly Detector
MAP Military Assistance Program
MATS Military Air Transport Service
MCAS Marine Corps Air Station
MRAAM Medium-Range Air-to-Air Missile
MSIP Multi-Stage Improvement Program

NACES Navy AirCrew Escape System
NAS Naval Air Station
NASA National Aeronautics and Space Administration
NATC Naval Air Test Center
NEACP National Emergency Airborne Command Post
NOAA National Oceanic and Atmospheric Administration
NOGS Night Observation Gunship System
NOS Night Observation System
NOTARR NO TAil RotoR
NWC Naval Weapons Center
NWL Naval Weapons Laboratory

OAS Offensive Attack System
OSA Operational Support Aircraft

PACAF Pacific Air Forces
PLSS Precision Location Strike System
PNVS Pilot's Night Vision Sensor

RAAF Royal Australian Air Force
RAF Royal Air Force
RCAF Royal Canadian Air Force
RHAWS Radar Homing And Warning System
RNZAF Royal New Zealand Air Force
ROKAF Republic Of Korea Air Force
RPV Remotely-Piloted Vehicle
RTNAF Royal Thai Naval Air Facility
RWR Radar Warning Receiver

SAC Strategic Air Command
SAM Surface-to-Air Missile
SAR Search And Rescue
SDC Situation Display Console
SEAM Sidewinder Expanded-Acquisition Mode
Sigint Signals intelligence
SLAMMR Sideways-Looking Airborne Multi-Mode Radar
SLAR Sideways-Looking Airborne Radar
SMA Special Missions Aircraft
SNOE Smart Noise Operation Equipment
SOR Specific Operational Requirement
SR Strategic Reconnaissance

SRAAM Short-Range Air-to-Air Missile
SRAM Short-Range Attack Missile
SSBN Nuclear-powered, ballistic missile-armed submarine
STAR Surface-To-Air Retrievals
STOL Short Take-Off and Landing
STOVL Short Take-Off, Vertical Landing

TAC Tactical Air Command
TACAMO Take Charge And Move Out
TACAN Tactical Air Navigation
TADS Target Acquisition and Designation Sight
TARPS Tactical Air Reconnaissance Pod System
TERCOM Terrain Contour Matching
Terprom Terrain profile matching
TISEO Target Identification System Electro-Optical
TOW Tube-launched, Optically-tracked, Wire-guided (anti-tank missile)
TR Tactical Reconnaissance
TRAM Target Recognition and Attack Multi-sensor

USAFE United States Air Forces in Europe
USEUCOM United States European Command

VERTREP/Vertrep Vertical Replenishment
VFR Visual Flight Rules
VIFFing Vectoring In Forward Flight
VNAF South Vietnamese Air Force
VOR VHF Omni-directional Range
VTAS Visual Target-Acquisition System
VTO Vertical Take-Off
VTOL Vertical Take-Off and Landing
VVIP Very, Very Important Person

WSIP Weapon System Improvement Program

INTRODUCTION

A Boeing B-52G of 416th BW carrying ALCMs

As this book makes clear, the US armed forces operate an astonishing number and variety of aircraft: the United States Air Force alone has around 7,000 in its inventory. The Air National Guard (ANG) and Air Force Reserve have more than 2,000 between them. The US Navy maintains an active fleet of more than 5,000 fixed-wing aircraft and around 1,350 helicopters, supplemented by four Marine Aircraft Wings, each with about 160 aeroplanes and 155 helicopters. The US Army operates some 8,500 helicopters and 550 fixed-wing aircraft. And even the US Customs Service and Coast Guard muster respectable air arms, with airborne early warning P-3s and attack helicopters fronting the war on drug smuggling. What are all these aircraft for?

The short answer is that, like the rest of the US military, they exist, in the words of the Joint Staff, 'to assure the physical security of the United States as a democracy and protect US interests abroad'. And since the basis of US military strategy is to deter aggression, its air and other forces are 'organised, manned, trained and equipped to deter and if necessary defeat aggression across the entire spectrum of potential conflict'.

The spectrum is a broad one. At one extreme, enormous resources are devoted to strategic deterrence, with the existing force of manned bombers and intercontinental and submarine-launched ballistic missiles planned to be bolstered by new space-based systems being developed under the 'star wars' Strategic Defense Initiative. At the other, special operations forces must be ready at any time to intervene in minor 'bush-league' conflicts to protect the interests of either the US itself or its allies.

Strategic air power

The US Air Force Strategic Air Command is responsible for the air-breathing leg of the US nuclear triad. US Navy carrier-based attack aircraft were tasked with delivering nuclear weapons during the 1950s and early 1960s, before ballistic missile submarines assumed the Navy's share of deterrence and left manned nuclear bombers to the Air Force. Today SAC operates 194 cruise missile-armed B-52G/H Stratofortresses intended to launch stand-off attacks, and nearly 100 B-1B penetrators, which would carry short-range attack missiles and gravity bombs inside hostile airspace to attack fixed targets. During the 1990s the B-2 Advanced Technology Bomber (ATB) will become operational: with its extremely low observability, the B-2 is designed to be able to search for, locate and destroy mobile ICBMs and other high-value targets even in the face of improved air defences.

Of course, the bombers do not exist in isolation. SAC also operates more than 600 KC-135 Stratotanker and KC-10 Extender tankers, as well as SR-71 Blackbird, U-2, TR-1 and RC-135 reconnaissance aircraft. There are also EC-135 and E-4B airborne command and control aircraft designed to provide a survivable alternative to the ground-based command network in the aftermath of a nuclear attack.

Nor is SAC purely a nuclear force. Two B-52H wings are tasked with short-notice, long-range support of conventional forces, and two 15-aircraft squadrons of B-52Gs are equipped with Harpoon anti-ship missiles to support Navy surface warfare operations. Minelaying is another of the B-52's tasks. And SAC's two wings of FB-111 all-weather strike aircraft are being switched to the non-nuclear role in preparation for a transfer to Tactical Air Command in the early 1990s.

Land-based tactical aircraft

Nearly half of all US Air Force aircraft are the responsibility of Tactical Air Command and its associated ANG and Air Force Reserve units. Forty per cent of TAC's 4,000-plus aircraft are multi-role types, 30 per cent are air-to-air fighters and a similar proportion are dedicated to ground-attack missions.

Easily the most important type in terms of numbers is the F-16 Fighting Falcon, which is the multi-role fighter replacement for the F-4 Phantom.

While current-production F-16C/Ds continue to be delivered to front-line tactical fighter squadrons, early models are taking over the air defence fighter role from the F-4, and the Air Force is also planning to deploy a specialised RF-16 reconnaissance version and to replace some of its A-10 Thunderbolt close support aircraft with an A-16 variant. The A-16s will be supported by modernised A-7F Corsairs with afterburning engines and night-attack avionics.

Back-up for the tactical teeth

Air superiority is the province of the F-15 Eagle, whose F-15E 'Strike Eagle' multi-role derivative will complement the long-range F-111 in the attack role. In the late 1990s the F-111s are scheduled to be replaced by an Air Force version of the Navy's A-12 Advanced Tactical Aircraft (ATA).

Back-up for the tactical teeth comes in various forms, including E-3 Sentrys for airborne warning and control, OV-10 Broncos and OA-37 Dragonflys for forward air control, F-4G 'Wild Weasel' Phantoms for defence suppression, EF-111 Raven airborne jamming platforms and EC-130s and EC-135s equipped for various electronic warfare and battlefield command and control missions.

TAC is not the only operator of tactical fighters. The major overseas commands, US Air Forces in Europe and Pacific Air Forces, have the same range of fighters and attack aircraft, while the smaller Alaskan Air Command operates F-15s, A-10s and OV-10s.

Given the US commitment to force projection on a global scale, rapid long-range transport is clearly a prime requirement. This is reflected in the number of aircraft operated by the US Air Force Military Airlift Command – more than 1,000 in the active-duty force, with another 400 in MAC-assigned ANG and Reserve units.

Transport and training

Biggest of all US military aircraft is the C-5 Galaxy, capable of air-lifting two M60 tanks or three Chinook helicopters and carrying a 200,000lb payload 2,700 miles without refuelling. MAC's other strategic transport is the C-141 StarLifter, whose roles include paratroop delivery. The annual Reforger (return of forces to Germany) exercises regularly involve C-141s, along with commercial transports operating under contract, in ferrying tens of thousands of troops and hundreds of tons of equipment across the Atlantic.

MAC's standard tactical transport, the C-130 Hercules, has also formed the basis for numerous specialised derivatives. As well as extended-range airlifters, Arctic transports with ski undercarriages, gunships, electronic warfare and special forces versions, there are variants equipped for such missions as in-flight refuelling of helicopters, the mid-air retrieval of space capsules, the recovery of aircrew and communications jamming.

Smaller numbers of other types, usually military versions of commercial transports, are operated for specialised roles. There is a range of VIP transports, from the C-137 (Boeing 707) Stratoliner *Air Force One* used by the US President to the C-20 Gulfstream III and the C-21A military version of the Learjet 35A. C-9 Nightingale derivatives of the DC-9 airliner are used for aeromedical transport.

Another major requirement is training for the hundreds of new pilots needed each year. For decades the standard Air Force primary trainer has been the T-37

The advanced Head-Up and Head-Down Displays of a McDonnell Douglas simulator.

Tweet, and as a result of the cancellation of the T-46 which was to replace it, the T-37 is expected to remain in service for some time to come. After completing their basic course on the T-37, Air Force trainee pilots graduate to the T-38 Talon, another design with years of history behind it and decades of service ahead.

While the Air Force is having to think again about a replacement for the T-37, the Navy has decided on the T-45 Goshawk naval version of the British Aerospace Hawk advanced trainer as its replacement for both the T-2 Buckeye and TA-4 Skyhawk advanced trainers. Navy pilots receive their basic training on the T-34 Turbo-Mentor (Beech Model 45) and pilots selected for multi-engine training go on to the T-44

Learning to fly is only half the story, however. Specialised training is required in navigation, systems operation and a host of other specialities, and small numbers of trainers are operated for such purposes. For example, the T-43 derivative of the Boeing 737 is used by the Air Force for navigation training, while the Navy's radar operators are trained aboard T-47 Citation IIs.

Even operational pilots need to hone their skills, so all three services operating fixed-wing fighters have aggressor squadrons for air-combat training. Aircraft used for this purpose in recent years include F-5s, A-4s and even Kfirs leased from the Israelis under the designation F-21. However, both the Air Force and the Navy are now standardising on the ubiquitous F-16.

Naval aviation

There are some sceptics who see a two-billion-dollar aircraft carrier sailing the oceans with billions of dollars' worth of aircraft on board as a clear case of too many eggs in a single basket. However, a naval task force that comes complete with its own air force is clearly a power-projection tool without equal, and the Navy is committed to expanding its force of large aircraft carriers to a total of 15 vessels.

Nevertheless, an aircraft carrier represents an investment of such size that its protection is vital, and the F-14 Tomcat that forms a carrier group's first line of defence is certainly the most potent interceptor in service today. For offensive operations a typical carrier air wing also includes two squadrons of A-7s – or their replacement, the F/A-18 Hornet – for daylight attack missions, and one of all-weather A-6 Intruders.

To support the fighters and bombers each carrier also operates four KA-6 tankers and four EA-6B Prowler electronic warfare aircraft; four E-2C Hawkeyes for airborne early warning; an anti-submarine warfare squadron of S-3 Vikings; and SH-3 Sea King anti-submarine helicopters. C-1 Traders and C-2 Greyhounds are also used for on-board delivery of personnel and cargo.

Not all Navy aircraft are based aboard aircraft carriers. One vital component of the Navy's anti-submarine effort is the shore-based P-3 Orion, and

*ABOVE: The second Fairchild **T-46A** on its first flight.*

other land-based aircraft for specialised tasks include the EP-3 for electronic reconnaissance and the EC-130 used to provide very low frequency communications with ballistic missile submarines. And helicopters such as the SH-60 Seahawk serve aboard frigates and destroyers.

BELOW: S-3A Vikings on the Lockheed production line.

The Navy's future plans involve improvements to almost its entire current inventory, plus the development of the new A-12 Advanced Tactical Aircraft, which is due to become operational in the late 1990s. Upgrades to existing types include re-engining some F-14s and the acquisition of the F-14D, whose new avionics will enable targets to identified at much longer ranges than is possible with the current F-14A. F/A-18s are being provided with forward-looking infra-red navigation and targeting pods to give them a night attack capability, while various schemes for enhancing the A-6's capabilities have been considered. However, plans to produce an enhanced A-6F have been abandoned, and the long-range deep strike mission will be assumed by the ATA. And just as the Air Force will use a land-based version of the ATA to replace its F-111s in the next century, it is hoped the follow-on to the Navy's F-14 will be a naval version of the Air Force Advanced Tactical Fighter (ATF).

Marine Corps wings

There will be other new aircraft in the supporting roles. An anti-submarine variant of the V-22 Osprey is planned as a replacement for the S-3, but the projected Advanced Multi-sensor System, a single airframe that would be fitted with appropriate mission equipment to take over the roles of the E-2, S-3 and KA-6 seems to have receded into the future.

The Marines expect to fight amphibious battles, going ashore from assault ships to establish a beachhead before taking the battle inland. Accordingly

the primary purpose of their air arm is to support Marines on the ground. So while the Corps continues to operate F/A-18s and A-6s from conventional carriers alongside Navy fighter and attack squadrons, it is moving toward an all-VSTOL force for amphibious warfare.

The Marines were early converts to the virtues of the Harrier, and the original AV-8As bought by the Corps have given way to the bigger, more powerful and much more capable AV-8B Harrier II. Alongside the Harrier, the Marines operate AH-1 Sea Cobra attack and UH-1 light transport helicopters, plus the big CH-46 Sea Knight assault transport and CH-53 Sea Stallion and Super Stallion heavy-lift choppers.

As their future assault transport, the Marines are buying the V-22 Osprey tilt-rotor, which takes off like a helicopter but swivels its engines and rotors after becoming airborne to cruise like an aeroplane. In the meantime, pending their replacement by F/A-18s and AV-8Bs respectively, Phantoms are still used by four fighter-attack squadrons and three squadrons of A-4 Skyhawks remain in service more than 30 years after the first example joined the Marines. KC-130 tankers are used to refuel aircraft on transoceanic deployments, and OV-10s serve as forward air control aircraft.

Army aviation

When the US Air Force was separated from the Army in 1947 the Army was prohibited from operating armed fixed-wing aircraft. That prohibition has remained in force ever since, and the

Army has made up for its lack of aeroplanes by developing whole new breeds of helicopter.

The main roles for the helicopter in the current US Army organisation are reconnaissance, attack, troop deployment and logistic transport. To fulfil the attack mission the Army deploys AH-64 Apache and AH-1S attack machines supported by OH-58 Kiowa and OH-6 Cayuse reconnaissance helicopters. The fleet of UH-1 Hueys is being replaced by UH-60 Blackhawks for combat assault and utility transport while the CH-54 heavy transports are nearing the end of their lives and CH-47 Chinooks are the principal vehicle for combat support and replenishment – that is, shifting everything from fuel and ammunition to 155mm howitzers.

The Army's big programme for the future is the Light Helicopter Experimental, or LHX. One sign of the way helicopters are evolving is the fact that the LHX mission of light attack and armed reconnaissance will require it to have an air-to-air combat capability.

Special operations forces

The recognition that low-intensity conflicts are the most likely source of trouble for the foreseeable future led to the establishment of a joint-service Special Operations Command in 1986, and the specialised variants of existing aircraft developed for use by special operations forces are among the most exotic machines in the current inventory.

Special operations forces need to be able to operate in the dark at low altitudes, so precision navigation systems involving terrain-following radar and forward-looking infra-red equipment are installed on such types as the MH-53 Pave Low and MH-60 Pave Hawk helicopters, AC-130 Spectre gunships, EC-130 'Volant Solo' electronic surveillance aircraft and MC-130 Combat Talon transports. These aircraft are operated by Military Airlift Command's 23rd Air Force, while the US Navy is reported to have deployed MH-6 'Killer Egg' scout helicopters in the Persian Gulf.

Of course, the complexity of modern military aircraft means there is still plenty of work for companies which are no longer prime contractors for airframes. Having lost out in the mid-1970s FX competition won by the F/A-18, LTV (Ling-Temco-Vought) decided that it could not afford to maintain its status as a prime contractor while it waited for

the next opportunity. In 1980, after 63 years in the business, it decided to continue as a subcontractor only, and the decision has been justified. Today LTV is thriving on contracts to build the nacelles, fin and tailplane for the C-17 plus major components for the B-2, and is bidding for a major A-7 upgrade programme.

For the future, analysts predict that the boom years of the Reagan era will be followed by a period of flat sales. The end of B-1B and C-5 production has helped avoid the need for major cuts in military aerospace programmes, but with no similar terminations scheduled for the near future, the US may have to choose between shrinking armed forces or substantial increases in defence spending.

The next generation

US manufacturers are currently working on a whole new generation of military aircraft. And this time round they are working in teams – a reflection of the sheer effort and expense involved in developing modern military aircraft. So General Dynamics and McDonnell Douglas have joined forces to develop the A-12 Advanced Tactical Aircraft for the US Navy, having beaten the rival team of Grumman, Northrop and LTV for the contract.

McDonnell Douglas and General Dynamics are also bidding for the US

A McDonnell Douglas Helicopters AH-64A Apache carrying 8 Hellfire ATGMs and a Sidewinder and a Stinger AAM

Air Force Advanced Tactical Fighter contract, though for the A-12 ATF they are in opposition: the former is backing Northrop's YF-23A, while GD, along with Boeing, is partnered with Lockheed in the rival YF-22A programme. Similarly, Bell and Boeing are jointly working on the V-22 Osprey tilt-rotor for all four services but are in opposition for the US Army's Light Helicopter Experimental competition, Boeing having joined forces with Sikorsky while Bell is partnered with McDonnell Douglas Helicopters.

There will be new aircraft in other roles, too. McDonnell Douglas is developing the C-17 strategic transport. Lockheed is working on a new anti-submarine warfare derivative of the P-3 under the unwieldy designation LRAAC (Long-Range ASW-Capable Aircraft). And Grumman is providing mission avionics for the E-8 Joint STARS (Surveillance Target Attack Radar System), a modified Boeing 707 which will locate targets and direct aircraft to attack them via the Joint Tactical Information Distribution System.

The manufacturing base

The Second World War was a boom time for US aircraft manufacturers. A fledgeling concern like North American Aviation, given a good design, hard work and a little luck, could find itself transformed almost overnight into a major supplier of combat aircraft and trainers; one that would turn out thousands of P-51 Mustangs and T-6 Texans in the space of a few years.

The post war era brought new challenges. Jet engines and supersonic speeds, guided missiles that could be carried under a fighter's wing and airborne radars small enough to fit in its nose: all posed new challenges for companies whose floods of wartime orders had suddenly come to an end. The onset of the Cold War, highlighted by a hot war in Korea, accelerated the pace of development, and barely ten years after North America had produced the first supersonic fighter in the shape of the F-86 Sabre, the Century-series fighters of the late 1950s, epitomised by Lockheed's F-104 Starfighter, were routinely exceeding Mach 2.

Fastest aircraft ever built

The efforts of the manufacturers were supported by the government via the National Advisory Committee for Aeronautics (NACA, subsequently to become NASA, or the National Aeronautics and Space Administration), which funded such projects as the Bell X-1 and the North American X-15. The former was the first aircraft to break the sound barrier, the latter the fastest aircraft ever built, and both made enormous contributions to aeronautical knowledge.

Since the heady days of the 1950s, however, aircraft development has become much more complicated, time-consuming and expensive. Fewer types have been funded, fewer still have been built in quantity, and the number of manufacturers has shrunk in consequence. North American itself, which had gone on from the X-15 to build two prototypes of the remarkable XB-70 Valkyrie Mach 3 bomber, found itself merging with automotive component and general aviation manufacturer Rockwell-Standard. Today the Rockwell International Corporation ranks 27th among US industrial concerns, and its North American Operations division has extensive space interests, but its aircraft activities have shrunk dramatically: the 100th and last B-1B was delivered in 1988 and it has no current aircraft production programme, though it is involved in the X-30 and X-31A research projects.

A dominant force

On the other hand, success in the competition for new military aircraft contracts can spell enormous prosperity. The McDonnell Aircraft Corporation was founded in 1939, at about the same time as North American, and a string of successful designs (notably that of the F-4), a merger with Douglas Aircraft in 1966 and the more recent acquisition of Hughes Helicopters have made it a dominant force in US combat aircraft design and manufacturing. As well as current production of the F-15, F/A-18 and AV-8B fighters, the AH-64 attack helicopter and the US Navy's new T-45 trainer, it is involved in both the ATF and ATA programmes, apart from building the C-17 strategic airlifter.

One particularly intriguing new scheme is the Marine Corps plan to replace its entire current range of fixed-wing combat aircraft with a single new ASTOVL (Advanced Short Take Off/Vertical Landing) type. This would take

The Bell Textron XV-15 tilt rotor aircraft – forerunner of the V-22 Osprey

over all the missions currently performed by the A-6, AV-8B and F/A-18, and would fulfil the Marines' ambition to be an all-STOVL force by the year 2015. In the meantime, the radar-equipped Harrier II Plus, currently under study by McDonnell Douglas and British Aerospace, is a likely short-term addition to Marine air power.

Meanwhile, new versions of existing types continue to appear, and old airframes are put to new uses. So the early l990s should see air defence, reconnaissance and – if the Air Force has its way – close-support versions of the F-16 in service alongside the Strike Eagle attack variant of the F-15; the A-10s displaced by the close-support F-16 will be converted as forward air control aircraft; US Marine Corps AV-8Bs will incorporate night attack equipment; the re-engined F-14D Super Tomcat will take its place on US Navy carrier decks alongside upgraded A-6 Intruders; and

virtually every other front-line aircraft, from the AH-64 Apache attack helicopter to the B-1B strategic bomber, will eventually be upgraded with new systems, avionics, engines and weapons as part of a planned improvement programme.

Hypersonic hybrid

Looking beyond even the next generation, there are the research aircraft which will lay the foundations of twenty-first century military aircraft technology. The Grumman X-29, with its forward-swept wings, seems almost old-hat already, but it has demonstrated levels of manoeuvrability unobtainable by an aircraft of conventional planform. Another approach to enhanced manoeuvrability is being explored by Rockwell, which has joined forces with MBB (Messerschmitt-Boelkow-Blohm) to develop the X-31A. This will use thrust vectoring and roll-coupled fuselage aim-

ing for improved dogfighting agility. Rockwell is also involved in the design of the X-30 National Aero-Space Plane, a hypersonic hybrid vehicle capable of operating both within the atmosphere and in low earth orbit.

Whatever the twenty-first century holds in store, by late 1988 there was graphic confirmation that future US combat aircraft are likely to look startlingly different from anything that has gone before. The publication in November of the first photograph of the elusive F-117 stealth fighter, ending years of speculation about the aircraft's designation and appearance, was followed within days by the public debut of the B-2 ATB. According to the Pentagon, 52 of the 59 F-117s ordered had been delivered, and the fighter was operational with TAC's 4450th Tactical Training Group at Nellis Air Force Base, Nevada.

A Grumman X-29 undergoing vibration tests

Agusta-Sikorsky AS-61

Argentina Brazil Egypt Iran Iraq Italy Libya Peru Saudi Arabia

Agusta-Sikorsky AS-61-TS of the 93° Gruppo, 31° Stormo, Italian air force.

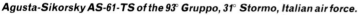

Sikorsky production of the extensively-built S-61 has ended, but the basic type continues in production with the company's licensees, namely Agusta in Italy, Mitsubishi in Japan and Westland in the UK. Agusta began licence-construction of the civil S-61 and military SH-3D in 1967, delivering its first **Agusta-Sikorsky ASH-3D** anti-submarine version to the Italian navy in 1969. Generally similar to the Sikorsky S-61, the Agusta production model differs by introducing some local strengthening of the airframe, a revised horizontal tail, uprated powerplant, and variations in armament and internal equipment.

Agusta is currently building the military **ASH-3H**, which is basically equivalent to the US Navy's SH-3H, and this can be equipped for roles that include ASV, ASW, anti-surface-missile defence, casevac, EW, SAR, tactical transport and Vertrep. Primary use of the ASH-3D/ASH-3H has been in the ASV and ASW roles, for which it has advanced avionics, carrying for ASW two or four Mk 44/46 or Moto Fides A 244/S homing torpedoes, or four depth charges. Armament for the ASV role can include four medium-range

Aérospatiale AS.12 missiles, or two Oto Melara Marte Mk 2, AM.39 Exocet or Harpoon type long-range missiles. ASH-3D and ASH-3H helicopters have been supplied to Argentina, Brazil, Iran and Peru, but the Italian navy is the major operator. An unarmed version for VIP transport, variously designated **ASH-3D/TS** (Trasporto Speciale), **AS-61A-4** and **AS-61VIP**, has been built for Iran, Iraq, Italy and Saudi Arabia.

With an end to Sikorsky construction of the S-61N, Agusta obtained production rights and modified the design to provide reduced capacity and increased range. Designated commercial **AS-61N1 Silver**, the prototype flew initially on 25 July 1984; this and initial aircraft retain the General Electric CT58 powerplant of the Sikorsky S-61N, but two 1312-kW (1,760-shp) CT7 turboshafts may be adopted later. Agusta also builds the very different Sikorsky S-61R transport under the designation **HH-3F** for use in SAR and utility roles. The Aeronautica Militare Italiana received 20 in the period 1977-80 and uses them in the SAR role from four bases; 10 more are being built for export.

Agusta-Sikorsky ASH-3H

The ASH-3H carries state-of-the-art submarine detection gear, communications and weapons, similar to the US Navy's SH-3H. This pair are operated by Brazil's naval air arm.

Agusta builds the HH-3F, similar to its US counterpart. This is primarily used by the Italian navy for SAR. This example displays its amphibious capability.

Specification: Agusta-Sikorsky ASH-3H (ASW role)
Origin: USA/Italy
Type: twin-turbine all-weather ASW helicopter
Powerplant: two 1118-kW (1,500-shp) General Electric T58-GE-100 turboshaft engines
Performance: cruising speed 120 kts (222 km/h; 138 mph); initial rate of climb 2,200 ft (670 m) per minute; service ceiling 12,205 ft (3720 m); hovering ceiling in ground effect 8,200 ft (2500 m); range with standard fuel 1165 km (724 miles)
Weights: empty 5895 kg (12,995 lb); maximum take-off 9525 kg (21,000 lb)
Dimensions: main-rotor diameter 18.90 m (62 ft 0 in); length, rotors turning 21.91 m (71 ft 10.7 in); height 4.93 m (16 ft 2 in); main-rotor disc area 280.47 m² (3,019.1 sq ft)
Armament: as detailed in text for ASW and ASV role.

Role	
Fighter	
Close support	
Counter-insurgency	
Tactical strike	
Strategic bomber	
Tactical reconnaissance	
Strategic reconnaissance	
Maritime patrol	■
Anti-ship strike	■
Anti-submarine warfare	■
Search and rescue	■
Assault transport	
Transport	■
Liaison	
Trainer	
Inflight-refuelling tanker	
Specialized	
Performance	
All-weather capability	■
Rough field capability	
STOL capability	
VTOL capability	■
Airspeed 0-250 mph	■
Airspeed 250 mph-Mach 1	
Airspeed Mach 1 plus	
Ceiling 0-20,000 ft	■
Ceiling 20,000-40,000 ft	
Ceiling 40,000 ft plus	
Range 0-1,000 miles	■
Range 1,000-3,000 miles	
Range 3,000 miles plus	
Weapons	
Air-to-air missiles	
Air-to-surface missiles	■
Cruise missiles	
Cannon	
Trainable guns	
Naval weapons	■
Nuclear-capable	
Rockets	
'Smart' weapon kit	
Weapon load 0-4,000 lb	■
Weapon load 4,000-15,000 lb	
Weapon load 15,000 lb plus	
Avionics	
Electronic Counter Measures	
Electronic Support Measures	
Search radar	■
Fire control radar	
Look-down/shoot-down radar	
Terrain-following radar	
Forward-looking infra-red	
Laser	
Television	

■ Primary capability
▨ Secondary capability

An AS-61 of the Peruvian Navy

Beech Model 45/T-34 Mentor

Algeria Argentina Chile Colombia Dominican Rep Ecuador El Salvador Gabon Indonesia Japan Mexico Morocco

Peru Philippines Spain Taiwan Turkey

United States Uruguay Venezuela

Beech T-34C-1 Mentor of the Ecuadorean air force.

Beech flew on 2 December 1948 the prototype (N8591A) of the **Beech Model 45**, a new tandem-seat trainer with a conventional single-fin-and-rudder tail unit; this was based on the structure of the Model 35 V-tailed Bonanza, to which it had some 80 per cent commonality. In early 1950 the US Air Force acquired three Model 45s under the designation **YT-34,** using them for competitive evaluation. It was not until 4 March 1953 that it was ordered into production for the USAF, under the designation **T-34A Mentor,** a total of 450 being acquired; on 17 June 1954 the type was adopted also by the US Navy, which procured a total of 423 **T-34B Mentor** aircraft. The Canadian Car and Foundry Company built 100 of the 450 T-34As for the USAF, plus 25 for the RCAF; all but one of this last order later went to the Turkish air force. Fuji built 160 under licence for service in Japan and with the Philippine air force, and in Argentina the Fábrica Militar de Aviones assembled 75 under licence for the Fuerza

Aérea Argentina. In addition to these military procurements, US-built aircraft were also supplied to recipients of aid from the Military Assistance Program.

In early 1973 the US Navy awarded Beech a contract to develop a turboprop-powered version, the first of two **YT-34C** prototypes flying initially on 21 September 1973. These also had improved avionics and air-conditioning, and following successful evaluation an initial contract was finalized for 184 new production **T-34C** aircraft; delivery of the last of an additional 150 aircraft was made in April 1984. Beech has also developed an armed version suitable for forward air control and tactical strike weapons training. Designated **T-34C-1,** this has four underwing hardpoints for a maximum 544-kg (1,200-lb) weapon load which can include anti-tank missiles, bombs, Minigun pods and rockets. T-34C-1s have been supplied to the air arms of Argentina, Ecuador, Gabon, Indonesia, Morocco, Peru and Uruguay.

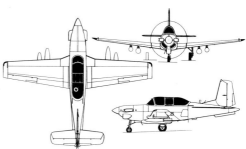

Beech T-34C-1 Mentor

Specification: Beech Model 45/T-34C
Origin: USA
Type: tandem-seat primary trainer
Powerplant: one 533-kW (715-shp) Pratt & Whitney Canada PT6A-25 turboprop engine flat-rated at 410 kW (550 shp)
Performance: maximum cruising speed 214 kts (396 km/h; 246 mph) at 17,000 ft (5182 m); initial rate of climb 1,480 ft (451 m) per minute; service ceiling 30,000 ft (9144 m); maximum range with maximum fuel 1310 km (814 miles)
Weights: empty 1343 kg (2,960 lb); maximum take-off 1950 kg (4,300 lb)
Dimensions: span 10.16 m (33 ft 3.9 in); length 8.75 m (28 ft 8.5 in); height 2.92 m (9 ft 7 in); wing area 16.68 m² (179.6 sq ft)
Armament: none

Morocco uses the T-34C-1 mainly for training duties. However, the aircraft retain weapons capability, and they can be used for counter-insurgency duties.

The US Navy has used the Beech T-34 as its basic trainer since 1954 in two successive versions. Current aircraft are the turboprop-powered T-34Cs, here represented by an aircraft of TAW-5.

Role
Fighter
Close support
Counter-insurgency
Tactical strike
Strategic bomber
Tactical reconnaissance
Strategic reconnaissance
Maritime patrol
Anti-ship strike
Anti-submarine warfare
Search and rescue
Assault transport
Transport
Liaison
Trainer
Inflight-refuelling tanker
Specialized

Performance
All-weather capability
Rough field capability
STOL capability
VTOL capability
Airspeed 0-250 mph
Airspeed 250 mph-Mach 1
Airspeed Mach 1 plus
Ceiling 0-20,000 ft
Ceiling 20,000-40,000 ft
Ceiling 40,000ft plus
Range 0-1,000 miles
Range 1,000-3,000 miles
Range 3,000 miles plus

Weapons
Air-to-air missiles
Air-to-surface missiles
Cruise missiles
Cannon
Trainable guns
Naval weapons
Nuclear-capable
Rockets
'Smart' weapon kit
Weapon load 0-4,000 lb
Weapon load 4,000-15,000 lb
Weapon load 15,000 lb plus

Avionics
Electronic Counter Measures
Electronic Support Measures
Search radar
Fire control radar
Look-down/shoot-down
Terrain-following radar
Forward-looking infra-red
Laser
Television

Beech Model 50 Twin Bonanza/Model 65 Queen Air/U-8 Seminole

Taiwan Thailand United States Uruguay Venezuela

Argentina Dominican Rep Ecuador Israel Japan

Pakistan Peru Switzerland

Beech Model 65 Queen Air of the Peruvian air force.

Beech Model 65 Queen Air (U-8F)

Seeking an 'off-the-shelf' light communications/transport aircraft in 1951, the US Army procured for evaluation four examples of the six-seat **Beech Model 50 Twin Bonanza** under the designation **YL-23**. Testing soon confirmed the type to be suitable and an initial order for 55 **L-23A** aircraft was placed in 1952, followed in 1953 by an order for 40 **L-23B** aircraft with steel instead of wooden propeller blades. From 1956 the US Army procured 85 **L-23D** machines with more powerful Lycoming O-480 engines, and the 93 surviving L-23A/L-23Bs were converted to this configuration, all being redesignated **U-8D** and acquiring the name **Seminole** in 1962. Subsequent procurements included 20 **RL-23D (RU-8D)** radar reconnaissance aircraft tested with APQ-86 side-looking airborne radar (SLAR), UPD-1 battlefield surveillance radar in a ventral fair-

ing, and AVQ-50 or similar weather radar. The final Twin Bonanza contract covered six **L-23E (U-8E)** aircraft, which were equivalent to the commercial **Twin Bonanza D50**.

Further procurement then centred on the **Beech Model 65 Queen Air,** which had flown in prototype form on 28 August 1958, and which differed from the Twin Bonanza by having an improved and enlarged fuselage accommodating a crew of one or two and up to nine passengers. Three were acquired initially for evaluation, under the designation **L-23F (U-8F),** and subsequently 76 additional examples were procured with accommodation for a crew of two and six passengers. As well as being used by the US Army, Twin Bonanzas or Model 65 Queen Airs have seen service with the air arms of Chile, Ecuador, Japan, Pakistan, Peru, Switzerland and Venezuela.

Specification: Beech Model 65 Queen Air/U-8F
Origin: USA
Type: light communications/transport aircraft
Powerplant: two 254-kW (340-hp) Lycoming IGSO-480-A1B6 flat-six piston engines
Performance: maximum speed 208 kts (386 km/h; 240 mph) at 12,000 ft (3658 m); maximum cruising speed 186 kts (344 km/h; 214 mph) at 15,200 ft (4633 m); initial rate of climb 1,300 ft (396 m) per minute; service ceiling 31,000 ft (9449 m); maximum range with auxiliary fuel and 45-minute reserves 1963 km (1,220 miles)
Weights: empty 2105 kg (4,640 lb); maximum take-off 3493 kg (7,700 lb)
Dimensions: span 13.98 m (45 ft 10.5 in); length 10.16 m (33 ft 4 in); height 4.32 m (14 ft 2 in); wing area 25.73 m² (277.0 sq ft)
Armament: none

The US Army has used the Seminole for light liaison duties since 1952. Several U-8Ds are still in service with the National Guard, this example being from Alabama.

Although covered by the same designation as the Seminole, the U-8F is the US Army derivative of the Queen Air. These are being used for communications duties.

20

Beech Model 80 Queen Air/ Model 90 King Air/U-21 Ute/T-44

Argentina | Chile | Colombia | Ecuador | Indonesia | Ivory Coast | Jamaica

Japan | Mexico | Morocco | Peru | Spain

Thailand | United States | Venezuela

Beech TC-90 King Air of No. 202 Sqn, Japan Maritime Self-Defence Force.

Improved capability for the Model 80 Queen Air became reality from May 1963 when Beech began flight testing one of these aircraft with its Lycoming piston engines replaced by two Pratt & Whitney Canada PT6A-6 turboprops. Designated as the **Beech Model 65-90T,** this variant represented a development stage for the true **King Air Model 90** which, first flown on 20 January 1964, was even more advanced in introducing a pressurized fuselage. In March 1964 the US Army acquired the Model 65-90T for evaluation under the designation **NU-8F,** and in 1966 it was decided to adopt the type for service in this unpressurized form. In that same year Beech was awarded an initial contract for 48 of these aircraft under the designation **U-21A Ute,** and eventually 141 of the type were built. The fuselage interior was modified to give increased utility: the cabin was equipped to seat in a transport role 10 fully equipped troops; as a staff transport there was more comfortable seating for six; and in a casevac role three stretchers, three ambulatory patients and medical attendants

could be carried. For use as a freighter all passenger seating could be removed easily, allowing for the carriage of up to 1361 kg (3,000 lb) of cargo.

Specialized variants, conversions of U-21As, have included the **EU-21A, RU-21A** and **RU-21D,** plus **RU-21B, RU-21C** and **RU-21E** aircraft which have 462-kW (620-shp) engines. Most of these variants were operated in an electronic reconnaissance role by the Army Security Agency, equipped with extensive aerial arrays, advanced avionics equipment, all-weather navigation systems and comprehensive communications. Under the designation **U-21F** the US Army acquired five examples of the **King Air A100** for evaluation; these have a pressurized fuselage and 507-kW (680-shp) PT6A-28 engines. The US Navy also adopted a version of the **King Air C90** to meet its requirement for an advanced pilot trainer: designated **T-44A** this has 559-kW (750-shp) PT-6A-34B turboprops flat rated at 410 kW (550 shp) and extensive avionics. A total of 61 was delivered from 5 April 1977.

Beech Model 80 Queen Air

Specification: Beech Model 65-A90-1C/U-21A Ute
Origin: USA
Type: military utility transport
Powerplant: two 410-kW (550-shp) Pratt & Whitney Canada PT6A-20 turboprop engines
Performance: maximum speed 216 kts (401 km/h; 249 mph) at 11,000 ft (3353 m); maximum cruising speed 213 kts (394 km/h; 245 mph) at 10,000 ft (3048 m); initial rate of climb 2,000 ft (609 m) per minute; service ceiling 25,500 ft (7772 m); range with maximum payload and 30-minute reserves 1878 km (1,167 miles); range with maximum fuel and 30-minute reserves 2697 km (1,676 miles)
Weights: empty 2478 kg (5,464 lb); maximum take-off 4377 kg (9,650 lb)
Dimensions: span 13.98 m (45 ft 10.5 in); length 10.82 m (35 ft 6 in); height 4.33 m (14 ft 2.5 in); wing area 25.98 m² (279.7 sq ft)
Armament: none

For advanced twin-engined pilot and navigator training, the US Navy uses the T-44A, a version of the civil King Air C90. This example is based at Corpus Christi NAS.

The US Army uses the U-21 series widely for liaison duties. This aircraft is the standard U-21A Ute, which can be used as a light troop transport, medevac aircraft or inter-theatre VIP transport.

Role
Fighter
Close support
Counter-insurgency
Tactical strike
Strategic bomber
Tactical reconnaissance
Strategic reconnaissance
Maritime patrol
Anti-ship strike
Anti-submarine warfare
Search and rescue
Assault transport
Transport
Liaison
Trainer
Inflight-refuelling tanker
Specialized

Performance
All-weather capability
Rough field capability
STOL capability
VTOL capability
Airspeed 0-250 mph
Airspeed 250 mph-Mach 1
Airspeed Mach 1 plus
Ceiling 0-20,000 ft
Ceiling 20,000-40,000 ft
Ceiling 40,000 ft plus
Range 0-1,000 miles
Range 1,000-3,000 miles
Range 3,000 miles plus

Weapons
Air-to-air missiles
Air-to-surface missiles
Cruise missiles
Cannon
Trainable guns
Naval weapons
Nuclear-capable
Rockets
'Smart' weapon kit
Weapon load 0-4,000 lb
Weapon load 4,000-15,000 lb
Weapon load 15,000 lb plus

Avionics
Electronic Counter Measures
Electronic Support Measures
Search radar
Fire control radar
Look-down/shoot-down
Terrain-following radar
Forward-looking infra-red
Laser
Television

Primary capability
Secondary capability

Beech Model 95-55 Baron/T-42A Cochise

Beech T-42A Cochise of the US Army.

The extensively-built (about 6,000 by the end of 1984) Beech Baron series of four/six-seat light twin-engined aircraft embrace the company's Models 55, 56 and 58. All stem from the four/five-seat Baron Model 95-55, first flown on 29 February 1960, and which was itself derived from the Beech Travel Air of 1956. The Model 95-55 differed, however, by introducing more powerful engines, was equipped as standard with full blind-flying instrumentation and had provision for the installation of optional de-icing equipment and weather radar, endowing it with far better all-weather capability than its predecessor.

When in 1964 the US Army established a requirement for a new twin-engined instrument trainer, a competition was initiated to determine the most suitable 'off-the-shelf' buy from a number of similar types then in production by US manufacturers. In February 1965 the **Beech Model 95-B55** was selected by the Army as the most suitable for its purpose, Beech then receiving an order for

65 of these aircraft, which were identified by the company as the **Model 95-B55B**. Delivered during 1965-6, these were allocated the designation **T-42A** and named **Cochise**, entering service with the US Army's Aviation Flying School at Fort Rucker, Alabama. Generally similar to the standard production Model 95-B55 of the period, they have swept vertical tail surfaces and electrically-retractable tricycle landing gear; they differ primarily from the commercial version by having US Army-specified avionics, communications and navigation aids.

In addition to those T-42As mentioned above, in 1971 the US Army procured five generally similar aircraft for supply to the Turkish army under the US Military Assistance Program. These are not, of course, the only Barons in military use; small numbers have directly, or indirectly, entered service with several armed forces and are deployed in communication, training or utility roles.

Beech Model 95-55 Baron

The T-42 Cochise is used by the US Army for training and other light duties. Many serve with the Army National Guard, including this aircraft at Burlington, Vermont.

The Army's T-42s differ little from the Model 95-B55 civil Baron, the major difference being a military avionics and navigation fit. Sixty-five were supplied to the US Army.

Specification: Beech Baron Model 95-B55/T-42A Cochise
Origin: USA
Type: lightweight cabin monoplane
Powerplant: two 194-kW (260-hp) Continental IO-470-L flat-six piston engines
Performance: maximum speed 201 kts (372 km/h; 231 mph) at sea level; economic cruising speed 173 kts (320 km/h; 199 mph) at 12,000 ft (3660 m); initial rate of climb 1,700 ft (518 m) per minute; service ceiling 19,300 ft (5885 m); maximum range at economic cruising speed with allowances and 45-minute reserves 1835 km (1,140 miles)
Weights: empty 1468 kg (3236 lb); maximum take-off 2313 kg (5,100 lb)
Dimensions: span 11.53 m (37 ft 10 in); length 8.53 m (28 ft 0 in); height 2.92 m (9ft 7 in); wing area 18.51 m² (199.20 sq ft)
Armament: none

Beech Model 99

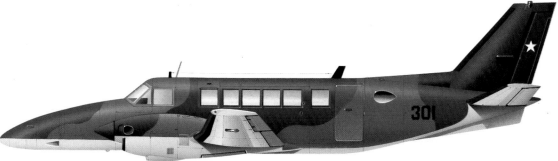

Chile   Peru

Beech Model 99 of the Chilean air force.

The prototype of the **Beech Model 99,** when flown for the first time during July 1966, represented the largest aircraft to be manufactured in quantity by the company. Intended for operators of commuter airlines, it was a low-wing monoplane powered by twin turboprop engines, the roomy fuselage incorporating a flight deck with side-by-side seats for pilot and co-pilot, and the cabin was equipped with easily removable seats in a 15-passenger high-density layout. A double-width door was optional, to simplify the loading of cargo, and a movable cabin divider was available so that the aircraft could operate in an all-passenger, all-cargo or combined passenger/cargo role. Initial reaction to the aircraft was excellent and there were plans to build 100 units per year by mid-1968 to meet a healthy order book.

Such plans were probably 'sales office' enthusiasm, for it was not until 2 May 1968 that the first production aircraft was delivered to Commuter Airliners Inc. in the USA, and

when production of what was then designated the **B99 Airliner** was suspended in 1977, a total of only 164 had been built.

Of this total, small numbers entered military service, and most of these were second hand. Peru and Thailand acquired examples, but of these only Peru still operates the type. By far the largest user is Chile, which had nine built as new. These have been used as liaison and general transports, but have been steadily refitted within Chile to perform a variety of other functions. Navigation training is an important facet, and others have been given search and rescue capability, with limited maritime patrol ability.

Political friction with Argentina has led to several Model 99s being fitted with a locally-built electronic intelligence set, called the ITATA. This has been employed for determining Argentina's electronic order of battle, and for developing countermeasures. All Chilean Model 99s serve with 11 Grupo.

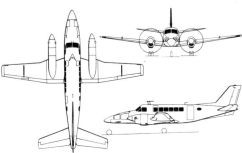

Beech Model 99

Chile is the major user of the Beech Model 99, using its aircraft for maritime patrol, Elint duties and navigation training. Nine aircraft were supplied.

Seen prior to delivery, this Beech 99 now serves with Chile's 11 Grupo. Chile has modified her aircraft for various duties indigenously, and few remain in this airliner-type configuration.

Specification: Beech 99 Airliner
Origin: USA
Type: commuter/cargo/VIP transport
Powerplant: two 410-kW (550-shp) Pratt & Whitney Canada PT6A-20 turboprop engines
Performance: maximum speed 221 kts (409 km/h; 254 mph) at 8,000 ft (2438 m); initial rate of climb 1,700 ft (518 m) per minute; service ceiling 23,650 ft (7209 m); range with maximum payload and 45-minute reserves 805 km (500 miles); range with maximum fuel and 816-kg (1,800-lb) payload 1770 km (1,100 miles)
Weights: empty 2667 kg (5,880 lb); maximum take-off 4717 kg (10,400 lb)
Dimensions: span 13.98 m (45 ft 10.5 in); length 13.58 m (44 ft 6.75 in); height 4.38 m (14 ft 4.25 in)
Armament: none

Role
Fighter
Close support
Counter-insurgency
Tactical strike
Strategic bomber
Tactical reconnaissance
Strategic reconnaissance
Maritime patrol
Anti-ship strike
Anti-submarine warfare
Search and rescue
Assault transport
Transport
Liaison
Trainer
Inflight-refuelling tanker
Specialized

Performance
All-weather capability
Rough field capability
STOL capability
VTOL capability
Airspeed 0-250 mph
Airspeed 250 mph-Mach 1
Airspeed Mach 1 plus
Ceiling 0-20,000 ft
Ceiling 20,000-40,000 ft
Ceiling 40,000ft plus
Range 0-1,000 miles
Range 1,000-3,000 miles
Range 3,000 miles plus

Weapons
Air-to-air missiles
Air-to-surface missiles
Cruise missiles
Cannon
Trainable guns
Naval weapons
Nuclear-capable
Rockets
'Smart' weapon kit
Weapon load 0-4,000 lb
Weapon load 4,000-15,000 lb
Weapon load 15,000 lb plus

Avionics
Electronic Counter Measures
Electronic Support Measures
Search radar
Fire control radar
Look-down/shoot-down
Terrain-following radar
Forward-looking infra-red
Laser
Television

Bell Model 204/UH-1 Iroquois

Austria Costa Rica Honduras Indonesia Italy Japan South Korea Malta

Role
Fighter
Close support
Counter-insurgency
Tactical strike
Strategic bomber
Tactical reconnaissance
Strategic reconnaissance
Maritime patrol
Anti-ship strike
Anti-submarine warfare
Search and rescue
Assault transport
Transport
Liaison
Trainer
Inflight-refuelling tanker
Specialized

Performance
All-weather capability
Rough field capability
STOL capability
VTOL capability
Airspeed 0-250 mph
Airspeed 250 mph-Mach 1
Airspeed Mach 1 plus
Ceiling 0-20,000 ft
Ceiling 20,000-40,000 ft
Ceiling 40,000ft plus
Range 0-1,000 miles
Range 1,000-3,000 miles
Range 3,000 miles plus

Weapons
Air-to-air missiles
Air-to-surface missiles
Cruise missiles
Cannon
Trainable guns
Naval weapons
Nuclear-capable
Rockets
'Smart' weapon kit
Weapon load 0-4,000 lb
Weapon load 4,000-15,000 lb
Weapon load 15,000 lb plus

Avionics
Electronic Counter Measures
Electronic Support Measures
Search radar
Fire control radar
Look-down/shoot-down
Terrain-following radar
Forward-looking infra-red
Laser
Television

Bell Model 204 of the Austrian air force.

In the early 1950s the US Army notified its requirement for a helicopter with a primary casevac mission, but suitable also for utility use and as an instrument trainer; in 1955 the design submitted by Bell was announced the winner, three prototypes of the **Bell Model 204** being ordered under the designation **XH-40**. The first of these (55-4459) was flown initially on 22 October 1956, its 615-kW (825-shp) Lycoming XT53-L-1 turboshaft engine, derated to 522-kW (700-shp), making it the first turbine-powered aircraft to be acquired by the US Army. The XH-40s were followed by six **YH-40** service trials aircraft with small changes, the most important being a 30.5cm (1.0-ft) fuselage 'stretch'. When ordered into production, the designation **HU-1A** was allocated, the HU prompting the 'Huey' nickname that survived the 1962 redesignation to UH-1, and which became far better known than the official title of **Iroquois**. Initial production version was the HU-1A, with a crew of two, plus six passengers or two stretchers, and with the T53-L-1 engine. It was followed by the **HU-1B** with revised main rotor blades and an enlarged cabin seating two crew, plus seven passengers or three stretchers; early-production helicopters had the 716-kW (960-shp)

Lycoming T53-L-5, late-production machines the 820-kW (1,100-shp) T53-L-11. In 1962 the HU-1A and HU-1B were redesignated **UH-1A** and **UH-1B** respectively, and in 1965 the UH-1B was superseded in production by the **UH-1C**. This had a 'door-hinge' main rotor with wide-chord blades, giving improvements in performance and manoeuvrability. Other military versions include the US Marine Corps **UH-1E** (with rescue hoist, rotor brake and special avionics); the USAF **UH-1F** and similar **TH-1F** trainer (962-kW/1,290-shp General Electric T58-GE-3 and increased-diameter rotor); the US Navy search and rescue **HH-1K** (similar to UH-1E but with 1044-kW/1,400-shpT53-L-13), plus the **TH-1L** (training) and **UH-1L** (utility) versions of the UH-1E with T53-L-13 engine; and the US Army **UH-1M** with night sensor equipment (three acquired for evaluation). In addition to production for the US armed forces Bell also built the Model 204B for military export, and this version was extensively licence-built for both civil and military use by Agusta in Italy (**Agusta-Bell AB.204**) and by Fuji in Japan, the latter also developing the **Fuji-Bell 204B-2** with increased engine power and a tractor tail rotor.

Bell Model 204 (UH-1B)

Specification: Bell UH-1E Iroquois
Origin: USA
Type: assault support helicopter
Powerplant: one 820-kW (1,100-shp) Lycoming T53-L-11 turboshaft engine
Performance: maximum speed 120 kts (222 km/h; 138 mph); initial rate of climb 2,350 ft (716 m) per minute; service ceiling 16,700 ft (5090 m); range with maximum fuel 341 km (212 miles)
Weights: empty 2155 kg (4,750 lb); maximum take-off 3856 kg (8,500 lb)
Dimensions: main rotor diameter 13.41 m (44 ft 0 in); length of fuselage 12.98 m (42 ft 7 in); height 4.44 m (14 ft 7 in); main rotor disc area 141.26 m² (1,520.5 sq ft)
Armament: some UH-1A/-1Bs were operated in Vietnam with up to four side-mounted 7.62-mm (0.3-in) machine-guns, or two similarly mounted packs each containing 24 rockets

The Bell 204 has been licence-built by Agusta and Fuji. The former built this example for the Austrian air force, which uses it for many co-operation duties and mountain rescue.

HT-18 at Whiting Field operates this UH-1E as part of the US Navy's helicopter training force. The Huey is a good trainer for pilots moving on to large helicopters.

Bell Model 205/UH-1D/UH-1H Iroquois

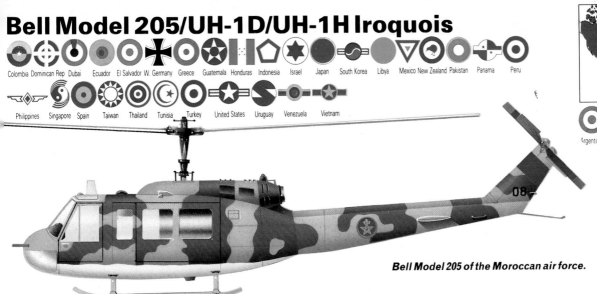

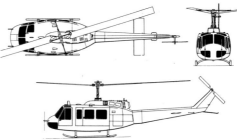

Bell Model 205 of the Moroccan air force.

With production of the Model 204 for the US armed services totalling some 2,500 examples, it is not surprising that an improved **Bell Model 205**, proposed in 1960, was of interest to the US Army; a contract followed in July 1960 for seven service test **YUH-1D** helicopters. These retained the Lycoming T53-L-11 turboshaft, but differed from the Model 204 by having a larger-diameter main rotor; a lengthened fuselage for a pilot and 12-14 troops, or six stretchers and a medical attendant, or 1814 kg (4,000 lb) of freight; and increased fuel capacity and provision for auxiliary fuel. The first was flown on 16 August 1961 and the type was ordered into production for the US Army under the designation **UH-1D**, the first being delivered on 9 August 1963. A total of 2,008 was built for the US Army, followed by the generally similar **UH-1H**, which differed by introducing the 1044-kW (1,400-shp) T53-L-13 turboshaft; final production of the UH-1H (40 for the Turkish army) is scheduled to end in 1986. Variants include three **EH-1H** ECM conversions from the UH-1H, with many more planned before the intended mission was taken over by the Sikorsky EH-60A, plus some 220 **UH-1V** medevac con-

versions from UH-1Hs, carried out by the US Army Electronics Command. Other military versions of the Model 205, generally similar to the UH-1H, have included 10 **CUH-1H** operational trainers for the Canadian Armed Forces (which designated them **CH-118**) and 30 **HH-1H** rescue helicopters for the USAF. Production of the UH-1H for the US Army totalled 3,573, and it is planned to retain some 2,700 in service into the 21st century. Under a product improvement programme these have gained new avionics and equipment, and new composite main rotor blades are to be introduced, as well as Doppler navigation and an improved cockpit. In addition to military exports by Bell, a multi-role utility helicopter for both civil and military use has been extensively licence-built by Agusta in Italy as the **Agusta-Bell AB.205**, with production continuing; Fuji in Japan is also building the Model 205 under the designation UH-1H. Dornier in Germany completed 352 equivalent to the UH-1D, which serve with the Luftwaffe and Heeresfliegertruppen, and in Taiwan AIDC built 118 similar to the UH-1H for the Chinese Nationalist army.

Bell Model 205 (UH-1D/H)

Fuji builds the Model 205 as the UH-1H for local use. This aircraft is typical of Japanese Hueys, which are used for general duties and search and rescue.

The US Army plans to retain masses of the UH-1H until the 21st century, despite widespread introduction of Sikorsky's Black Hawk. Many now serve with the National Guard.

Specification: Bell UH-1H
Origin: USA
Type: general-purpose helicopter
Powerplant: one 1044-kW (1,400-shp) Lycoming T53-L-13 turboshaft engine
Performance: maximum speed 110 kts (204 km/h; 127 mph); initial rate of climb 1,600 ft (488 m) per minute; service ceiling 12,600 ft (3840 m); range with maximum fuel 318 miles (512 km)
Weights: empty 2363 kg (5,210 lb); maximum take-off 4309 kg (9,500 lb)
Dimensions: main rotor diameter 14.63 m (48 ft 0 in); length, rotors turning 17.62 m (57 ft 9.7 in); height 4.41 m (14 ft 5.5 in); main rotor disc area 168.11 m² (1,809.56 sq ft)
Armament: none in this version

Role
Fighter
Close support
Counter-insurgency
Tactical strike
Strategic bomber
Tactical reconnaissance
Strategic reconnaissance
Maritime patrol
Anti-ship strike
Anti-submarine warfare
Search and rescue
Assault transport
Transport
Liaison
Trainer
Inflight-refuelling tanker
Specialized

Performance
All-weather capability
Rough field capability
STOL capability
VTOL capability
Airspeed 0-250 mph
Airspeed 250 mph-Mach 1
Airspeed Mach 1 plus
Ceiling 0-20,000 ft
Ceiling 20,000-40,000 ft
Ceiling 40,000ft plus
Range 0-1,000 miles
Range 1,000-3,000 miles
Range 3,000 miles plus

Weapons
Air-to-air missiles
Air-to-surface missiles
Cruise missiles
Cannon
Trainable guns
Naval weapons
Nuclear-capable
Rockets
'Smart' weapon kit
Weapon load 0-4,000 lb
Weapon load 4,000-15,000 lb
Weapon load 15,000 lb plus

Avionics
Electronic Counter Measures
Electronic Support Measures
Search radar
Fire control radar
Look-down/shoot-down
Terrain-following radar
Forward-looking infra-red
Laser
Television

Bell Model 206 Army versions/OH-58 Kiowa

Austria	Canada	Israel	Spain	United States

The US Army's competition for a Light Observation Helicopter (LOH), announced in 1960, appeared a reasonably uncomplicated problem. It was only when they read the 'small print' that prospective contenders realized that the term LOH covered a helicopter suitable not only for an observation role, but for missions that included also casevac, close support, photo-reconnaissance and light transport. This demanding challenge spurred interest, no fewer than 12 US manufacturers making design proposals for this four-seat helicopter, for which a payload of 181 kg (400 lb) and cruising speed of some 104 kts (193 km/h; 120 mph) was specified. Bell, Hiller and Hughes each gained contracts to build five prototypes for evaluation, the Hughes contender finally being chosen by the US Army. Nevertheless, convinced that its design had merit, Bell built a new five-seat prototype, the **Bell Model 206A JetRanger.** Flown on 10 January 1966 and certificated nine months later, the Model 206A was soon produced commercially and also built by Agusta in Italy.

In 1967 the US Army, worried by delivery rate and rising cost of the Hughes OH-6A reopened its LOH competition; on 8 March 1968 the Bell Model 206A was declared winner and ordered into production as the **OH-58A Kiowa.** Deliveries to the US Army began on 23 May 1969, and over five years a total of 2,200 were procured; the Canadian Armed Forces also acquired 74 as **COH-58A** (later **CH-136**) helicopters. On 30 June 1976 the US Army awarded Bell a development contract to convert one OH-58A to improved **OH-58C** standard; this introduced a flat glass canopy, uprated engine, and an installation for infra-red suppression, and two more OH-58C conversions followed before modification of 275 OH-58As to OH-58C standard began in March 1978.

In September 1981 the **Bell Model 406** proposal won the Army Helicopter Improvement Program (AHIP) to provide close combat reconnaissance and an ability to support attack helicopters and direct artillery fire. The Model 406 thus introduces a mast-mounted sight, specialized avionics and a cockpit control and display subsystem. The US Army expect that testing of five Model 406 prototypes, which ended in 1985, will result in the modification of 578 OH-58A Kiowas to this new AHIP standard under the designation **OH-58D.**

Bell OH-58A Kiowa of the 25th Aviation Company, US Army based in Germany.

Bell OH-58A Kiowa

Most early Kiowas are expected to be converted to OH-58D standard, featuring four-blade rotor and mast-mounted sight. Completely revised avionics will also be fitted.

The OH-58A serves in large numbers with the US Army, used in the spotting role. A six-barrel machine-gun provides suppressive fire whilst operating in hostile areas.

Specification: Bell OH-58C Kiowa

Origin: USA
Type: light observation helicopter
Powerplant: one 313-kW (420-shp) Allison T63-A-720 turboshaft engine
Performance: maximum speed 120 kts (222 km/h; 138 mph) at sea level; cruising speed 102 kts (188 km/h; 117 mph); initial rate of climb 1,780 ft (543 m) per minute; service ceiling 18,900 ft (5760 m); maximum range on armed scout mission at sea level with no reserves 491 km (305 miles)
Weights: empty 719 kg (1,585 lb); maximum take-off 1451 kg (3,200 lb)
Dimensions: main rotor diameter 10.77 m (35 ft 4 in); length, rotors turning 12.49 m (40 ft 11.75 in); height 2.91 m (9 ft 6.5 in); main rotor disc area 91.09 m² (980.56 sq ft)
Armament: the M27 armament kit incorporating a 7.62-mm (0.3-in) Minigun is standard

Bell Model 206/206L TexasRanger/TH-57 SeaRanger and AB.206

Argentina · Australia · Austria · Bangladesh · Brazil · Brunei · Canada · Chile · Colombia · Dubai · Greece · Guatemala · Guyana · Indonesia · Iran · Israel · Italy · Jamaica · South Korea · Kuwait · Libya

Malta · Mexico · Morocco · Oman · Pakistan · Peru · Philippines · Saudi Arabia · Spain

Sri Lanka · Tanzania · Thailand · Turkey · Uganda

United States · Venezuela · Yemen

The US Navy showed little interest in the US Army's light observation OH-58 Kiowa, but with a requirement identified in 1967 for a light turbine primary training helicopter it was decided, if possible, to procure an off-the-shelf aircraft in current production. On 31 January 1968 the US Navy ordered from Bell 40 examples of what was basically a standard civil Model 206A JetRanger II; these differed only by having US Navy avionics and the optional dual controls installed. Designated **TH-57A SeaRanger,** they were delivered during 1968 to Training Squadron HT-8 at NAS Whiting Field, Milton, Florida, and more than 85 per cent of them remain in service. Expanding requirements have led to 21 new-production **TH-57B** primary trainers, the last of them delivered in late 1984; these are based on the later Model 206B JetRanger III, and introduce a number of detail improvements suggested by use of the TH-57As. In January 1982 the US Navy ordered the **TH-57C,** a new-production advanced instrument trainer. Also based on the JetRanger III, it introduces full IFR instrumentation, plus

Bell Model 206 of the Pakistani army.

other improvements, and all of the 76 ordered have now been delivered.

In 1980 Bell began development of a military **Bell Model 206L TexasRanger** which, so far, has not proceeded beyond a demonstration aircraft. Powered by a 373-kW (500-shp) Allison 250-C28B turboshaft, it incorporates the lengthened fuselage of the Model 206L LongRanger to seat a pilot and up to six passengers, but for anti-armour/armed reconnaissance sorties has the pilot and weapons operator on side-by-side armoured seats. Weapons include air-to-air or TOW missiles, or two pods containing folding-fin rockets or 7.62-mm (0.3-in) machine-guns.

Agusta in Italy has built versions equivalent to Bell's Model 206A JetRanger, 206B JetRanger II and 206B JetRanger III under equivalent AB.206 designations. The most recent version of the **Agusta-Bell AB.206B JetRanger III** has a quieter Allison 250-C20J engine, increased fuel capacity and other improvements. Italian production, for civil and military use, exceeds 1,000 aircraft.

Bell Model 206A JetRanger

Specification: Bell TH-57C SeaRanger
Origin: USA
Type: advanced instrument training helicopter
Powerplant: one 313-kW (420-shp) Allison 250-C20J turboshaft engine, flat-rated at 236 kW (317 shp)
Performance: maximum cruising speed 114 kts (211 km/h; 131 mph) at sea level; initial rate of climb 1,540 ft (469 m) per minute; range with maximum fuel at sea level 692 km (430 miles); maximum range 848 km (527 miles) at 10,000 ft (3050 m)
Weights: empty 840 kg (1,852 lb); maximum take-off 1520 kg (3,350 lb)
Dimensions: main rotor diameter 10.16 m (33 ft 4 in); length, rotors turning 11.82 m (38 ft 9.5 in); height 2.91 m (9 ft 6.5 in); main rotor disc area 81.07 m² (872.67 sq ft)
Armament: none in this version

Australia is one of the many operators of the Model 206, which has been successfully sold around the world. Several have been converted to carry guns and light missiles.

Differing little from the civil JetRanger, the TH-57 SeaRanger forms the bulk of the US Navy's helicopter training fleet. This TH-57A serves with HT-8 at NAS Whiting Field, Florida.

Role
Fighter
Close support
Counter-insurgency
Tactical strike
Strategic bomber
Tactical reconnaissance
Strategic reconnaissance
Maritime patrol
Anti-ship strike
Anti-submarine warfare
Search and rescue
Assault transport
Transport
Liaison
Trainer
Inflight-refuelling tanker
Specialized

Performance
All-weather capability
Rough field capability
STOL capability
VTOL capability
Airspeed 0-250 mph
Airspeed 250 mph-Mach 1
Airspeed Mach 1 plus
Ceiling 0-20,000 ft
Ceiling 20,000-40,000 ft
Ceiling 40,000 ft plus
Range 0-1,000 miles
Range 1,000-3,000 miles
Range 3,000 miles plus

Weapons
Air-to-air missiles
Air-to-surface missiles
Cruise missiles
Cannon
Trainable guns
Naval weapons
Nuclear-capable
Rockets
'Smart' weapon kit
Weapon load 0-4,000 lb
Weapon load 4,000-15,000 lb
Weapon load 15,000 lb plus

Avionics
Electronic Counter Measures
Electronic Support Measures
Search radar
Fire control radar
Look-down/shoot-down
Terrain-following radar
Forward-looking infra-red
Laser
Television

Bell Model 209 (single-engine)/AH-1 HueyCobra

Greece   Israel   Japan   Jordan   Pakistan   Turkey   United States

Role
- Fighter
- Close support
- Counter-insurgency
- Tactical strike
- Strategic bomber
- Tactical reconnaissance
- Strategic reconnaissance
- Maritime patrol
- Anti-ship strike
- Anti-submarine warfare
- Search and rescue
- Assault transport
- Transport
- Liaison
- Trainer
- Inflight-refuelling tanker
- Specialized

Performance
- All-weather capability
- Rough field capability
- STOL capability
- VTOL capability
- Airspeed 0-250 mph
- Airspeed 250 mph-Mach 1
- Airspeed Mach 1 plus
- Ceiling 0-20,000 ft
- Ceiling 20,000-40,000 ft
- Ceiling 40,000ft plus
- Range 0-1,000 miles
- Range 1,000-3,000 miles
- Range 3,000 miles plus

Weapons
- Air-to-air missiles
- Air-to-surface missiles
- Cruise missiles
- Cannon
- Trainable guns
- Naval weapons
- Nuclear-capable
- Rockets
- 'Smart' weapon kit
- Weapon load 0-4,000 lb
- Weapon load 4,000-15,000 lb
- Weapon load 15,000 lb plus

Avionics
- Electronic Counter Measures
- Electronic Support Measures
- Search radar
- Fire control radar
- Look-down/shoot-down
- Terrain-following radar
- Forward-looking infra-red
- Laser
- Television

Primary capability
Secondary capability

Bell AH-1S HueyCobra of the Israeli air force (Heyl Ha'Avir).

When details were issued of the Army's AAFSS (Advanced Aerial Fire Support System) requirement to replace the failed Lockheed Cheyenne, Bell initiated crash development of a company-funded prototype derived from the Model 204; it had the powerplant, transmission and wide-chord rotor of the UH-1C but introduced a new fuselage seating the gunner in the nose and the pilot higher in the rear. The fuselage was very narrow, only 0.97 m (3 ft 2 in) at its widest point and this, coupled with a low silhouette, made the aircraft easy to conceal on the ground and a more difficult target in the air. Designated **Bell Model 209 Huey-Cobra,** the prototype (N209J) was flown for the first time on 7 September 1965. It began service tests in December 1965, and then gained an order for two pre-production **AH-1G** helicopters on 4 April 1966 and an initial contract for 110 production AH-1Gs nine days later; such was the degree of urgency. Initial production deliveries reached the US Army in June 1967 and within weeks the type had become operational in Vietnam. AH-1G production totalled 1,119 for the US Army, of which 38 were transferred to the US Marine

Corps for training; some US Army AH-1Gs were converted as **TH-1G** dual-control trainers. Later variants include 92 **AH-1Q** conversions from AH-1Gs to fire TOW missiles, and the **AH-1R** conversion with a 1342-kW (1,800-shp) T53-L-703 turboshaft and no TOW capability. The designation **Modified AH-1S** applies to 315 AH-1Gs retrofitted with a TOW system and the powerplant of the AH-1R, plus the 92 AH-1Qs brought up to this same standard. They were followed by 100 **Production AH-1S** which have improved avionics, uprated powerplant and transmission; 98 similar **Up-gun AH-1S** which introduce a universal 20/30-mm gun turret and other refinements; and the current **Modernised AH-1S.** This last incorporates the updates of the Production and Up-gun AH-1S, and improvements that include new air data, Doppler navigation and fire-control systems, and continuing programmes are under development to enhance the capability of the HueyCobra. In addition to the production of Modernised AH-1S Hueys for the US Army, others are in the process of manufacture and delivery for foreign air arms.

Specification: Bell Modernised AH-1S
Origin: USA
Type: anti-armour attack helicopter
Powerplant: one 1342-kW (1,800-shp) Lycoming T53-L-703 turboshaft engine, flat-rated at 820kW (1,100 shp)
Performance: maximum speed with TOW missiles 122 kts (227 km/h; 141 mph); initial rate of climb 1,620 ft (494 m) per minute; service ceiling 12,200 ft (3720 m); range with maximum fuel and reserves 507 km (315 miles) at sea level
Weights: empty 2939 kg (6,479 lb); maximum take-off 4536 kg (10,000 lb)
Dimensions: main rotor diameter 13.41 m (44 ft 0 in); length, rotors turning 16.14 m (52 ft 11.5 in); height 4.12 m (13 ft 6.25 in); main rotor disc area 141.26 m^2 (1,520.53 sq ft)
Armament: eight TOW missiles, one General Electric universal turret for 20-mm or 30-mm cannon, plus launcher pods for 2.75-in (69.85-mm) folding-fin rockets

Bell AH-1S HueyCobra

Early AH-1Gs are still in service with the US Army National Guard. This example serves in Utah.

Aircraft of modernized AH-1S standard are now being supplied in some numbers to foreign users. The Pakistani army are to receive 20 for anti-armour duties, coming complete with TOW missiles.

Bell Model 209 (twin-engine)/AH-1J/T SeaCobra

Iran | Israel | South Korea | United States

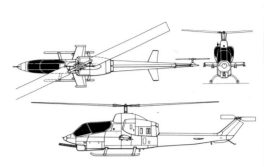

Bell AH-1J SeaCobra of the US Marine Corps.

US Marine Corps interest in a well-armed close-support helicopter was heightened by the US Army's procurement of the Bell AH-1G HueyCobra. Following USMC evaluation of the AH-1G it was decided to acquire this for service, but with the extra reliability of a twin-engine powerplant. In May 1968 the USMC ordered 49 **AH-1J SeaCobra** helicopters, and as an interim measure procured 38 AH-1G HueyCobras which were used for training and initial deployment until delivery of the SeaCobras during 1970-1. This initial AH-1J retained basically the same airframe as the AH-1G, with some detail changes to cater for the higher output of the Pratt & Whitney Canada T400-CP-400 powerplant, a revolutionary engine with two powerplants which ran for the first time in July 1968. Flat-rated at 820 kW (1,100 shp) and with a take-off and emergency power rating of 932 kW (1,250 shp), the T400 is a militarized version of Pratt & Whitney Canada's PT6T-3 Turbo Twin-Pac, incorporating aluminium instead of magnesium in its construction, which is essential for a maritime or seaboard environment. Bell was also to build for Iran 202 similar AH-1Js, but these incorporated TOW-capability.

An additional 20 AH-1Js were delivered to the USMC in 1974-5, the last two of this batch being modified subsequently to serve as prototypes for the **AH-1T Improved Sea-Cobra.** Retaining many features of the AH-1J airframe, these have a slightly lengthened fuselage (to increase fuel capacity), a lengthened tail boom, improved main and tail rotors as developed for the Bell Model 214, and an uprated transmission to handle the full rated power of the upgraded T400-WV-402 powerplant, developing 1469 kW (1,970 shp). The first of 57 AH-1Ts (59228) was flown on 20 May 1976 and delivered to the USMC on 15 October 1977. Of these, 51 have now been equipped to carry TOW missiles.

In 1980 Bell was loaned an AH-1T by the USMC, and demonstrated this machine with two General Electric T700-GE-700 turboshafts having a combined output of 2386 kW (3,200 shp). From this was planned an improved AH-1T which, in production form, will have T700-GE-401 turboshafts developing together 2424 kW (3,250 shp), a new combining gearbox and other improvements. Designated **AH-1T+ SuperCobra,** 44 have been ordered by the USMC with initial deliveries scheduled for March 1986.

Bell AH-1T SeaCobra

Specification: Bell AH-1T SeaCobra
Origin: USA
Type: twin-turbine close-support/attack helicopter
Powerplant: one 1469-kW (1,970-shp) Pratt & Whitney Canada T400-WV-402 twin-turbine unit, which has a maximum continuous rating of 1248 kW (1,673 shp)
Performance: maximum speed 149 kts (277 km/h; 172 mph) at sea level; initial rate of climb 1,785 ft (544 m) per minute; service ceiling 7,400 ft (2255 m); range with maximum fuel 420 km (261 miles)
Weights: empty 3642 kg (8,030 lb); maximum take-off 6350 kg (14,000 lb)
Dimensions: main rotor diameter 14.63 m (48 ft 0 in); length, rotors turning 17.68 m (58 ft 0 in); height 4.32 m (14 ft 2 in); main rotor disc area 168.11 m² (1,809.56 sq ft)
Armament: chin turret housing a 20-mm M197 three-barrel cannon, plus underwing attachments for 2.75-in (69.85-mm) rocket pods, flare dispensers, grenade dispensers, parachute flares, Minigun pods, or alternative TOW or Hellfire missile installations

Sporting the new black markings, this AH-1J displays the far bulkier engine bay of the twin-engined version. These helicopters have recently had infra-red countermeasures fitted.

The Marine Corps Cobras are used for supporting ground operations, especially beach assaults. TOW missiles are used, and the new Rockwell Hellfire missile is also entering service.

Role	
Fighter	
Close support	■
Counter-insurgency	
Tactical strike	
Strategic bomber	
Tactical reconnaissance	
Strategic reconnaissance	
Maritime patrol	
Anti-ship strike	
Anti-submarine warfare	
Search and rescue	
Assault transport	
Transport	
Liaison	
Trainer	
Inflight-refuelling tanker	
Specialized	

Performance	
All-weather capability	
Rough field capability	
STOL capability	
VTOL capability	
Airspeed 0-250 mph	■
Airspeed 250 mph-Mach 1	
Airspeed Mach 1 plus	
Ceiling 0-20,000 ft	■
Ceiling 20,000-40,000 ft	
Ceiling 40,000 ft plus	
Range 0-1,000 miles	■
Range 1,000-3,000 miles	
Range 3,000 miles plus	

Weapons	
Air-to-air missiles	
Air-to-surface missiles	■
Cruise missiles	
Cannon	■
Trainable guns	■
Naval weapons	
Nuclear-capable	
Rockets	■
'Smart' weapon kit	
Weapon load 0-4,000 lb	■
Weapon load 4,000-15,000 lb	
Weapon load 15,000 lb plus	

Avionics	
Electronic Counter Measures	
Electronic Support Measures	
Search radar	
Fire control radar	
Look-down/shoot-down	
Terrain-following radar	
Forward-looking infra-red	
Laser	
Television	

Bell Model 212 Twin Two-Twelve/UH-1N

Following negotiations in early 1968 between Bell Helicopters, the Canadian government and Pratt & Whitney Canada, it was mutually agreed to initiate a jointly-funded programme covering the development of a twin-turbine version of the Bell Model 205/UH-1H Iroquois. Selected as powerplant for this new venture was the PT6T Turbo Twin-Pac. It comprised two turboshaft engines mounted side-by-side to drive, through a combining gearbox, a single output shaft. An advantage was provided by sensing torquemeters in the gearbox which, in the event of an engine failure, could signal the still-operative turbine to develop either emergency or continuous power in order that the flight could be concluded in safety.

Adaptation of the initial production PT6T-3 Turbo Twin-Pac to the airframe of the Bell Model 205 proceeded without serious problem, and the first deliveries of **Bell Model 212** helicopters to the US Air Force began during 1970 under the tri-service designation **UH-1N.** The USAF acquired a total of 79 UH-1Ns which have seen service worldwide in support of Special Operations Force counter-insurgency activities. A larger number went to the US Navy and Marine Corps, which by 1978 received a total of 221. Those of the US Marine Corps include two UH-1Ns converted to **VH-1N** VIP transports, plus six built as new to this configuration. The Canadian Armed Forces acquired 50 Bell 212s, the first of them handed over on 3 May 1971 and the last of them being delivered just over a year later. These were designated initially **CUH-1N,** but have since been re-designated **CH-135.**

The improved safety offered by the Twin-Pac powerplant made this helicopter attractive to companies providing support to offshore gas/oil operations, and while Bell soon had a commercial Twin Two-Twelve in full-scale production, it also built small numbers of military helicopters for other nations. Agusta in Italy soon acquired a licence for the Model 212, producing the AB.212 for civil and military customers, and has developed a specialized maritime version as the AB.212ASW, these being described in an earlier issue.

Specification: Bell UH-1N
Origin: USA
Type: utility and transport helicopter
Powerplant: one Pratt & Whitney Canada T400-CP-400 (military designation of PT6T) Twin-Pac flat-rated at 962 kW (1,290 shp) for take-off
Performance: maximum speed 110 kts (204 km/h; 127 mph) at sea level; initial rate of climb 1,745 ft (532 m) per minute; service ceiling 17,300 ft (5275 m); maximum range 460 km (286 miles)
Weights: empty 2722 kg (6,000 lb); maximum take-off 4536 kg (10,000 lb)
Dimensions: main rotor diameter 14.69 m (48 ft 2.25 in); length, rotors turning 17.46 m (57 ft 3.25 in); height 4.53 m (14 ft 10.25 in); main rotor disc area 173.90 m² (1,871.91 sq ft)
Armament: none

Bell Model 212, as used by CAAC in China. These are used for quasi-civil duties, but would be used by the military in times of war.

Bell Model 212 (UH-1N)

The twin-engined Huey version is used in numbers by the US Marine Corps. Eight aircraft are used as VIP transports under the designation VH-1N. This example is a UH-1N, used for general transport duties.

Most of the UH-1Ns supplied to the USAF are employed on covert duties with Special Operations forces. These two sport a jungle camouflage for counter-insurgency duties in the Panama Canal Zone.

30

Bell/Boeing Vertol V-22 Osprey

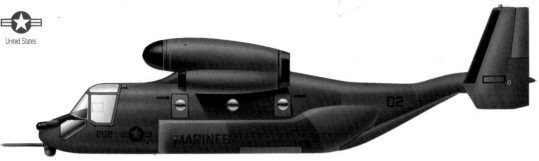

United States

Bell/Boeing V-22 Osprey as it is expected to appear in US Marine Corps service.

The basic helicopter has in its normally accepted configuration (with either a single main rotor and anti-torque tail rotor or twin counter-rotating rotors to overcome torque) two major shortcomings, its comparatively low forward speed and high operating costs. Many manufacturers have explored means of overcoming these disadvantages, to give improved performance and lower operating costs to an aircraft with the helicopter's VTOL capability, but there is not the space here to review the many different approaches to the problem. However, Bell has been working for almost 40 years on tilt-rotor systems and as early as 18 December 1958 demonstrated, with its second Model 200 prototype (US Army designation XV-3), that it was possible to take off or land vertically with twin rotors that could be tilted progressively forward to act as propellers for horizontal flight. Continuing research and development by Bell led to the company's Model 301 (US Army designation XV-15), which is a twin tilt-rotor research aircraft powered by two 1156-kW (1,550-shp) Lycoming LTC1K-4K turboshaft

engines. The first of the two XV-15 research prototypes was flown on 3 May 1977 and they have since demonstrated helicopter forward speeds of up to 100 kts (185 km/h; 115 mph), and with the rotors tilted fully forward horizontal flight cruising speeds of 301 kts (558 km/h; 347 mph).

Bell teamed up with Boeing Vertol to submit a design proposal for the US government's Joint Services Advanced Vertical Lift Aircraft (JVX), and on 26 April 1983 the team was awarded a contract covering the preliminary design phase. Based on the XV-15 techniques, the **Bell/Boeing Vertol JVX,** which has since been designated **V-22 Osprey,** is a twin engine tilt-rotor aircraft for deployment by all US armed services for amphibious assault carrying up to 24 troops, and suitable also for such roles as combat SAR, electronic warfare and special operations. If a go-ahead for full-scale development is given during 1985, Bell and Boeing Vertol have estimated that a first flight will be made during August 1987, with initial entry into service following in 1991.

Specification: Bell/Boeing Vertol JVX
Origin: USA
Type: tilt-rotor multi-role aircraft
Powerplant: two General Electric T64-GE-717 turboshaft engines, each with a maximum power rating of 3620 kW (4,855 shp)
Performance: (provisional) maximum cruising speed 261 kts (483 km/h; 300 mph); range with pilot and 24 troops 740 km (460 miles) at 3,000 ft (915 m)
Weights: (provisional) maximum take-off VTOL 19,867 kg (43,800 lb); maximum take-off STOL 24,948 kg (55,000 lb)
Dimensions: (provisional) rotor diameter, each 11.58 m (38 ft 0 in); width overall 25.76 m (84 ft 6 in); length 17.32 m (56 ft 10 in); height, rotors in take-off position 6.15 m (20 ft 2 in); rotor disc area, total 210.72 m² (2,268.24 sq ft)
Armament: nose-mounted 12.7-mm (0.5-in) multi-barrel machine-gun

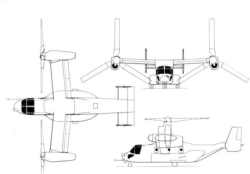

Bell/Boeing V-22 Osprey

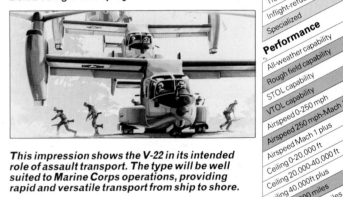

This impression shows the V-22 in its intended role of assault transport. The type will be well suited to Marine Corps operations, providing rapid and versatile transport from ship to shore.

The prime tilt-rotor V-22 development aircraft is the Bell XV-15. It is seen here demonstrating a vertical landing during carrier suitability trials aboard the USS Tripoli.

Role	
Fighter	
Close support	
Counter-insurgency	
Tactical strike	
Strategic bomber	
Tactical reconnaissance	
Strategic reconnaissance	
Maritime patrol	
Anti-ship strike	
Anti-submarine warfare	
Search and rescue	
Assault transport	
Transport	
Liaison	
Trainer	
Inflight-refuelling tanker	
Specialized	

Performance	
All-weather capability	
Rough field capability	
STOL capability	
VTOL capability	
Airspeed 0-250 mph	
Airspeed 250 mph-Mach 1	
Airspeed Mach 1 plus	
Ceiling 0-20,000 ft	
Ceiling 20,000-40,000 ft	
Ceiling 40,000ft plus	
Range 0-1,000 miles	
Range 1,000-3,000 miles	
Range 3,000 miles plus	

Weapons	
Air-to-air missiles	
Air-to-surface missiles	
Cruise missiles	
Cannon	
Trainable guns	
Naval weapons	
Nuclear-capable	
Rockets	
'Smart' weapon kit	
Weapon load 0-4,000 lb	
Weapon load 4,000-15,000 lb	
Weapon load 15,000 lb plus	

Avionics	
Electronic Counter Measures	
Electronic Support Measures	
Search radar	
Fire control radar	
Look-down/shoot-down	
Terrain-following radar	
Forward-looking infra-red	
Laser	
Television	

Primary capability
Secondary capability

Boeing B-52G Stratofortress

Boeing B-52G Stratofortress of the 2nd Bomb Wing, US Air Force.

The remarkable **Boeing B-52 Strato-fortress** originated from two prototypes designated **XB-52** and **YB-52**, the latter (49-231) making the type's maiden flight on 15 April 1952. Early production versions were the **B-52B** (23 built), **RB-52B** (27), **B-52C** (35), **B-52D** (170), **B-52E** (100) and **B-52F** (89); the RB-52B was the first delivered for service with the USAF, equipping Strategic Air Command's 93rd Heavy Bombardment Wing at Castle AFB, California, from 29 June 1955. The ability of the Stratofortress to carry nuclear weapons to almost any target in the world (with the aid of inflight-refuelling) made it a vital component of SAC's inventory, but all of these early variants are now withdrawn from service.

The major version was the structurally re-designed **B-52G** (193 built), the first being flown on 26 October 1958. Important changes included a 'wet' wing to increase fuel capacity, an improved pressurized com-partment for all six crew, remotely-operated tail guns and provisions for Quail decoy mis-siles and AGM-28 Hound Dog ASMs. The 1962 switch from conventional high-level bombing to low-level penetration demanded better avionics to enhance navigation and ensure accurate weapon delivery, and since then the B-52G has been involved in continual update programmes. By August 1972 they were modified to carry 20 Boeing SRAMs (short-range attack missiles) and soon gained the ASQ-151 EVS (Electro-optical Viewing System) with chin-turrets housing FLIR and LLLTV to improve low-level forward view. They are now advanced in updating with Phase VI avionics which includes AFSAT-COM worldwide communications via satel-lite, ALQ-155(V) advanced ECM, ALQ-177 ECM system, ALR-46 digital RWR, ALQ-153 tail-warning radar and ALQ-122 SNOE (Smart Noise Operation Equipment); 99 B-52Gs have also been modified to carry 12 ALCMs (Air-Launched Cruise Missiles). Scheduled for completion by 1990 is the installation of an Offensive Attack System (OAS) which in-cludes an AHRS, ASQ-38 bombing/naviga-tion system, Doppler and modernized radar, ASN-131 INS, radar altimeter and TERCOM (TERrain COmparison Matching) for greater accuracy in penetration/weapon delivery. Instead of being equipped to carry ALCMs, some 70 B-52Gs are to fulfil the maritime surveillance/support mission and conven-tional bombing role of the now withdrawn B-52Ds; for the former task some are being equipped to carry AGM-84A Harpoon and GBU-15V anti-shipping missiles.

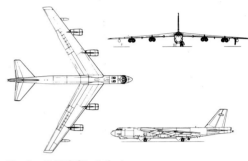

Boeing B-52G Stratofortress

Specification: Boeing B-52G Stratofortress
Origin: USA
Type: long-range cruise missile carrier/maritime support aircraft
Powerplant: eight 6237-kg (13,750-lb) thrust Pratt & Whitney J57-P-43WB turbojet engines
Performance: maximum speed 516 kts (956 km/h; 594 mph) at optimum altitude; cruising speed 442 kts (819 km/h; 509 mph) at optimum altitude; maximum penetration speed 365 kts (676 km/h; 420 mph) at low level; service ceiling 40,000 ft (12192 m); range with maximum internal fuel 12070 km (7,500 miles)
Weight: maximum take-off more than 221353 kg (488,000 lb)
Dimensions: span 56.39 m (185 ft 0 in); length 49.04 m (160 ft 10.8 in); height 12.40 m (40 ft 8 in); wing area 371.60 m² (4,000.0 sq ft)
Armament: as detailed in text to a maximum weapon load of approximately 22680 kg (50,000 lb)

This front view of the B-52 shows the enormous flaps fitted to the aircraft. The wing is extremely flexible, and bends down considerably when the aircraft is parked with fuel in the wings.

Seen in landing posture, this B-52G demonstrates the unusual landing gear arrangement, with bicycle-type main gear and wingtip outriggers. The main gear twists to counteract crosswinds.

Boeing B-52H Stratofortress

United States

Boeing B-52H Stratofortress of the US Air Force.

Quite obviously the **Boeing B-52H Stratofortress** shared the same derivation as the B-52G, but because it was intended for a new task it was not merely a slightly-improved variant but differed in some important ways. Instead of being required for a bomber role, like its predecessors, the B-52H was intended to serve as a carrier for the Douglas GAM-87A Skybolt air-launched ballistic missile then under development. The most significant of the changes for this mission was to ensure that the B-52H would be able to penetrate enemy airspace at low level, below the radar, and this required extensive structural modification to ensure the airframe would be able to withstand the effects of low-level turbulence. The changes were barely visible externally, but two other modifications were to provide external features that allowed of identification. One of the early-build B-52Gs (57-6471) had flown in July 1960 as a testbed for the Pratt & Whitney TF33-P-1 turbofan, and more powerful versions of the same engine were installed in revised cowlings to enhance performance of the B-52H, giving a range increase of almost a third by comparison with the B-52G. The last externally-

noticeable change was replacement of the four 12.7-mm (0.5-in) machine-guns in the tail turret of the B-52G by a Vulcan cannon with six 20-mm barrels. Internal changes for the new role brought revised ECM equipment and the provision of terrain-avoidance radar.

A total of 102 B-52H Stratofortresses was built, the first (60-006) being flown on 6 March 1961. Within 16 months, in June 1962, the last of them had been completed; six months later President John F. Kennedy cancelled the Skybolt programme for which the B-52H had been developed. Since then this aircraft has followed similar modification programmes to those described for the B-52G, being equipped to carry 20 SRAMs and gaining the ASQ-151 Electro-optical Viewing System. It is also in the process of Phase VI avionics and Offensive Avionics System updating. In addition, it is planned that towards the end of the 1980s the B-52H will be modified to carry eight more AGM-86 ALCMs, these being mounted on a lengthened internal rotary launcher. Before they are retired from service, SAC's B-52G/H Stratofortresses may yet see more updates, particularly of avionics.

Boeing B-52H Stratofortress

The prime differences between the B-52H and other marks are the turbofan engines with distinctive cowlings, and the six-barrel rotary cannon in the tail turret.

Present USAF planning for the B-52H fleet calls for modifications to cruise missile carrier. These will have 12 ALCMs on the wing pylons and a further eight on an internal rotary launcher.

Specification: Boeing B-52H Stratofortress
Origin: USA
Type: long-range strategic cruise missile carrier
Powerplant: eight 7711-kg (17,000-lb) thrust Pratt & Whitney TF33-P-3 turbofan engines
Performance: maximum speed 516 kts (956 km/h; 594 mph) at optimum altitude; cruising speed 442 kts (819 km/h; 509 mph) at optimum altitude; maximum penetration speed 365 kts (676 km/h; 420 mph) at low level; service ceiling 55,000 ft (16765 m); range with maximum internal fuel 16093 km (10,000 miles)
Weight: maximum take-off more than 221353 kg (488,000 lb)
Dimensions: span 56.39 m (185 ft 0 in); length 49.04 m (160 ft 10.8 in); height 12.40 m (40 ft 8 in); wing area 371.60 m² (4,000.0 sq ft)
Armament: as detailed in text to a maximum weapon load of approximately 22680 kg (50,000 lb)

Role
Fighter
Close support
Counter-insurgency
Tactical strike
Strategic bomber
Tactical reconnaissance
Strategic reconnaissance
Maritime patrol
Anti-ship strike
Anti-submarine warfare
Search and rescue
Assault transport
Transport
Liaison
Trainer
Inflight-refuelling tanker
Specialized

Performance
All-weather capability
Rough field capability
STOL capability
VTOL capability
Airspeed 0-250 mph
Airspeed 250 mph-Mach 1
Airspeed Mach 1 plus
Ceiling 0-20,000 ft
Ceiling 20,000-40,000 ft
Ceiling 40,000ft plus
Range 0-1,000 miles
Range 1,000-3,000 miles
Range 3,000 miles plus

Weapons
Air-to-air missiles
Air-to-surface missiles
Cruise missiles
Cannon
Trainable guns
Naval weapons
Nuclear-capable
Rockets
'Smart' weapon kit
Weapon load 0-4,000 lb
Weapon load 4,000-15,000 lb
Weapon load 15,000 lb plus

Avionics
Electronic Counter Measures
Electronic Support Measures
Search radar
Fire control radar
Look-down/shoot-down
Terrain-following radar
Forward-looking infra-red
Laser
Television

Boeing C-135/KC-135

France   United States

71445

OHIO AIR GUARD

U.S. AIR FORCE

Boeing KC-135A Stratotanker of the 145th Air Refueling Squadron, 160th ARG, Ohio Air National Guard.

On 15 July 1954 Boeing flew its private-venture Model 367-80 prototype for the first time. For the company it represented an enormous gamble, one that depended on winning orders from the US Air Force. In consequence the 'Dash-80' prototype, as it soon became known, was initially a military demonstrator equipped with a Boeing-developed inflight-refuelling boom. This boom, controlled by an operator, was thought to be more practical than the 'probe-and-drogue' system developed in the UK, and its effective demonstration in the 'Dash-80' convinced the USAF that not only was Boeing's rigid 'flying boom' an efficient refuelling system, but that the aircraft had important potential as a tanker/transport. In August 1954, a few weeks after the maiden flight of the 'Dash-80', the USAF placed its first contract for the Model 717 as the **Boeing KC-135A Stratotanker**; the first (55-3118) was flown on 31 August 1956 and initial deliveries, to Castle AFB, California, began on 28 June 1957; production totalled 724.

Generally similar to the 'Dash-80', but smaller than even the first Boeing Model 707 developed from it, the KC-135A was powered by four J57 turbojets. In the tanker role fuel system capacity was 118105 litres (31,200 US gal), but the cabin could be used alternatively to carry cargo, loaded via a large door

in the port forward fuselage, or up to 80 passengers or a mixture of freight and passengers; with reduced fuel a maximum of 160 troops could be airlifted. Variants include a small number of KC-135As rebuilt for special duties as **JC-135A** and **JKC-135A**, subsequently becoming **NC-135A** and **NKC-135A** which was the designation of some 20 rebuilds for test and research programmes; 17 new-build **KC-135B** tankers had improved equipment, increased fuel capacity, TF33-5 turbofan engines and provisions for use as airborne command posts; and 56 conversions of KC-135As to transfer JP-7 fuel to Lockheed SR-71 'Blackbirds' were redesignated **KC-135Q**. The Model 717 airframe was adopted also as a cargo/troop transport for MATS (later MAC) as the **C-135A Stratolifter** accommodating 126 troops or 44 stretchers and 54 seated casualties. The C-135A (18 built) was followed by the **C-135B** (30 with TF33-5 engines), but the **C-135F** was a tanker/transport of which 12 were built for France. Seven **VC-135A** staff transports were conversions of C/KC-135A aircraft, two of them retaining tanker capability; five **VC-135B** staff transports were conversions of C-135Bs, as were 11 **WC-135B** weather reconnaissance aircraft, three of which later became reconverted as **C-135C** freighters.

Specification: Boeing KC-135A
Origin: USA
Type: inflight-refuelling tanker/cargo/transport aircraft
Powerplant: four 6237-kg (13,750-lb) thrust Pratt & Whitney J57-59W turbojet engines
Performance: average cruising speed 460 kts (853 km/h; 530 mph) between 30,500 and 40,000 ft (9300 and 12190 m); initial rate of climb 1,290 ft (393 m) per minute; time to climb to 30,500 ft (9300 m) 27 minutes; transfer radius with 3040-kg (6,702-lb) reserve fuel 1850 km (1,150 miles)
Weight: empty 44663 kg (98,466 lb); maximum take-off 136078 kg (300,000 lb); maximum fuel load 86047 kg (189,702 lb)
Dimensions: span 39.88 m (130 ft 10 in); length 41.53 m (136 ft 3 in); height, short fin 11.68 m (38 ft 4 in); wing area 226.03 m² (2,433.0 sq ft)
Armament: none

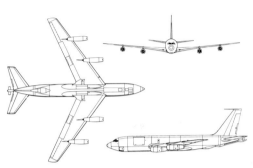

Boeing KC-135A Stratotanker

A dozen tankers were built for France under the designation C-135F. Eleven survive, and these are shortly to be re-engined with the CFM 56 turbofan.

This is typical of the many KC-135As in service with SAC. Most report to the strategic bomber force, being based with the B-52s and B-1s. This aircraft is from the 92nd BW at Fairchild.

U.S. AIR FORCE

Boeing C-137

United States

Boeing VC-137C used for Presidential transport.

As mentioned in the entry for the KC-135 Stratotanker, this Model 707 was derived from Boeing's private-venture Model 367-80 prototype. The 'Dash-80', as it became known, proved an important aircraft for the USAF, for from it has come the family of C-135, EC-135, KC-135 and RC-135 tankers, transports and special-purpose aircraft, all of them described separately. It was an equally important aircraft for The Boeing Airplane Company (as it then was), which had gambled on gaining USAF interest and contracts for a tanker version equipped with the Boeing-developed refuelling boom; income from this source would then enable the company to develop a new range of civil transports. This gamble paid off, the company gaining USAF contracts plus approval to proceed with design and production of a civil version. The 'Dash-80', then equipped as a civil demonstrator, gained on 13 October 1955 its first order from Pan American World Airways.

The original civil version was identified as the Model 707-120 and differed from the USAF tanker/transports, the biggest change being in the fuselage which was increased in width by 0.41 m (1 ft 4 in) to a maximum of 3.76 m (12 ft 4 in), and lengthened to 42.32 m (138 ft 10 in) to seat up to 181 passengers in a high-density configuration; at

the same time it gained the closely-spaced cabin windows absent from the military aircraft. There were also, of course, many detail changes to suit these aircraft for civil rather than military use, and when the USAF decided to acquire the civil version, as a transport for VIP personnel or high-priority cargo, the combination of changes was considered sufficient for the new designation **Boeing C-137** to be allocated.

USAF procurement was very limited, amounting to three Model 707-153s allocated the designation **VC-137A**. When delivered in 1959 these had four 6123-kg (13,500-lb) thrust Pratt & Whitney JT3C-6 turbojet engines; when subsequently re-engined with 8165-kg (18,000-lb) thrust TF33-5 turbofans they were redesignated **VC-137B**. Only one other version serves with the USAF, the Presidential transport **VC-137C** (Air Force One when the President is on board), the two examples of which, apart from interior furnishings, are similar to the civil Model 707-320B Intercontinental. However, several other air arms operate small numbers of Boeing Model 707s in special VIP/transport/tanker roles. As well as the VC-137s, the USAF converted several C-135 airframes to **VC-135** VIP standard. These have been used for staff transport, mainly within the United States, and supplement the VC-137 fleet.

Specification: Boeing VC-137C
Origin: USA
Type: VIP transport
Powerplant: four 8165-kg (18,000-lb) thrust Pratt & Whitney JT3D-3 turbofan engines
Performance: maximum speed 544 kts (1009 km/h; 627 mph); maximum cruising speed 521 kts (966 km/h; 600 mph) at 25,000 ft (7620 m); range with maximum fuel, with allowances but no reserves 12247 km (7,610 miles)
Weights: maximum take-off 148325 kg (327,000 lb)
Dimensions: span 44.42 m (145 ft 9 in); length 46.61 m (152 ft 11 in); height 12.93 m (42 ft 5 in); wing area 279.63 m² (3,010.0 sq ft)
Armament: none

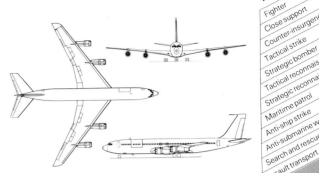

Boeing VC-137C

As well as the VC-137, several C-135 airframes have been adapted for staff transport, including this VC-135B. Some have been returned to cargo configuration.

'Air Force One' is the Presidential transport. Two aircraft are used for this but are nearing the end of their useful lives. They are based at Andrews AFB in Maryland, near Washington DC.

Role
Fighter
Close support
Counter-insurgency
Tactical strike
Strategic bomber
Tactical reconnaissance
Strategic reconnaissance
Maritime patrol
Anti-ship strike
Anti-submarine warfare
Search and rescue
Assault transport
Transport
Liaison
Trainer
Inflight-refuelling tanker
Specialized

Performance
All-weather capability
Rough field capability
STOL capability
VTOL capability
Airspeed 0-250 mph
Airspeed 250 mph-Mach 1
Airspeed Mach 1 plus
Ceiling 0-20,000 ft
Ceiling 20,000-40,000 ft
Ceiling 40,000ft plus
Range 0-1,000 miles
Range 1,000-3,000 miles
Range 3,000 miles plus

Weapons
Air-to-air missiles
Air-to-surface missiles
Cruise missiles
Cannon
Trainable guns
Naval weapons
Nuclear-capable
Rockets
'Smart' weapon kit
Weapon load 0-4,000 lb
Weapon load 4,000-15,000 lb
Weapon load 15,000 lb plus

Avionics
Electronic Counter Measures
Electronic Support Measures
Search radar
Fire control radar
Look-down/shoot-down
Terrain-following radar
Forward-looking infra-red
Laser
Television

Boeing E-6

United States

Boeing E-6 as it is expected to appear with the US Navy.

To maintain a survivable all-oceans communications link between the US National Command Authorities in Washington (or one of the National Emergency Airborne Command Post aircraft) and the US Navy's fleet of 'Ohio' class nuclear submarines (SSBNs), the US Navy currently operates a fleet of Lockheed EC-130Q Hercules aircraft. In this vital mission, known as TACAMO (TAke Charge And Move Out), the US Navy plans to complement a reduced number of EC-130Qs with a more capable aircraft.

On 29 April 1983 the Boeing Aerospace Company was contracted to develop such an aircraft, using the basic Model 707 airframe of the E-3 Sentry to carry the essential communications equipment and crew. It is planned to procure a total of 15 aircraft under the designation **Boeing E-6**. The first is scheduled to fly in 1987. The US Navy expects to attain initial operational capability with six E-6s by November 1988. The full fleet of 15 E-6 and 10 EC-130Q TACAMO aircraft should be operational by 1993, when eight of the former will be allocated for the Pacific area and the remaining seven to the Atlantic/ Mediterranean, with one E-6 in each area then required to be airborne at all times. Pending delivery of the first E-6 in 1987-8 the US Navy has procured two specially equipped NKC-135As which are being used in the training role.

The key to this mission is the provision of a secure and reliable communications system for the E-6 aircraft, which can link them to the nation's ABCP aircraft, the Presidential E-4 AABNCP, communication satellites and an emergency rocket communications system (ERCS). However, this is of little use unless positive contact can be maintained with the Trident-armed SSBNs, far away and deep in the ocean. This relies upon a VLF radio system with a trailing wire aerial about 7.9 km (4.9 miles) long and requiring some 200 kW of power for signal transmission to the buoyant wire antenna towed by the SSBNs. This aerial wire has to be maintained in an almost vertical position for reliable links with the SSBNs. This is achieved by having a heavy drogue attached to the lower end and keeping the E-6 in a tight circular orbit.

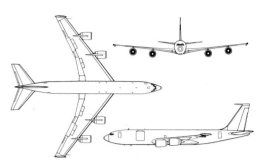

Boeing E-6

Specification: Boeing E-6 TACAMO
Origin: USA
Type: communications relay aircraft
Powerplant: four 9979-kg (22,000-lb) thrust CFM International CFM56-2 turbofan engines
Performance: cruising speed 445 kts (824 km/h; 512 mph) at 40,000 ft (12190 m); operating altitude between 25,000 and 30,000 ft (7620 and 9145 m); endurance on-station with internal fuel 16 hours; maximum on-station endurance with inflight-refuelling 72 hours
Weights: not known
Dimensions: span 44.42 m (145 ft 9 in); length 46.61 m (152 ft 11 in); height 12.93 m (42 ft 5 in); wing area 283.35 m² (3,050.0 sq ft)
Armament: none

The US Navy operates two NKC-135A aircraft for electronic warfare training duties. These will pave the way for the operational E-6 TACAMO aircraft.

This impression shows the E-6 TACAMO. In its role as a radio relay station, the E-6 comes packed with communications aerials for keeping in contact with submarines and other command posts.

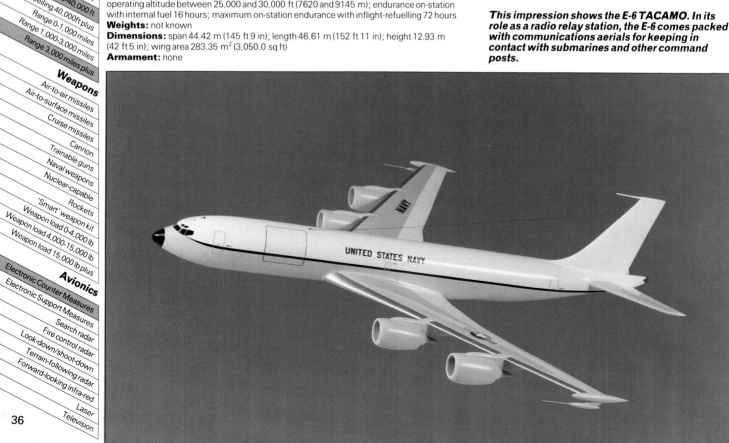

Boeing EC-135

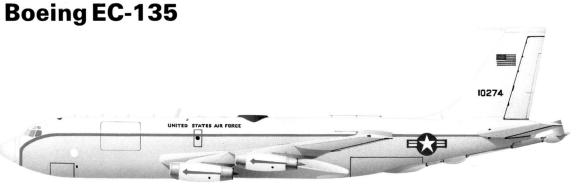

United States

Boeing EC-135H assigned to the 6th ACCS, 1st Tactical Fighter Wing.

In the early days of KC-135A production, the USAF's Strategic Air Command identified the requirement for an airborne command post (ABCP). The idea was for an aircraft equipped for this role to be airborne at all times so that, in the event of a devastating strike against SAC's fixed-position ground control centres, it would be possible to maintain command of its strategic retaliatory force from a command post that was on the move and high above the ground. Accordingly the 17 T33-engined KC-135B tankers delivered to the command also had comprehensive communications systems, were equipped to receive fuel in flight, and had work areas and living quarters laid out within the large cabin area. By 1964 the fact that these aircraft were dedicated ABCPs was recognized by redesignation as the **Boeing EC-135C**, and in mid-1985 13 of the original 17 remained in service in this role.

Over the years the number of EC-135 variants has grown, the EC-135C being joined first by six conversions from J57-engined KC-135A tankers to provide communications relay aircraft able to double in the ABCP role; designated **EC-135A**, five of these aircraft are still operating as relay aircraft. Other variants are in use, although the numbers

quoted have been altered by subsequent further conversions. The **EC-135G** (three converted from KC-135A) serve as airborne control centres for ballistic missile launch but can double for communications relay. Five advanced airborne national command posts (ABNCP) have the designation **EC-135H** (from four KC-135As and one VC-135A) and other ABNCPs include the **EC-135J** (four upgraded from EC-135C). There were originally three **EC-135K** ABNCP conversions from KC-135As for Tactical Air Command, but one was later taken to serve as a zero-gravity astronaut trainer; two **EC-135P** ABNCP conversions now with the Pacific Air Forces are similar but have changes in communications equipment for use in that theatre. Also in current service are five **EC-135L** radio relay aircraft which have reverse refuelling capability to allow for extended missions. Another known variant is the **EC-135N**, of which eight were equipped for satellite tracking and other space projects. At least four **EC-135B ARIA** (Advanced Range Instrumentation Aircraft) each with a steerable antenna in a bulbous nose were derived as conversions of the C-135B.

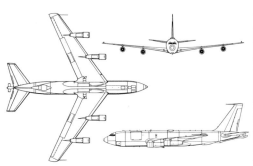

Boeing EC-135C

Specification: Boeing EC-135A
Origin: USA
Type: communications relay aircraft
Powerplant: four 6237-kg (13,750-lb) thrust Pratt & Whitney J57-59W turbojet engines
Performance: maximum speed 508 kts (941 km/h; 585 mph) at 30,000 (9145 m); average cruising speed 460 kts (853 km/h; 430 mph) between 30,500 and 40,000 ft (9300 and 12190 m); initial rate of climb 2,000 ft (610 m) per minute; service ceiling 50,000 ft (15240 m)
Weights: empty 46633 kg (98,466 lb); maximum take-off 134717 kg (297,000 lb)
Dimensions: span 39.88 m (130 ft 10 in); length 41.53 m (136 ft 3 in); height 12.70 m (41 ft 8 in); wing area 226.03 m² (2,433.0 sq ft)
Armament: none

This collection of EC-135B and EC-135N ARIA aircraft was brought together for Apollo space missions. The large antenna in the bulbous nose is for tracking missiles and rockets.

The EC-135J is a rebuild of the EC-135C for airborne command post duties. These are typical of the ABNCP EC-135s and are active with the 9th ACCS, 15th ABW.

Role
Fighter
Close support
Counter-insurgency
Tactical strike
Strategic bomber
Tactical reconnaissance
Strategic reconnaissance
Maritime patrol
Anti-ship strike
Anti-submarine warfare
Search and rescue
Assault transport
Transport
Liaison
Trainer
Inflight-refuelling tanker
Specialized

Performance
All-weather capability
Rough field capability
STOL capability
VTOL capability
Airspeed 0-250 mph
Airspeed 250 mph-Mach 1
Airspeed Mach 1 plus
Ceiling 0-20,000 ft
Ceiling 20,000-40,000 ft
Ceiling 40,000ft plus
Range 0-1,000 miles
Range 1,000-3,000 miles
Range 3,000 miles plus

Weapons
Air-to-air missiles
Air-to-surface missiles
Cruise missiles
Cannon
Trainable guns
Naval weapons
Nuclear-capable
Rockets
'Smart' weapon kit
Weapon load 0-4,000 lb
Weapon load 4,000-15,000 lb
Weapon load 15,000 lb plus

Avionics
Electronic Counter Measures
Electronic Support Measures
Search radar
Fire control radar
Look-down/shoot-down
Terrain-following radar
Forward-looking infra-red
Laser
Television

Boeing E-3A Sentries of the US Air Force

Boeing EC-137D/E-3 Sentry

NATO   United States

Boeing E-3A Sentry of the NATO Airborne Early Warning Force, based at Geilenkirchen, West Germany.

One of the most vital roles fulfilled by the Model 707 airframe is that of the USAF's and NATO's Airborne Warning And Control System (AWACS) aircraft, which carries the designation **Boeing E-3 Sentry**. It is, in effect, an airborne radar station serving also as a command, control and communications (C^3) centre. Operating in three dimensions it is regarded as survivable under wartime conditions, as it is highly resistant to jamming, and in addition to the C^3 function provides long-range surveillance over all terrains.

On 23 July 1970 the Boeing Aerospace Company, previously concerned only with missiles and space, became prime contractor/integrator for the AWAC System, proposing the Model 707-320B as its carrier and recommending that the aircraft be powered by eight TF34 engines, a choice later changed back to four TF33 turbofans to save cost. Under the designation **EC-137D**, two prototypes evaluated competing radar systems proposed by Hughes Aircraft and Westinghouse, the latter finally being named winner. The most notable external feature of these aircraft is the 9.14-m (30-ft) diameter rotodome pylon-mounted above the rear fuselage, which streamlines the back-to-back antennas for the radar and IFF. In January 1973 the USAF authorized development of the AWACS, designating these aircraft E-3 and later naming them Sentry. The first USAF **E-3A** was delivered to TAC's 552nd AWAC

Wing on 24 March 1977, and the force of 34 was completed in 1985. NATO's 18 Luxemburg-registered multi-national crew E-3As were delivered from 22 January 1982 to 25 April 1985.

The USAF's first 24 Sentries were equipped to **Core E-3A** standard, which provides pulse-Doppler radar, a CC-1 computer, nine situation display consoles (SDCs), two auxiliary display units (ADUs) and 13 communication links. These 24 aircraft are in the process of updating to **E-3B** standard with the secure Joint Tactical Information Distribution System (JTIDS), faster CC-2 computer, some maritime reconnaissance capability and other equipment. The remaining 10 USAF and 18 NATO aircraft, designated **Standard E-3A**, have maritime (overwater) reconnaissance capability plus the JTIDS and CC-2 computer. Under modifications started in 1984 the 10 USAF Standard E-3As are being updated to **E-3C** configuration, gaining five more SDCs, additional UHF radios and provision for 'Have Quick' anti-jamming improvements.

Five **E-3A/Saudi** AWACS have been contracted for the Royal Saudi Air Force, with initial deliveries planned for 1986; like the tanker/transports on order for this air arm under the designation KE-3A, they are powered by 9979-kg (22,000-lb) thrust CFM International CFM56-2 turbofan engines.

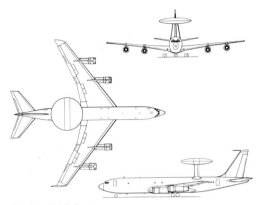

Boeing E-3A Sentry

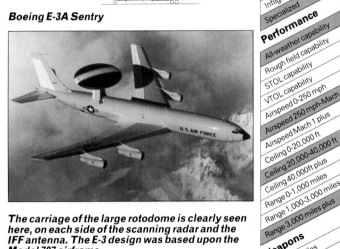

The carriage of the large rotodome is clearly seen here, on each side of the scanning radar and the IFF antenna. The E-3 design was based upon the Model 707 airframe.

E-3s now serve in some numbers, most in USAF service having been updated to E-3B or E-3C standard as better equipment has become available to the AWACS force.

Specification: Boeing E-3A Sentry
Origin: USA
Type: airborne early-warning and C^3 aircraft
Powerplant: four 9525-kg (21,000-lb) thrust Pratt & Whitney TF33-100/100A turbofan engines
Performance: maximum speed 460 kts (853 km/h; 530 mph); operating ceiling 29,000 ft (8840 m); loiter time on station 1609 km (1,000 miles) from base 6 hours; maximum endurance on internal fuel 11 hours
Weights: maximum take-off 147418 kg (325,000 lb)
Dimensions: span 44.42 m (145 ft 9 in); length 46.61 m (152 ft 11 in); height 12.73 m (41 ft 9 in); wing area 283.35 m² (3,050.0 sq ft)
Armament: none

Role	
Fighter	
Close support	
Counter-insurgency	
Tactical strike	
Strategic bomber	
Strategic reconnaissance	■
Tactical reconnaissance	■
Maritime patrol	
Anti-ship strike	
Anti-submarine warfare	
Search and rescue	
Assault transport	
Transport	
Liaison	
Trainer	
Inflight-refuelling tanker	
Specialized	■

Performance	
All-weather capability	■
Rough field capability	
STOL capability	
VTOL capability	
Airspeed 0-250 mph	
Airspeed 250 mph-Mach 1	■
Airspeed Mach 1 plus	
Ceiling 0-20,000 ft	
Ceiling 20,000-40,000 ft	■
Ceiling 40,000ft plus	
Range 0-1,000 miles	
Range 1,000-3,000 miles	
Range 3,000 miles plus	■

Weapons	
Air-to-air missiles	
Air-to-surface missiles	
Cruise missiles	
Cannon	
Trainable guns	
Naval weapons	
Nuclear-capable	
Rockets	
'Smart' weapon kit	
Weapon load 0-4,000 lb	
Weapon load 4,000-15,000 lb	
Weapon load 15,000 lb plus	

Avionics	
Electronic Counter Measures	■
Electronic Support Measures	■
Search radar	■
Fire control radar	
Look-down/shoot-down	
Terrain-following radar	
Forward-looking infra-red	
Laser	
Television	

Primary capability
Secondary capability

United States

Boeing KC-135E and KC-135R

Boeing KC-135E Stratotanker of the 108th ARS, 126th ARW, Illinois Air National Guard.

Modern performance requirements for fighter/interceptor aircraft are an antithesis to range, yet the policy of major air forces to react quickly when needed in a far distant policing role demands unprecedented range. It is a constantly growing demand, one which makes the requirement for inflight-refuelling tankers increase by leaps and bounds, and it is important for an air arm to get the maximum utilization from its existing fleet.

When production of Boeing KC-135 tankers for the US Air Force ended a total of 724 had been built, of which about 650 remain in use. It was decided to ensure they would remain operational into the next century, the major requirement being replacement of the underwing skin. This task, started in 1975, has progressed steadily and by mid-1985 more than 500 KC-135s had benefited from this modification which should extend service life by some 27,000 hours. It was followed by a programme to re-engine Air National Guard and Air Force Reserve KC-135s with JT3D engines (civil equivalent of the TF33). These powerplants were removed and refurbished from ex-commercial Boeing 707s acquired by the USAF, and at the same time the KC-135s gain also tail units, engines pylons and cowlings from the Model 707s. Simultaneously new brakes and anti-skid units are installed and, upon completion of the work, the aircraft are redesignated **KC-135E**.

Far more comprehensive is the programme to update the main tanker fleet with the 9979-kg (22,000-lb) thrust CFM International F108-CF-100 turbofan (equivalent to the civil CFM56-2B-1), existing contracts covering 108 conversions. With this powerplant revision comes also an APU to give self-start capability; more advanced autopilot, avionics, controls and displays on the flight deck; strengthened main landing gear incorporating anti-skid units; revised hydraulic/pneumatic systems; and an enlarged tailplane. Redesignated **KC-135R** on completion of this update, the first example was redelivered to SAC's 384th Air Refueling Wing at McConnell AFB, Wichita in July 1984. Improved capability enables the KC-135R to operate from shorter runways (civil airports if necessary) and to transfer more fuel, to an extent that two can cover the workload of three KC-135A tankers. In addition to KC-135R conversions for the USAF, Boeing received a contract to modify seven of the 11 remaining French C-135F tankers to this same standard.

Specification: Boeing KC-135R
Origin: USA
Type: inflight-refuelling tanker/cargo/transport aircraft
Powerplant: four 9979-kg (22,000-lb) thrust CFM International F108-CF-100 turbofan engines
Performance: average cruising speed 460 kts (853 km/h; 530 mph) between 30,500 and 40,000 ft (9300 and 12190 m); able to transfer 150 per cent more fuel than the KC-135A at a radius of 4627 km (2,875 miles)
Weight: maximum take-off 146284 kg (322,500 lb); maximum fuel-load 92210 kg (203,288 lb)
Dimensions: span 39.88 m (130 ft 10 in); length 41.53 m (136 ft 3 in); height 12.70 m (41 ft 8 in); wing area 226.03 m² (2,433.0 sq ft)
Armament: none

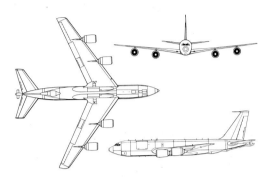

Boeing KC-135R Stratotanker

An early KC-135R shows the large high-bypass ratio CFM F108 turbofans which have replaced the thirsty J57s. Fuel receiving capability has also been added.

The whole first-line KC-135 fleet will eventually be re-engined, giving a planned service life into the 21st century. This example is from the 384th ARW at McConnell AFB.

Boeing Model 707 Tanker/Transport/C-18

Boeing Model 707 in service with the Chilean air force.

When production of Boeing's Model 707 airliner ended in 1981 a total of 962 civil aircraft had been sold. But the basic airframe is of early 1950s technology, now being superseded by more advanced and thus more efficient designs, and there is a growing number of Model 707s coming onto the secondhand market. The Boeing Military Airplane Company appreciated that these aircraft, available at comparatively very low cost, could be easily converted for use as inflight-refuelling tanker/transport aircraft; this would make it possible for smaller air arms to gain an inflight-refuelling capability at a fraction of the capital cost of a new tanker. Furthermore, the large cabin was suitable for a variety of roles.

Acquiring an ex-TWA 707-320C in 1982, BMAC immediately began its conversion as a 707 tanker/transport demonstrator aircraft. It has three hose-and-drogue refuelling outlets, one on the fuselage centreline and two, in pods, at the wingtips. In the interior cargo-handling equipment, furnishings, partitions and seats are mounted on tracks wherever possible, and given quick-disconnect fittings to make the cabin easily convertible for aeromedical, cargo, passenger, combination cargo/passenger or VIP transport roles. An optional large fuel tank in the lower cargo hold makes it possible for the tanker to rendezvous with client aircraft up to 1610 km (1000 miles) from base and transfer up to 55792 kg (123,000 lb) of fuel; if required the aircraft can be equipped with a refuelling boom. There are some structural changes and internal revisions, and military avionics are standard. So far almost 30 have been contracted, and many of them are already in service; eight ordered for the Royal Saudi Air Force under the designation **KE-3A**, and scheduled for delivery in 1986-8, will have CFM56 turbofan engines.

In a separate programme, the USAF's Aeronautical Systems Division acquired six ex-American Airlines' Model 707-320s. Under the designation **EC-18B** these are being equipped with avionics and a large steerable nose antenna to serve as Advanced Range Instrumentation Aircraft. The first of them began flight testing at Wright Patterson AFB in March 1985 and was scheduled to enter USAF service in autumn 1985; they are to be used to expand the ARIA capability, supporting worldwide missile and space tracking. They are particularly valuable in areas where there are no ground stations able to undertake this task.

Boeing Model 707-320

Specification: Boeing Model 707 tanker/transport
Origin: USA
Type: airliner converted for tanker/transport role
Powerplant: four 8618-kg (19,000-lb) thrust Pratt & Whitney JT3D-7 turbofan engines
Performance: maximum cruising speed 525 kts (974 km/h; 605 mph) at 25,000 ft (7620 m); initial rate of climb 4,000 ft (1219 m) per minute; service ceiling 39,000 ft (11890 m); range with 36287-kg (80,000 lb) payload 5834 km (3,625 miles)
Weights: empty, cargo configuration 63957 kg (141,000 lb); maximum payload (other than fuel) 40324 kg (88,900 lb); maximum take-off 151318 kg (333,600 lb)
Dimensions: span 44.42 m (145 ft 9 in); length 46.61 m (152 ft 11 in); height 12.93 m (42 ft 5 in); wing area 283.35 m² (3,050.0 sq ft)
Armament: none

Several ex-airliner Model 707s are used by the Israeli air force. A handful have been converted to the Elint role with cheek SLARs; others serve in the stand-off ECM role. This example is a standard transport.

Many air forces operate the Model 707 for general and VIP transport duties. Canada is a major user, under the designation CC-137.

Boeing Model 727

Jordan Mexico New Zealand Nigeria Panama Qatar Senegambia Taiwan United States

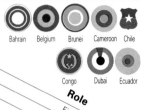

Bahrain Belgium Brunei Cameroon Chile

Congo Dubai Ecuador

Boeing Model 727.

In the late 1950s there was a major upsurge in the air travel market, and even before the Boeing Model 707 was in service the company was thinking about the design and development of a new and more advanced short/medium-range airliner which would supplement the Model 707/720 line. The basic aim was to put in service initially an aircraft with greater efficiency than the Model 720, with sufficient 'stretch' potential to grow to Model 707 size when needed. The finalization of powerplant and layout was protracted, with the benefits of a 'clean' wing (first demonstrated by the Sud-Aviation Caravelle) considered most desirable. The decision to adopt such a wing dictated a rear-engine layout, and the selection of three rear-mounted turbofan engines to power the new design resulted in one being installed in the tail of the fuselage, its inlet forward of the fin, and the incorporation of a T-tail. For reasons of economy there was maximum possible commonality between the Model 707/720 line and the new aircraft in terms of structure, components and systems, and the first **Boeing Model 727** was flown on 9 February 1963; initiation into revenue service by Eastern Air Lines was made on 1 February 1964.

Production of the Model 727 continued for almost 20 years, and when the last was rolled out in mid-1984 a total of 1,832 had been built, which is still a record for jet airliners. A key to this success story was the economy and reliability of the 727, plus the fact that it was built in a number of versions including the **Model 727-100C** and **Model 727-100QC** which were convertible passenger/cargo versions with a large cargo door and strengthened floor. There was also a **Model 727-200F** pure freighter without windows and incorporating a strengthened fuselage structure. These latter versions, as they have come on to the market from commercial airlines, have proved of interest to several governments and are to be found in service with their air arms as VIP/multi-role transports. In view of the large numbers that remain in commercial service it would seem likely that far more will eventually fulfil an important military role.

Boeing Model 727-200

Specification: Boeing Model 727-100C
Origin: USA
Type: convertible cargo-passenger airliner
Powerplant: three 6350-kg (14,000-lb) thrust Pratt & Whitney JT8D-7 turbofan engines
Performance: maximum cruising speed 527 kts (977 km/h; 607 mph) at 21,000 ft (6400 m); economic cruising speed 495 kts (917 km/h; 570 mph) at 30,000 ft (9145 m); service ceiling 36,500 ft (11125 m); range with maximum payload 3259 km (2,025 miles)
Weights: empty 41322 kg (91,100 lb); maximum take-off 76657 kg (169,000 lb)
Dimensions: span 32.92 m (108 ft 0 in); length 35.41 m (116 ft 2 in); height 10.36 m (34 ft 0 in); wing area 157.93 m² (1,700.0 sq ft)
Armament: none

Two Boeing 727 aircraft were transferred from the Belgian national airline SABENA to the Belgian air force. These handle VIP and staff transport operations.

Several countries operate ex-airliner Model 727s for personnel transport. Mexico has this aircraft, along with six others, flying with the presidential flight.

Boeing Model 737/T-43A

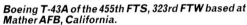

Brazil Dubai Egypt India Mexico Saudi Arabia Thailand United States Venezuela

31152

U.S. AIR FORCE

Boeing T-43A of the 455th FTS, 323rd FTW based at Mather AFB, California.

Busy with civil/military sales of the Model 707/717/720 family of airliners/tankers/transports, none of them small-capacity twin-jet aircraft, Boeing regarded with concern the success being gained in this area by its rival Douglas Aircraft Company with the DC-9; more alarming was the fact that British Aircraft Corporation was breaking into the US market with its One-Eleven twin-jet. It was not until 19 February 1965 that Boeing announced it would build a short-range twin-jet **Boeing Model 737-100,** and the prototype first flew on 9 April 1967.

The Model 737 was immediately seen to be different from its rivals, for its two turbofan engines were mounted against the under-surface of the wings, whereas both the DC-9 and One-Eleven had rear-engine installations. A less visible but important difference was adoption of a fuselage similar in cross-section to that of the Model 727, with more width and headroom than the competitors and giving six- rather than five-abreast seating. The Model 737 also extended as far as possible the component commonality with earlier members of the family, not just for reasons of economy, but with similar short-, medium-

and long-range aircraft available it could encourage fleet sales to the bigger airlines.

It seems unlikely that Boeing could have expected the Model 737 to enter the military field, but experience in Vietnam showed the US Air Force had inadequate training facilities for navigators. Requiring an aircraft to replace the Convair T-29 (a militarized version of the Convair-Liner), the USAF announced on 27 May 1971 that it had decided to buy the Model 737 'off-the-shelf'. Designated **T-43A,** this was based on the airframe of the lengthened-fuselage (by 1.93 m/6 ft 4 in) **Model 737-200,** and had the interior equipped with 19 navigator stations to seat three instructors, 12 students and four advanced students. A total of 19 T-43As were procured (**Boeing Model 737-253**), the first being flown on 10 April 1973, and all were delivered to Mather AFB, California by the end of July 1974. Although (with one other exception) not procured as a military aircraft, ex-airline Model 737s are now used by a number of governments and air arms in a variety of transport roles, carrying cargo, personnel and VIP passengers.

Specification: Boeing Model 737-253/T-43A
Origin: USA
Type: navigation trainer
Powerplant: two 6577-kg (14,500-lb) thrust Pratt & Whitney JT8D-9 turbofan engines
Performance: maximum cruising speed 493 kts (914 km/h; 568 mph) at 21,000 ft (6400 m); economic cruising speed 459 kts (851 km/h; 529 mph) at 30,000 ft (9145 m); range with maximum fuel 3862 km (2,400 miles)
Weight: maximum take-off 51936 kg (114,500 lb)
Dimensions: span 28.35 m (93 ft 0 in); length 30.53 m (100 ft 2 in); height 11.28 m (37 ft 0 in); wing area 91.04 m² (980 sq ft)
Armament: none

Boeing Model 737 Series 200

The Boeing T-43A is a militarized Model 737. The USAF flies 19 aircraft for navigation training duties, also using Honeywell simulators.

Sole USAF user of the T-43A is the 455th FTS, 323rd FTW based at Mather AFB. Navigators trained on the T-43A are destined for service in large USAF aircraft.

US AIR FORCE USAF 11403

Role
Fighter
Close support
Counter-insurgency
Tactical strike
Strategic bomber
Tactical reconnaissance
Strategic reconnaissance
Maritime patrol
Anti-ship strike
Anti-submarine warfare
Search and rescue
Assault transport
Transport
Liaison
Trainer
Inflight-refuelling tanker
Specialized

Performance
All-weather capability
Rough field capability
STOL capability
VTOL capability
Airspeed 0-250 mph
Airspeed 250 mph-Mach 1
Airspeed Mach 1 plus
Ceiling 0-20,000 ft
Ceiling 20,000-40,000 ft
Ceiling 40,000 ft plus
Range 0-1,000 miles
Range 1,000-3,000 miles
Range 3,000 miles plus

Weapons
Air-to-air missiles
Air-to-surface missiles
Cruise missiles
Cannon
Trainable guns
Naval weapons
Nuclear-capable
Rockets
'Smart' weapon kit
Weapon load 0-4,000 lb
Weapon load 4,000-15,000 lb
Weapon load 15,000 lb plus

Avionics
Electronic Counter Measures
Electronic Support Measures
Search radar
Fire control radar
Look-down/shoot-down radar
Terrain-following radar
Forward-looking infra-red
Laser
Television

Primary capability
Secondary capability

Boeing Model 747/E-4

Iran   Saudi Arabia   United States

Boeing E-4 operated by the 55th SRW at Offutt AFB, Nebraska.

The **Boeing Model 747,** which entered revenue service with Pan American World Airways on 22 January 1970, was the world's first wide-body civil transport. Since then more than 630 have been sold and in 1985 the worldwide fleet of Model 747s was carrying some 5 million passengers each month, fully confirming their heavy-lift capability. Under a programme for completion in 1988, Boeing is modifying 19 of PanAm's Model 747s for military use by the Civil Reserve Air Fleet in wartime or for quick-reaction policing. This involves strengthening of floors, and provision of wider cargo doors plus cargo-handling equipment. Modification of the first was completed in mid-1985. More important in the current military scene is the USAF's procurement of the Model 747 for its Advanced Airborne Command Post (AABNCP) programme. The USAF planned for six such **E-4** aircraft to provide a survivable airborne command and communications post capability: their task is to link in time of war the US National Command Authority and its strategic retaliatory force, both conventional and nuclear. By July 1973 the USAF had contracted for three 747s: designated **E-4A** and

initially carrying equipment removed from EC-135s, these entered service in 1974-5 as National Emergency Airborne Command Posts (NEACPs). A fourth aircraft, procured in December 1973 as an **E-4B,** had more advanced equipment, and the E-4As have since been updated to this standard. All four E-4Bs are now operational from Offutt AFB, Nebraska. Funding for the two additional E-4Bs has not yet been allocated.

The E-4B is equipped to accommodate 94 crew members on three deck levels: the upper incorporates the flight deck and flight crew rest area; the main deck is allocated to the National Command Authority; and the lower areas are for equipment, maintenance and a winch operator's station for deployment of the 8-km (5-mile) long VLF antenna. Other secure communications comprise SHF satellite links (with its antennae in a dorsal fairing), HF and UHF, and there are also MF and VHF transceivers; the E-4Bs also have nuclear thermal shielding and inflight-refuelling receptacles.

In addition to these military 747s described, small numbers serve with other air arms for military and government use.

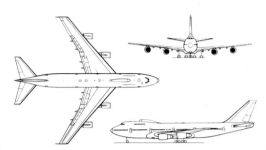

Boeing E-4B

Seen in pre-revolution days, this Boeing 747 is typical of the 16 supplied to Iran. These suffer from lack of spares, and it is thought that only four are serviceable.

The Boeing 747 provided the necessary volume for a national emergency airborne command post (NEACP). Inflight-refuelling increases the endurance.

Specification: Boeing Model 747-200B/E-4B
Origin: USA
Type: Advanced Airborne Command Post aircraft
Powerplant: four 23814-kg (52,500-lb) thrust General Electric F103-GE-100 (military equivalent of CF6-50E2) turbofan engines
Performance: maximum speed 523 kts (969 km/h; 602 mph) at 30,000 ft (9145 m); unrefuelled endurance 12 hours; maximum endurance with inflight-refuelling 72 hours
Weight: maximum take-off 362874 kg (800,000 lb)
Dimensions: span 59.64 m (195 ft 8 in); length 70.51 m (231 ft 4 in); height 19.33 m (63 ft 5 in); wing area 510.95 m² (5,500.0 sq ft)
Armament: none

Role

Fighter
Close support
Counter-insurgency
Tactical strike
Strategic bomber
Tactical reconnaissance
Strategic reconnaissance
Maritime patrol
Anti-ship strike
Anti-submarine warfare
Search and rescue
Assault transport
Transport
Liaison
Trainer
Inflight-refuelling tanker
Specialized

Performance

All-weather capability
Rough field capability
STOL capability
VTOL capability
Airspeed 0-250 mph
Airspeed 250 mph-Mach 1
Airspeed Mach 1 plus
Ceiling 0-20,000 ft
Ceiling 20,000-40,000 ft
Ceiling 40,000ft plus
Range 0-1,000 miles
Range 1,000-3,000 miles
Range 3,000 miles plus

Weapons

Air-to-air missiles
Air-to-surface missiles
Cruise missiles
Cannon
Trainable guns
Naval weapons
Nuclear-capable
Rockets
'Smart' weapon kit
Weapon load 0-4,000 lb
Weapon load 4,000-15,000 lb
Weapon load 15,000 lb plus

Avionics

Electronic Counter Measures
Electronic Support Measures
Search radar
Fire control radar
Look-down/shoot-down
Terrain-following radar
Forward-looking infra-red
Laser
Television

Boeing RC-135

Boeing RC-135V of the 55th Strategic Reconnaissance Wing.

The capability of the Boeing Model 707 in tanker/transport versions suggested its suitability for deployment in a reconnaissance role; initial procurement covered four new-build aircraft. Given the company identification Model 739-700, these were delivered for use by the 1,370th Photo Mapping Wing of the USAF's MAC under the designation **RC-135A**. Similar to the Boeing C-135A and with J57-59W engines, they had cameras behind three ports in the underfuselage, aft of the nosewheel. Special equipment was carried for electronic surveillance. These four RC-135As were subsequently converted to serve as transports, and again in 1980 to tanker configuration as **KC-135D**. In the mid-1960s the RC-135As were followed by 10 new-build **RC-135B** electronic reconnaissance aircraft (Boeing Model 739-445B) with an airframe similar to that of the KC-135B but with TF33-9 turbofan engines; used for a variety of purposes, there was no standardization in the electronics installed by various military establishments. Later the RC-135Bs were rebuilt, losing their inflight-refuelling booms but gaining side-looking airborne radar (SLAR), undernose radomes and a ventral camera bay to become redesignated **RC-135C**. Four

conversions from KC-135A (one) and C-135A (three) produced the **RC-135D** with modified SLAR and 'thimble-nose' radome, and one **RC-135E** (formerly C-135B) was similar but with a wide glassfibre radome around the forward fuselage. By conversion of C/VC-135B transports at least six electronic reconnaissance **RC-135M** aircraft appeared with 'thimble-nose', teardrop fairings each side of the fuselage forward of the tailplane and a twin-lobe ventral aerial; these were associated with the 'Rivet Card' and 'Rivet Quick' programmes. Other rebuilds for the reconnaissance role include the **RC-135S** (numbers uncertain) with large external dipole aerials and a variety of blisters and pods; one **RC-135T** for classified electronic surveillance in support of SAC; two or three **RC-135U** aircraft with SLAR, a chin radome and a variety of aerials; at least seven **RC-135V** rebuilds (from RC-135Cs and an RC-135U) with 'thimble-nose', SLAR and a farm of under-fuselage blade aerials; plus similar and more recent **RC-135W** rebuilds. It would seem likely that many more variants will become known as they lose their classified status.

Specification: Boeing RC-135C
Origin: USA
Type: electronic reconnaissance aircraft
Powerplant: four 8165-kg (18,000-lb) thrust Pratt & Whitney TF33-9 turbofan engines
Performance: maximum speed 535 kts (991 km/h; 616 mph) at 25,000 (7620 m); cruising speed 486 kts (901 km/h; 560 mph) at 35,000 ft (10670 m); service ceiling 40,600 ft (12375 m); operational radius 4305 km (2,675 miles); ferry range 9100 km (5,655 miles)
Weight: empty 46403 kg (102,300 lb); maximum take-off 124965 kg (275,500 lb)
Dimensions: span 39.88 m (130 ft 10 in); length 39.20 m (128 ft 7.3 in); height (tall fin) 12.70 m (41 ft 8 in); wing area 226.03 m² (2,433.0 sq ft)
Armament: none

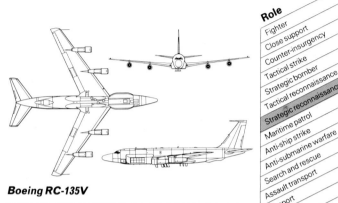

Boeing RC-135V

Two RC-135U aircraft are on the strength of the 55th SRW. These do not have the 'thimble' nose, but have extra aerials on the wingtips, cheeks and tail area.

Six RC-135Ws serve on general Elint duties around the world. These aircraft have been modified from the RC-135M, introducing SLAR cheeks and extra blade aerials.

Role
Fighter
Close support
Counter-insurgency
Tactical strike
Strategic bomber
Tactical reconnaissance
Strategic reconnaissance
Maritime patrol
Anti-ship strike
Anti-submarine warfare
Search and rescue
Assault transport
Transport
Liaison
Trainer
Inflight-refuelling tanker
Specialized

Performance
All-weather capability
Rough field capability
STOL capability
VTOL capability
Airspeed 0-250 mph
Airspeed 250 mph-Mach 1
Airspeed Mach 1 plus
Ceiling 0-20,000 ft
Ceiling 20,000-40,000 ft
Ceiling 40,000ft plus
Range 0-1,000 miles
Range 1,000-3,000 miles
Range 3,000 miles plus

Weapons
Air-to-air missiles
Air-to-surface missiles
Cruise missiles
Cannon
Trainable guns
Naval weapons
Nuclear-capable
Rockets
'Smart' weapon kit
Weapon load 0-4,000 lb
Weapon load 4,000-15,000 lb
Weapon load 15,000 lb plus

Avionics
Electronic Counter Measures
Electronic Support Measures
Search radar
Fire control radar
Look-down/shoot-down
Terrain-following radar
Forward-looking infra-red
Laser
Television

A KC-135 of SAC refuelling an RC-135

Boeing Vertol Model 107/CH-46 Sea Knight

Canada   Sweden   United States

The Piasecki Helicopter Corporation, formed in 1955, had a change of management in March 1956 and was renamed the Vertol Aircraft Corporation. Almost at once the company began design and development of a twin-rotor transport helicopter, ostensibly for civil use, but engineered to be suitable for military procurement if sales could be won. Identified as the **Vertol Model 107,** the new type had design features such as light but powerful twin turboshaft engines, mounted above the fuselage to give maximum cabin volume; a large and robust loading ramp in the upswept rear fuselage, strong enough for direct onloading of wheeled vehicles; and a sealed and compartmented fuselage for emergency operation from water.

The Model 107 prototype (N74060), flown on 22 April 1958, soon gained a US Army order for 10 similar **YHC-1A** helicopters, the first (58-5514) flying on 27 August 1959; the order was later reduced to only seven when the Army became interested in a larger helicopter being developed by Vertol. At the end of March 1960 Vertol became a division of the Boeing Airplane Company with the name Boeing Vertol Company; by then the US Marine Corps was looking closely at one of the YHC-1As then flying with General Electric T58 turboshafts, and in February 1961 a modification of this helicopter, the **Boeing**

Vertol Model 107M, won a USMC design competition and was ordered into production as the **HRB-1 Sea Knight** (becoming **CH-46A** in 1962) for use mainly as an assault or logistics transport helicopter. Production of CH-46As (with 932-kW/1,250-shp T58-GE-8/8B engines) totalled 164, the first entering USMC service in early 1965. Subsequent production for the USMC includes the **CH-46D** (266 built) with more powerful T68-GE-10 engines, and the **CH-46F** (186) with improved avionics and equipment. US Navy procurement of the Sea Knight includes the **UH-46A** (14 built) and **UH-46D** (10 plus two conversions), respectively similar to the CH-46A and CH-46D, and used in the VERTREP role. Almost 300 USMC Sea Knights have been updated to **CH-46E** standard with 1394-kW (1,870-shp) T58-GE-16 turboshafts and other improvements. Other naval versions, conversions of the related basic aircraft, include small numbers of **HH-46A** and **HH-46D** for SAR, and a few **RH-46** helicopters for use in the minesweeping role.

In addition to civil production of the Model 107, Boeing Vertol supplied the type to other air forces, and in 1965 Kawasaki in Japan acquired worldwide sales rights for the improved Model 107-II. Under the designation KV-107 Kawasaki has developed and continues to build several variants of this aircraft, which will be described in a later issue.

Boeing Vertol Model 107 (CH-113 Labrador/Voyageur) of the Canadian Armed Forces.

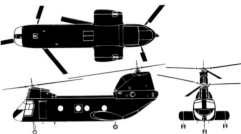

Boeing Vertol CH-46 Sea Knight

The CH-46 is a true warhorse, having seen action in Vietnam, Lebanon and Grenada. Marines aircraft operate from assault carriers.

These CH-46s are lined up on deck on an assault carrier sailing off Grenada. The type acquitted itself well in this campaign.

Specification: Boeing Vertol CH-46D
Origin: USA
Type: twin-rotor military transport
Powerplant: two 1044-kW (1,400-shp) General Electric T58-GE-10 turboshaft engines
Performance: maximum cruising speed 140 kts (259 km/h; 161 mph); economic cruising speed 134 kts (248 km/h; 154 mph); initial rate of climb 1,660 ft (506 m) per minute; service ceiling 14,000 ft (4265 m); range at maximum weight with 10 per cent fuel reserve 380 km (236 miles)
Weight: empty 5827 kg (13,067 lb); maximum take-off 10433 kg (23,000 lb)
Dimensions: rotor diameter, each 15.54 m (51 ft 0 in); length, rotors turning 25.40 m (83 ft 4 in); height 5.09 m (16 ft 8.5 in); rotor disc area, total 379.56 m² (4,085.65 sq ft)
Armament: none

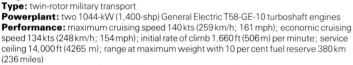

Role
Fighter
Close support
Counter-insurgency
Tactical strike
Strategic bomber
Tactical reconnaissance
Strategic reconnaissance
Maritime patrol
Anti-ship strike
Anti-submarine warfare
Search and rescue
Assault transport
Transport
Liaison
Trainer
Inflight-refuelling tanker
Specialized

Performance
All-weather capability
Rough field capability
STOL capability
VTOL capability
Airspeed 0-250 mph
Airspeed 250 mph-Mach 1
Airspeed Mach 1 plus
Ceiling 0-20,000 ft
Ceiling 20,000-40,000 ft
Ceiling 40,000 ft plus
Range 0-1,000 miles
Range 1,000-3,000 miles
Range 3,000 miles plus

Weapons
Air-to-air missiles
Air-to-surface missiles
Cruise missiles
Cannon
Trainable guns
Naval weapons
Nuclear-capable
Rockets
'Smart' weapon kit
Weapon load 0-4,000 lb
Weapon load 4,000-15,000 lb
Weapon load 15,000 lb plus

Avionics
Electronic Counter Measures
Electronic Support Measures
Search radar
Fire control radar
Look-down/shoot-down
Terrain-following radar
Forward-looking infra-red
Laser
Television

Boeing Vertol Model 114/CH-47 Chinook

United States Vietnam

Further development by Vertol of the YHC-1A resulted in a considerably larger aircraft with more powerful engines and all-weather capability to meet a US Army requirement for a medium transport helicopter in this category. Evaluation of the **Vertol Model 114** design submission, and those from four other manufacturers, resulted in Vertol receiving a contract for five pre-production **YCH-1B** helicopters; these were redesignated **YCH-47A** in 1962 and the name **Chinook** was allocated. By comparison with the CH-46D, the production **CH-47A** had a fuselage lengthened by 1.88 m (6 ft 2 in), increased-diameter rotors, 1641-kW (2,200-shp) Lycoming T55-5 engines (later 1976-kW/2,650-shp T55-7s), fixed quadricycle landing gear, and retained the CH-46 style of fuselage for operation from water. The enhanced capability of the Chinook meant it could carry a maximum 44 troops or external cargo load of 7257 kg (16,000 lb), compared with the CH-46's 25 troops and external load of 4536 kg (10,000 lb).

Production of the C-47A for the US Army totalled 354 (including the pre-production aircraft). Subsequent versions have included two **YCH-47B** prototypes for the production **CH-47B** (108 built), these introducing modified rotor blades, detail improvements and 2125-kW (2,850-shp) T55-7C turboshafts. Final production version for the US Army was the **CH-47C** (270) with 2796-kW (3,750-shp) T55-11A turboshafts, strengthened transmissions and increased internal fuel; under a 1978 contract Boeing Vertol has uprated the transmissions of surviving CH-47A/47Bs to CH-47C standard. Since then one of each version served as prototype conversions to the latest **CH-47D** standard to which the Army plans to upgrade 436 aircraft for operation into the next century. After undergoing airframe refurbishment, these gain higher rated T55 turboshafts, an advanced uprated transmission, composite rotor blades, an improved flight deck, and more advanced systems and equipment. Some 136 CH-47Ds have been funded, the first 'production' conversion being redelivered to the US Army on 20 May 1982.

In addition to civil versions of the Chinook (Model 234), Boeing Vertol has supplied the military **Model 414 Chinook** to several other air arms, and in 1968 Meridionali SpA in Italy acquired production and marketing rights for the CH-47C and has since built considerable numbers for Italian army aviation and other armed forces.

Specification: Boeing Vertol CH-47D
Origin: USA
Type: medium transport helicopter
Powerplant: two Lycoming T55-712 turboshaft engines, each with a standard rating of 2796 kW (3,750 shp) and emergency rating of 3356 kW (4,500 shp)
Performance: maximum speed 157 kts (291 km/h; 181 mph); cruising speed at maximum take-off weight 138 kts (256 km/h; 159 mph); initial rate of climb 1,330 ft (405 m) per minute; ferry range 2020 km (1,255 miles)
Weight: empty 10475 kg (23,093 lb); maximum take-off 22680 kg (50,000 lb)
Dimensions: rotor diameter, each 18.29 m (60 ft 0 in); length, rotors turning 30.18 m (99 ft 0 in); height 5.68 m (18 ft 7.8 in); rotor area, total 525.34 m² (5,654.88 sq ft)
Armament: none

Boeing Vertol CH-47 Chinook.

Boeing Vertol CH-47C Chinook

The Chinook is the main heavylift helicopter for the US Army's airborne divisions. These are used to airlift artillery and heavy equipment following infantry landings.

The RAF has belatedly adopted the Chinook for army support, principally in Germany. Nos 7 and 18 Sqns are the users, as well as No. 1310 Flt in the Falklands.

British Aerospace/McDonnell Douglas AV-8A/C Harrier

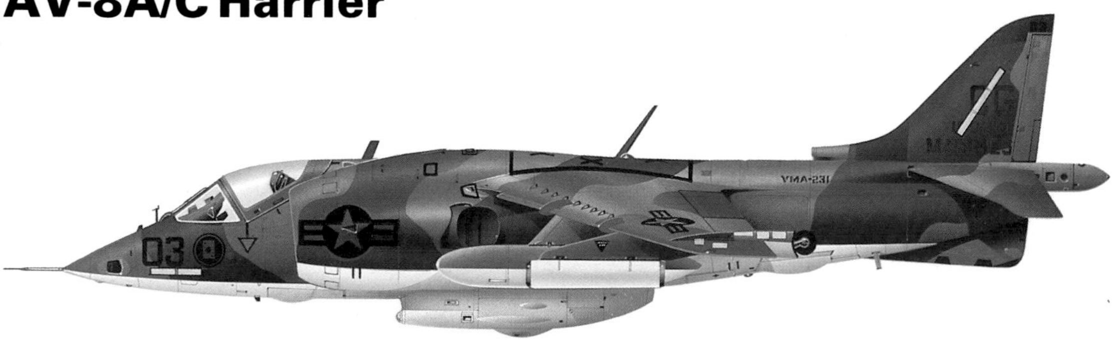

British Aerospace/McDonnell Douglas AV-8C Harrier of VMA-231, US Marine Corps, NAS Cherry Point.

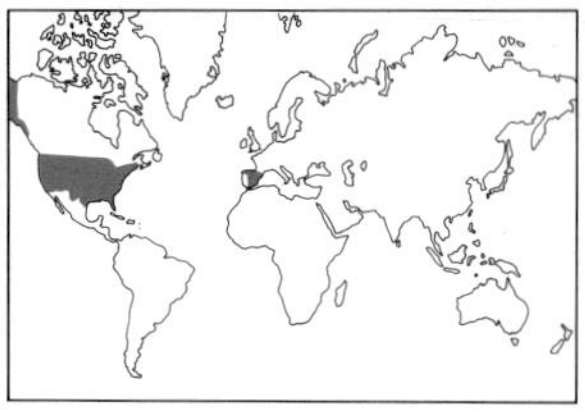

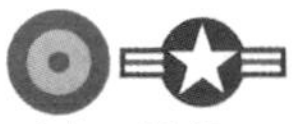

Spain United States

Throughout the early 1960s the US Marine Corps was urgently seeking an aircraft that could provide firepower to protect a beach assault on a hostile shore. The choices seemed to be an armed helicopter, or ship-loads of complex prefab airfield hardware, or total reliance on US Navy carriers. In 1968 the USMC evaluated the Hawker Siddeley Harrier, then still immature, and found it almost the weapon they had dreamed of. Plans were drawn up for a buy of 114 aircraft, designated **AV-8A**, though this was cut to 102 plus eight **TAV-8A** two-seaters because of the higher price of the two-seaters. Delivery began in January 1971, and in 1972 all were recycled through NAS Cherry Point to bring them to a common standard, without inertial system, laser nose or British radar warning receiver; they gained a manual fuel control (later fitted to RAF Harriers) to keep the engine running after birdstrike or other severe disturbance, and wiring and racks for Sidewinder AAMs. The American Stencel SIII-S3 seat was fitted on US policy grounds, a non-toppling attitude/heading system was installed, together with tactical VHF radio using a large inclined mast aerial amidships, and the TAV-8As also received UHF for airborne command of ground forces.

The Marines pioneered VIFFing (vectoring in forward flight), and accomplished a great deal with the relatively tricky and limited AV-8A. From 1979 a total of 47 have been reworked to **AV-8C** standard with airframe life extension, lift-improvement devices, ALR-45 radar warning, ALE-39 chaff/flare dispenser, on-board oxygen generation, secure voice link and new UHF.

A Spanish naval order was placed via the US government, with final assembly by McDonnell at St Louis. The buy comprised 10 **AV-8S** (Spanish **VA-1 Matador**) to AV-8A Mod standard, and three **TAV-8S** (**VAE-1**), to TAV-8A Mod standard, again with tactical VHF. They equip Escuadrilla 008.

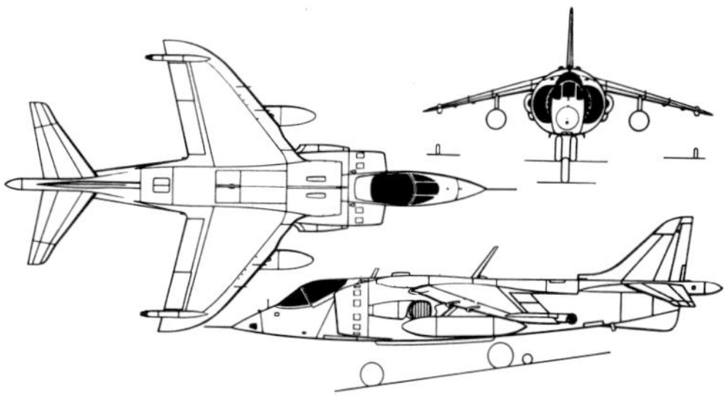

British Aerospace/McDonnell Douglas AV-8A

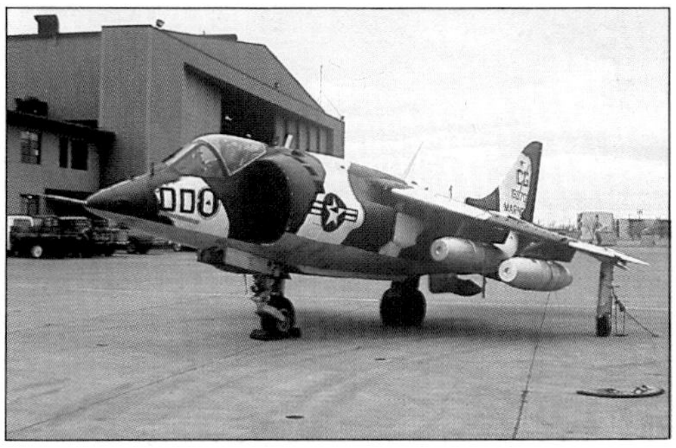

An AV-8A Harrier of VMA-231, normally based at NAS Cherry Point, wears an unusual winter camouflage scheme. VMA-231 was the last of the three USMC AV-8 units to form.

***An AV-8A, locally designated as the VA-1 Matador, of Escuadrilla 008 of the Spanish navy. The unit is based at Rota, and frequently operates from the carrier* Dedalo.**

Specification: BAe/McDonnell Douglas AV-8C Harrier
Origin: UK/USA
Type: STOVL land or shipboard tactical attack fighter
Powerplant: one 9752-kg (21,500-lb) thrust Rolls-Royce F402-RR-402 vectored-thrust turbofan engine
Performance: maximum speed over Mach 1, or at sea level 643 kts (1191 km/h; 740 mph); initial rate of climb at VTO weight 50,000 ft (15240 m) per minute; service ceiling 51,200 ft (15605 m); range on a ferry mission 3766 km (2,340 miles)
Weights: empty 5699 kg (12,565 lb) maximum take-off 11340 kg (25,000 lb)
Dimensions: span 7.70 m (25 ft 3 in); length 13.89 m (45 ft 7 in); height 3.45 m (11 ft 4 in); wing area 18.68 m^2 (201.1 sq ft)
Armament: two 30-mm Aden cannon each with 130 rounds, two AIM-9 Sidewinder AAMs and up to 2268 kg (5,000 lb) of weapons and tanks carried externally

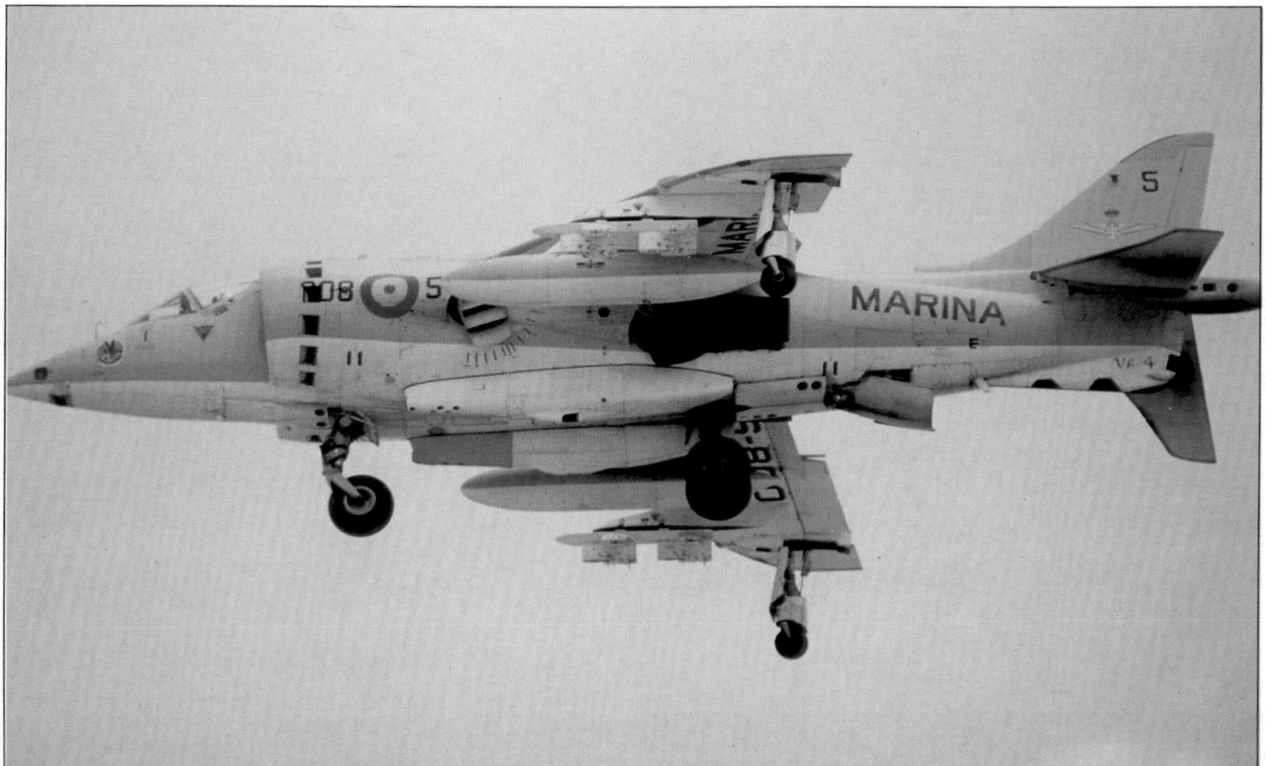

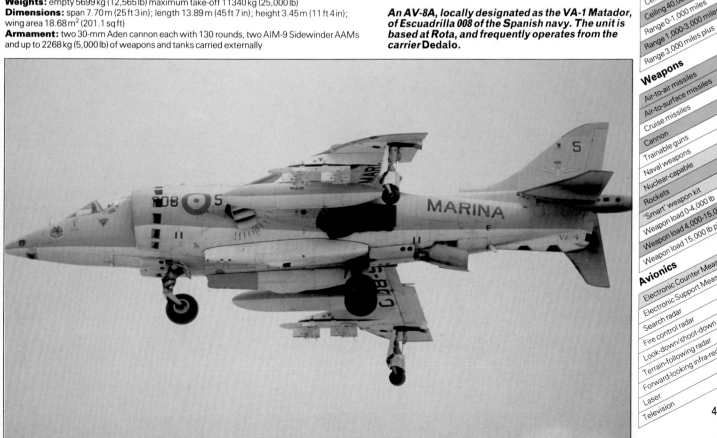

Role
- Fighter
- Close support
- Counter-insurgency
- Tactical strike
- Strategic bomber
- Tactical reconnaissance
- Strategic reconnaissance
- Maritime patrol
- Anti-ship strike
- Anti-submarine warfare
- Search and rescue
- Assault transport
- Transport
- Liaison
- Trainer
- Inflight-refuelling tanker
- Specialized

Performance
- All-weather capability
- Rough field capability
- STOL capability
- VTOL capability
- Airspeed 0-250 mph
- Airspeed 250 mph-Mach 1
- Airspeed Mach 1 plus
- Ceiling 0-20,000 ft
- Ceiling 20,000-40,000 ft
- Ceiling 40,000ft plus
- Range 0-1,000 miles
- Range 1,000-3,000 miles
- Range 3,000 miles plus

Weapons
- Air-to-air missiles
- Air-to-surface missiles
- Cruise missiles
- Cannon
- Trainable guns
- Naval weapons
- Nuclear-capable
- Rockets
- 'Smart' weapon kit
- Weapon load 0-4,000 lb
- Weapon load 4,000-15,000 lb
- Weapon load 15,000 lb plus

Avionics
- Electronic Counter Measures
- Electronic Support Measures
- Search radar
- Fire control radar
- Look-down/shoot-down
- Terrain-following radar
- Forward-looking infra-red
- Laser
- Television

British Aerospace/McDonnell Douglas T-45 Goshawk

British Aerospace/McDonnell Douglas T-45 Goshawk in US Navy colours.

In November 1981 the US Navy decided that in its search for a comprehensive VTXTS training system to replace the Rockwell T-2 Buckeye the clear winner was the BAe Hawk, partnered by McDonnell Douglas and with Sperry providing academics, simulators and support. The aircraft selected, the **T-45 Goshawk**, will differ appreciably from the Hawk T.Mk 1, notably in having full carrier capability including a strong nose-tow nose gear with twin wheels, strengthened long-stroke main gear, an arrester hook and twin side airbrakes instead of a single ventral airbrake. Other changes include an advanced US Navy cockpit, US Navy avionics and modest use of CFRP (carbonfibre reinforced plastics) throughout the structure. The engine, like every other functioning item, has been deliberately designed not for high per-

formance but for the lowest cost of ownership and of operation over a service life expected to be at least 20 years and possibly 40. Fuel burn is expected to be only about 40 per cent that of the current T-2 and McDonnell Douglas TA-4, and maintenance man-hours will be dramatically reduced. The seat will be the new NACES (Navy AirCrew Escape System) of Martin-Baker design and joint US manufacture.

Total procurement will exceed 300 aircraft. First flight is due in 1987, with service entry in 1990. There are possibilities of BAe and McDonnell Douglas jointly developing further derived designs, not only for the US Navy. McDonnell Douglas is prime contractor, BAe being 'principal subcontractor for the airframe'. Assembly will be at the Douglas Aircraft Company plant at Long Beach.

British Aerospace/McDonnell Douglas T-45 Goshawk

Specification: BAe/McDonnell Douglas T-45 Goshawk
Origin: joint UK/USA with USA assembly and flight test
Type: carrier-equipped naval pilot trainer
Powerplant: one Rolls-Royce Turboméca Adour Mk 861-49 turbofan engine derated to 2472-kg (5,450-lb) thrust
Performance: maximum speed Mach 0.85 or 487 kts (903 km/h; 561 mph) clean at high altitude, or 529 kts (980 km/h; 609 mph) at 8,000 ft (2440 m); initial rate of climb 6,740 ft (2054 m) per minute; service ceiling 42,500 ft (12955 m); ferry range, clean 1851 km (1,150 miles)
Weights: empty 4234 kg (9,335 lb); maximum take-off 5761 kg (12,700 lb)
Dimensions: span 9.40 m (30 ft 10 in); length including probe 11.97 m (39 ft 3.3 in); height 4.12 m (13 ft 6.2 in); wing area 16.68 m² (179.54 sq ft)
Armament: none

A convincing-looking mock-up of the T-45 Goshawk appeared at the 1984 Farnborough airshow, giving a realistic impression of how the finished aircraft will look.

The T-45 Goshawk has yet to fly, but this artist's impression shows the aircraft in typical US Navy training livery, with bright red conspicuity markings.

A T-45 Goshawk at the Long Beach plant.

Cessna Model 172, T-41 and Skyhawk

El Salvador Greece Guatemala Honduras Indonesia Iran Israel South Korea Liberia Madagascar Nicaragua Pakistan Panama Paraguay Peru Philippines Saudi Arabia

Thailand Turkey United States Uruguay

Angola Argentina Bolivia Chile Colombia

Dominican Rep Ecuador Eire

Cessna T-41 of the Greek air force.

Role

Fighter
Close support
Counter-insurgency
Tactical strike
Strategic bomber
Tactical reconnaissance
Strategic reconnaissance
Maritime patrol
Anti-ship strike
Anti-submarine warfare
Search and rescue
Assault transport
Transport
Liaison
Trainer
Inflight-refuelling tanker
Specialized

Performance

All-weather capability
Rough field capability
STOL capability
VTOL capability
Airspeed 0-250 mph
Airspeed 250 mph-Mach 1
Airspeed Mach 1 plus
Ceiling 0-20,000 ft
Ceiling 20,000-40,000 ft
Ceiling 40,000ft plus
Range 0-1,000 miles
Range 1,000-3,000 miles
Range 3,000 miles plus

Weapons

Air-to-air missiles
Air-to-surface missiles
Cruise missiles
Cannon
Trainable guns
Naval weapons
Nuclear-capable
Rockets
'Smart' weapon kit
Weapon load 0-4,000 lb
Weapon load 4,000-15,000 lb
Weapon load 15,000 lb plus

Avionics

Electronic Counter Measures
Electronic Support Measures
Search radar
Fire control radar
Look-down/shoot-down
Terrain-following radar
Forward-looking infra-red
Laser
Television

From the **Model 170** of the immediate post-war era the company developed the **Cessna Model 172** by 1955 with tricycle landing gear as its basic four-seat design in its range of high-wing cabin machines. Since then this family has at last surpassed the wartime Soviet Ilyushin Il-2 as the best-selling aircraft of all time with total sales of about 36,000 commercial aircraft in the Model 172/Skyhawk family plus 864 **T-41 Mescalero** military trainers.

All are all-metal aircraft with a high wing braced by a single strut, electrically-driven slotted flaps, two front and two rear seats with a door on each side, swept vertical tail and fixed landing gear with the familiar Land-O-Matic main legs in the form of cantilever spring-steel struts which deflect by bending. Customer options include wheel spats, floats or skis. The French Reims company builds the **F 172**, the total of some 2,180 so far having been included in the above figure. The various **Skyhawk** models are slightly up-graded Model 172s with full blind-flying instruments, augmented avionics and more luxurious interiors.

To meet an urgent need for a new primary (ab initio) trainer in 1964 the US Air Force ordered the T-41A Mescalero, almost identical with the Model 172 of that period, with dual controls. The USAF eventually bought 204, another 26 being bought by the Peruvian, eight by the Ecuadorean and five by the Honduran air forces. The **R172E** was specially designed in 1963-5 with increased tankage and the 157-kW (210-hp) Continental IO-360-D six-cylinder engine with a constant-speed propeller, and various special equipment items. The US Army purchased 255 as the **T-41B Mescalero** for training and installation support duties, and the USAF took 52 **T-41C** aircraft with fixed-pitch propellers for cadet flight training at the Air Force Academy, and this series ended with 238 **T-41D** aircraft with constant-speed propellers, for supply to nations receiving MAP aid (initially Colombia).

Cessna Model 172

Specification: Cessna Model 172 (landplane)/T-41A
Origin: USA; versions also made by Reims in France
Type: four-seat light aircraft and trainer
Powerplant: one 112-kW (150-hp) Avco Lycoming O-320-E2D horizontally opposed four-cylinder air-cooled piston engine
Performance: maximum speed 121 kts (224 km/h; 139 mph) at sea level; economic cruising speed 102 kts (188 km/h; 117 mph); initial rate of climb 645 ft (196 m) per minute; service ceiling 13,100 ft (3995 m); range with standard tanks and no reserve 990 km (615 miles)
Weights: empty 558 kg (1,230 lb); maximum take-off 1043 kg (2,300 lb)
Dimensions: span 10.92 m (35 ft 10 in); length 8.20 m (26 ft 11 in); height 2.68 m (8 ft 9.5 in); wing area 16.16 m² (174.0 sq ft)
Armament: none

One of 25 Cessna T-41Ds delivered to the Turkish air force, and used by the Primary Flying School (123 Filo) at Cumaovasi. After primary training pilots graduate to the Beech T-34A.

The Peruvian air force operates a number of Cessna T-41As with the Academia del Aire at Las Palmas. This aircraft was pictured before delivery.

Cessna Model 318E/A-37 Dragonfly

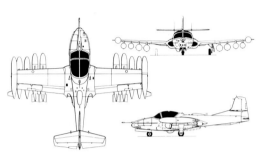

Chile   Colombia   Ecuador   El Salvador   Guatemala

Honduras   South Korea   Peru   Thailand   United States   Uruguay   Vietnam

Cessna A-37 Dragonfly of the Chilean air force.

Around 1960 there was a sharp increase in American interest in light COIN (counter-insurgency) aircraft for so-called brushfire wars. The USAF set up a Special Air Warfare Center and began evaluating suitable aircraft, one being the Cessna T-37B trainer. Later two were re-engined with the J85 engine giving more than twice the original power, and these **YAT-37D** aircraft were tested with increasing loads of external stores until the total aircraft weight reached 6350 kg (14,000 lb), well over twice that of the T-37B.

Involvement in Vietnam led to a 1966 contract for the conversion of 39 T-37B trainers to **Cessna A-37A Dragonfly** standard, with J85-5 engines, much stronger structure, fixed tip tanks to increase internal fuel to 1920 litres (507 US gal), and eight underwing pylons for a great diversity of weapons and other stores. In late 1967 a squadron equipped with 25 A-37As served in Vietnam, and eventually remained in that country.

In 1967 design was finalized of the definitive **A-37B**, and by 1977 a total of 577 had

been delivered. Most were supplied to friendly nations, though large numbers were transferred to the US Air National Guard. Very economical to operate, the A-37B has a further strengthened and refined airframe, hydraulically operated landing gear, belly speed brake and slotted flaps, unpressurized cockpit with side-by-side fixed seats, flak curtains of layered nylon in place of armour, very comprehensive night and bad-weather avionics (except for any sensors or night vision devices), an inflight-refuelling probe in the nose, and provision for four auxiliary underwing tanks on the inner pylons. All flight controls are manual, the tailplane being fixed, though all three axes have electric trim tabs.

One of the major recipients was the VNAF (air force of South Vietnam) and the A-37B is one of very few US types still flown by the Vietnamese People's air force. Most recipients were in Latin America (Paraguay, Uruguay, Chile, Peru, Ecuador, Guatemala and Honduras among them), and a squadron of 16 was supplied to Thailand.

Cessna Model 318 A-37 Dragonfly

Specification: Cessna A-37B Dragonfly

Origin: USA

Type: light attack and reconnaissance aircraft and weapons trainer

Powerplant: two 1293-kg (2,850-lb) thrust General Electric J85-17A turbojets

Performance: maximum speed (maximum weight at 16,000 ft/4875 m) 440 kts (816 km/h, 507 mph); maximum cruising speed (maximum weight at 25,000 ft/7620 m) 425 kts (787 km/h, 489 mph); initial rate of climb 6,990 ft (2130 m) per minute; service ceiling 41,765 ft (12730 m); range with maximum load including 1860 kg (4,100 lb) of ordnance at high altitude 740 km (460 miles)

Weights: empty 2817 kg (6,211 lb); maximum loaded 6350 kg (14,000 lb)

Dimensions: span (over tanks) 10.93 m (35 ft 10.3 in); length (excluding probe) 8.62 m (28 ft 3.4 in); height 2.70 m (8 ft 10.3 in); wing area 17.09 m² (183.9 sq ft)

Armament: one 7.62-mm (0.3-in) GAU-2B/A Minigun in forward fuselage; eight underwing pylons, four inners each rated at 394 kg (870 lb), next pair 272 kg (600 lb) and outers at 227 kg (500 lb), for almost all tactical bombs, tanks, rocket launchers and other ordnance to total exceeding 2268 kg (5,000 lb)

A Cessna A-37 Dragonfly of the Chilean air force, a major user of this handy little COIN/attack machine. The aircraft wears the original colour scheme, which is now being replaced.

Another Latin American operator of the Cessna A-37 is the Peruvian air force. Thirty-six were delivered, and serve alongside Canberras with Grupo 21 and Mirages with Grupo 13.

Role

Fighter
Close support
Counter-insurgency
Tactical strike
Strategic bomber
Tactical reconnaissance
Strategic reconnaissance
Maritime patrol
Anti-ship strike
Anti-submarine warfare
Search and rescue
Assault transport
Transport
Liaison
Trainer
Inflight-refuelling tanker
Specialized

Performance

All-weather capability
Rough field capability
STOL capability
VTOL capability
Airspeed 0-250 mph
Airspeed 250 mph-Mach 1
Airspeed Mach 1 plus
Ceiling 0-20,000 ft
Ceiling 20,000-40,000 ft
Ceiling 40,000 ft plus
Range 0-1,000 miles
Range 1,000-3,000 miles
Range 3,000 miles plus

Weapons

Air-to-air missiles
Air-to-surface missiles
Cruise missiles
Cannon
Trainable guns
Naval weapons
Nuclear-capable
Rockets
'Smart' weapon kit
Weapon load 0-4,000 lb
Weapon load 4,000-15,000 lb
Weapon load 15,000 lb plus

Avionics

Electronic Counter Measures
Electronic Support Measures
Search radar
Fire control radar
Look-down/shoot-down
Terrain-following radar
Forward-looking infra-red
Laser
Television

Cessna O-2 and Model 337 Skymaster

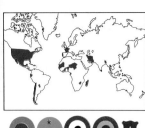

Bangladesh | Benin! | Burkina-Faso | Chad | Chile

Ecuador | El Salvador | France

Cessna O-2 of the Sri Lanka air force.

Gabon | Guinea-Bissau | Haiti | Iran | Ivory Coast | Jamaica | South Korea | Liberia | Madagascar | Mauretania | Mexico | Nicaragua | Niger | Paraguay | Portugal | Senegambia | Sri Lanka | Thailand | Togo | United States | Zimbabwe

On 28 February 1961 Cessna flew the prototype **Cessna Skymaster** (at that time the **Model 336**) in an endeavour to produce a twin that could be easily and safely flown by any private pilot, without needing a twin rating. The unusual push/pull layout did not significantly degrade flight performance or increase cabin noise, and the Model 336 and later **Model 337** (largely redesigned, and with retractable landing gear) sold well into the 4/6-seat civil market, a proportion being made by Reims Aviation in France. The Model 337 is an all-metal machine with single wing bracing struts, manual flight controls (with twin rudders), electric flaps, hydraulic landing gear and optional pneumatic de-icers on the wings and tail.

In 1967-70 Cessna delivered to the USAF 501 of a FAC (forward air control) version designated **O-2A**; another 12 were supplied to the Iranian air force. The O-2A was equipped for reconnaissance, target identification and marking, ground/air co-ordination and damage assessment. Very comprehensive

communications radios were fitted, as well as four wing pylons for a wide range of stores and equipment including weapons.

In 1968 Cessna also delivered 31 **O-2B** psy-war (psychological warfare) aircraft. These were unused ex-civil machines equipped with a massive broadcasting system with three highly directional 600-watt speakers. Other equipment included a leaflet dispenser. Almost all the O-2s saw combat duty in Vietnam.

Only prototypes were made of the twin-turboprop **O-2TT**, with Allison 250 (T63) engines. Among numerous Model 337 variants produced by Reims was the **FTMA Milirole**, first flown on 26 May 1970. This was a versatile military aircraft able to carry two pilots side-by-side (as in the O-2) and either four passengers or two stretchers. It had four wing pylons, and STOL performance with special high-lift flaps. Small numbers of commercial Model 337s were sold to foreign air forces and navies, various sub-species having different designations.

Specification: Cessna O-2A
Origin: USA
Type: FAC and observation aircraft
Powerplant: two 157-kW (210-hp) Teledyne Continental IO-360-C/D six-cylinder horizontally opposed air-cooled piston engines
Performance: maximum speed at sea level 173 kts (320 km/h; 199 mph); initial rate of climb 1,100 ft (334 m) per minute; service ceiling 18,000 ft (5490 m); range 1705 km (1,060 miles)
Weights: empty 1291 kg (2,848 lb); maximum loaded 2450 kg (5,400 lb)
Dimensions: span 11.63 m (38 ft 2 in); length 9.07 m (29 ft 9 in); height 2.84 m (9 ft 4 in); wing area 18.81 m² (202.5 sq ft)
Armament: wing pylons can carry 7.62-mm (0.3-in) Minigun pods and a variety of rocket launchers

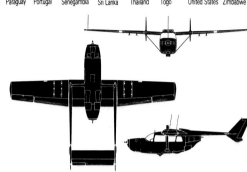

Cessna Model O-2A

A Cessna O-2A of VA-122, US Navy. The US Navy O-2s are used for a variety of support and liaison tasks, but only a small number are in service.

The Portuguese air force operates the Cessna FTB 337G mainly with Esquadra 401 of Grupo 12 and Esquadrons 701 and 702 of Grupo 21.

Cessna T-37 Tweet

South Korea Pakistan Paraguay Peru Portugal Thailand Turkey United States

Cessna T-37B of the Chilean air force.

After prolonged study, the USAF decided in 1952 to procure a jet primary trainer. The winning design was the **Cessna Model 318**, using a pair of imported French Turboméca Marboré turbojets in the thickened wing roots. A clean stressed-skin machine, first flown on 12 October 1954, it was noteworthy for its wide cockpit with side-by-side lightweight ejection seats and upward-opening clamshell canopy, extremely short landing gear with a steerable nosewheel and inwards-retracting main units with hydraulic actuation, high-mounted fixed tailplane, manual flight controls with electric trimmers, hydraulic slotted flaps, and an internal fuel capacity of 1170 litres (309 US gal), several times more than in previous primary trainers.

After 11 **T-37A** aircraft had been evaluated, the type was at last put into production, with engines made under licence by Continental (today Teledyne CAE), and full service use began in early 1957. Cessna built 537 T-37As with the 417-kg (920-lb) J69-T-9 engine, all these being later upgraded to **T-37B** stan-dard (see specification), with more power and new Omni and UHF radio; Cessna also built 447 new T-37Bs. This version was also supplied to several foreign air forces, and 47 at Sheppard AFB belong to the Luftwaffe, though wearing USAF insignia. From 1961 USAF pupils completed their entire training on jets, but in 1965 an initial 30 hours was added on the Cessna T-41 Mescalero to weed out pupils who would otherwise have 'washed out' only after costly T-37 flying. In 1970 all USAF T-37 windscreens were replaced by thick polycarbonate screens proof against virtually all birdstrikes.

In 1962 the USAF began procuring the **Model 318C (T-37C)** for delivery to foreign air forces under MAP aid. This has provision for reconnaissance cameras, combat camera, gunsight and two wing pylons for gun pods, rocket launchers, two 113-kg (250-lb) bombs or four Sidewinder AAMs. Cessna delivered 252 of this model, which can also carry the tip tanks first developed for the T-37B.

Specification: Cessna T-37B

Origin: USA
Type: primary pilot trainer
Powerplant: two 465-kg (1,025-lb) thrust Teledyne CAE J69-T-25 turbojets
Performance: maximum speed at 25,000 ft (7620 m) 370 kts (685 km/h; 426 mph); initial rate of climb 3,370 ft (1027 m) per minute; service ceiling 39,200 ft (11950 m); range at 25,000 ft (7620 m) with 5 per cent reserve 1400 km (870 miles)
Weights: empty 1755 kg (3,870 lb); maximum loaded 2993 kg (6,600 lb)
Dimensions: span (no tip tanks) 10.30 m (33 ft 9.3 in); length 8.92 m (29 ft 3 in); height 2.80 m (9 ft 2.3 in); wing area 17.09 m² (183.9 sq ft)
Armament: none

Burma Chile Colombia W. Germany Greece Jordan

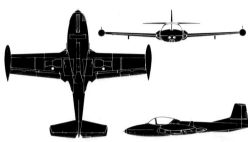

Cessna T-37C

The 'Tweety Bird', as it is fondly known, remains an integral part of the US Air Force's training programme. Replacement by the Fairchild T-46A looks increasingly unlikely.

A Cessna T-37 of the Pakistan air force. The T-37s are operated by Nos 1 and 2 Basic Flying Squadrons of the Basic Flying Wing at Risalpur. No replacement is yet in sight.

Role

Fighter
Close support
Counter-insurgency
Tactical strike
Strategic bomber
Tactical reconnaissance
Strategic reconnaissance
Maritime patrol
Anti-ship strike
Anti-submarine warfare
Search and rescue
Assault transport
Transport
Liaison
Trainer
Inflight-refuelling tanker
Specialized

Performance

All-weather capability
Rough field capability
STOL capability
VTOL capability
Airspeed 0-250 mph
Airspeed 250 mph-Mach 1
Airspeed Mach 1 plus
Ceiling 0-20,000 ft
Ceiling 20,000-40,000 ft
Ceiling 40,000 ft plus
Range 0-1,000 miles
Range 1,000-3,000 miles
Range 3,000 miles plus

Weapons

Air-to-air missiles
Air-to-surface missiles
Cruise missiles
Cannon
Trainable guns
Naval weapons
Nuclear-capable
Rockets
'Smart' weapon kit
Weapon load 0-4,000 lb
Weapon load 4,000-15,000 lb
Weapon load 15,000 lb plus

Avionics

Electronic Counter Measures
Electronic Support Measures
Search radar
Fire control radar
Look-down/shoot-down
Terrain-following radar
Forward-looking infra-red
Laser
Television

Primary capability
Secondary capability

Convair CV-240 to CV-580

Convair CV-440-86 of No. 2 Squadron, Sri Lanka air force.

On 1 June 1948 the **Convair CV-240** entered service with American Airlines. Planned as a 'DC-3 replacement', it was a modern pressurized 40-seater with neat twin-wheel main and nose gears, a built-in rear airstairs and paddle-blade reversing propellers driven by powerful R-2800 engines whose twin exhaust pipes were carried back over the wing to induce cooling air and give extra propulsive thrust. Well over 1,000 Convair-Liners were built at San Diego, the airframes developing through three main versions. After the CV-240 came the **CV-340** with span increased from 27.96 m (91 ft 9 in) to the figure given in the specification, and with a longer fuselage. The **CV-440** introduced numerous improvements to reduce drag and noise, typical seating going up to 52. Many of all three models are still flying.

The USAF bought hundreds of **T-29** crew trainers (CV-240 type) and **C-131 Samari-** tan aircraft for transport, casevac, Elint and other tasks (CV-340). The US Navy CV-340 model was the **R4Y**. A few C-131s and R4Ys still fly with foreign air forces, as do some ex-civil CV-440s.

From 1954 there were many turboprop versions, mostly rebuilds. Convair produced the **CV-600** and **CV-640** with the Dart Mk 542 of 2256 kW (3,025 ehp). PacAero rebuilt 130 CV-340 and CV-440 aircraft with the Allison 501, and nearly all these **CV-580s** are still flying including a handful with military operators. Canadair built 10 Eland-engined **CL-66B Cosmopolitan** transports, recently replaced in the CAF by Challengers after having spent most of their life re-engined with the Allison 501. Though the C-131 and R4Y remained in service until at least 1981, today all these 'Convairs' are very seldom seen and are likely to be retired even from minor air forces before about 1988.

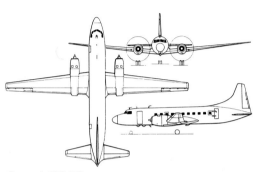

Convair CV-440

A Miami-based Convair HC-131F of the US Coast Guard. These aircraft are rapidly being replaced by more modern types.

The Canadian Armed Forces still operate a handful of Allison-engined, licence-built Cosmopolitans. This aircraft belongs to No. 412 Squadron.

Specification: Convair/PacAero CV-580
Origin: USA
Type: transport
Powerplant: two 2796-kW (3,750-shp) Allison 501-D13 turboprops
Performance: maximum speed 297 kts (550 km/h; 342 mph); typical cruising height 20,000 ft (6095 m); range with maximum payload about 2250 km (1,400 miles), or with maximum fuel 4611 km (2,865 miles)
Weights: empty 13835 kg (30,500 lb); maximum loaded 26371 kg (58,140 lb)
Dimensions: span 32.12 m (105 ft 4 in); length 24.84 m (81 ft 6 in); height 8.89 m (29 ft 2 in); wing area 85.47 m² (920 sq ft)
Armament: none

A CV-440 in Luftwaffe service in 1967

Curtiss C-46 Commando

Bolivia China Colombia South Korea Mexico

Taiwan

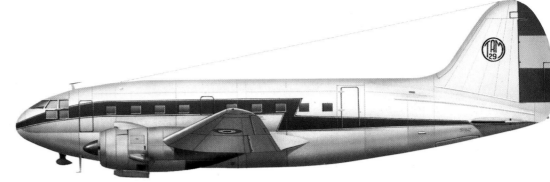

Super Smith 46-C (custom-built variant) of the Bolivian air force.

Spurred by the global success of the Douglas DC-3, Curtiss-Wright in 1937 began design of a much larger transport with the new Wright R-2600 engine and a pressurized fuselage. The **Curtiss-Wright CW-20** flew on 26 March 1940. It was later sold to BOAC, but it triggered off massive wartime production of a developed version for the USAAF. A switch to the R-2800 engine allowed weights to increase greatly, features including single-strut tailwheel landing gears, a heavy freight floor, wide double doors on the left and, usually, folding seats along each side for 40 equipped troops. Production lines were set up at Buffalo, St Louis and Louisville.

In service the **C-46 Commando** proved very valuable, despite what is today seen as an inconvenient layout with a steeply sloping floor and side doors high above the ground.

Many had glider-tow cleats, and paratroops and externally carried containers could be dropped. Large numbers served 'over the Hump' to China, the R-2800-51 engine giving better altitude performance. The **C-46E** had a stepped windscreen, but oddly was withdrawn in 1953, while most of the many other versions soldiered on until the Vietnam War. The US Navy version was the **R5C**. Altogether 3,341 of these exceptionally large twin-engined machines were built, and despite having performance unacceptable by modern airworthiness standards large numbers continued flying into the 1970s, mostly in Latin America and the Caribbean. In these areas a handful were still flying in 1986, including several with military and government operators. Most have a few passenger seats but are used mainly for cargo.

Specification: Curtiss C-46A Commando
Origin: USA
Type: utility transport
Powerplant: two 1492-kW (2,000-hp) Pratt & Whitney R-2800-51 18-cylinder radial piston engines
Performance: maximum speed 234 kts (433 km/h; 269 mph) at 15,000 ft (4570 m); cruising speed 150 kts (278 km/h; 173 mph); service ceiling 24,500 ft (7470 m); maximum range with full standard fuel 5069 km (3,150 miles)
Weights: empty 14060 kg (31,000 lb); maximum loaded 20412 kg (45,000 lb) though some are illegally operated to wartime weight limit of 25400 kg (56,000 lb)
Dimensions: span 32.91 m (108 ft 0 in); length 23.26 m (76 ft 4 in); height 6.62 m (21 ft 9 in); wing area 126.34 m² (1,360 sq ft)
Armament: none

Curtiss C-46 Commando

Still thought to be in service with the Republic of Korea Air Force in small numbers, the C-46 has enjoyed a long and distinguished career.

A number of Commandos are flown in military markings in the United States, this ex-Chinese Nationalist C-46 wearing its original colours. Taiwan still operates a large number of C-46s.

Douglas A-3 Skywarrior

United States

An EA-3B of VQ-1, headquartered at Guam, but serving on board USS Constellation.

Originally conceived in response to a US Navy requirement of 1947 calling for a carrierborne strategic strike attack-bomber, the **Douglas XA3D-1 Skywarrior** prototype first flew on 28 October 1952 with a pair of Westinghouse XJ40-WE-3 turbojet engines. Complete failure of this engine required urgent redesign of most Navy fighters and bombers, and the Skywarrior switched to the J57.

The first production model was the **A3D-1** (later redesignated **A-3A**) which made its maiden flight on 16 September 1953 and which began to enter service with heavy attack squadrons of the US Navy during March 1956. In the event the A3D-1 was produced in only modest quantities, giving way to the definitive **A3D-2** (**A-3B** from late 1962), which remained in use as a strike aircraft until well into the 1960s.

Post-production modification of the A-3B model resulted in the appearance of several specialized variants including the **KA-3B** inflight-refuelling tanker and the **EKA-3B**, which married the ECM role to the inflight-refuelling mission. By the late 1960s no pure bomber Skywarriors remained in the inventory, but the Navy did possess a fairly sizeable fleet of KA-3Bs and EKA-3Bs which per-

formed valuable work in Vietnam.

Other new-build models include the **A3D-2P** (later **RA-3B**) for photo-reconnaissance and the **A3D-2Q** (later **EA-3B**) for ECM duties, the latter now being the only Skywarrior sub-type still found in the front-line inventory, equipping squadrons based at Guam and in Spain, and operating alongside the Lockheed EP-3E Orion on the acquisition of electronic. intelligence. For training purposes, a small number of **A3D-2T** (later **TA-3B**) aircraft were completed, and some of these are also still employed today.

Despite the fact that it has virtually disappeared from front-line units, quite a few Skywarriors remain active, a few KA-3Bs equipping a couple of US Navy Reserve squadrons whilst, as already noted, the EA-3B is still very much an operational aircraft. As well as these machines, the Skywarrior has proved a particularly valuable research tool, being employed as a radar testbed, for instance, and this is still a task undertaken by some aircraft. Finally, several **ERA-3B** 'ECM aggressors' serve with two squadrons in the USA, being used to evaluate Navy ECM capability and to test new items of ECM gear.

Douglas TA-3B Skywarrior

VAK-308's KA-3Bs serve as inflight-refuelling aircraft for the aircraft of Reserve Carrier Air Wing 30, and are based at NAS Alameda. The service life of the KA-3B is now drawing to a close.

Two squadrons, VAQ-33 and VAQ-34, operate the A-3 in the fleet ECM training support role, acting as electronic aggressors. The aircraft shown is a TA-3B.

Specification: Douglas EA-3B Skywarrior
Origin: USA
Type: land/carrier-based electronic reconnaissance platform
Powerplant: two 5625-kg (12,400-lb) thrust Pratt & Whitney J57-P-10 turbojet engines
Performance: maximum speed 530 kts (982 km/h; 610 mph) at 10,000 ft (3050 mph); cruising speed 452 kts (837 km/h; 520 mph); service ceiling 41,000 ft (12495 m); maximum range 4667 km (2,900 miles)
Weights: empty 17856 kg (39,409 lb); maximum take-off 33112 kg (73,000 lb)
Dimensions: span 22.10 m (72 ft 6 in); length 23.27 m (76 ft 4 in); height 6.95 m (22 ft 9.5 in); wing area 75.43 m² (812 sq ft)
Armament: none

Role
Fighter
Close support
Counter-insurgency
Tactical strike
Strategic bomber
Tactical reconnaissance
Strategic reconnaissance
Maritime patrol
Anti-ship strike
Anti-submarine warfare
Search and rescue
Assault transport
Transport
Liaison
Trainer
Inflight-refuelling tanker
Specialized

Performance
All-weather capability
Rough field capability
STOL capability
VTOL capability
Airspeed 0-250 mph
Airspeed 250 mph-Mach 1
Airspeed Mach 1 plus
Ceiling 0-20,000 ft
Ceiling 20,000-40,000 ft
Ceiling 40,000ft plus
Range 0-1,000 miles
Range 1,000-3,000 miles
Range 3,000 miles plus

Weapons
Air-to-air missiles
Air-to-surface missiles
Cruise missiles
Cannon
Trainable guns
Naval weapons
Nuclear-capable
Rockets
'Smart' weapon kit
Weapon load 0-4,000 lb
Weapon load 4,000-15,000 lb
Weapon load 15,000 lb plus

Avionics
Electronic Counter Measures
Electronic Support Measures
Search radar
Fire control radar
Look-down/shoot-down radar
Terrain-following radar
Forward-looking infra-red
Laser
Television

Douglas C-47 Skytrain/Dakota

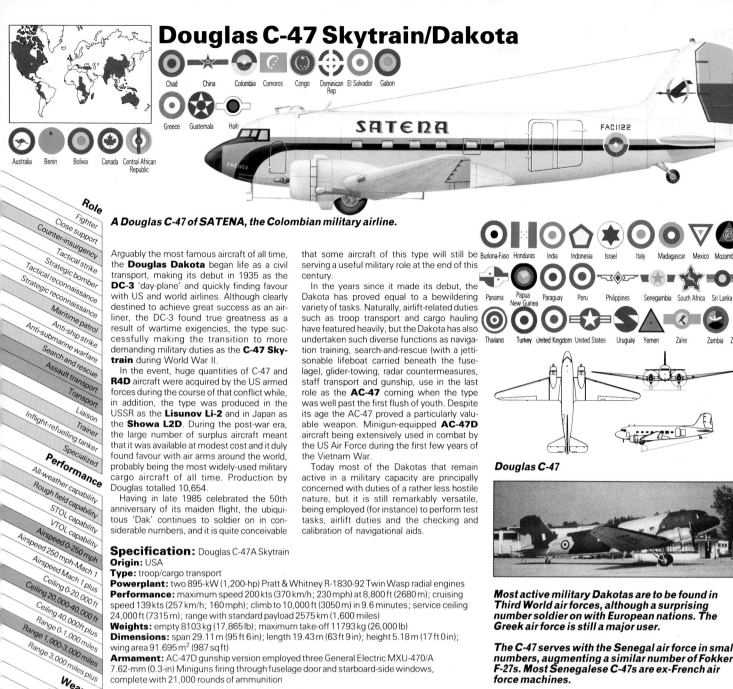

Chad · China · Colombia · Comoros · Congo · Dominican Rep · El Salvador · Gabon

Greece · Guatemala · Haiti

Australia · Benin · Bolivia · Canada · Central African Republic

Burkina-Faso · Honduras · India · Indonesia · Israel · Italy · Madagascar · Mexico · Mozambique

Panama · Papua New Guinea · Paraguay · Peru · Philippines · Senegambia · South Africa · Sri Lanka

Thailand · Turkey · United Kingdom · United States · Uruguay · Yemen · Zaïre · Zambia · Zimb...

Douglas C-47

A Douglas C-47 of SATENA, the Colombian military airline.

Arguably the most famous aircraft of all time, the **Douglas Dakota** began life as a civil transport, making its debut in 1935 as the **DC-3** 'day-plane' and quickly finding favour with US and world airlines. Although clearly destined to achieve great success as an airliner, the DC-3 found true greatness as a result of wartime exigencies, the type successfully making the transition to more demanding military duties as the **C-47 Skytrain** during World War II.

In the event, huge quantities of C-47 and **R4D** aircraft were acquired by the US armed forces during the course of that conflict while, in addition, the type was produced in the USSR as the **Lisunov Li-2** and in Japan as the **Showa L2D**. During the post-war era, the large number of surplus aircraft meant that it was available at modest cost and it duly found favour with air arms around the world, probably being the most widely-used military cargo aircraft of all time. Production by Douglas totalled 10,654.

Having in late 1985 celebrated the 50th anniversary of its maiden flight, the ubiquitous 'Dak' continues to soldier on in considerable numbers, and it is quite conceivable

that some aircraft of this type will still be serving a useful military role at the end of this century.

In the years since it made its debut, the Dakota has proved equal to a bewildering variety of tasks. Naturally, airlift-related duties such as troop transport and cargo hauling have featured heavily, but the Dakota has also undertaken such diverse functions as navigation training, search-and-rescue (with a jettisonable lifeboat carried beneath the fuselage), glider-towing, radar countermeasures, staff transport and gunship, use in the last role as the **AC-47** coming when the type was well past the first flush of youth. Despite its age the AC-47 proved a particularly valuable weapon. Minigun-equipped **AC-47D** aircraft being extensively used in combat by the US Air Force during the first few years of the Vietnam War.

Today most of the Dakotas that remain active in a military capacity are principally concerned with duties of a rather less hostile nature, but it is still remarkably versatile, being employed (for instance) to perform test tasks, airlift duties and the checking and calibration of navigational aids.

Specification: Douglas C-47A Skytrain
Origin: USA
Type: troop/cargo transport
Powerplant: two 895-kW (1,200-hp) Pratt & Whitney R-1830-92 Twin Wasp radial engines
Performance: maximum speed 200 kts (370 km/h; 230 mph) at 8,800 ft (2680 m); cruising speed 139 kts (257 km/h; 160 mph); climb to 10,000 ft (3050 m) in 9.6 minutes; service ceiling 24,000 ft (7315 m); range with standard payload 2575 km (1,600 miles)
Weights: empty 8103 kg (17,865 lb); maximum take-off 11793 kg (26,000 lb)
Dimensions: span 29.11 m (95 ft 6 in); length 19.43 m (63 ft 9 in); height 5.18 m (17 ft 0 in); wing area 91.695 m² (987 sq ft)
Armament: AC-47D gunship version employed three General Electric MXU-470/A 7.62-mm (0.3-in) Miniguns firing through fuselage door and starboard-side windows, complete with 21,000 rounds of ammunition

Most active military Dakotas are to be found in Third World air forces, although a surprising number soldier on with European nations. The Greek air force is still a major user.

The C-47 serves with the Senegal air force in small numbers, augmenting a similar number of Fokker F-27s. Most Senegalese C-47s are ex-French air force machines.

Role
Fighter
Close support
Counter-insurgency
Tactical strike
Strategic bomber
Tactical reconnaissance
Strategic reconnaissance
Maritime patrol
Anti-ship strike
Anti-submarine warfare
Search and rescue
Assault transport
Transport
Liaison
Trainer
Inflight-refuelling tanker
Specialized

Performance
All-weather capability
Rough field capability
STOL capability
VTOL capability
Airspeed 0-250 mph
Airspeed 250 mph-Mach 1
Airspeed Mach 1 plus
Ceiling 0-20,000 ft
Ceiling 20,000-40,000 ft
Ceiling 40,000ft plus
Range 0-1,000 miles
Range 1,000-3,000 miles
Range 3,000 miles plus

Weapons
Air-to-air missiles
Air-to-surface missiles
Cruise missiles
Cannon
Trainable guns
Naval weapons
Nuclear-capable
Rockets
'Smart' weapon kit
Weapon load 0-4,000 lb
Weapon load 4,000-15,000 lb
Weapon load 15,000 lb plus

Avionics
Electronic Counter Measures
Electronic Support Measures
Search radar
Fire control radar
Look-down/shoot-down
Terrain-following radar
Forward-looking infra-red
Laser
Television

Elicotteri Meridionali CH-47C Chinook

A second source for the successful Boeing Vertol CH-47 Chinook twin-rotor medium-lift helicopter was established in Italy following the agreement of a manufacturing licence with the American parent firm in 1968. Elicotteri Meridionali (EM) had begun operations in the previous year as a subsidiary of Agusta overhauling helicopters, but by 1970 was assembling the **Elicotteri Meridionali CH-47C Chinook** to meet an order for 26 placed by Italian army light aviation (Aviazione Leggera dell'Esercito, or ALE). EM has built only the CH-47C version of the helicopter, of which over 160 have been supplied from the assembly facilities at Vergiate.

Allocated the little-used ALE designation **ETM-1** (Elicottero da Trasporto Medio, or medium transport helicopter), two Chinooks were delivered for evaluation in 1973. On 1 February 1976, the 11° and 12° Gruppi Squadroni were formed at Viterbo to fly the Chinook operationally, their 26th helicopter being completed in May 1977. Two attrition replacements followed in 1984. The major customer, however, was pre-revolutionary Iran, which ordered batches of 16, 26 and 50: two for the air force and the remainder for the army. Only 67 of these had been delivered by April 1981, when the USA embargoed further supplies, and so in recompense for lost

business the US Army purchased 11 unsold CH-47Cs from EM in 1984. These have been assigned to units in Europe and will probably undergo conversion to CH-47D standard at a later time.

Further customers have included Libya, which has been permitted to receive 20 EM-built Chinooks despite the otherwise strict US controls on trade with Colonel Ghadaffi's regime. Delivered between July 1976 and early 1980, six have gone to the air force and the remainder to the army for logistic support of radar and missile sites. Morocco's first six CH-47Cs were received in 1979 and employed in the Western Sahara conflict against Polisario guerrillas. Deliveries of at least three more began in June 1982. An Egyptian requirement for 15 CH-47Cs was quickly satisfied as the result of Iranian cancellations, permitting deliveries to begin to the base at Kom Amshim late in 1981. At the same time, Greece began to take delivery of 10 Chinooks, equally divided between the air force and army aviation. A further customer, Tanzania, ordered two EM-built CH-47Cs in 1981 for delivery in the following year, but the contract appears to have lapsed. Most recently, the Italian disaster relief organization, SNPC, has revealed a requirement for six Chinooks, probably to be flown on its behalf by the ALE.

An Italian-built Chinook of the Egyptian air force.

Elicotteri Meridionali CH-47C Chinook

Imperial Iran was the main customer for the Elicotteri Meridionali CH-47C Chinook, and 67 had been delivered by April 1981 when the USA embargoed further deliveries.

An Elicotteri Meridionali-built CH-47C Chinook of the Italian army. The aircraft has also been supplied to Libya, Morocco, Greece, Tanzania, and Egypt, and even the US Army.

Specification: Elicotteri Meridionali CH-47C Chinook

Origin: USA (via Italy)
Powerplant: two 2796-kW (3,750-shp) maximum rating Avco Lycoming T55-L-11D turboshaft engines
Performance: cruising speed 115 kts (213 km/h; 132 mph) at maximum weight; limiting speed 119 kts (220 km/h; 137 mph); initial rate of climb 1,150 ft (351 m) per minute; service ceiling 8,000 ft (2440 m); range 500 km (311 miles) at 2,000 ft (609 m)
Weights: empty equipped 9398 kg (20,719 lb); maximum take-off 20866 kg (46,000 lb); useful load 11468 kg (25,281 lb)
Dimensions: rotor diameter, each 18.29 m (60 ft 0 in); fuselage length 15.54 m (51 ft 0 in); effective length (rotors turning) 30.18 m (99 ft 0 in); height 5.69 m (18 ft 8 in); total rotor disc area 525.34 m² (5,654.9 sq ft)
Armament: none

Egypt Italy Libya Greece Iran Morocco

Tanzania United States

Role
Fighter
Close support
Counter-insurgency
Tactical strike
Strategic bomber
Tactical reconnaissance
Strategic reconnaissance
Maritime patrol
Anti-ship strike
Anti-submarine warfare
Search and rescue
Assault transport
Transport
Liaison
Trainer
Inflight-refuelling tanker
Specialized

Performance
All-weather capability
Rough field capability
STOL capability
VTOL capability
Airspeed 0-250 mph
Airspeed 250 mph-Mach 1
Airspeed Mach 1 plus
Ceiling 0-20,000 ft
Ceiling 20,000-40,000 ft
Ceiling 40,000ft plus
Range 0-1,000 miles
Range 1,000-3,000 miles
Range 3,000 miles plus

Weapons
Air-to-air missiles
Air-to-surface missiles
Cruise missiles
Cannon
Trainable guns
Naval weapons
Nuclear-capable
Rockets
'Smart' weapon kit
Weapon load 0-4,000 lb
Weapon load 4,000-15,000 lb
Weapon load 15,000 lb plus

Avionics
Electronic Counter Measures
Electronic Support Measures
Search radar
Fire control radar
Look-down/shoot-down
Terrain-following radar
Forward-looking infra-red
Laser
Television

A10A Thunderbolt IIs of 23rd TFW

Fairchild Republic A-10A Thunderbolt II

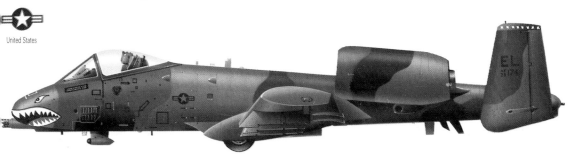

United States

A Fairchild Republic A-10A Thunderbolt II of the 23rd Tactical Fighter Wing, US Air Force, England AFB, Louisiana.

Designed from the outset to perform the battlefield interdiction and close air support missions, the **Fairchild Republic A-10A Thunderbolt II** is undoubtedly one of the most grotesque warplanes to have made its debut in the years since World War II.

More or less built around the fearsome GAU-8/A Avenger 30-mm 'Gatling' type rotary cannon, the A-10A was one of two candidates for the USAF's A-X (Attack, Experimental) design competition and eventually fought off the challenge posed by Northrop's A-9A, two prototypes of each type being completed for a comparative evaluation programme conducted during the early 1970s. Eventually, in January 1973, the Fairchild submission was adjudged more suitable and was ordered into quantity production.

Subsequently, it was introduced to Europe in 1978 when the Bentwaters-based 81st Tactical Fighter Wing received the first of more than 100 aircraft, and since then the Thunderbolt II has been assigned to elements of the Alaskan Air Command, the Air National Guard and the Air Force Reserve, production terminating in February 1984 when the 713th example was handed over to the USAF.

Powered by a pair of General Electric TF34 turbofan engines, the A-10A possesses remarkable payload capability, being able to operate with up to 7258 kg (16,000 lb) of ordnance, although in this configuration it cannot carry a full fuel load.

As far as internal systems are concerned, the A-10A was relatively unsophisticated in its original form but it is to be the subject of a major improvement initiative in 1987, this involving fitment of the LANTIRN night nav/attack pod system incorporating FLIR and laser sensors as well as terrain-following radar. A wide-angle HUD will also be installed to display FLIR imagery to the pilot.

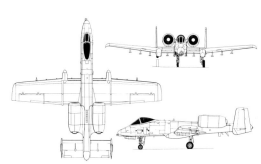

Fairchild Republic A-10A Thunderbolt II

This 81st TFW A-10 is seen manoeuvring hard at low level over North Wales. The 81st TFW is based at Bentwaters and Woodbridge, England, with Forward Operating Locations in Germany.

An A-10A of the 81st TFW is about to edge in and refuel from an SAC KC-135 high above the North Sea. The A-10 force routinely practises air-to-air refuelling and forward deployments.

Specification: Fairchild A-10A Thunderbolt II
Origin: USA
Type: single-seat close air support and battlefield interdiction aircraft
Powerplant: two 4112-kg (9,065-lb) thrust General Electric TF34-GE-100 high-bypass turbofan engines
Performance: maximum speed 381 kts (706 km/h; 439 mph) at sea level; cruise speed in clean configuration 336 kts (623 km/h; 387 mph) at 5,000 ft (1525 m); loiter time at 402 km (250 miles) from base with 18 Mk 82 bombs plus 750 rounds of gun ammunition 2 hours: take-off distance at maximum weight 1220 m (4,000 ft)
Weights: operating empty 11321 kg (24,959 lb); forward airstrip 14865 kg (32,771 lb); maximum take-off 22680 kg (50,000 lb)
Dimensions: span 17.53 m (57 ft 6 in); length 16.26 m (53 ft 4 in); height 4.47 m (14 ft 8 in); wing area 47.01 m² (506 sq ft)
Armament: one integral GAU-8/A 30-mm rotary cannon with capacity for up to 1,350 rounds of ammunition, plus maximum external payload of 7,258 kg (16,000 lb) of ordnance on 11 hardpoints; weapons options include conventional bombs, incendiary bombs, Rockeye cluster bomb units, AGM-65 Maverick air-to-surface missiles, laser and electro-optically guided 'smart' bombs and SUU-23 gun pods

Role
Fighter
Close support
Counter-insurgency
Tactical strike
Strategic bomber
Tactical reconnaissance
Strategic reconnaissance
Maritime patrol
Anti-ship strike
Anti-submarine warfare
Search and rescue
Assault transport
Transport
Liaison
Trainer
Inflight-refuelling tanker
Specialized

Performance
All-weather capability
Rough field capability
STOL capability
VTOL capability
Airspeed 0-250 mph
Airspeed 250 mph-Mach 1
Airspeed Mach 1 plus
Ceiling 0-20,000 ft
Ceiling 20,000-40,000 ft
Ceiling 40,000 ft plus
Range 0-1,000 miles
Range 1,000-3,000 miles
Range 3,000 miles plus

Weapons
Air-to-air missiles
Air-to-surface missiles
Cruise missiles
Cannon
Trainable guns
Naval weapons
Nuclear-capable
Rockets
'Smart' weapon kit
Weapon load 0-4,000 lb
Weapon load 4,000-15,000 lb
Weapon load 15,000 lb plus

Avionics
Electronic Counter Measures
Electronic Support Measures
Search radar
Fire control radar
Look-down/shoot-down
Terrain-following radar
Forward-looking infra-red
Laser
Television

Gates Learjet C-21A

A US Air Force Military Airlift Command Gates Learjet C-21A.

On 19 September 1983 the Gates Learjet Corporation secured what must surely rank as its most prestigious deal to date when it was awarded a $175.4 million contract covering the supply and support of no less than 80 Learjet Model 35As to the US Air Force. Known by that service as the **Gates Learjet C-21A**, the Learjet was basically intended to replace the 1960s-vintage North American Rockwell CT-39A Sabreliner with the Military Airlift Command (MAC), forming just one part of the so-called OSA (Operational Support Aircraft) programme, the other major component being Beechcraft's C-12F Super King Air.

Breaking new ground in that it marked the first time that the USAF had entered into a major leasing agreement, the deal initially covers a five-year period but includes options to extend for three more years and, eventually, to purchase the aircraft outright should the USAF so desire. Utilized on a variety of support-related tasks such as the delivery of priority cargo, proficiency training, personnel movement and medical evacuation, the first

C-21A made its debut at the company's Tucson, Arizona, facility during March 1984, from where it was delivered to MAC headquarters at Scott AFB, Illinois, fairly soon afterwards.

With production for MAC quickly building up to a peak rate of four aircraft per month, all of the 80 Learjets involved had been delivered by late 1985. Understandably, the majority are based with MAC elements located within the continental USA but modest numbers (probably not exceeding 10 or so aircraft in all) have been deployed overseas, most notably with the small units operating in support of PACAF (Pacific Air Forces) and USAFE (United States Air Forces in Europe) in Japan and West Germany respectively.

As far as operational reliability is concerned, MAC clearly has good cause to be delighted with the C-21A which, during its first year of service, demonstrated a mission-capable rate exceeding 95 per cent whilst accumulating the quite respectable total of just under 19,000 flying hours.

Specification: Gates Learjet C-21A
Origin: USA
Type: light transport aircraft
Powerplant: two 1588-kg (3,500-lb) thrust Garrett TFE731-2-2B turbofan engines
Performance: maximum speed 471 kts (872 km/h; 542 mph) at 25,000 ft (7620 m); economical cruising speed 418 kts (774 km/h; 481 mph) at 45,000 ft (13715 m); initial rate of climb 4,760 ft (1451 m) per minute; service ceiling 45,000 ft (13715 m)
Weights: empty equipped 4341 kg (9,571 lb); maximum payload 1588 kg (3,500 lb); maximum take-off 7711 kg (17,000 lb)
Dimensions: span over tip tanks 12.04 m (39 ft 6 in); length 14.83 m (48 ft 8 in); height 3.73 m (12 ft 3 in); wing area 23.53 m² (253.3 sq ft)
Armament: none

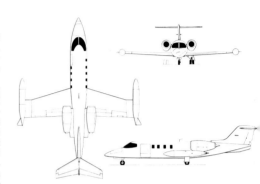

Gates Learjet C-21A

This Gates Learjet C-21A is one of three used by the 58th Military Airlift Squadron, a light communication unit based at Ramstein, West Germany. A further three are used by the HQ USEUCOM.

A C-21A is seen at Tucson prior to delivery to the 1375th MAS of the 375th Air Ambulance Wing at Scott AFB. Tucson International Airport is home to an ANG A-7 unit.

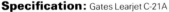

Gates Learjet 20 series

Bolivia Ecuador Yugoslavia Mexico Peru

Saudi Arabia

One of two Gates Learjet 25Bs used by the Peruvian air force for photo-survey duties.

With its roots in the Swiss-designed Flug und Fahrzeugwerke AG (FFA) P-1604 fighter that was evaluated by the Swiss air force during the mid-1950s, the **Gates Learjet** is without doubt one of the most successful 'biz-jets' yet conceived, and progressive development of the line has enabled it to remain in great demand for more than 20 years.

The first variant to appear was the **Learjet 23** which made its maiden flight from Wichita, Kansas, as long ago as October 1963. Clear evidence of its origins in the P-1604 project lay in the fact that it employed a basically similar wing planform, complete with tip tanks. Possessing sparkling performance, it quickly found favour on the commercial market and deliveries duly got under way in October 1964.

Subsequently, in 1966, the Lear Jet Corporation announced an improved version known as the **Learjet 24** which was slightly heavier and featured an improved pressurization system, further development of this model resulting in the appearance of the **Learjet 24B** with more powerful CJ610-6 turbojet engines, the short-range **Learjet 24C** and the slightly smaller **Learjet 24D** with a revised window arrangement similar to that adopted by the **Learjet 25**.

The Learjet 25 was in fact basically a stretched aircraft with capacity for two more

passengers, and this too has appeared in several guises, most notably as the **Learjet 25B**, **Learjet 25D** and **Learjet 25G**, the last subtype being probably the most advanced of the Learjet 20 series in that it features a number of improvements to the wing, engine pylons and tip tank attachment points. Between them, these 'fine tuning' efforts have resulted in substantially greater range capability, the current Learjet 25G variant possessing a range which exceeds that of the standard Learjet 25D by more than 20 per cent. Making its debut in the early 1980s, the Learjet 25G is no longer in production but the older Learjet 25D is still being built in modest numbers although, understandably, demand for this version has declined in recent years.

As far as military use is concerned, the Learjet has only achieved limited success, being employed on such tasks as high-speed transportation, photo-mapping and target towing, customers including the air forces of Bolivia (one Learjet 25B and one Learjet 25D), Peru (two Learjet 25Bs), Saudi Arabia (one Learjet 25B and one Learjet 25D) and Yugoslavia (two Learjet 25Bs). In addition, single examples of the Learjet 24D have been purchased by the Ecuadorian army and the Mexican navy.

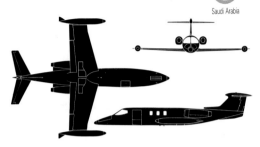

Gates Learjet 25

One Learjet 24 is used by the Mexican navy for executive transport duties, operating from bases shared with the Mexican air force. The Learjet's speed and altitude capability are impressive.

This Learjet 25B is used by the Fuerza Aérea Boliviana for reconnaissance and survey duties with the Servicio Nacional Aerofotogrametrica based at La Paz.

Specification: Gates Learjet 25D
Origin: USA
Type: 10-seat light executive jet aircraft
Powerplant: two 1338-kg (2,950-lb) thrust General Electric CJ610-8A turbojet engines
Performance: maximum operating speed 475 kts (880 km/h; 547 mph) at 25,000 ft (7620 m); economical cruising speed at 47,000 ft (14325 m) 428 kts (793 km/h; 493 mph); initial rate of climb at sea level 6,830 ft (2082 m) per minute; service ceiling 51,000 ft (15545 m); range with four passengers, maximum fuel and 45-minute reserves 2650 km (1,647 miles)
Weights: empty equipped 3606 kg (7,950 lb); maximum take-off 6804 kg (15,000 lb)
Dimensions: span over tip tanks 10.84 m (35 ft 7 in); length 14.50 m (47 ft 7 in); height 3.73 m (12 ft 3 in); wing area 21.53 m² (231.77 sq ft)
Armament: none

Role
Fighter
Close support
Counter-insurgency
Tactical strike
Strategic bomber
Tactical reconnaissance
Strategic reconnaissance
Maritime patrol
Anti-ship strike
Anti-submarine warfare
Search and rescue
Assault transport
Transport
Liaison
Trainer
Inflight-refuelling tanker
Specialized

Performance
All-weather capability
Rough field capability
STOL capability
VTOL capability
Airspeed 0-250 mph
Airspeed 250 mph-Mach 1
Airspeed Mach 1 plus
Ceiling 0-20,000 ft
Ceiling 20,000-40,000 ft
Ceiling 40,000ft plus
Range 0-1,000 miles
Range 1,000-3,000 miles
Range 3,000 miles plus

Weapons
Air-to-air missiles
Air-to-surface missiles
Cruise missiles
Cannon
Trainable guns
Naval weapons
Nuclear-capable
Rockets
'Smart' weapon kit
Weapon load 0-4,000 lb
Weapon load 4,000-15,000 lb
Weapon load 15,000 lb plus

Avionics
Electronic Counter Measures
Electronic Support Measures
Search radar
Fire control radar
Look-down/shoot-down
Terrain-following radar
Forward-looking infra-red
Laser
Television

General Dynamics F-16 experimental models

The production F-16 has spawned several interesting developments and some of these have resulted in flying prototypes. When the US government authorized an FX (Fighter Experimental) programme, to develop aircraft for countries where a front-line US fighter type could not be exported or was not required, the company responded by developing the **General Dynamics F-16/79**. The F-16/79 is basically a standard F-16, but powered by the older General Electric J79 turbojet. This makes possible a substantial reduction in unit cost, but without compromising performance too severely. A number of nations have evaluated the F-16/79, but most potential customers are prepared to pay the extra to procure the F-16C/D, and have been allowed by the US government to do so. Nevertheless, the F-16/79 remains available for export, in both single- and two-seat variants. The prototype first flew on 29 October 1980.

The **F-16/101** was another re-engined F-16 variant, but this aircraft was never intended to be anything more than a single prototype, converted to evaluate the General Electric F101-DFE (Derivative Fighter Engine) developed from the F101-GE-100 designed to power the Rockwell B-1 strategic bomber.

The F-16/101 concluded its 58-sortie, 75-hour flight test programme well ahead of schedule.

During December 1978 the US Air Force selected the F-16 as the testbed for its Advanced Fighter Technology Integration (AFTI) programme, following in the footsteps of the earlier experimental **CCV/YF-16** programme. The **AFTI/F-16**, which first flew on 10 July 1982, incorporates a digital fly-by-wire control system, with canard foreplanes mounted under the forward fuselage. These allow the aircraft to demonstrate radically new flight techniques. Interactive avionics technology is also being tested during the flight programme, including direct voice command of certain functions usually controlled by manual switch selections.

Flight testing of the AFTI/F-16 is continuing at NASA's Dryden Flight Research Center at Edwards Air Force Base, and new avionics equipment is being integrated with the new type. While it has never been intended that the AFTI/F-16 should enter production, the technology provided by the type is certain to be incorporated into the next generation of US fighter aircraft, and some spin-offs may benefit today's fighters, including the F-16 itself.

Specification: General Dynamics F-16/79
Origin: USA
Type: single-seat air-combat (F-16/79A) and two-seat (F-16/79B) operational trainer/multi-role fighter
Powerplant: one 8165-kg (18,000-lb) thrust General Electric J79-GE-119 afterburning turbojet engine
Performance: maximum speed at high altitude more than Mach 2 or 1146 kts (2124 km/h; 1,320 mph); service ceiling more than 50,000 ft (15240 m); combat radius more than 925 km (575 miles); ferry range more than 3887 km (2,415 miles)
Weights: empty 8088 kg (17,832 lb); maximum take-off, clean 11805 kg (26,025 lb) maximum with full external load 16057 kg (35,400 lb)
Dimensions: span over missiles 10.01 m (32 ft 10 in); length 15.01 m (49 ft 3 in); height 5.09 m (16 ft 8.5 in); wing area 27.87 m² (300 sq ft)
Armament: one 20-mm M61A1 Vulcan cannon with 500 rounds, and up to 9276 kg (20,450 lb) of external ordnance on one underfuselage, six underwing and two tip hardpoints, this total declining to 5420 kg (11,950 lb) for sorties including 9-*g* manoeuvres; the ordnance can include AIM-9 Sidewinder and AIM-120 AMRAAM air-to-air missiles, a wide range of disposable ordnance (free fall and guided), drop tanks and electronic pods (ECM, reconnaissance and targeting)

The second F-16B development aircraft became the prototype F-16/79, also testing the British Aerospace Terprom (Terrain Profile Matching) navigation system.

General Dynamics AFTI F-16

The F-16/101 was a one-off prototype intended to evaluate the General Electric F101-DFE (Derivative Fighter Engine) and wore the same red, white and blue colours as the YF-16.

Flight testing of the AFTI F-16 is being conducted from NASA's Dryden Flight Center at Edwards AFB, and the results will be incorporated into any future US fighters.

General Dynamics F-16A/C/N Fighting Falcon

Belgium Denmark Egypt Greece Israel South Korea Netherlands Norway Pakistan

Singapore Thailand Turkey Venezuela United States

Today's **General Dynamics F-16 Fighting Falcon** is a direct descendant of the successful General Dynamics submission in the 1972 USAF Light-Weight Fighter (LWF) competition. Two **YF-16** prototypes were built for trials and for evaluation against the competing Northrop YF-17 prototypes. The first YF-16 made an unscheduled and unplanned first flight when test pilot Phillip Oestricher took off following an incident during a high speed taxi run. An official first flight followed on 2 February 1974.

During January 1975 it was announced that the YF-16 had been selected for full scale engineering development, largely on account of its superb manoeuvrability and its use of an existing engine. Although the LWF programme had been undertaken to produce a cheap, simple, clear-air air-superiority fighter, the role of the production F-16 has widened considerably to include a significant all-weather and air-to-surface capability. Eight pre-production aircraft, six of them single-seat **F-16A** fighters, were procured from July 1975.

When the USAF announced its F-16 requirement it was for some 1,388 aircraft to replace the McDonnell F-4 Phantom (and other types) in the active and reserve inventories. The USAF now intends to procure 2,795 F-16s and production is continuing at a rate of 150 per year. The rate of production will increase to 180 in 1987, and perhaps to 216 in 1989. In June 1975 Belgium, Denmark, the Netherlands and Norway finally selected the F-16 to replace their ageing Lockheed F-104 Starfighters. The four nations initially ordered a combined total of 348 aircraft, with final assembly of these NATO aircraft undertaken in Belgium and the Netherlands. Other foreign orders for the F-16 have been received from Egypt, Greece, Israel, Singapore, South Korea, Pakistan, Thailand, Turkey and Venezuela.

The **F-16C** is basically an improved development of the F-16A incorporating various structural, systems and avionics changes developed under the Multi-national Staged Improvement Program (MSIP). The **F-16N** is a more specialized variant, a derivative of the F-16C modified for use by the US Navy as a land-based 'aggressor' aircraft. Modifications for this role (currently fulfilled by Northrop F-21s and leased IAI Kfirs) include the deletion of the cannon, underwing missile launchers and pylons, airborne self-protection jammer and global positioning system. The older APG-66 radar of the F-16A is retained, and the General Electric F110-GE-100 afterburning turbofan is used. The wings are structurally strengthened to meet the increased frequency of g loading in the adversary role. The delivery of 26 aircraft is expected to begin in February 1987.

A General Dynamics F-16A of the 4th TFS, 388th TFW, Hill AFB, Utah.

General Dynamics F-16A Fighting Falcon

This Belgian air force General Dynamics F-16A is fitted with twin AIM-9 Sidewinder launchers on its wingtips. European F-16s are assembled in Belgium and the Netherlands.

Egypt is one of the many overseas operators of the F-16 Fighting Falcon, using the aircraft to replace its ageing Soviet-built MiGs, primarily in the air defence role.

Specification: General Dynamics F-16C Fighting Falcon
Origin: USA
Type: single-seat air-combat and multi-role fighter
Powerplant: one 10810-kg (23,450-lb) thrust Pratt & Whitney F100-PW-220 afterburning turbofan engine
Performance: maximum speed more than Mach 2 or 1146 kts (2124 km/h; 1,320 mph) at 40,000 ft (12190 m); service ceiling more than 50,000 ft (15240 m); combat radius more than 925 km (575 miles); ferry range with maximum internal and external fuel 3886 km (2,415 miles)
Weights: empty 7618 kg (16,794 lb); maximum take-off 17010 kg (37,500 lb)
Dimensions: span over missiles 10.01 m (32 ft 10 in); length 15.01 m (49 ft 3 in); height 5.09 m (16 ft 8.5 in); wing area 27.87 m² (300 sq ft)
Armament: one 20-mm M61A1 Vulcan cannon with 500 rounds, and up to 9276 kg (20,450 lb) of external ordnance on one underfuselage, six underwing and two tip hardpoints, this total declining to 5420 kg (11,950 lb) for sorties including 9-g manoeuvres; the ordnance can include AIM-9 Sidewinder and AIM-120 AMRAAM air-to-air missiles, a wide range of disposable ordnance (free-fall and guided), drop tanks and electronic pods (ECM, reconnaissance and targeting)

Role
- Fighter
- Close support
- Counter-insurgency
- Tactical strike
- Strategic bomber
- Tactical reconnaissance
- Strategic reconnaissance
- Maritime patrol
- Anti-ship strike
- Anti-submarine warfare
- Search and rescue
- Assault transport
- Transport
- Liaison
- Trainer
- Inflight-refuelling tanker
- Specialized

Performance
- All-weather capability
- Rough field capability
- STOL capability
- VTOL capability
- Airspeed 0-250 mph
- Airspeed 250 mph-Mach 1
- Airspeed Mach 1 plus
- Ceiling 0-20,000 ft
- Ceiling 20,000-40,000 ft
- Ceiling 40,000ft plus
- Range 0-1,000 miles
- Range 1,000-3,000 miles
- Range 3,000 miles plus

Weapons
- Air-to-air missiles
- Air-to-surface missiles
- Cruise missiles
- Cannon
- Trainable guns
- Naval weapons
- Nuclear-capable
- Rockets
- 'Smart' weapon kit
- Weapon load 0-4,000 lb
- Weapon load 4,000-15,000 lb
- Weapon load 15,000 lb plus

Avionics
- Electronic Counter Measures
- Electronic Support Measures
- Search radar
- Fire control radar
- Look-down/shoot-down
- Terrain-following radar
- Forward-looking infra-red
- Laser
- Television

General Dynamics F-16B/D Fighting Falcon

Pakistan · Singapore · Thailand · Turkey · Venezuela · United States

South Korea · Netherlands · Norway

Belgium · Denmark · Egypt · Greece · Israel

Role
Fighter
Close support
Counter-insurgency
Tactical strike
Strategic bomber
Tactical reconnaissance
Strategic reconnaissance
Maritime patrol
Anti-ship strike
Anti-submarine warfare
Search and rescue
Assault transport
Transport
Liaison
Trainer
Inflight-refuelling tanker
Specialized

Performance
All-weather capability
Rough field capability
STOL capability
VTOL capability
Airspeed 0-250 mph
Airspeed 250 mph-Mach 1
Airspeed Mach 1 plus
Ceiling 0-20,000 ft
Ceiling 20,000-40,000 ft
Ceiling 40,000 ft plus
Range 0-1,000 miles
Range 1,000-3,000 miles
Range 3,000 miles plus

Weapons
Air-to-air missiles
Air-to-surface missiles
Cruise missiles
Cannon
Trainable guns
Naval weapons
Nuclear-capable
Rockets
'Smart' weapon kit
Weapon load 0-4,000 lb
Weapon load 4,000-15,000 lb
Weapon load 15,000 lb plus

Avionics
Electronic Counter Measures
Electronic Support Measures
Search radar
Fire control radar
Look-down/shoot-down
Terrain-following radar
Forward-looking infra-red
Laser
Television

Two of the eight pre-production F-16s were two-seaters, designated **General Dynamics F-16B Fighting Falcon**, and the first of these made its maiden flight on 8 August 1977. The F-16B retained full operational equipment and capability, with the second cockpit taking the place of one fuselage fuel tank, reducing internal fuel capacity by about 17 per cent.

Some 204 of the 1,388 F-16s originally ordered by the USAF were to be two-seat F-16Bs, and the proportion of two-seaters has remained constant with each increase in total F-16 procurement. Most foreign F-16 operators have opted for a similar mix of single- and two-seat F-16s. USAF F-16Bs are being given the same Multi-national Staged Improvement Program (MSIP) modifications as the F-16As, and production MSIP two-seaters are designated **F-16D**. There are three basic stages to the MSIP programme, which is being undertaken to allow the F-16 to remain a viable front-line fighter well into the 1990s. Stage one of the programme covers the installation of structural and wiring provisions for future systems to production F-16As and F-16Bs delivered between November 1981 and March 1985. Stage two began in July 1984, when production F-16Cs and F-16Ds started being delivered, and these aircraft incorporated core avionic, cockpit and airframe provisions to accommodate new systems. Stage three of the programme will cover the installation, during

production or by retrofitting, of advanced systems as they become available.

MSIP F-16s incorporate a Westinghouse APG-68 radar in place of the earlier APG-66, giving increased range, sharper resolution and expanded air-to-air and air-to-surface modes. MSIP-configured aircraft also have an advanced versatile cockpit, with a new GEC wide-angle HUD, while structural improvements allow an increased maximum take-off weight and increased gross weight limitations for the application of maximum *g*. Advanced weapons and systems will be added, including AMRAAM, LANTIRN and PLSS, significantly increasing the F-16's multi-role capability and survivability. The adoption of a 'common engine bay' by F-16Cs and F-16Ds will permit the installation of either the Pratt & Whitney F100-PW-220 or the General Electric F110-GE-100 in any aircraft.

During September 1984 the USAF placed a contract with General Dynamics to develop a reconnaissance variant of the F-16D as a potential replacement for the USAF's ageing McDonnell Douglas RF-4C Phantoms. The reconnaissance equipment, including a video camera to provide display information to the crew and for real-time transmission to ground stations, will be housed in an underfuselage pod. Some 400 such pods are likely to be ordered for carriage on the F-16D or possibly the F-16E.

Specification: General Dynamics F-16D Fighting Falcon
Origin: USA
Type: two-seat operational trainer and multi-role fighter
Powerplant: one 10810-kg (23,840-lb) thrust Pratt & Whitney F100-PW-200 afterburning turbofan engine (or one General Electric F110-GE-100 or Pratt & Whitney F100-PW-220 afterburning turbofan engine)
Performance: maximum speed at high altitude more than Mach 2 or 1146 kts (2124 km/h; 1,320 mph); service ceiling more than 50,000 ft (15240 ft); combat radius more than 925 km (575 miles); ferry range 3887 km (2,415 miles)
Weights: empty 7896 kg (17,408 lb); maximum take-off 17010 kg (37,500 lb)
Dimensions: span over missiles 10.01 m (32 ft 10 in); length 15.01 m (49 ft 3 in); height 5.09 m (16 ft 8.5 in); wing area 27.87 m² (300 sq ft)
Armament: one 20-mm M61A1 Vulcan cannon with 500 rounds, and up to 9276 kg (20,450 lb) of external ordnance on one underfuselage, six underwing and two tip hardpoints, this total declining to 5421 kg (11,950 lb) for sorties including 9-*g* manoeuvres; the ordnance can include AIM-9 Sidewinder and AIM-120 AMRAAM air-to-air missiles, a wide range of disposable ordnance (free-fall and guided), drop tanks and electronic pods (ECM, reconnaissance and targeting)

A General Dynamics F-16B of the Volkel-based 311 Squadron, Netherlands air force.

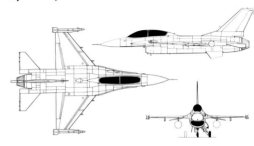

General Dynamics F-16B Fighting Falcon

An early F-16B fires an AGM-65 Maverick air-to-surface missile. Two-seat F-16s retain full mission equipment and combat capability, with slightly reduced fuel tankage.

The Israeli air force has used its F-16s over the Lebanon, and on the raids on Tunis and the Iraqi nuclear plant at Baghdad. F-16Bs may have participated in these attacks.

F-16s of the USAF take-off on a mission over Korea

General Dynamics F-16XL and F-16E

This is the second prototype F-16XL, now redesignated F-16E.

The **General Dynamics F-16XL** is a company-funded development of the standard F-16 which was designed to incorporate advances in aerodynamics and systems. The USAF provided a measure of support by leasing the company two F-16A development airframes, engines and an F-16B forward fuselage. Two prototypes, one a single-seater and one a two-seater, were constructed and delivered to Fort Worth during 1981, where they made their respective first flights on 3 July and 29 October 1982.

The F-16XL was designed with a huge cranked arrow planform wing, with compound sweep of 50° and 70° on the leading edge. The aircraft was also given two fuselage plugs, which increase the fuselage length by 1.42 m (4 ft 8 in) and the internal fuel capacity by 85 per cent, as well as providing increased equipment space. The new wing has more than twice the area of that fitted to the standard F-16, yet it generates significantly less drag.

Weapons are carried semi-conformally, with a consequent increase in aerodynamic efficiency, and amongst the various types of weapon that can be carried are four semi-submerged AMRAAM missiles. The new wing has given the aircraft much improved cruise efficiency, which combines with increased fuel capacity and lower drag to result in a 48 per cent increase in combat radius on internal fuel with twice the payload, or 87 per cent with external fuel tanks, when compared with the F-16C. Higher penetration speeds are possible, and manoeuvring capabilities are maintained or enhanced.

The F-16XL was not selected by the USAF as the new dual-role air-defence ground-attack fighter, however, the McDonnell Douglas F-15E Strike Eagle emerging as the preferred aircraft. Development of the F-16XL, now redesignated **F-16E**, continues and the aircraft is clearly still under consideration, even though no orders have been placed. The future of the F-16 is assured regardless of whether or not the F-16E enters production, but it is interesting to note how far removed today's Fighting Falcon is from the unsophisticated and cheap day fighter envisaged by the original Light-Weight Fighter competition.

Both F-16Es are continuing flight testing at Edwards AFB, and full-scale development is planned to begin during 1987. If this happens the first new development aircraft will fly in 1989 for a production start in 1991.

General Dynamics F-16E

Specification: General Dynamics F-16E
Origin: USA
Type: dual-role tactical fighter prototype
Powerplant: one 13150-kg (29,000-lb) thrust General Electric F110-GE-100 afterburning turbofan engine
Performance: maximum speed at high altitude more than Mach 2 or 1146 kts (2124 km/h; 1,320 mph); range more than 4630 km (2,875 miles)
Weights: design mission 19504 kg (43,000 lb); maximum take-off 21722 kg (48,000 lb)
Dimensions: span 10.43 m (34 ft 2.8 in); length 16.51 m (54 ft 1.86 in); height 5.36 m (17 ft 7 in); wing area 61.59 m² (663 sq ft)
Armament: up to 6804 kg (15,000 lb) of disposable air-to-air and air-to-surface stores on 17 underfuselage and underwing stations

This view of the single seat F-16E prototype shows its radical new cranked-arrow tailless delta wing, which is more than twice as large as the standard wing but generates less drag.

The second prototype F-16E is a two-seater, and wears an attractive three-tone grey colour scheme, having lost its distinctive royal blue spine and tailfin.

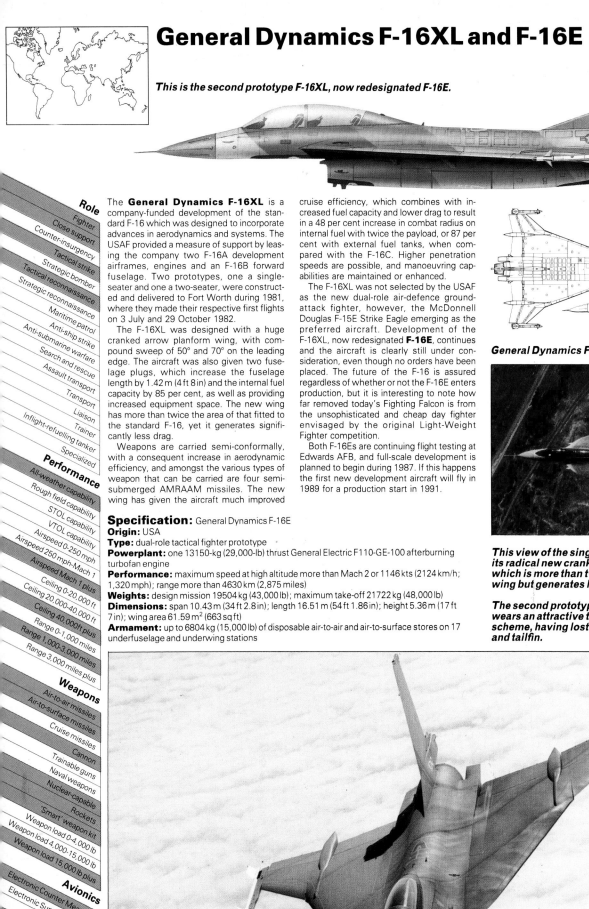

General Dynamics F-111

Australia   United States

The remarkable **General Dynamics F-111** was the first tactical aircraft in the world with variable-geometry wings and also the first in the world with afterburning turbofan engines, yet despite a troubled and controversial birth, it has set a new standard of tactical strike capability. Combat experience in Vietnam, and more recently in the USAF's April 1985 night attack on Libya, have proved it to be an unbeatable all-weather precision tactical bomber which has overcome its early faults and weaknesses.

The F-111 was developed to fulfil two separate but superficially similar requirements, one from the USAF for a long-range interdictor and strike aircraft, and one from the US Navy for a carrier-borne long-range interceptor. The first **YF-111A** made its maiden flight on 21 December 1964 and it was followed by 17 pre-series aircraft and 141 production **F-111A** aircraft. The **F-111B**, the Navy's fleet fighter variant, was an almost unmitigated disaster, and was cancelled after only nine had been built.

The only export customer for the F-111 has been the Royal Australian Air Force, who received 24 aircraft designated **F-111C**. These aircraft were similar to the USAF F-111As, but with the longer-span wing of the F-111B, strengthened landing gear and eight wing pylons instead of four. These were delivered in 1978, after a 10-year delay. The

next USAF variant should have been the **F-111D** with more powerful TF30-P-9 engines in place of the TF30-P-3 engines used by earlier variants. It also featured new engine air inlets and sophisticated new avionics, the analog computer of the F-111A being replaced by a new digital computer, and the original radar replaced by an Autonetics APQ-130 multi-mode radar. Development problems plagued the F-111D, but 96 eventually entered service with the 27th TFW at Cannon AFB.

Delays with the F-111D led to the development of an interim machine, the **F-111E**. This was basically an F-111A with the new inlets, and various ECM and avionics improvements, as well as a new weapon management system. Today the F-111E, of which 94 were built, serves with the 20th TFW at RAF Upper Heyford. The advanced F-111D was replaced in production by the **F-111F**, which combined new avionics with the vastly more reliable and considerably more powerful TF30-P-100 turbofan, which also gives improved fuel economy. The F-111F also introduced strengthened wing pivots, and the aircraft are today equipped with the 'Pave Tack' laser acquisition and designating system in a removable belly pod. Production of the F-111F amounted to 106 aircraft, and the type now serves with the 48th TFW at RAF Lakenheath.

Specification: General Dynamics F-111F
Origin: USA
Type: two-seat all-weather tactical strike aircraft
Powerplant: two 11385-kg (25,100-lb) thrust Pratt & Whitney TF30-P-100 afterburning turbofan engines
Performance: maximum speed at high altitude Mach 2.5 or 1433 kts (2655 km/h; 1,650 mph), or at low altitude Mach 1.2 or 792 kts (1468 km/h; 912 mph); service ceiling 60,000 ft (18290 m); range more than 4707 km (2,925 miles) with maximum internal fuel
Weights: empty 21398 kg (47,175 lb); maximum take-off 45359 kg (100,000 lb)
Dimensions: span 19.20 m (63 ft 0 in) spread and 9.74 m (31 ft 11.4 in) swept; length 22.40 m (73 ft 6 in); height 5.22 m (17 ft 1.4 in); wing area 48.77 m² (525 sq ft) spread
Armament: carried in an internal bay and on four underwing hardpoints, this can amount to 14228 kg (31,500 lb) of disposable stores including nuclear or conventional bombs, glide bombs and air-to-surface missiles.

A General Dynamics F-111F of the 48th TFW, based at RAF Lakenheath, Suffolk.

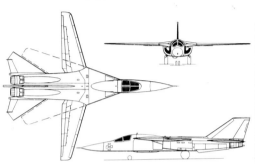

General Dynamics F-111A

This Lakenheath-based F-111F belongs to the 494th Tactical Fighter Squadron, and carries 'Pave Tack', four laser guided bombs, and an AN/ALQ-131V jamming pod.

The blue and white chequered fin-cap identifies this F-111E as an aircraft of the 55th Tactical Fighter Squadron, part of the 20th TFW based at RAF Upper Heyford.

Role
Fighter
Close support
Counter-insurgency
Tactical strike
Strategic bomber
Tactical reconnaissance
Strategic reconnaissance
Maritime patrol
Anti-ship strike
Anti-submarine warfare
Search and rescue
Assault transport
Transport
Liaison
Trainer
Inflight-refuelling tanker
Specialized

Performance
All-weather capability
Rough field capability
STOL capability
VTOL capability
Airspeed 0-250 mph
Airspeed 250 mph-Mach 1
Airspeed Mach 1 plus
Ceiling 0-20,000 ft
Ceiling 20,000-40,000 ft
Ceiling 40,000ft plus
Range 0-1,000 miles
Range 1,000-3,000 miles
Range 3,000 miles plus

Weapons
Air-to-air missiles
Air-to-surface missiles
Cruise missiles
Cannon
Trainable guns
Naval weapons
Nuclear-capable
Rockets
'Smart' weapon kit
Weapon load 0-4,000 lb
Weapon load 4,000-15,000 lb
Weapon load 15,000 lb plus

Avionics
Electronic Counter Measures
Electronic Support Measures
Search radar
Fire control radar
Look-down/shoot-down
Terrain-following radar
Forward-looking infra-red
Laser
Television

United States

General Dynamics FB-111A

This FB-111A carries special 2nd Air Force insignia applied for a 'Giant Voice' bombing contest in the early 1970s.

Strategic Air Command had been the operator of the world's first supersonic bomber, the revolutionary Convair B-58 Hustler, but this aircraft was withdrawn from service in 1970 on the grounds of cost to be replaced by a strategic bomber derivative of the F-111 tactical fighter. The possibility of such a variant had been discussed since the beginning of the F-111 project.

The **General Dynamics FB-111A** programme was eventually announced in December 1965, promising twice the speed of the early Boeing B-52 variant with approximately the same range. General Dynamics was easily able to achieve the required speed, but the FB-111A (especially with maximum weapon load) was seriously deficient in range when compared with the B-52. The first FB-111A, actually a converted F-111A, flew for the first time on 30 July 1967, and the first production machine followed almost one year later. Initial aircraft were delivered to the 340th Bomb Group in September 1969.

Due to cost escalation procurement of the FB-111A was cut back from 263 to 76 aircraft, equipping two 30-aircraft bomber wings, the 380th at Plattsburgh and the 509th at Pease. The FB-111A has been a much more important aircraft than the small number

delivered might suggest. Since its introduction into service in 1969 it has provided SAC with its only supersonic bomber, and the type has consistently achieved better accuracy than the B-52s, as well as being more survivable. FB-111 crews have frequently taken the prizes at USAF bombing competitions.

Typical loads for the FB-111A include six free-fall nuclear bombs, four carried underwing and two in the internal weapons bay. Against more heavily-defended targets the FB-111A can carry six Short-Range Attack Missiles (SRAMs). The SRAM has a range of more than 160km (100 miles) and is highly supersonic. It is also extremely agile and capable of flight at tree-top height. It is small and presents minimal radar cross section, and thus still stands a good chance of getting through to its target. SRAM carries a small thermonuclear warhead with an impressive yield.

The introduction of the Rockwell B-1B will finally give SAC a supersonic strategic bomber with a genuine intercontinental range, but the FB-111A's life is by no means over, and the type will remain an integral part of the USA's strategic nuclear deterrent forces for some years to come.

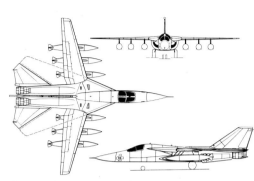

General Dynamics FB-111A

Although it only equips two USAF Bomb Wings, the FB-111A is an enormously important aircraft, being more penetrable and more accurate than the more numerous B-52s.

The FB-111A will remain a vital part of the SAC inventory for many years, and the aircraft are now receiving a new 'lizard' type colour scheme to replace their distinctive grey/green colours.

Specification: General Dynamics FB-111A
Origin: USA
Type: two-seat strategic bomber
Powerplant: two 9231-kg (20,350-lb) thrust Pratt & Whitney TF30-P-7 afterburning turbofan engines
Performance: maximum speed at high altitude Mach 2 or 1146 kts (2124 km/h; 1,320 mph), range with internal SRAMs, external fuel but no inflight-refuelling 2897 km (1,800 miles); range with inflight-refuelling and a 2226-km (1,383-mile) low-level dash 9817 km (6,100 miles)
Weights: empty 21545 kg (47,500 lb); maximum take-off 48534 kg (107,000 lb)
Dimensions: span spread 21.34 m (70 ft 0 in) and 10.34 m (33 ft 11 in) swept; length 23.02 m (75 ft 6.25 in); height 5.22 m (17 ft 1.4 in)
Armament: carried in an internal bay and on eight underwing hardpoints, this can amount to 14288 kg (31,500 lb) of disposable stores including nuclear and conventional bombs, and air-to-surface missiles

General Dynamics MSIP F-16, F-16R, F-16 (ADF) and Agile Falcon

The General Dynamics F-16 Fighting Falcon has been subject to a continuing series of updates and improvements, radically increasing its capabilities. USAF F-16s in particular have been the subject of several new programmes to incorporate the latest avionics and weapons systems. A Multinational Staged Improvement Programme was initiated during February 1980, giving all aircraft delivered after November 1981 structural, system and wiring provisions to accept future developments to expand the aircraft's multirole capabilities.

Provision for advanced cockpit displays, improved fire control radar, AIM-120 AMRAAM air-to-air missiles, LANTIRN nav/attack system and ALQ-165 ASPJ jammer were among early improvements to be incorporated. From late 1988, automatic terrain-following, a diffractive optics HUD, digital flight-control system, IFF update, Navstar Global Positioning System, HARM/Shrike capability, on-board oxygen generation and various RWR enhancements are to be introduced.

In September 1984 General Dynamics was awarded a $62 million contract to develop a two-seat reconnaissance variant of the F-16, as a potential RF-4C replacement. An initial paper evaluation of the aircraft was followed by a flight test phase, with a production F-16D being modified under the designation F-16R to carry a General Dynamics-developed reconnaissance pod. Electro-optical, infra-red and video sensors are built into the pod, which also incorporates extendable digital data link equipment for real-time transmission of reconnaissance images to end users. Four hundred and ten of these semiconformal pods may be procured for USAF F-16Ds from FY 1991.

The F-16 has also been flown with four different European reconnaissance pods, and the F-16s of No. 306 Squadron, Royal Netherlands Air Force, based at Volkel, have been operational since 1983 with the Orpheus camera pods previously used by Dutch F-104 Starfighters.

The rising cost of the F-16C/D, with its sophisticated avionics and multi-role capability, led General Dynamics to offer a cheaper F-16 variant dedicated to the air defence role, for use by Air National Guard units tasked with the air defence of the CONUS. This aircraft was eventually ordered in October 1986, after a fierce competition with the Northrop F-20 Tigershark.

Two hundred and seventy F-16As will be uprated to F-16 (ADF) standard to replace McDonnell Douglas F-4 Phantom and Convair F-106 Delta Dart aircraft previously used for the defence of the USA. The aircraft will receive a flight data recorder, HF transceiver, IFF, AIM-7 Sparrow AAMs, and the F-16A standard APG-66 radar will be modified to incorporate an AMRAAM data link, and will be given improved ECCM capabilities.

The LN-39 inertial navigation system will be modified to provide very rapid alignment for scramble type take-offs. The F-16 (ADF), also known in some quarters as the Specially Configured F-16C, has been offered with a guaranteed hourly maintenance cost.

General Dynamics has proved to be extremely adept at devising new variants of the basic F-16, including the cranked-arrow winged F-16XL ground-attack aircraft, the F-16 AFTI (Advanced Fighter Technology Integration) demonstrator, the F-16R tactical recce platform, and a plethora of F-16s powered by various other powerplants.

The latest variant proposed by the company is the Agile Falcon, essentially an F-16C with a new wing of 25 per cent greater area. This would reduce the wing loading of the rather heavy F-16C, restoring the sparkling performance of the less heavily-laden F-16A. The Agile Falcon is intended to complement the new ATF (Advanced Tactical Fighter) in the 1990s, with a price tag of about $15 million per aircraft, or $2 million more than the current F-16C.

The USAF and the four NATO operators of the F-16 have yet to express any interest in the aircraft.

The General Dynamics F-16R testbed, a converted F-16B.

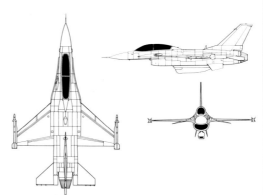

General Dynamics F-16R Fighting Falcon

Some Dutch F-16s are used in the tactical reconnaissance role, carrying the 1970s-technology Orpheus reconnaissance pod. These aircraft equip No. 306 Squadron.

The F-16R carries a sophisticated modern reconnaissance pod under its fuselage. This pod contains electro-optical sensors covering the visual and the infra-red spectrum.

Role

Fighter
Close support
Counter-insurgency
Tactical strike
Strategic bomber
Tactical reconnaissance
Strategic reconnaissance
Maritime patrol
Anti-ship strike
Anti-submarine warfare
Search and rescue
Assault transport
Transport
Liaison
Trainer
Inflight-refuelling tanker
Specialized

Performance

All-weather capability
Rough field capability
STOL capability
VTOL capability
Airspeed 0-250 mph
Airspeed 250 mph-Mach 1
Airspeed Mach 1 plus
Ceiling 0-20,000 ft
Ceiling 20,000-40,000 ft
Ceiling 40,000ft plus
Range 0-1,000 miles
Range 1,000-3,000 miles
Range 3,000 miles plus

Weapons

Air-to-air missiles
Air-to-surface missiles
Cruise missiles
Cannon
Trainable guns
Naval weapons
Nuclear-capable
Rockets
'Smart' weapon kit
Weapon load 0-4,000 lb
Weapon load 4,000-15,000 lb
Weapon load 15,000 lb plus

Avionics

Electronic Counter Measures
Electronic Support Measures
Search radar
Fire control radar
Look-down/shoot-down
Terrain-following radar
Forward-looking infra-red
Laser
Television

United States

Grumman A-6 Intruder

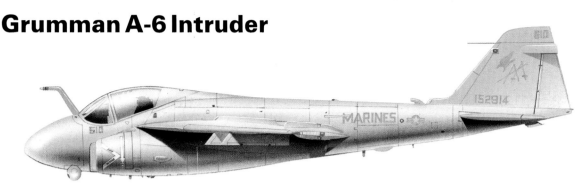

A Grumman A-6E Intruder of VMA(AW)-533, a Marine attack unit based at El Toro, California.

Role
Fighter
Close support
Counter-insurgency
Tactical strike
Strategic bomber
Tactical reconnaissance
Strategic reconnaissance
Maritime patrol
Anti-ship strike
Anti-submarine warfare
Search and rescue
Assault transport
Transport
Liaison
Trainer
Inflight-refuelling tanker
Specialized

Performance
All-weather capability
Rough field capability
STOL capability
VTOL capability
Airspeed 0-250 mph
Airspeed 250 mph-Mach 1
Airspeed Mach 1 plus
Ceiling 0-20,000 ft
Ceiling 20,000-40,000 ft
Ceiling 40,000ft plus
Range 0-1,000 miles
Range 1,000-3,000 miles
Range 3,000 miles plus

Weapons
Air-to-air missiles
Air-to-surface missiles
Cruise missiles
Cannon
Trainable guns
Naval weapons
Nuclear-capable
Rockets
'Smart' weapon kit
Weapon load 0-4,000 lb
Weapon load 4,000-15,000 lb
Weapon load 15,000 lb plus

Avionics
Electronic Counter Measures
Electronic Support Measures
Search radar
Fire control radar
Look-down/shoot-down
Terrain-following radar
Forward-looking infra-red
Laser
Television

In continuous production since the late 1950s and with a new improved version likely to make its debut later in the present decade, the **Grumman A-6 Intruder** seems certain to establish a production longevity record that is unlikely to be equalled by any combat aircraft type manufactured in the West.

Development of the Intruder dates back to 1957, when 11 companies responded to a US Navy request for proposals for a new jet-powered attack aircraft capable of operating at night or in the worst conceivable weather conditions. Close study of the various contenders resulted in Grumman's model **G-128** being selected at the end of 1957 for further development as the **A2F** and eight development examples of the **A2F-1 (A-6A** from late 1962) were duly ordered, the first making a succesful maiden flight on 19 April 1960.

Its distinctly utilitarian appearance perhaps belied the fact that it was indeed a most sophisticated machine, effectively marrying computer technology with a sturdy airframe to produce a remarkably effective warplane. Despite teething troubles with the early avionics systems, the A-6A eventually went on to compile an impressive combat record in Vietnam, often being the only aircraft able to fly and fight effectively in that theatre.

Production of the basic A-6A ceased in late 1969 after just under 500 had been built, but by then plans were well in hand for the next major attack-dedicated model, this being the

A-6E which took full advantage of progress made in the field of avionics, being fitted with Norden APQ-148 multi-mode nav/attack radar and numerous other bits and pieces of new kit.

Still in production at the time of writing, the A-6E has been progressively modernized since attaining operational status in the early 1970s, visible evidence of this process being best exemplified by the TRAM (Target Recognition Attack Multi-sensor) turret beneath the nose radome. Basically, TRAM consists of FLIR (Forward-Looking Infra-Red) and laser detection gear to provide greater accuracy in weapons delivery in all weather conditions.

Other Intruder models, most of them produced by converting existing airframes, have included the **EA-6A** ECM platform for the US Marine Corps, the **A-6B** for SAM suppression, the **A-6C** with improved night attack capability and the **KA-6D** inflight-refuelling tanker. Of these models, only the KA-6D remains active in a truly operational capacity with the US Navy.

With regard to the future, the upcoming **A-6F** will be the 'third-generation' Intruder and this model is expected to enter full production in 1990 with the new General Electric F404 unreheated turbofan. The A-6F's avionics suite will be a vast improvement over existing gear and is to include high-resolution synthetic-aperature radar and completely revised cathode ray tube-based cockpit displays.

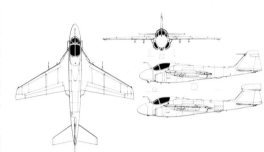

A-6E (TRAM) Intruder (lower side view: EA-6A)

Specification: Grumman A-6E Intruder
Origin: USA
Type: medium two-seat land/sea-based all-weather attack aircraft
Powerplant: two 4,218-kg (9,300-lb) thrust Pratt & Whitney J52-P-8A turbojet engines
Performance: maximum speed 563 kts (1043 km/h; 648 mph) at sea level; initial rate of climb 'clean' 7,620 ft (2322 m) per minute; service ceiling 'clean' 47,500 ft (14480 m); range with full weapon load 1627 km (1,011 miles)
Weights: empty 12132 kg (26,746 lb); maximum take-off (catapult launch) 26581 kg (58,600 lb); maximum take-off (field) 27397 kg (60,400 lb)
Dimensions: span 16.15 m (53 ft 0 in); length 16.69 m (54 ft 9 in); height 4.93 m (16 ft 2 in); wing area 49.13 m² (528.9 sq ft)
Armament: five external stores stations capable of accommodating maximum payload of 8165 kg (18,000 lb); options include nuclear weapons, conventional bombs, 'smart' bombs, air-to-surface missiles such as Harpoon; alternatively, auxiliary fuel tanks may be fitted to increase range at some penalty in offensive payload

An unmarked A-6E Intruder takes off from USS Coral Sea during the recent operations off Libya, which culminated in the bombing of Benghazi by US Navy A-6s.

A KA-6D of VA-55 takes off from Coral Sea, with underwing tanks and an underfuselage refuelling pod clearly visible. Attack A-6 units usually go to sea with four of these useful tankers.

An A-6E of VA-75 prepares for a mission

Grumman C-1 Trader

A US Navy Grumman C-1 Trader assigned to USS Nimitz.

Basically a derivative of the highly successful S-2 Tracker anti-submarine warfare aircraft, the **Grumman C-1A Trader** is still employed in an operational capacity by the US Navy at the time of writing, but numbers have been in decline in recent years, largely as a result of difficulties in obtaining suitable fuel for the elderly reciprocating engines which power the C-1A. With procurement of additional examples of the larger and much more capable turbine-powered C-2A Greyhound now under way, it seems certain that the process of withdrawal of the long-serving Trader will accelerate in the very near future but it will have secured the distinction of being the last piston-powered type to operate from US Navy aircraft-carriers on a regular basis.

Known by the parent company as the model **G-96**, no fewer than 87 examples of the Trader were purchased by the Navy for service from shore stations in the USA, Europe and the Far East. Reaching navy support-dedicated organizations during the mid-1950s, the C-1A (originally designated **TF-1** up to late 1962) fulfilled COD (Carrier On-board Delivery) functions and featured a greatly redesigned and enlarged fuselage which was able to accommodate up to nine passengers or, alternatively, cargo such as engines, mail or other urgently required supplies.

Possessing rather greater payload capability than previous COD-dedicated types like the Douglas AD Skyraider and Beech SNB-5 Expediter, the Trader quickly became a familiar sight aboard Navy carriers around the world and it was usual until quite recently for a single example of the type to be assigned to each aircraft-carrier on a permanent basis.

Although none now appear to be allocated directly to the carrier fleet, a modest number of Traders are still active from major Navy installations in the USA and overseas. A derivative of the type (the **EC-1A (TF-1Q)** engaged in electronic countermeasures training functions) disappeared from the scene quite a few years back, whilst the **TF-1W** airborne early warning proposal incorporating APS-82 radar in a prominent dorsal fairing eventually evolved into the **WF-2 Tracer** which also enjoyed a long front-line career with AEW-dedicated units.

Specification: Grumman C-1A Trader
Origin: USA
Type: utility transport aircraft
Powerplant: two 1137-kW (1,525-hp) Wright R-1820-82 air-cooled radial piston engines
Performance: maximum speed 252 kts (467 km/h; 290 mph) at 4,500 ft (1370 m); economical cruise speed 178 kts (330 km/h; 205 mph); typical range at economical cruise speed at 10,000 ft (3050 m) 1288 km (800 miles)
Weight: maximum take-off 12247 kg (27,000 lb)
Dimensions: span 22.12 m (72 ft 7 in); length 13.26 m (43 ft 6 in); height 5.05 m (16 ft 7 in); wing area 46.36 m² (499 sq ft)
Armament: none

Grumman C-1 Trader

This VRC-40 Grumman C-1A Trader displays a close family resemblance with the S-2 Tracker and the E-1 Tracer. The Trader is the only member of the family still in US Navy service.

Seen at Sigonella, Sicily, during the early 1980s is a COD C-1A Trader of VR-24. VR-24 is based at Sigonella and operates a mix of Hercules, Trader and Greyhound aircraft.

Grumman C-2 Greyhound

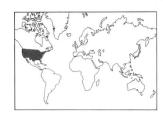

United States

As had happened earlier with the S-2 Tracker, so the turbine-engined E-2 Hawkeye provided the basis for a COD (Carrier On-board Delivery) transport for service with the US Navy in the vital role of transferring urgently required personnel and material from shore bases to aircraft-carriers operating at sea and vice versa.

Although its origins in the E-2 Hawkeye are readily apparent, the resulting **Grumman C-2A Greyhound** is significantly different. Perhaps the most notable change related to the fuselage, which is of much greater cross-section, incorporating an upswept aft fuselage section complete with cargo door and an integral loading ramp permitting bulky items like turbojet engines to be manhandled with relative ease.

Less apparent, but no less important, is the fact that the horizontal and vertical tail surfaces were redesigned, the absence of the Hawkeye's distinctive 'pancake' radome smoothing out airflow patterns in this area and eliminating the requirement for dihedral and inwardly-canted fins and rudders. Of the other changes, perhaps the most notable involved strengthening the nose wheel unit to permit operation at higher gross weights.

Fuel capacity is also rather greater.

As far as payload is concerned, the Greyhound can accommodate up to 39 passengers or 20 stretchers and four attendants or, alternatively, approximately 8165 kg (18,000 lb) of palletized cargo.

Flying for the first time as the **YC-2A** in the latter half of 1964, the Greyhound was initially built in only modest numbers, just 19 aircraft being accepted for service with the Navy between 1965 and 1968. Plans to acquire 12 more at this time fell victim to cancellation and, by the early 1970s, attrition had reduced the quantity in service to just a dozen, these operating alongside even older C-1A Traders from Navy installations in the Pacific and Mediterranean theatres.

Faced with the question of replacing the vintage C-1A, the Navy opted to reinstate the C-2A in production during 1982 and the first examples of 39 additional Greyhounds were delivered to VR-24 at Sigonella, Sicily shortly before the end of 1985. Under the terms of the $678 million multi-year contract, procurement is expected to continue until 1989, by which time the C-2A will be operational from a number of fleet support bases situated in the USA, the Far East and Europe.

Specification: Grumman C-2A Greyhound, second series
Origin: USA
Type: carrier on-board delivery transport aircraft
Powerplant: two 3915-kW (5,250-shp) Allison T56-A-427 turboprop engines
Performance: maximum speed 310 kts (574 km/h; 357 mph); cruising speed 260 kts (481 km/h; 299 mph); initial rate of climb 2,610 ft (796 m) per minute; service ceiling 33,500 ft (10210 m); range with maximum COD payload, more than 1931 km (1,200 miles)
Weights: empty 16486 kg (36,346 lb); maximum take-off 24655 kg (54,354 lb)
Dimensions: span 24.56 m (80 ft 7 in); length 17.32 m (56 ft 10 in); height 5.14 m (16 ft 10.5 in); wing area 65.03 m² (700 sq ft)
Armament: none

This Grumman C-2A Greyhound serves with VR-24 'The World's Biggest Little Airline', based at Sigonella, Sicily.

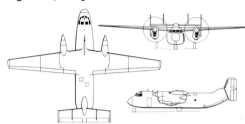

Grumman C-2A Greyhound

The C-2A Greyhound has been reinstated in production as a replacement for the ageing C-1A Trader, in preference to the Lockheed US-3A Viking.

One of the units serving the Pacific Fleet is VRC-50, based at Cubi Point in the Philippines, and with a detachment at Atsugi, Japan. C-2As are in service in Europe, the Far East and the USA.

Role
Fighter
Close support
Counter-insurgency
Tactical strike
Strategic bomber
Tactical reconnaissance
Strategic reconnaissance
Maritime patrol
Anti-ship strike
Anti-submarine warfare
Search and rescue
Assault transport
Transport
Liaison
Trainer
Inflight-refuelling tanker
Specialized

Performance
All-weather capability
Rough field capability
STOL capability
VTOL capability
Airspeed 0-250 mph
Airspeed 250 mph-Mach 1
Airspeed Mach 1 plus
Ceiling 0-20,000 ft
Ceiling 20,000-40,000 ft
Ceiling 40,000 ft plus
Range 0-1,000 miles
Range 1,000-3,000 miles
Range 3,000 miles plus

Weapons
Air-to-air missiles
Air-to-surface missiles
Cruise missiles
Cannon
Trainable guns
Naval weapons
Nuclear-capable
Rockets
'Smart' weapon kit
Weapon load 0-4,000 lb
Weapon load 4,000-15,000 lb
Weapon load 15,000 lb plus

Avionics
Electronic Counter Measures
Electronic Support Measures
Search radar
Fire control radar
Look-down/shoot-down radar
Terrain-following radar
Forward-looking infra-red
Laser
Television

Grumman E-2 Hawkeye

Role
Fighter
Close support
Counter-insurgency
Tactical strike
Strategic bomber
Tactical reconnaissance
Strategic reconnaissance
Maritime patrol
Anti-ship strike
Anti-submarine warfare
Search and rescue
Assault transport
Transport
Liaison
Trainer
Inflight-refuelling tanker
Specialized

Performance
All-weather capability
Rough field capability
STOL capability
VTOL capability
Airspeed 0-250 mph
Airspeed 250 mph-Mach 1
Airspeed Mach 1 plus
Ceiling 0-20,000 ft
Ceiling 20,000-40,000 ft
Ceiling 40,000 ft plus
Range 0-1,000 miles
Range 1,000-3,000 miles
Range 3,000 miles plus

Weapons
Air-to-air missiles
Air-to-surface missiles
Cruise missiles
Cannon
Trainable guns
Naval weapons
Nuclear-capable
Rockets
'Smart' weapon kit
Weapon load 0-4,000 lb
Weapon load 4,000-15,000 lb
Weapon load 15,000 lb plus

Avionics
Electronic Counter Measures
Electronic Support Measures
Search radar
Fire control radar
Look-down/shoot-down
Terrain-following radar
Forward-looking infra-red
Laser
Television

First flown as long ago as 21 October 1961, the **Grumman E-2 Hawkeye** has demonstrated a remarkable ability to keep pace with developments in the airborne early warning field, being perhaps a classic example of cramming a quart into a pint pot. In its latest guise as the **E-2C**, it is infinitely superior to the original E-2A model which entered service with Navy AEW squadron VAW-11 at the beginning of 1964 and which played an important role in controlling Navy strike packages during the Vietnam War.

Early AEW-dedicated aircraft such as the Grumman TBF Avenger and Grumman WF-2 Tracer were adequate for the time, but were unable to cope with more than a handful of targets at once. It gradually became clear, therefore, that some form of computerization was required if radar systems operators were to take full advantage of all information at their disposal. However, it was not until the late 1950s that miniaturization of computers reached the stage at which it was possible to install such devices in an airframe small enough for operation from Navy carriers.

What resulted was the **W2F-1** (E-2A from late 1962) Hawkeye, instantly recognizable by the pancake-shaped dorsal radome which housed the antenna for the General Electric APS-96 surveillance radar. Including proto-

types and test specimens, a total of 59 E-2As was built and delivered to the US Navy between 1962 and 1967, most being later modfied to **E-2B** standard through installation of a Litton L-304 general-purpose computer. A few E-2Bs remain operational with the Navy early in 1986.

Further upgrading of the avionics systems led to the appearance of the E-2C model, perhaps the most significant change entailing fitment of rather more capable General Electric APS-120 radar, since replaced by the even more effective APS-125. Attention was also paid to improving data-processing capability to a point where the aircraft is capable of automatically tracking more than 250 targets at any given time, whilst also controlling 30 or more interceptions.

Flown for the first time in prototype form on 20 January 1971, the E-2C became operational with VAW-123 aboard the USS *Saratoga* in the autumn of 1974 and variants of the type now equip most Navy AEW squadrons. In addition, small quantities have also been purchased by Egypt (4), Israel (4), Japan (8) and Singapore (4) whilst production continues for the US Navy, which plans to buy no fewer than 102, later examples benefiting from installation of the recently-developed APS-138 surveillance radar.

Specification: Grumman E-2C Hawkeye
Origin: USA
Type: airborne early warning and control aircraft
Powerplant: two 3661-ekW (4,910-ehp) Allison T56-A-425 turboprop engines
Performance: maximum speed 325 kts (602 km/h; 374 mph); cruising speed for maximum range 269 kts (499 km/h; 310 mph); service ceiling 30,800 ft (9390 m); patrol endurance 6 hours; maximum ferry range 2583 km (1,605 miles)
Weights: empty 17265 kg (38,063 lb); maximum take-off 23556 kg (51,933 lb)
Dimensions: span 24.56 m (80 ft 7 in); length 17.54 m (57 ft 6.75 in); height 5.58 m (18 ft 3.75 in); wing area 65.03 m² (700 sq ft)
Armament: none

A Grumman E-2C of the Israeli air force.

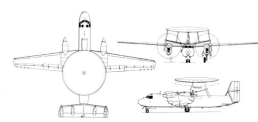

Grumman E-2C Hawkeye

A Grumman E-2C Hawkeye of VAW-126 is shown during a Pacific fleet deployment on board USS Constellation as a part of CVW-9. The Hawkeye provides Fleet airborne early warning cover.

This E-2C of VAW-124 'Bear Aces' is seen landing back on an Atlantic Fleet carrier. The Hawkeye's turboprop powerplants confer great economy and endurance.

Grumman EA-6B Prowler

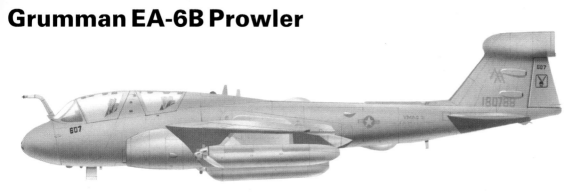

United States

A Grumman EA-6B Prowler of VMAQ-2, assigned to USS America during the Libyan operations.

Inheriting responsibility for electronic countermeasures duties from the veteran Douglas EKA-3B Skywarrior at the beginning of the 1970s, the **Grumman EA-6B Prowler** evolved from the highly successful A-6 Intruder. Although produced in relatively modest quantities, the Prowler does nevertheless form an important part of the modern carrier air wing, fulfilling functions which range from 'riding shotgun' for Navy strike aircraft intent on penetrating enemy defences through providing a protective screen around carrier task forces to acquisition of electronic intelligence.

Development of the Prowler began in the latter half of the 1960s when it was decided to purchase a new-build aircraft to perform this increasingly important role. Grumman's A-6 seemed to provide a good starting point for an ECM-dedicated type and was duly selected to provide the basis for the Prowler, which eventually appeared as a four-seater with a crew consisting of a pilot to fly the aircraft and three electronic warfare officers (EWOs) to manage the sophisticated array of ECM and electronic support measures (ESM) systems.

At the heart of the EA-6B is the ALQ-99 tactical jamming system, this being basically a package capable of detecting, sorting, classifying and dealing with electronic 'threats' across a broad spectrum of frequency bands. Operation may be accomplished automatically, semi-automatically or manually, various antennas located around the airframe being employed to detect electronic emissions whilst up to five external pods can be carried to generate 'noise' jamming signals designed to render enemy radar ineffective.

Not surprisingly, Prowler capability has been steadily enhanced since the type first attained operational status with VAQ-132 in the summer of 1972. Early production machines were to 'Basic' standard and these have since been followed by 'ExCap' (Expanded Capability), 'ICap' (Improved Capability) and 'ICap-2' aircraft, the last being the current production model. Looking to the future, development of an 'AdvCap' (Advanced Capability) version is now in hand, and this will feature a number of improvements, including better communications jamming equipment, increased jamming power and electronically-steered antennas.

In late 1984 some 76 EA-6Bs of various subtypes were to be found in the Navy and Marine Corps inventory whilst procurement of a further 12 was in hand, and it seems likely that production will eventually surpass the 100 mark. In addition to new-build Prowlers, the Navy has also been pursuing the CILOP (conversion in lieu of procurement) policy with regard to the EA-6B, many older aircraft having been updated to late-standard configuration, and this process also looks likely to continue.

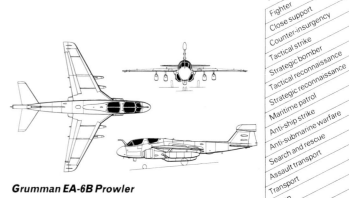

Grumman EA-6B Prowler

This US Navy Grumman EA-6B is seen in an unfamiliar environment, in front of a HAS at Zweibrücken, West Germany, during a rare off-ship deployment from USS Nimitz.

Grumman EA-6Bs, in common with most front-line US Navy aircraft, are receiving toned-down overall grey colour schemes, although many still carry white underwing ECM pods.

Specification: Grumman EA-6B Prowler with five jamming pods
Origin: USA
Type: electronic countermeasures platform
Powerplant: two 5080-kg (11,200-lb) thrust Pratt & Whitney J52-P-408 turbojet engines
Performance: maximum speed 530 kts (982 km/h; 610 mph) at sea level; cruising speed 418 kts (774 km/h; 481 mph); initial rate of climb 10,030 ft (3057 m) per minute; service ceiling 38,000 ft (11580 m); combat range with maximum external fuel 1769 km (1,099 miles)
Weights: empty 14588 kg (32,162 lb); stand-off jamming configuration take-off 24703 kg (54,461 lb); maximum take-off 29484 kg (65,000 lb)
Dimensions: span 16.15 m (53 ft 0 in); length 18.24 m (59 ft 10 in); height 4.95 m (16 ft 3 in); wing area 49.13 m (528.9 sq ft)
Armament: none

Role

Fighter	
Close support	
Counter-insurgency	
Tactical strike	
Strategic bomber	
Tactical reconnaissance	■
Strategic reconnaissance	
Maritime patrol	
Anti-ship strike	
Anti-submarine warfare	
Search and rescue	
Assault transport	
Transport	
Liaison	
Trainer	
Inflight-refuelling tanker	
Specialized	■

Performance

All-weather capability	■
Rough field capability	
STOL capability	
VTOL capability	
Airspeed 0-250 mph	
Airspeed 250 mph-Mach 1	■
Airspeed Mach 1 plus	
Ceiling 0-20,000 ft	
Ceiling 20,000-40,000 ft	■
Ceiling 40,000 ft plus	
Range 0-1,000 miles	■
Range 1,000-3,000 miles	
Range 3,000 miles plus	

Weapons

Air-to-air missiles	
Air-to-surface missiles	
Cruise missiles	
Cannon	
Trainable guns	
Naval weapons	
Nuclear-capable	
Rockets	
'Smart' weapon kit	
Weapon load 0-4,000 lb	
Weapon load 4,000-15,000 lb	
Weapon load 15,000 lb plus	

Avionics

Electronic Counter Measures	■
Electronic Support Measures	■
Search radar	
Fire control radar	
Look-down/shoot-down	
Terrain-following radar	
Forward-looking infra-red	
Laser	
Television	

A Grumman EA-6B Prowler of the US Navy

Grumman (General Dynamics) EF-111A Raven

A Grumman EF-111A Raven, 'Spark Vark', of the 42nd ECS, based at RAF Upper Heyford.

The importance of aircraft able to provide wide-area ECM jamming coverage for friendly attacking forces was underlined by events in the air war over Vietnam during the late 1960s and early 1970s. Thus in 1974 the USAF awarded study contracts to General Dynamics and Grumman for the development of a suitable conversion of the General Dynamics F-111A tactical strike fighter. Evaluation of the proposals led to Grumman receiving a contract in 1975 for the conversion of two F-111As as **Grumman (General Dynamics) EF-111A** ECM jamming prototypes; the first was flown on 15 December 1975. The second was the first fully aerodynamic prototype, flown on 10 March 1977 and incorporating the reinforced fin with large fin-tip pod housing the jamming system's receiver and antennas, a conspicuous identification feature. The whole system was flown initially on 10 March 1977. Three operational modes are possible: stand-off, with the EF-111A staying in its own airspace to screen the routes of its strike aircraft; escort, with the EF-111A accompanying strike aircraft in penetration of enemy defences; and neutralization of enemy radars in the close air support role.

Primary role equipment of the EF-111A is the Eaton Corporation ALQ-99E tactical jamming system (housed in the weapons bay), which is claimed to have sufficient power to allow the aircraft to penetrate the most concentrated electronic defences. The ALQ-99E's advanced configuration permits the electronic warfare officer to counter differing threats as they develop, and with the aid of an IBM 4 Pi computer to cope with a workload that previously required several operators. Essential accuracy of navigation is ensured by INS, Tacan, UHF/DF and terrain-following radar, and the ALQ-99E system is backed by electronic countermeasures dispenser, radar countermeasures receiver, self-protection and terminal threat-warning systems.

Development of the complete electronics system and comprehensive testing occupied more than four years, the first fully operational EF-111A, by then named **Raven**, entering service with TAC in November 1981; in December 1983, the 390th Electronic Combat Squadron became the first fully operational unit. In all 42 F-111As have been converted to EF-111A configuration, the last of them being delivered to the USAF during 1985.

Grumman EF-111A Raven

The EF-111A Raven carries its sensitive ALQ-99 emission receiver system in its fin-top fairing. This system's inputs activate the 10 powerful jammers mounted in the weapons bay.

Twenty-four of the USAF's EF-111s are based at Mountain Home AFB, with the 388th ECS, while 12 serve with the 42nd ECS at Upper Heyford, and six are held in reserve as attrition replacements.

Specification: Grumman (General Dynamics) EF-111A Raven, penetration role
Origin: USA
Type: two-seat ECM tactical jamming aircraft
Powerplant: two 8391-kg (18,500-lb) afterburning thrust Pratt & Whitney TF30-P-3 turbofan engines
Performance: (estimated) maximum speed 1227 kts (2272 km/h; 1,412 mph); speed in combat area 507 kts (940 km/h; 584 mph); initial rate of climb 3,300 ft (1006 m) per minute; service ceiling 45,000 ft (13715 m); combat radius 1495 km (929 miles); unrefuelled endurance more than 4 hours
Weights: empty 25072 kg (55,275 lb); combat take-off 31751 kg (70,000 lb)
Dimensions: span, spread 19.20 m (63 ft 0 in) and swept 9.74 m (31 ft 11.4 in); length 23.16 m (76 ft 0 in); height 6.10 m (20 ft 0 in); wing area, spread 48.77 m² (525.0 sq ft)
Armament: none

Role
Fighter
Close support
Counter-insurgency
Tactical strike
Strategic bomber
Tactical reconnaissance
Strategic reconnaissance
Maritime patrol
Anti-ship strike
Anti-submarine warfare
Search and rescue
Assault transport
Transport
Liaison
Trainer
Inflight-refuelling tanker
Specialized

Performance
All-weather capability
Rough field capability
STOL capability
VTOL capability
Airspeed 0-250 mph
Airspeed 250 mph-Mach 1
Airspeed Mach 1 plus
Ceiling 0-20,000 ft
Ceiling 20,000-40,000 ft
Ceiling 40,000 ft plus
Range 0-1,000 miles
Range 1,000-3,000 miles
Range 3,000 miles plus

Weapons
Air-to-air missiles
Air-to-surface missiles
Cruise missiles
Cannon
Trainable guns
Naval weapons
Nuclear-capable
Rockets
'Smart' weapon kit
Weapon load 0-4,000 lb
Weapon load 4,000-15,000 lb
Weapon load 15,000 lb plus

Avionics
Electronic Counter Measures
Electronic Support Measures
Search radar
Fire control radar
Look-down/shoot-down
Terrain-following radar
Forward-looking infra-red
Laser
Television

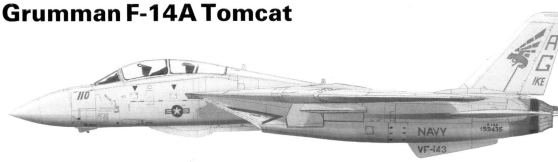

Grumman F-14A Tomcat

Iran   United States

Role
Fighter
Close support
Counter-insurgency
Tactical strike
Strategic bomber
Tactical reconnaissance
Strategic reconnaissance
Maritime patrol
Anti-ship strike
Anti-submarine warfare
Search and rescue
Assault transport
Transport
Liaison
Trainer
Inflight-refuelling tanker
Specialized

Performance
All-weather capability
Rough field capability
STOL capability
VTOL capability
Airspeed 0-250 mph
Airspeed 250 mph-Mach 1
Airspeed Mach 1 plus
Ceiling 0-20,000 ft
Ceiling 20,000-40,000 ft
Ceiling 40,000ft plus
Range 0-1,000 miles
Range 1,000-3,000 miles
Range 3,000 miles plus

Weapons
Air-to-air missiles
Air-to-surface missiles
Cruise missiles
Cannon
Trainable guns
Naval weapons
Nuclear-capable
Rockets
'Smart' weapon kit
Weapon load 0-4,000 lb
Weapon load 4,000-15,000 lb
Weapon load 15,000 lb plus

Avionics
Electronic Counter Measures
Electronic Support Measures
Search radar
Fire control radar
Look-down/shoot-down
Terrain-following radar
Forward-looking infra-red
Laser
Television

Arguably the finest interceptor flying anywhere in the world today, the **Grumman F-14 Tomcat** would probably not even have existed had it not been for the failure of the earlier General Dynamics F-111B. Nevertheless, although it fared significantly better than the General Dynamics machine, the **F-14A** variant has not steered entirely clear of trouble, engine-related problems probably being responsible for most of the headaches as well as a substantial proportion of those aircraft lost in accidents to date. However, recent developments (described more fully in the entry for the F-14D) will address most of the engine-related shortcomings.

What eventually evolved into the Tomcat was already well established on Grumman's drawing boards even before the ill-fated F-111B was cancelled, and the company was thus well placed to bid for the Navy's new fighter competition launched soon after the General Dynamics machine passed into history. Competing against three other proposals, the **G-303** was duly selected by the US Navy in January 1969, an initial contract for six (later increased to 12) development aircraft being placed later in the same year.

The first F-14A eventually got airborne on 21 December 1970 but was destroyed nine days later on only its second flight when it suffered catastrophic hydraulic failure. Despite this setback, the development programme seems to have gone well and culminated in production Tomcats being assigned to Navy training squadron VF-125 at Miramar, California, in October 1972.

Thereafter, a fairly lengthy period of training followed before the type made its operational debut aboard the USS *Enterprise* with VF-1 and VF-2 in September 1974. Since then, the F-14A has gone on to become the Navy's premier fleet defence fighter, progressive re-equipment enabling it to replace both the Vought F-8 Crusader and McDonnell Douglas F-4 Phantom, and the type now serves with 26 front-line and reserve fighter squadrons of the US Navy.

In addition to the 500 or so F-14As procured by the US Navy, a further 80 were supplied to Iran during the era of the Shah although it seems that very few of these are still maintained in an airworthy condition, clandestine attempts to re-purchase the surviving aircraft having been doomed to failure.

As far as weaponry is concerned, it is the Hughes AIM-54 Phoenix air-to-air missile which undoubtedly gives the F-14A the edge over other contemporary interceptors, this AAM possessing the ability to destroy aircraft at ranges far in excess of any other missile. However, in the event of combat being conducted at medium to close ranges, the Tomcat may also carry both the IR-homing AIM-9 Sidewinder and the radar-guided AIM-7 Sparrow. A single M61 Vulcan 20-mm cannon completes the F-14's arsenal.

Specification: Grumman F-14A Tomcat
Origin: USA
Type: fleet defence fighter

Powerplant: two 9480-kg (20,900-lb) static thrust Pratt & Whitney TF30-P-412A afterburning turbofan engines
Performance: maximum speed at altitude 1,359 kts (2517 km/h; 1,564 mph); maximum speed at sea level 791 kts (1465 km/h; 910 mph); initial rate of climb at normal gross weight more than 30,000 ft (9145 m) per minute; service ceiling more than 56,000 ft (17070 m); range in interceptor configuration with external fuel about 3220 km (2,000 miles)
Weights: empty 18191 kg (40,104 lb); take-off 'clean' 26633 kg (58,715 lb); take-off with six AIM-54 Phoenix AAMs 32098 kg (70,764 lb); maximum take-off 33724 kg (74,349 lb)
Dimensions: span unswept 19.55 m (64 ft 1.5 in); span swept 11.65 m (38 ft 2.5 in); length 19.10 m (62 ft 8 in); height 4.88 m (16 ft 0 in); wing area 52.49 m² (565 sq ft)
Armament: one M61A1 Vulcan 20-mm Gatling-type rotary cannon in forward fuselage with 675 rounds of ammunition, plus various combinations of AIM-7F Sparrow, AIM-9L Sidewinder and AIM-54 Phoenix air-to-air missiles; alternatively, up to 6577 kg (14,500 lb) of Mk 82/83/84 bombs or other weaponry can be carried in the attack role

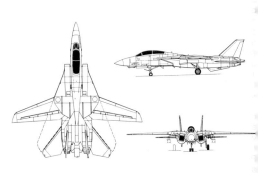

A Grumman F-14A Tomcat of VF-143 'Pukin' Dogs'

Grumman F-14A Tomcat

This Grumman F-14A Tomcat, seen on the deck of USS America, wears the markings of VF-33 'Tarsiers'. The aircraft in the background is from VF-102 'Diamondbacks'.

VF-102 'Diamondbacks' is one of the squadrons trained to use the TARPS reconnaissance pod. Four pods are carried on each carrier, and may be replaced by reconnaissance-configured RF-18 Hornets.

Grumman F-14D Tomcat

Anyone who has followed the F-14's career closely will be well aware that the type has been plagued by engine-related problems for much of its life. Attempts to eliminate some of the TF30's worst vices have met with a measure of success but the Pratt & Whitney engine was still a source of major concern until quite recently, when it was decided to install a derivative of General Electric's F110 turbofan in a new variant of the fighter to be known as the **Grumman F-14D Tomcat**.

In fact, the TF30 was initially viewed as merely an interim powerplant pending the availability of a 'definitive' engine which would be installed in a new version known as the **F-14B**. At one time it seemed certain that Pratt & Whitney's F100 turbofan would serve as the basis around which the F-14B would be built and a variant of this (given the designation F401-PW-400) was installed and flown in the seventh Tomcat in 1973, the modified aircraft itself being redesignated as the F-14B. Unfortunately, plans to convert a second machine to take the F401 engine fell by the wayside, largely as a result of financial restraint which led to the TF30-engined F-14A becoming the standard variant.

Several years later and in a more equable financial climate, the question of re-engining Tomcat re-emerged and this time the proposal met with much greater success. General Electric's F101 engine (selected to power the Rockwell B-1) served as the basis for the F101DFE (Derivative Fighter Engine) and was test flown in the sole F-14B for the first time in July 1981.

Now known by the parent company as the **Super Tomcat**, the re-engined prototype demonstrated remarkable performance benefits in a fairly short period of evaluation and this eventually prompted the decision in October 1982 to proceed with full-scale development of the F110. Even then, it was to be another couple of years before the Navy puts its full weight behind this engine, the service preferring to adopt something akin to a 'belt and braces' approach by carefully monitoring progress made with Pratt & Whitney's basically similar PW1128N powerplant.

Eventually, in early 1984, the Navy came down in favour of the F110-GE-400, selecting this to power the F-14D which will also benefit from major updating of the Hughes AWG-9 weapons control system in light of experience gained with the same company's APG-70 radar which forms part of McDonnell Douglas F-15 Eagle MSIP (Multi-Stage Improvement Program) initiatives. Other developments will entail major redesign of cockpit instrumentation whilst a number of Pentagon-sponsored items, most notably the ALQ-165 ASPJ (Airborne Self-Protection Jammer) and the Joint Tactical Information Distribution System, will also be fitted.

As far as the new engine is concerned, this will in fact make its debut in the **F-14A(Plus)**, 29 examples of which are due to be delivered to the Navy later in the present decade. Changes on these aircraft will, however, be confined just to the engine. Then, a couple of years later, the F-14D will enter service.

Grumman F-14B 'Super Tomcat' prototype.

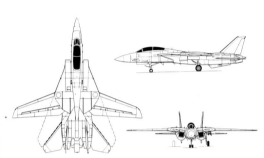

Grumman F-14D Tomcat

The seventh F-14A was fitted with Pratt & Whitney F401-PW-400 engines to become the F-14B during 1973. It was later converted to fly with General Electric F101DFE turbofans.

The F-14D will be a considerably more capable fighting machine than the F-14A, with improved avionics and instruments as well as more powerful engines.

Specification: Grumman F-14D Tomcat
Origin: USA
Type: fleet defence fighter
Powerplant: two 13154-kg (29,000-lb) thrust General Electric F110 turbofan engines
Performance: none so far quoted, but combat radius and patrol time on station are estimated to be increased by 60 and 35 per cent respectively
Weights: not known
Dimensions: as F-14A
Armament: one M61A1 Vulcan 20-mm Gatling-type rotary cannon with 675 rounds of ammunition, plus various combinations of AIM-7 Sparrow, AIM-9 Sidewinder and AIM-54 Phoenix air-to-air missiles; the type will also be compatible with the AIM-120 AMRAAM; conventional bombs can also be carried in the attack role

Role
Fighter
Close support
Counter-insurgency
Tactical strike
Strategic bomber
Tactical reconnaissance
Strategic reconnaissance
Maritime patrol
Anti-ship strike
Anti-submarine warfare
Search and rescue
Assault transport
Transport
Liaison
Trainer
Inflight-refuelling tanker
Specialized

Performance
All-weather capability
Rough field capability
STOL capability
VTOL capability
Airspeed 0-250 mph
Airspeed 250 mph-Mach 1
Airspeed Mach 1 plus
Ceiling 0-20,000 ft
Ceiling 20,000-40,000 ft
Ceiling 40,000 ft plus
Range 0-1,000 miles
Range 1,000-3,000 miles
Range 3,000 miles plus

Weapons
Air-to-air missiles
Air-to-surface missiles
Cruise missiles
Cannon
Trainable guns
Naval weapons
Nuclear-capable
Rockets
'Smart' weapon kit
Weapon load 0-4,000 lb
Weapon load 4,000-15,000 lb
Weapon load 15,000 lb plus

Avionics
Electronic Counter Measures
Electronic Support Measures
Search radar
Fire control radar
Look-down/shoot-down
Terrain-following radar
Forward-looking infra-red
Laser
Television

Grumman OV-1 Mohawk

During the operational lifetime of the **Grumman OV-1 Mohawk**, tremendous strides have been taken in the realm of army airborne reconnaissance, and what began as a traditional visual and photographic aircraft is today packed with sophisticated sensors. The **G-134**, unusual for its time in being an army aviation turboprop (two 708-kW/950-hp Lycoming T53-L-3s), was initially designated **AO-1** when the first of nine development aircraft flew on 14 April 1959, these later being redesignated **YOV-1A**. A further four were ordered to meet US Marine Corps requirements, but this proposed **OF-1** model was cancelled before the aircraft could be completed. A comprehensive array of avionics was included in the initial production **OV-1A** to enable the aircraft to meet the all-weather battlefield surveillance requirement, and two underwing stores pylons enabled up to 1225 kg (2,700 lb) of ordnance to be carried. Grumman built 64 OV-1As, equipped with KA-30 high resolution camera systems and removable pods above the wing roots for 52 upward-firing night photography flares. A small number were modified with six underwing pylons for bombs, guns and rockets to provide close support during the Vietnam War.

The **OV-1B** (90 built) introduced APS-94 side-looking airborne radar (SLAR) in a large underfuselage container, an AKT-16 VHF data link, and a further 1.83 m (6 ft 0 in) of wing span. Fuselage airbrakes were deleted, as was provision for dual controls for the two-man crew in their armour-protected, Martin-Baker J5 ejector seats. Later OV-1Bs had 858-kW (1,150-hp) T53-L-15s. Built in parallel, the **OV-1C** was an updated OV-1A with short-span wings and UAS-4 infra-red ground surveillance equipment in the underside of the rear fuselage, and late models of the 129 built also progressed to T53-L-15 engines. In the four **YOV-1D** and 37 **OV-1D** large-span aircraft which followed up to the end of production in December 1970, the SLAR could be exchanged for IR sensors within an hour, combining OV-1B/C functions in an airframe powered by further uprated engines. In addition, 72 OV-1B/C aircraft were converted to OV-1D standard by 1984, with equipment including new model APS-94F SLAR. All retain 180° visual spectrum photographic capability. The US Army will operate 110 OV-1Ds, plus 36 **RV-1D** conversions with ALQ-133 'Quicklook II' equipment for pinpointing enemy radars, up to the end of the century. At least two OV-1Ds were supplied to Israel in mid-1976, and four OV-1s were offered to Pakistan in 1984, although delivery has not yet taken place.

A Grumman OV-1C of the US Army.

Grumman OV-1B Mohawk

A Grumman RV-1D of the 73rd Combat Intelligence Company, US Army, based at Stuttgart in the Federal Republic of Germany. The RV-1D is equipped with ALQ-133 'Quicklook II'.

The OV-1D carries an APS-94 SLAR in its underfuselage pod, and this can be augmented by photographic and infra-red sensors. One hundred and ten will remain in service into the next century.

Specification: Grumman OV-1D Mohawk

Origin: USA
Type: tactical reconnaissance aircraft
Powerplant: two 1044-kW (1,400-shp) Lycoming T53-L-701 turboprop engines
Performance: maximum speed 265 kts (491 km/h; 305 mph) with IR sensors, or 251 kts (465 km/h; 289 mph) with SLAR; cruising speed 210 kts (389 km/h; 242 mph) service ceiling 25,000 ft (7620 m); range 1738 km (1,080 miles) with IR, or 1653 km (1,027 miles) with SLAR
Weights: empty 5333 kg (11,757 lb); maximum take-off 8085 kg (17,826 lb) with IR, or 8164 kg (18,000 lb) with SLAR
Dimensions: span 14.63 m (48 ft 0 in); overall length 13.69 m (44 ft 11 in); fuselage length 12.50 m (41 ft 0 in); height 3.86 m (12 ft 8 in); wing area 33.45 m² (360 sq ft)

Grumman S-2 Tracker

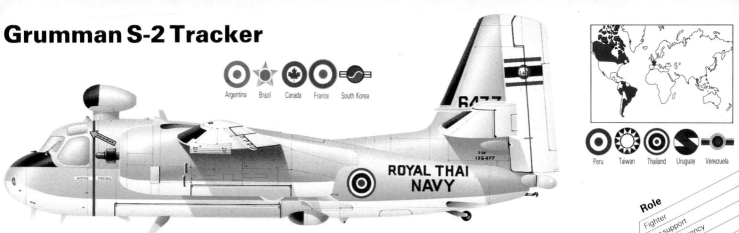

Making its maiden flight as long ago as December 1952, the **Grumman S-2 Tracker** is still used by a respectable number of air arms throughout the world, although it no longer remains operational with the US Navy, having been replaced by the Lockheed S-3A Viking during the course of the 1970s.

A successful marriage of the previously separate search and destroy aspects of anti-submarine warfare, the Tracker can be said to have revolutionized shipborne ASW and was produced in large numbers for the US Navy, successive updating of the basic **G-89** design permitting it to keep abreast of developments in this vital field and, incidentally, ensuring that it remained in production until well into the 1960s.

Powered by a pair of Wright Cyclone radial engines, the first model of the Tracker to enter quantity production was the **S2F-1 (S-2A** from late 1962), this being by far the most numerous subtype with well over 700 being completed for service with the US Navy and a number of friendly nations including Italy, Japan and the Netherlands.

Later updating of the S2F-1 led to the appearance of the **S2F-1S (S-2B)** and **S2F-1S1 (S-2F)**, modification work mainly entailing addition of 'Julie' and 'Jezebel' active and passive detection equip-ment but, following the advent of later and more modern ASW models of the Tracker, a substantial number of these aircraft were reconfigured for utility-type missions as the **US-2A** and **US-2B**. Many more were re-assigned to multi-engine training duties as the **S2F-1T (TS-2A)**, and some of these claimed the distinction of being amongst the last Trackers to be employed by the US Navy.

In addition to the initial production model, subsequent newbuild versions of the Tracker comprised the **S2F-2 (S-2C)**, **S2F-3 (S-2D)** and **S2F-3S (S-2E)**, retrospective modification of these subtypes leading to the appearance of specialized aircraft engaged in a variety of tasks including target towing and utility functions (**US-2C** and **US-2D**), photo-graphic reconnaissance (**RS-2C**) and tele-metry relay/electronic missions (**ES-2D**).

As far as the basic ASW function is con-cerned, the last model to be specifically engaged in this task by the US Navy was the **S-2G** which was essentially an S-2E with enhanced electronics. Indeed, the S-2G was not produced as such, those aircraft which existed being simply conversions of S-2Es. Following service with the US Navy many of the survivors have found their way overseas, examples of the S-2G being supplied to Australia and Uruguay.

Specification: Grumman S-2E Tracker
Origin: USA
Type: anti-submarine warfare aircraft
Powerplant: two 1137-kW (1,525-hp) Wright R-1820-82WA Cyclone radial piston engines
Performance: maximum speed 230 kts (426 km/h; 265 mph) at sea level; patrol speed at 1,500 ft (460 m) 130 kts (241 km/h; 150 mph); ferry range 2092 km (1,300 miles); endurance with maximum fuel and reserves 9 hours
Weights: empty 8505 kg (18,750 lb); maximum take-off 13222 kg (29,150 lb)
Dimensions: span 22.12 m (72 ft 7 in); length 13.26 m (43 ft 6 in); height 5.05 m (16 ft 7 in); wing area 46.08 m^2 (496 sq ft)
Armament: one Mk 47 or Mk 101 nuclear depth bomb or similar store in the weapons bay, plus a variety of bombs, rockets or torpedoes on six underwing stores stations; search devices include 60 echo-sounding depth charges in fuselage and 32 sonobuoys in engine nacelles

A Grumman S-2A Tracker of the Royal Thai navy.

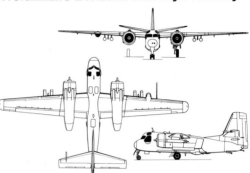

Grumman S-2G Tracker

The Japanese Maritime Self-Defence Force operates a number of S-2F Trackers with its 11 Kokutai, part of 1 Kokugun based at Kanoya, on the southern island of Kyushu.

The Canadian Armed Forces remain a major user of the Tracker, 18 aircraft equipping No. 880 Squadron at Summerside. Canada's Trackers act as a short-range supplement to the more capable Lockheed CP-140 Auroras.

Role
- Fighter
- Close support
- Counter-insurgency
- Tactical strike
- Strategic bomber
- Tactical reconnaissance
- Strategic reconnaissance
- Maritime patrol
- Anti-ship strike
- Anti-submarine warfare
- Search and rescue
- Assault transport
- Transport
- Liaison
- Trainer
- Inflight-refuelling tanker
- Specialized

Performance
- All-weather capability
- Rough field capability
- STOL capability
- VTOL capability
- Airspeed 0-250 mph
- Airspeed 250 mph-Mach 1
- Airspeed Mach 1 plus
- Ceiling 0-20,000 ft
- Ceiling 20,000-40,000 ft
- Ceiling 40,000 ft plus
- Range 0-1,000 miles
- Range 1,000-3,000 miles
- Range 3,000 miles plus

Weapons
- Air-to-air missiles
- Air-to-surface missiles
- Cruise missiles
- Cannon
- Trainable guns
- Naval weapons
- Nuclear-capable
- Rockets
- 'Smart' weapon kit
- Weapon load 0-4,000 lb
- Weapon load 4,000-15,000 lb
- Weapon load 15,000 lb plus

Avionics
- Electronic Counter Measures
- Electronic Support Measures
- Search radar
- Fire control radar
- Look-down/shoot-down
- Terrain-following radar
- Forward-looking infra-red
- Laser
- Television

A Bermudan Gulfstream II

Gulfstream Aerospace Gulfstream II

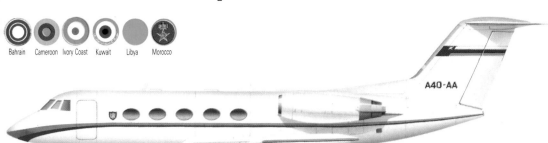

Bahrain　Cameroon　Ivory Coast　Kuwait　Libya　Morocco

Nigeria　Oman　Papua New Guinea　United States　Venezuela

This Gulfstream II is used by the Omani government for VIP transport duties.

Employed as a VIP transport by a small number of air arms, the **Gulfstream II** was conceived as a jet replacement for the turbo-prop-powered Grumman Gulfstream I. The Grumman Aircraft Engineering Corporation announced its launch decision on 17 May 1965, and the first production aircraft (there was no prototype) flew on 2 October 1966. A year later, on 17 October 1967, type certification was granted by the FAA, allowing deliveries to customers to begin on 6 December 1967. Grumman's policy had been to produce an aircraft with similar interior dimensions to the Gulfstream I, but with both trans-oceanic capability and short-field performance to meet the diverse needs of the business executive. The aims were met handsomely by installing Rolls-Royce Spey turbofans for a high power:weight ratio, and demonstrated by a nonstop flight from New Jersey to London in under seven hours.

Production of the aircraft ended in December 1979 after 256 had been built, and by which time the manufacturer had changed title to Gulfstream American Corporation (1978). The present name of Gulfstream Aerospace Corporation was adopted in 1982. Included alongside corporate deliveries have been examples of single Gulfstream IIs which

are currently operated by the air forces of the Ivory Coast, Morocco and Venezuela in VIP roles. Other governments have flown Gulfstream IIs in civil markings. In addition, one aircraft was supplied to the US Coast Guard for transport duties and, because of the service's paramilitary status, received the designation **VC-11A**.

No military aircraft have yet adopted the option offered by the manufacturer of retro-fitting with the more efficient wing of the Gulfstream III. The resultant **Gulfstream II-B** features the winglets of later aircraft, married to a wing swept at 27° 40′ at quarter chord, but is also modified structurally for a higher take-off weight, operating speed and cruising height. A revised electrical system, as in the Gulfstream III, is not incorporated. Greater fuel economy, and thus improved range, is available from the new wing, the first of which flew on a Gulfstream II-B on 17 March 1981 and completed its certification programme on 17 September the same year. Some 40 original Gulfstream IIs have been converted to G II-B standard, their former configuration including a wing span of 20.98 m (68 ft 10 in), a ceiling of 43,000 ft (13105 m) and a maximum range of 6635 km (4,123 miles)

Specification: Gulfstream Aerospace II-B
Origin: USA
Powerplant: two 5171-kg (11,400-lb) thrust Rolls-Royce Spey Mk 511-8 turbofan engines fitted with thrust reversers
Performance: maximum cruising speed Mach 0.85 or 500 kts (928 km/h; 576 mph) at 30,000 ft (9145 m), or Mach 0.77 or 441 kts (818 km/h; 508 mph) for maximum economy; initial rate of climb 3,800 ft (1158 m) per minute; maximum operating altitude 45,000 ft (13,715 m); range 7357 km (4,571 miles) with VFR reserves
Weights: empty operating 17736 kg (39,100 lb); maximum payload 1315 kg (2,900 lb); maximum take-off 31615 kg (69,700 lb)
Dimensions: span 23.72 m (77 ft 10 in); length 24.36 m (79 ft 11 in); height 7.47 m (24 ft 6 in); wing area 86.83 m² (934.6 sq ft)
Armament: none

Gulfstream Aerospace Gulfstream II

The single Gulfstream II delivered to the US Coast Guard is formally designated VC-11A, and was the 23rd Gulfstream II built. It is used as a fast executive transport.

This Gulfstream II is one of the huge fleet of aircraft operated by NASA, and is seen here at Biggs Army Airfield, Fort Bliss, Texas. It is used for VIP transport and liaison duties.

Role
- Fighter
- Close support
- Counter-insurgency
- Tactical strike
- Strategic bomber
- Tactical reconnaissance
- Strategic reconnaissance
- Maritime patrol
- Anti-ship strike
- Anti-submarine warfare
- Search and rescue
- Assault transport
- Transport
- Liaison
- Trainer
- Inflight-refuelling tanker
- Specialized

Performance
- All-weather capability
- Rough field capability
- STOL capability
- VTOL capability
- Airspeed 0-250 mph
- Airspeed 250 mph-Mach 1
- Airspeed Mach 1 plus
- Ceiling 0-20,000 ft
- Ceiling 20,000-40,000 ft
- Ceiling 40,000ft plus
- Range 0-1,000 miles
- Range 1,000-3,000 miles
- Range 3,000 miles plus

Weapons
- Air-to-air missiles
- Air-to-surface missiles
- Cruise missiles
- Cannon
- Trainable guns
- Naval weapons
- Nuclear-capable
- Rockets
- 'Smart' weapon kit
- Weapon load 0-4,000 lb
- Weapon load 4,000-15,000 lb
- Weapon load 15,000 lb plus

Avionics
- Electronic Counter Measures
- Electronic Support Measures
- Search radar
- Fire control radar
- Look-down/shoot-down
- Terrain-following radar
- Forward-looking infra-red
- Laser
- Television

Gulfstream Aerospace Gulfstream III

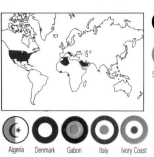

Saudi Arabia United Arab Emirates United States

Algeria Denmark Gabon Italy Ivory Coast

A Gulfstream Aerospace C-20A of the US Air Force.

Despite the considerable difference between the first two marks of Gulfstream, the **Gulfstream III** strongly resembles the Gulfstream II. Its principal differences are restricted to a revised wing of greater span with added winglets, a lengthened fuselage and greater fuel capacity. The last, in conjunction with the 18 per cent increase in fuel economy which the more efficient wing provides, gives a significant range increase compared with the Gulfstream II. First flight of the prototype Gulfstream III was made on 2 December 1979, with civil certification by the FAA following on 22 September 1980. The aircraft has also been approved for installation of an electronic flight information system (EFIS), in which TV displays replace conventional instruments.

The Royal Danish air force was the Gulfstream III's launch customer, taking delivery of three examples during the first half of 1982, having trained crews on a leased Gulfstream II. These are alternatively designated **SMA-3** (Special Missions Aircraft) and operated by Eskadril 721 from Vaerlose and a detachment at Sondrestrom, Greenland. Their varied duties include fishery patrol (with installed Texas Instruments APS-127 sea surveillance radar, plus a parachute-flare launching tube); SAR; light transport (for

which a special 1.60 by 2.11 m (63 by 83in) starboard side cargo door is fitted; air dropping; medical evacuation; and VVIP transport. In the primary fishery protection role the aircraft is flown by a crew of seven, which includes a radio operator, navigator, observer and photographer in addition to the pilot, co-pilot and flight engineer. The Gulfstream III's long duration is an added safety advantage in Greenland's changeable weather conditions.

Amongst operators of the standard Gulfstream III is the US Air Force, which leased three for a two-year period beginning September 1983, then purchased them outright and announced its intention of buying eight more. These USAF **C-20A** aircraft are operated by the 89th MAW at Andrews AFB, Maryland, and 58th MAS, Ramstein, West Germany, as replacements for Lockheed C-140 JetStars. Internal arrangements are for five crew and up to 14 passengers. A most creditable 99.2 per cent mission completion rate was achieved by the C-20A in its first year of service. Single Gulfstream IIIs have also been supplied to the air forces of Gabon, Ivory Coast, Venezuela and Italy for VIP transport duties, the last-mentioned receiving its aircraft in 1985 for 306° Gruppo of 31° Stormo at Rome/Ciampino in partial replacement for a pair of McDonnell Douglas DC-9s.

Specification: Gulfstream Aerospace III
Origin: USA
Powerplant: two 5171-kg (11,400-lb) thrust Rolls-Royce Spey Mk 511-8 turbofan engines fitted with thrust reversers
Performance: maximum cruising speed Mach 0.85 or 500 kts (928 km/h; 576mph) at 30,000ft (9145m), or Mach 0.77 or 441 kts (818 km/h; 508mph) for maximum economy; initial rate of climb 3,800ft (1158m) per minute; maximum operating altitude 45,000ft (13,715m); range 7598 km (4,721 miles) with VFR reserves
Weights: empty 14515kg (32,000lb); typical payload 726kg (1,600lb); maximum take-off 31615kg (69,700lb)
Dimensions: span 23.72m (77ft 10in); length 25.32m (83ft 1in); height 7.43m (24ft 4.5in); wing area 86.83m² (934.6 sqft)
Armament: none

Gulfstream Aerospace Gulfstream III

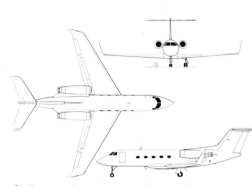

Three Gulfstream IIIs were leased for two years by the US Air Force before being bought outright. A further eight were ordered in 1985 to equip squadrons at Andrews AFB and Ramstein.

The Gulfstream IIIs of the Royal Danish air force are designated SMA-3. Eskadril 721 at Vaerlose uses them for fishery protection and liaison duties.

Gulfstream Aerospace Gulfstream IV

Further improvement of the Gulfstream series of executive jets led in 1982 to the start of design work on a Mk IV aircraft. Principal alterations include additional power obtained by a change of engine (although still from Rolls-Royce), an increase of 1.37 m (4 ft 6 in) in fuselage length (providing for a sixth window on each side of the cabin) and a redesigned structure to the wing, although this retains the same span as the Gulfstream III, plus winglets. Internally, the flight deck has been revised to feature advanced forms of digital avionics and TV displays. The first of three **Gulfstream IV** prototypes flew on 19 September 1985 and was expected to achieve certification in mid-1986. Civil deliveries followed immediately, a target of 17 having been set for hand-over before the end of the year. Production will thereafter be at the rate of between four and six per month, according to demand, the aircraft already having a healthy backlog of orders. The Gulfstream seats 14-19 passengers in addition to two or three crew, but a **Gulfstream IV-B** is on offer with a fuselage stretched by 5.64 m (18 ft 6 in) and room for 24 passengers and four crew.

It is likely that the Gulfstream IV will be offered in military versions pioneered by the Gulfstream III and known as the **SRA-1** (Surveillance and Reconnaissance Aircraft). The SRA-1 prototype first flew on 14 August 1984, initially displaying its ability to carry wingtip sensor or ECM pods before adopting the usual winglets. Apart from the expected VIP role, the SRA-1 can be equipped for electronic surveillance, stand-off high-altitude reconnaissance, maritime surveillance, airborne command post, anti-submarine patrol or combinations of these roles. Notably, there are six underwing hardpoints for weapons or other stores, in addition to the freight door and flare tube of the Danish SMA-3 on which the new model is based. In an early demonstration configuration, the SRA-1 flew with a Motorola SLAMMR (Sideways-Looking Airborne Multi-Mode Radar) in a 5.8m (19 ft) long pod beneath the lower front fuselage, later replacing this with a Goodyear Aerospace VP8D synthetic-aperture SLAR. Other equipment for the surveillance role can include a long-range optical camera. Maritime missions are flown with a nose radar such as the Texas Instrument APS-127, FLIR and ESM equipment, whilst the reconnaissance role is provided for by SLAR and long-range oblique photographic cameras. In most roles an endurance of more than nine hours is possible.

The prototype Gulfstream IV SRA-1 with underfuselage SLAMMR fitted.

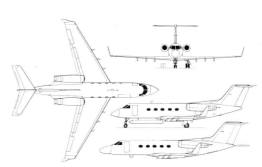

Gulfstream Aerospace SRA-1 SLAR version (lower side view: ASW version)

The prototype Gulfstream Aerospace SRA-1 is seen on its maiden flight on 14 August 1984; it appeared at Farnborough later the same year.

In surveillance configuration the SRA-1 can carry a Side-Looking Airborne Multi-Mode Radar under the nose. In maritime configuration a search radar and ESM equipment are carried.

Specification: Gulfstream Aerospace IV

Origin: USA
Powerplant: two 5634-kg (12,420-lb) thrust Rolls-Royce Tay Mk 610-8 turbofan engines fitted with thrust reversers
Performance: maximum cruising speed Mach 0.85 or 490 kts (908km/h; 564 mph) at 35,000 ft (10670m); initial rate of climb 4,350 ft (1326m) per minute; maximum operating altitude 45,000 ft (13715m); range with maximum payload and IFR reserves 6760 km (4,201 miles)
Weights: empty 15150 kg (33,400 lb); maximum payload 2132 kg (4,700 lb); maximum take of 31615 kg (69,700 lb)
Dimensions: span 23.72 m (77 ft 10 in); length 26.70 m (87 ft 7 in); height 7.42 m (24 ft 4 in); wing area 88.29 m² (950.39 sq ft)
Armament: (SRA-1 only; subject to flight-test clearance) homing torpedoes, missiles etc on six underwing pylons

Role	
Fighter	
Close support	
Counter-insurgency	
Tactical strike	
Strategic bomber	
Tactical reconnaissance	▓
Strategic reconnaissance	▓
Maritime patrol	▓
Anti-ship strike	
Anti-submarine warfare	▓
Search and rescue	
Assault transport	
Transport	
Liaison	
Trainer	
Inflight-refuelling tanker	
Specialized	▓

Performance	
All-weather capability	▓
Rough field capability	
STOL capability	
VTOL capability	
Airspeed 0-250 mph	
Airspeed 250 mph-Mach 1	▓
Airspeed Mach 1 plus	
Ceiling 0-20,000 ft	
Ceiling 20,000-40,000 ft	
Ceiling 40,000ft plus	▓
Range 0-1,000 miles	
Range 1,000-3,000 miles	
Range 3,000 miles plus	▓

Weapons	
Air-to-air missiles	
Air-to-surface missiles	
Cruise missiles	
Cannon	
Trainable guns	
Naval weapons	
Nuclear-capable	
Rockets	
'Smart' weapon kit	
Weapon load 0-4,000 lb	▓
Weapon load 4,000-15,000 lb	
Weapon load 15,000 lb plus	

Avionics	
Electronic Counter Measures	▓
Electronic Support Measures	▓
Search radar	▓
Fire control radar	
Look-down/shoot-down	
Terrain-following radar	
Forward-looking infra-red	▓
Laser	
Television	▓

Lockheed AC-130 Hercules

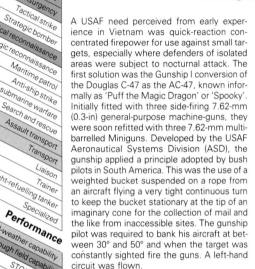

A USAF need perceived from early experience in Vietnam was quick-reaction concentrated firepower for use against small targets, especially where defenders of isolated areas were subject to nocturnal attack. The first solution was the Gunship I conversion of the Douglas C-47 as the AC-47, known informally as 'Puff the Magic Dragon' or 'Spooky'. Initially fitted with three side-firing 7.62-mm (0.3-in) general-purpose machine-guns, they were soon refitted with three 7.62-mm multibarrelled Miniguns. Developed by the USAF Aeronautical Systems Division (ASD), the gunship applied a principle adopted by bush pilots in South America. This was the use of a weighted bucket suspended on a rope from an aircraft flying a very tight continuous turn to keep the bucket stationary at the tip of an imaginary cone for the collection of mail and the like from inaccessible sites. The gunship pilot was required to bank his aircraft at between 30° and 50° and when the target was constantly sighted fire the guns. A left-hand circuit was flown.

With the system operational, there was a need to improve firepower, sensing equipment, targeting and armour. The Fairchild C-119 was adapted as the AC-119G Shadow and AC-119K Stinger with the 17th and 18th Special Operations Squadrons (SOS) respectively, while ASD began converting the 13th production C-130A (54-1626) to Gunship II standard in 1965. This involved installation of four 20-mm Vulcan cannon, four 7.62-mm Miniguns, flare equipment and improved sighting. This aircraft was tested operationally in Vietnam in late 1967, and LTV

Electrosystems was awarded an immediate contract to modify seven JC-130A missile trackers to Lockheed AC-130A standard. Weaponry remained the same but these aircraft were fittted with a searchlight, sensors, FLIR target-acquisition and direct-view image intensifiers. Four were in service in Vietnam by the end of 1968 with the 14th Air Commando Wing operating from Ubon in Thailand. A further single C-130 was converted in the 'Surprise Package' project with two 40-mm cannon replacing two of the 20-mm variety and with computerized fire control. Nine more C-130A conversions were delivered in the 'Pave Pronto' programme.

So successful was the project that 11 C-130E models were converted to AC-130E standard in the 'Pave Spectre' programme. The aircraft were given heavier armour, better avionics and provision for more ammunition; from 1973 they were brought up to AC-130H standard with the installation of the more powerful T56-A-15 engine. The final developments for use in South East Asia were the fitting of a 105-mm howitzer and laser target designator in the 'Pave Aegis' programme. At the end of the Vietnam War remaining AC-130A/H aircraft returned to the USA to serve with the 1st Special Operations Wing at Eglin AFB. The AC-130 was used operationally again with the US occupation of Grenada in October 1983. Temporarily based at Bridgetown, Barbados, and fitted with underwing ECM pods and exhaust shrouds, AC-130H aircraft of the 16th Special Operations Squadron operated against Cuban positions.

Specification: Lockheed AC-130E Hercules
Origin: USA
Type: multi-sensor ground-attack gunship
Powerplant: four 3020-ekW (4,050-eshp) Allison T56-A-7 turboprop engines
Performance: maximum speed 330 kts (612 km/h; 380 mph) at 30,000 ft (9145 m); cruising speed 320 kts (592 km/h; 368 mph); initial rate of climb 1,830 ft (558 m) per minute; endurance 5 hours
Weights: empty 33063 kg (72,892 lb); maximum take-off 70307 kg (155,000 lb)
Dimensions: span 40.41 m (132 ft 7 in); length 29.79 m (97 ft 9 in); height 11.66 m (38 ft 3 in); wing area 162.11 m² (1,745 sq ft)
Armament: (AC-130H) one 105-mm (4.13-in) howitzer, two 40-mm cannon, two 20-mm cannon and four 7.62-mm (0.3-in) Miniguns

A Lockheed AC-130H 'Pave Spectre' of the 16th SOS, 1st SOW, based at Hurlburt Field, Florida.

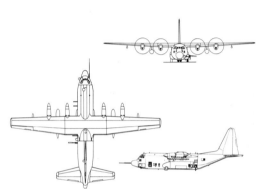

Lockheed AC-130H Spectre

The AC-130Hs of the 16th SOS have been used over Grenada during the US invasion, flying in the gunship role, and over Central America, as unarmed night reconnaissance aircraft.

This Spectre is an AC-130A (note the three-bladed props) of the 711th SOS, 919th SOG, AFRes, based at Duke Field AFB, Florida. This unit would be assigned to TAC during time of tension or war.

Lockheed C-5 Galaxy

A Lockheed C-5A Galaxy of Military Airlift Command, US Air Force.

Designed to meet requirements formulated by the USAF's MATS in 1963 for a very large logistics transport capable of lifting a 56700-kg (125,000-lb) payload over a range of 12875km (8,000 miles), the **Lockheed C-5 Galaxy** was selected in October 1965, the first **C-5A** being flown on 30 June 1968. The largest landplane then built, it featured a high-set swept wing with leading-edge slats, wide-span modified-Fowler trailing-edge flaps and aileron-cum-spoilers. Through-loading by means of upward-hingeing nose and drop-down rear fuselage ramp enabled large and heavy vehicles and missiles (such as two M60 tanks or 10 Pershing missiles with launch-tractors) to be loaded. Power was provided by four underslung, purpose-developed General Electric TF39-GE-1 turbofans.

By the end of 1970 30 C-5As out of an order for 81 aircraft had flown and deliveries made to MAC squadrons in the USA; already heavy-lift services were being flown to Europe and the Far East. In the meantime the entire specification had been extended to include a gross weight of 317515kg (700,000lb) and global deployment, calling for inflight-refuelling compatibility with the USAF's Boeing KC-135 tankers. Although the C-5's prime role was and remains heavy freighting

(such as global deployment of strategic missiles), its 28-wheel landing gear permitting operation from semi-prepared runways in potential combat areas, it is capable of lifting 345 fully-equipped troops, the entire upper deck and cargo hold being pressurized and air-conditioned.

In 1978 Lockheed gained authority to proceed with improved wings constructed of 7175-T73511 aluminium alloy for greater strength and corrosion resistance, intended to increase the service life to 30,000 hours, and all surviving C-5As are scheduled to be re-winged by the end of 1987. In 1982 a new production version, the C-5B, was authorized in which all modifications and improvements evolved in the C-5A were to be incorporated, including uprated TF39-GE-1C turbofans, extended-life wing, Bendix colour weather radar, triple Delco inertial navigators.

With C-5As now serving with the USAF's 60th, 436th, 437th and 443rd MAWs, as well as the 105th MAG of the New York ANG, C-5Bs are currently being delivered to the service, with the last of 50 scheduled aircraft being due for completion during 1987. For more than 15 years the Galaxy remained the world's largest military aircraft, only now being eclipsed by the Soviet Antonov An-124 'Condor'.

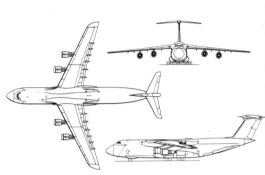

Lockheed C-5A Galaxy

The prototype C-5B Galaxy is towed into position before making its maiden flight on 10 September 1985 at the Lockheed plant at Marietta, Georgia.

A large number of C-5s have received this 'Euro One' camouflage scheme, but it has caused severe overheating problems and a lighter scheme is likely to be adopted.

Specification: Lockheed C-5B Galaxy
Origin: USA
Type: heavy logistics transport
Powerplant: four 19504-kg (43,000-lb) thrust General Electric TF39-GE-1C turbofan engines
Performance: maximum cruising speed 490 kts (908 km/h; 564 mph) at 25,000 ft (7620 m); initial rate of climb 1,725 ft (526 m) per minute; service ceiling at 278959-kg (615,000-lb) AUW 35,750 ft (10895 m); range with 118388-kg (261,000-lb) maximum payload 5526 km (3,434 miles)
Weights: empty equipped 169644 kg (374,000 lb); maximum take-off 379657 kg (837,000 lb)
Dimensions: span 67.88 m (222 ft 8.5 in); length 75.54 m (247 ft 10 in) height 19.85 m (65 ft 1.5 in); wing area 575.98 m² (6,200 sq ft)
Armament: none

Lockheed C-130A/G Hercules

Israel Jordan Pakistan Saudi Arabia Singapore South Africa Turkey United States Vietnam

Argentina Brazil Canada Indonesia Iran

There are few more important aircraft flying with the world's air forces than the ubiquitous **Lockheed C-130 Hercules**. In production since 1955, the aircraft has been successively developed to meet changing demands, but so sound was the basic design that current production models differ little externally from the first prototype. Built to a USAF specification for a turboprop-engined tactical transport, the prototype **YC-130** first flew on 23 August 1954. The requirement was for rough-base operation with good short-field performance. Rear ramp design was essential to facilitate loading of bulky items and to ensure paradrops with minimum dispersion: 11340 kg (25,000 lb) of cargo, 92 infantrymen or 64 paratroops were to be carried. Other features of the design were sturdy multi-wheel landing gear (the main units retracting into fuselage blisters) to keep the fuselage level at truck-bed height, and a high-set wing above the hold.

The first production **C-130A** flew on 7 April 1955, followed by 192 for the USAF and 12 for the RAAF. First USAF unit to fly the new transport ws the 463rd Tactical Control Wing at Ardmore AFB from December 1956. Gross weight of the early aircraft was 46266 kg (102,000 lb) and the clear cargo volume 12.19 by 3.05 by 2.74 m (40 by 10 by 9 ft). The **C-130B** entered production in 1958 and incorporated the Allison T56-A-7 with four-blade Hamilton Standard propellers permitting an increase in gross weight to 61,235 kg (135,000 lb) with increased fuel capacity. Speed was increased by 13 kts (24 km/h; 15 mph). A total of 186 was built

including 29 for export. Nine C-130Bs were converted to serve alongside five new-build WC-130Bs for weather reconnaissance missions.

The long-range **C-130E** was built to meet a Military Air Transport Service (MATS) requirement for a transoceanic-range interim aircraft pending delivery of the Lockheed C-141. Fitted with two 5148-litre (1,360-US gal) wing tanks on inboard pylons plus increased internal fuel and with a strengthened structure, gross weight was increased to 70307 kg (155,000 lb). Range with a 9072-kg (20,000-lb) payload is 7411 km (4,605 miles), and maximum payload is 20412 kg (45,000 lb). Acquired by Tactical Airlift Command (TAC) from 1963, this model bore the brunt of tactical transport work in Vietnam and has been widely exported. The civil **Hercules L-100** (21 built) is a demilitarized version of the C-130E and is flown by several air forces. Six C-130Es were converted to WC-130Es from 1965 to 1969, these featuring increased range and enhanced data-link technology compared to the WC-130Bs. All six continue to serve today.

The C-130 has been developed in many variants and most are covered separately. Of note were the sole **NC-130B** boundary layer control research conversion (of which the **C-130C** production version was not built) and the ski-equipped **C-130D** variant (12 built) of the C-130A for use in the Antarctic. In US Navy service the C-130B and C-130E became the **C-130F** (originally the **GV-1U**, of which seven were built) and **C-130G** (four built) respectively.

Specification: Lockheed C-130A Hercules
Origin: USA
Type: tactical transport
Powerplant: four 2796-ekW (3,750-eshp) Allison T56-A-1A turboprop engines
Performance: maximum speed 330 kts (612 km/h; 380 mph) at 30,000 ft (9145 m); cruising speed 290 kts (540 km/h; 335 mph); initial rate of climb 1,700 ft (518 m) per minute; service ceiling 41,300 ft (12590 m); range with 11703-kg (25,800-lb) payload 4667 km (2,900 miles)
Weights: empty 26911 kg (59,328 lb); maximum take-off 56336 kg (124,200 lb)
Dimensions: span 40.41 m (132 ft 7 in); length 29.79 m (97 ft 9 in); height 11.66 m (38 ft 3 in); wing area 162.11 m² (1,745 sq ft)
Armament: none

A Lockheed C-130E of No. 16 Squadron, Royal Saudi Air Force, based at Riyadh.

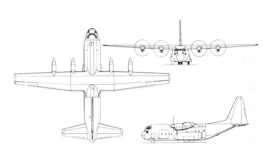

Lockheed C-130A (radar not fitted)

This C-130B Hercules serves with the Royal Jordanian Air Force, flying with No. 8 Squadron based at Amman-King Abdullah air base. This C-130B serves alongside four C-130Hs.

This is one of the few remaining C-130As still in original configuration, with three-bladed props and short nose. This aircraft serves with the 105th TAS, 118th TAG, Tennessee Air National Guard.

Lockheed C-130H/K Hercules

Algeria · Argentina · Australia · Belgium · Bolivia · Brazil · Cameroon · Canada · Chad · Chile · Denmark · Egypt · Gabon · Greece · Honduras

Indonesia · Iran · Israel · Italy · Japan · Jordan · Kuwait · Libya · Malaysia · Morocco · New Zealand · Niger · Nigeria · Norway · Oman

Peru · Philippines · Portugal · Saudi Arabia · Singapore

Spain · Sudan · Sweden

Thailand · Tunisia · United Arab Emirates · United Kingdom · United States · Venezuela · Yemen · Zaïre

This Lockheed C-130H is one of three serving with Eskadrille 721, Royal Danish Air Force.

Manufacture of the planned 503 copies of the C-130E version of the Hercules was completed in February 1975, but by then the company already had the next improved model in production with derated T56-A-15 engines, revised centre-section structure and improved brakes. This was the **Lockheed C-130H Hercules**, the current production transport type still rolling off the Marietta line at the rate of three aircraft per month. The first C-130H variant was the HC-130H ordered from 1964 for the Aerospace Rescue and Recovery Service for catching re-entering spacecraft. This specialized type first featured the more powerful Allison T56-A-15 engines of 3661 ekW (4,910 eshp) derated to 3362 ekW (4,508 eshp). Ferry range is extended to 8803 km (5,470 miles) and the aircraft enjoys an improved wing and more up-to-date avionics. The first transport version followed shortly after the recovery type from 1968. The **LC-130R** is the ski-equipped version for US Navy Antarctic use. A total of 15 WC-130Hs were produced from C-130H and HC-130H conversions to replace the early WC-130Bs. The WC-130H features an auxiliary fuel tank in the main cabin and an increased crew. One WC-130H has been lost.

Ordered from 1965 for the Royal Air Force was the **C-130K** designated **Hercules C.Mk 1**. Sixty-six were produced from 1966, and these were basically similar to the C-130H but with a British avionics fit. Marshall of Cambridge was awarded the UK support

contract and at an early stage converted one aircraft, XV208, to **Hercules W.Mk 2** standard for meteorological research.

With more than adequate power available, Lockheed produced a stretched version of the civil L-100 by adding 2.54 m (8 ft 4 in) to the fuselage to produce the **L-100-20**. Among other operators, this model is in service with the Gabonese, Peruvian and Philippine air forces. Dating from 1968, the L-100-20 was followed in 1970 by the **L-100-30** with a total stretch of 4.57 m (15 ft) increasing capacity to 128 infantrymen or 92 fully equipped paratroops. Thirty of the RAF Hercules have now been converted to this standard as the **Hercules C.Mk 3**, and the designation of such aircraft produced by the parent company is **C-130H-30**.

The versatility of the Hercules is clearly demonstrated through the specialized entries and there is no doubt that the type will continue to surprise through its longevity and adaptability. In Vietnam the aircraft dropped the USAF's heaviest bombs to create cleared landings for helicopter use, and the latest **C-130-MP** maritime patrol variant is in service with the Indonesian and Malaysian air forces. A high-technology testbed developed by Lockheed from the L-100-20, the **HTTB**, flew in June 1984 as a STOL research vehicle, and an AEW version with BAe Nimrod-type nose and tail fairings is planned. At the time of writing in spring 1986 total sales of all models had reached 1,804.

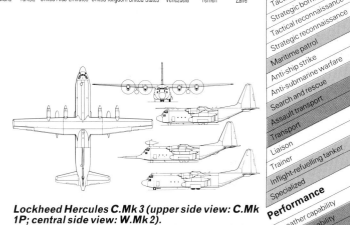

Lockheed Hercules C.Mk 3 (upper side view: C.Mk 1P; central side view: W.Mk 2).

This Lockheed C-130H serves with No. 36 Squadron, Royal Australian Air Force, flying from Richmond. No. 36 is one of two Hercules-equipped units, the other being No. 37, also at Richmond.

This Hercules C. Mk 3 shows its stretched fuselage to advantage. Thirty RAF Hercules were 'stretched' by Marshall of Cambridge, giving a marked improvement in payload capability.

Specification: Lockheed C-130H Hercules
Origin: USA
Type: tactical transport
Powerplant: four 3362-ekW (4,508-ehp) Allison T56-A-15 turboprop engines
Performance: maximum speed 333 kts (618 km/h; 384 mph) at 30,000 ft (9145 m); cruising speed 326 kts (603 km/h; 375 mph); initial rate of climb 1,900 ft (579 m) per minute; service ceiling 42,900 ft (13075 m); range with 9072-kg (20,000-lb) payload 8264 km (5,135 miles)
Weights: empty 34827 kg (76,780 lb); maximum take-off 79379 kg (175,000 lb)
Dimensions: span 40.41 m (132 ft 7 in); length 29.79 m (97 ft 9 in); height 11.66 m (38 ft 3 in); wing area 162.11 m² (1,745 sq ft)
Armament: none

Role
Fighter
Close support
Counter-insurgency
Tactical strike
Strategic bomber
Tactical reconnaissance
Strategic reconnaissance
Maritime patrol
Anti-ship strike
Anti-submarine warfare
Search and rescue
Assault transport
Transport
Liaison
Trainer
Inflight-refuelling tanker
Specialized

Performance
All-weather capability
Rough field capability
STOL capability
VTOL capability
Airspeed 0-250 mph
Airspeed 250 mph-Mach 1
Airspeed Mach 1 plus
Ceiling 0-20,000 ft
Ceiling 20,000-40,000 ft
Ceiling 40,000 ft plus
Range 0-1,000 miles
Range 1,000-3,000 miles
Range 3,000 miles plus

Weapons
Air-to-air missiles
Air-to-surface missiles
Cruise missiles
Cannon
Trainable guns
Naval weapons
Nuclear-capable
Rockets
'Smart' weapon kit
Weapon load 0-4,000 lb
Weapon load 4,000-15,000 lb
Weapon load 15,000 lb plus

Avionics
Electronic Counter Measures
Electronic Support Measures
Search radar
Fire control radar
Look-down/shoot-down
Terrain-following radar
Forward-looking infra-red
Laser
Television

Lockheed C-140 Jet Star

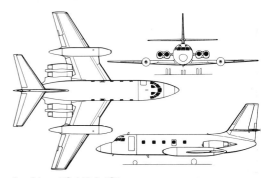

A Lockheed C-140A JetStar of Air Force Communications Command, US Air Force.

Role

Fighter
Close support
Counter-insurgency
Tactical strike
Strategic bomber
Tactical reconnaissance
Strategic reconnaissance
Maritime patrol
Anti-ship strike
Anti-submarine warfare
Search and rescue
Assault transport
Transport
Liaison
Trainer
Inflight-refuelling tanker
Specialized

Performance

All-weather capability
Rough field capability
STOL capability
VTOL capability
Airspeed 0-250 mph
Airspeed 250 mph-Mach 1
Airspeed Mach 1 plus
Ceiling 0-20,000 ft
Ceiling 20,000-40,000 ft
Ceiling 40,000 ft plus
Range 0-1,000 miles
Range 1,000-3,000 miles
Range 3,000 miles plus

Weapons

Air-to-air missiles
Air-to-surface missiles
Cruise missiles
Cannon
Trainable guns
Naval weapons
Nuclear-capable
Rockets
'Smart' weapon kit
Weapon load 0-4,000 lb
Weapon load 4,000-15,000 lb
Weapon load 15,000 lb plus

Avionics

Electronic Counter Measures
Electronic Support Measures
Search radar
Fire control radar
Look-down/shoot-down
Terrain-following radar
Forward-looking infra-red
Laser
Television

On 4 September 1957 the private-venture prototype (N329J) of Lockheed's Model 1329 jet-powered utility transport made its first flight from the Lockheed Air Terminal at Burbank, California. The design and development of the type had been initiated to meet a USAF requirement for a utility transport (UCX, utility transport experimental) which the service had intimated it wished to procure 'off-the-shelf' as soon as budgeting allowed.

Originating from a team headed by Clarence L. ('Kelly') Johnson, the aeroplane soon to be named **Lockheed JetStar** had a fuselage sized for a crew of two and 10 passengers, a low-set wing with 30° of sweepback, a tail unit with all-swept surfaces, and tricycle landing gear with twin wheels on each unit. Selected powerplant was the Curtiss-Wright TJ37 turbojet, a licence-built version of the 2200-kg (4,850-lb) thrust Bristol Orpheus, and the two prototypes were powered by British-built examples of this engine, one pod-mounted Caravelle fashion on each side of the rear fuselage. However, decision by Curtiss-Wright not to manufacture the TJ37 then resulted in selection of the 1361-kg (3,300-lb)

thrust Pratt & Whitney JT12A-6, whose lower thrust required the use of four engines, two in podded pairs on each side of the fuselage. Such an arrangement was first tested on the second prototype, which was also guinea pig for a slipper fuel tank on each wing. This finalized the overall configuration of the initial production **JetStar 6** that differed only in having a fuselage lengthened by 48.3 cm (1 ft 7 in) and pneumatic de-icing boots on all aerofoil leading edges. Production of JetStars of all versions totalled 204, including the prototypes, and included the **JetStar 8** with more powerful JT12A-8 engines and the **JetStar II** with 1678-kg (3,700-lb) thrust Garrett TFE731-3 turbofans and improved wing slipper tanks.

USAF procurement was small, comprising five **C-140A** navaid calibration aircraft, five **C-140B** utility transports and six **VC-140B** VIP transports; all were similar to initial production JetStar 6s, and the C-140Bs were soon converted to VC-140B configuration. Two similar **UV-1** aircraft for the US Navy were cancelled, and only small numbers were procured by foreign air arms.

Specification: Lockheed JetStar 8
Origin: USA
Type: light utility transport
Powerplant: four 1497-kg (3,300-lb) thrust Pratt & Whitney JT12A-8 turbojet engines
Performance: maximum speed 492 kts (911 km/h; 566 mph) at 21,200 ft (6460 m); economic cruising speed 440 kts (816 km/h; 507 mph) at 37,000 ft (11280 m); initial rate of climb 5,200 ft (1585 m) per minute; service ceiling 37,400 ft (11400 m); range with maximum payload and 45 minutes reserve fuel 3412 km (2,120 miles)
Weights: empty operating 10013 kg (22,074 lb); maximum take-off 19051 kg (42,000 lb)
Dimensions: span 16.59 m (54 ft 5 in); length 18.41 m (60 ft 5 in); height 6.22 m (20 ft 5 in); wing area 50.40 m² (542.5 sq ft)
Armament: none

Lockheed C-140 JetStar

This C-140A belongs to the 1866th FCS, AFCC, and wears the subdued 'European One' colour scheme. It is used for calibration of ground navaids.

The VC-140B JetStar is equipped for VIP transport duties. This example belongs to the 58th MAS, based at Ramstein. The VIP role of the VC-140B has allowed it to escape the 'European One' scheme.

Lockheed C-141 StarLifter

United States

A Lockheed C-141B StarLifter of Military Airlift Command, US Air Force.

With an air transport fleet composed almost entirely of piston-engined aircraft in the late 1950s, the USAF's Military Air Transport Service was inadequately equipped for its growing worldwide responsibility. In May 1960 the USAF's Specific Operational Requirement 182 was drawn up, and Requests for Proposals accordingly circulated to US manufacturers. From submissions received, Lockheed was announced winner and on 13 March 1961 awarded an initial contract for five DT & E aircraft. SOR 182 specified an aircraft to airlift a payload of 27216 kg (60,000 lb) over a range of 6477 km (4,025 miles), and Lockheed's proposal probably gained favour by using proven ideas adopted from the C-130 Hercules. Thus the new design had the C-130's high-wing configuration and main landing gear units retracting into fuselage side fairings to maximize cabin volume, and a similar main loading door/ramp in the rear fuselage for straight-in cargo/vehicle loading. Conspicuous differences, apart from size, were the T-tail and podded turbofan engines pylon-mounted beneath the wings.

Given the basic designation **Lockheed C-141**, the first example (61-2775) was flown on 17 December 1963; just over 16 months later, on 23 April 1965, the type had become operational with Military Airlift Command, the successor to MATS. Operated by a flight crew of five, these aircraft were soon providing a daily service across the Pacific, outward bound with up to 138 troops or some 28440 kg (62,700 lb) of cargo, and returning with the casualties of growing conflict in Vietnam, the main cabin having room for 80 stretchers and 23 medical attendants. The last of 284 **C-141A StarLifter** aircraft was delivered to the USAF in February 1968.

Experience showed that the C-141A frequently ran out of cabin volume long before its maximum payload weight had been loaded. This problem was resolved from 1976 onward by a programme that lengthened the fuselage by 7.11 m (23 ft 4 in) and at the same time provided an inflight-refuelling capability. The prototype **YC-141B** conversion was flown on 24 March 1977, and on 29 June 1982 the last of the 270 surviving C-141As had been converted to the new **C-141B** configuration, ahead of schedule and below projected cost. This programme has, in effect, provided MAC with 90 additional transports of C-141A capacity that require no extra crew.

Lockheed C-141B StarLifter

All surviving C-141s were converted to C-141B standard by stretching the fuselage. This prevents the aircraft 'bulking out' before maximum payload weight is reached.

The C-141B has seen active service in Vietnam and in the invasion of Grenada, as well as providing logistic support for countless smaller operations of equal importance.

Specification: Lockheed C-141B StarLifter
Origin: USA
Type: strategic troop/cargo transport
Powerplant: four 9526-kg (21,000-lb) thrust Pratt & Whitney TF33-7 turbofan engines
Performance: maximum cruising speed 492 kts (912 km/h; 567 mph); long-range cruising speed 430 kts (797 km/h; 495 mph); initial rate of climb 2,920 ft (890 m) per minute; range with maximum payload 4723 km (2,935 miles); ferry range 10284 km (6,390 miles)
Weights: empty 67186 kg (148,120 lb); maximum take-off 155582 kg (343,000 lb)
Dimensions: span 48.74 m (159 ft 11 in); length 51.29 m (168 ft 3.5 in); height 11.96 m (39 ft 3 in); wing area 299.88 m² (3,228.0 sq ft)
Armament: none

Role

Fighter
Close support
Counter-insurgency
Tactical strike
Strategic bomber
Tactical reconnaissance
Strategic reconnaissance
Maritime patrol
Anti-ship strike
Anti-submarine warfare
Search and rescue
Assault transport
Transport
Liaison
Trainer
Inflight-refuelling tanker
Specialized

Performance

All-weather capability
Rough field capability
STOL capability
VTOL capability
Airspeed 0-250 mph
Airspeed 250 mph-Mach 1
Airspeed Mach 1 plus
Ceiling 0-20,000 ft
Ceiling 20,000-40,000 ft
Ceiling 40,000 ft plus
Range 0-1,000 miles
Range 1,000-3,000 miles
Range 3,000 miles plus

Weapons

Air-to-air missiles
Air-to-surface missiles
Cruise missiles
Cannon
Trainable guns
Naval weapons
Nuclear-capable
Rockets
'Smart' weapon kit
Weapon load 0-4,000 lb
Weapon load 4,000-15,000 lb
Weapon load 15,000 lb plus

Avionics

Electronic Counter Measures
Electronic Support Measures
Search radar
Fire control radar
Look-down/shoot-down
Terrain-following radar
Forward-looking infra-red
Laser
Television

Lockheed EP-3 Orion

United States

For weapons to be applied most effectively, knowledge of the potential opposition is essential. Nowhere is this more true than in the area of electronics. Modern navies (especially) depend upon a wide range of communications and identification systems in order to function. It therefore follows that detailed information about the characteristics of radars and radios is necessary if they are to be avoided or (better still) neutralized. For this reason, the major navies have long employed a range of electronic intelligence (Elint) vehicles, including aircraft. The US Navy had used the Lockheed EC-121 version of the Constellation airliner, but by the mid-1960s these aircraft were becoming outdated.

Initially the US Navy converted one P-3A (BuNo 149673) to **Lockheed EP-3A Orion** configuration for use by the Naval Air Test Center (NATC), the Naval Weapons Laboratory (NWL) and latterly Air Test & Evaluation Squadron One (VX-1) at NAS Patuxent River. The aircraft was fitted with additional radomes and used to test a range of electronic surveillance equipment. The magnetic anomaly detector (MAD) boom on the tail was deleted. In 1969 two P-3Bs (BuNos 149669 and 149678) were converted into **EP-3B** aircraft for use with VQ-1; both were subsequently updated to **EP-3E** standard, but were maintained by the same squadron. Between 1971 and 1975, 10 more powerful EP-3Es entered service with the two operational fleet air reconnaissance countermeasures

squadrons, VQ-1 and VQ-2, which are assigned the task of giving 'signal warfare support' to various units, particularly to the large aircraft carriers. VQ-1 operates out of NAS Agana on Guam and VQ-2 covers the Mediterranean and Eastern Atlantic from its base at NAS Rota in Spain.

The EP-3E is a modification of the basic patrol P-3A with the anti-submarine warfare equipment replaced by electronic equipment for analysing radar signals. The new electronics installed within the EP-3E include the ALQ-110 signals-gathering system from United Technology Laboratory, the ALD-8 radio direction finder from E-Systems, the ALR-52 automatic frequency-measuring receiver from ARGO-Systems, and the ALR-60 from GTE-Sylvania for the multiple recording of radio communications. Externally, the main features which distinguish the EP-3E from the conventional P-3 is a flat, circular radome under the forward fuselage, and two oblong black antennae domes on top of and underneath the fuselage. The work of these aircraft involves collecting, storing, and analysing signals emitted by radar or radio: major surface vessels employ dozens of separate systems and if the signals are successfully analysed, it is possible to identify the installations, their purpose and range. To make the task of the squadrons as difficult as possible, the Soviet navy frequently alters the radiation patterns of its ships.

Specification: Lockheed EP-3 Orion
Origin: USA
Type: Elint platform
Powerplant: four 3661-kW (4,910-hp) Allison T56-A-15 turboprop engines
Performance: maximum speed 380 kts (703 km/h; 437 mph) at 15,000 ft (4570 m); patrol speed 180 kts (333 km/h; 207 mph); initial rate of climb 2,175 ft (663 m) per minute; service ceiling 28,000 ft (8535 m); maximum mission radius 4075 km (2,532 miles)
Weight: maximum take-off 64410 kg (142,000 lb)
Dimensions: span 30.38 m (99 ft 8 in); length 35.61 m (116 ft 10 in); height 10.27 m (33 ft 8.5 in); wing area 120.77 m² (1,300.0 sq ft)
Armament: none

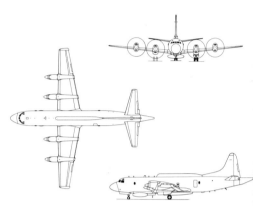

A Lockheed EP-3E of VQ-1, based at NAS Agana, Guam.

Lockheed EP-3E Orion

This EP-3A is one of those used by the Pacific Missile Test Center, based at Point Mugu, California, for miscellaneous missile tracking and calibration duties.

Squatting down on its nosewheel, this EP-3E of VQ-2 winds up to full power before taking off from RAF Wyton, an occasional port of call for this Rota-based Elint unit.

Lockheed F-19/RF-19

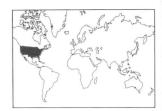

Increasingly sophisticated SAM defences had made direct overflights of hostile territory extremely dangerous even by the 1960s. Even the Mach 3+ Lockheed SR-71 cannot afford to make more than minor probing incursions of hostile territory that is protected by sophisticated radar and SAM defences, although it embodies many features to make it less conspicuous, particularly to radar. This low conspicuity to radar is now dubbed 'stealth' technology.

Pioneering work on radar-absorbent materials was conducted by the British company, Plessey, during the early 1950s, and flight trials were conducted mid great secrecy on Canberras and Lincolns of the Royal Aircraft Establishment. The experiments were at last partially successful, but the weight penalties of the early materials were such that they were not widely adopted. (There is some evidence to suggest that some Elint Canberras may have used small patches of the material.) The results of the experiments were passed on to the USA, who tested the material on at least one U-2C. No details have emerged of any operational use of the material.

Aircraft configuration, shape and structure were found to influence radar signature during the latter part of World War II, and there were several attempts to produce aircraft with extremely small radar signatures. Although no front line 'stealthy' aircraft types emerged, research continued, and by the late 1970s there were rumours that Lockheed was working on a 'stealth' project on behalf of the USAF Flight Dynamics Laboratory, possibly as an SR-71 replacement.

Tantalizing rumours about the new aircraft have emerged, but since even its funding has been kept secret any analysis of the aircraft must remain speculative. The aircraft is thought to be a product of the Lockheed 'Skunk Works', and may bear the USAF designation RF-19. (This would explain the apparent gap between the F/A-18 Hornet and F-20 Tigershark.) It is thought to bear the official acronym COSIRS, standing for COvert Survivable In-weather Reconnaisnce and Strike aircraft. About 30 are said to be operational, flying from a secret site in the massive Nellis Air Force Base area in the Nevada desert. The RF-19s, possibly known as 'Spectres', may operate from Tonopah, but this remains a matter for conjecture.

The RF-19 is said to use its structure and a sophisticated radar-absorbent skin to render it virtually invisible to radar. Sharp angles are avoided, and engines and their intakes are screened, as far as is possible. The latter feature also provides good protection from detection by infra-red seekers. Visual acquisition of the aircraft is difficult due to its small size and high speed.

The US Air Force continues to deny the existence of the RF-19 'Stealth', but questions about the project have been asked in the US Senate and Congress, and three mysterious crashes would seem to lend a little substance to the rumours. The latest crash occurred in August 1986; the crash site was immediately sealed off and no mention was made of the aircraft type involved. It soon emerged that the pilot was 'attached' to/ from the 4450th Tactical Group based at Nellis, and it seems likely that he was flying an RF-19. The aircraft are said to embody folding wings to allow transport on board Lockheed C-5 Galaxies, and the most fascinating rumours concern the operation of RF-19s from British airfields, variously reported as Alconbury, Binbrook, Mildenhall and Wethersfield.

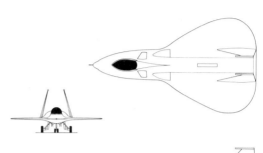

An artist's impression of the 'stealth fighter', thought to be a reconnaissance machine designated Lockheed RF-19. Rumours abound, but little hard fact has emerged.

Possible configuration of the Lockheed RF-19 'Stealth'

Up to 30 RF-19s are said to be operational with a USAF unit based somewhere in the massive Nellis AFB complex.

RF-19 has almost certainly already been deployed, and may have operated from British airfields. Rumours suggest that Wethersfield, Alconbury and Binbrook are the bases involved.

Specification: Lockheed F-19/RF-19 (provisional)
Origin: USA
Type: fighter/reconnaissance aircraft
Powerplant: two 7257-kg (16,000-lb) thrust General Electric F404-400 turbofan engines
Performance: maximum cruising speed more than Mach 2 or 1146 kts (2124 km/h; 1,320 mph) at high altitude; maximum operating height 65,600 ft (19995 m); maximum combat radius 1000 km (621 miles)
Weights: empty 10000 kg (22,046 lb); maximum take-off 15000 kg (33,069 lb)
Dimensions: span 9.65 m (31 ft 8 in); length 18.00 m (59 ft 0 in); height 4.00 m (13 ft 2 in)
Armament: unknown

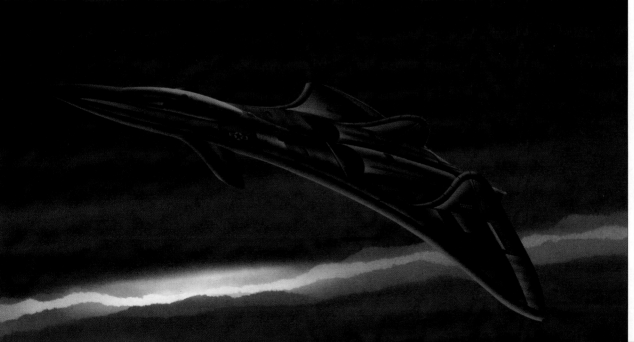

Role
- Fighter
- Close support
- Counter-insurgency
- Tactical strike
- Strategic bomber
- Tactical reconnaissance
- Strategic reconnaissance
- Maritime patrol
- Anti-ship strike
- Anti-submarine warfare
- Search and rescue
- Assault transport
- Transport
- Liaison
- Trainer
- Inflight-refuelling tanker
- Specialized

Performance
- All-weather capability
- Rough field capability
- STOL capability
- VTOL capability
- Airspeed 0-250 mph
- Airspeed 250 mph-Mach 1
- Airspeed Mach 1 plus
- Ceiling 0-20,000 ft
- Ceiling 20,000-40,000 ft
- Ceiling 40,000ft plus
- Range 0-1,000 miles
- Range 1,000-3,000 miles
- Range 3,000 miles plus

Weapons
- Air-to-air missiles
- Air-to-surface missiles
- Cruise missiles
- Cannon
- Trainable guns
- Naval weapons
- Nuclear-capable
- Rockets
- 'Smart' weapon kit
- Weapon load 0-4,000 lb
- Weapon load 4,000-15,000 lb
- Weapon load 15,000 lb plus

Avionics
- Electronic Counter Measures
- Electronic Support Measures
- Search radar
- Fire control radar
- Look-down/shoot-down
- Terrain-following radar
- Forward-looking infra-red
- Laser
- Television

A Lockheed HC-130B Hercules of the US Coast Guard

Lockheed HC-130 Hercules

First customer for a search-and-rescue variant of the Hercules was the US Coast Guard, 12 modified C-130Bs being ordered from 1958 as **Lockheed R8V-1G** aircraft, becoming **SC-130B** aircraft before the first deliveries in 1959. Later redesignated **HC-130B**, they featured additional crew posts and two scanner stations offering an unrestricted field of view. Space was provided for 74 stretchers. The basic avionics of the transport version were retained, including the APS-59 nose radar.

On 8 December 1964 Lockheed flew the first HC-130H, a rescue variant powered by Allison T-56-A-15s. Forty-three were ordered for the USAF Air Rescue Service and the Coast Guard have received 23 aircraft, with deliveries continuing. The HC-130H was ordered for a variety of work focusing on the recovery of downed aircrew but also including duties related to the space programme. The HC-130H carried additional equipment and two 6814-litre (1,800-US gal) fuel tanks in the cargo hold. Externally it mounted a large blister above the forward fuselage containing the Cook Electric re-entry tracking system for use in conjunction with the Gemini spacecraft. The most remarkable feature, however, is the Fulton recovery system: two 4.42-m (14.5-ft) nose-mounted tines are normally stowed back along the fuselage, but hinge forward to make a V-shaped fork. The aircraft

also carries recovery kits, including rafts and helium balloons. The latter, when inflated, carry aloft a 152-m (500-ft) line which is attached to a body harness. Flying at 122 kts (225 km/h; 140 mph) into wind the HC-130 snags the line with its recovery yoke, snatching the maximum 227-kg (500-lb) load from the surface. The balloon breaks away at a weak link and the rescued person or load is winched into the aircraft, the line being grapnelled to allow recovery into the cargo bay. Teflon lines from nose to fin and wingtips deflect the wire from the propellers in the event of a missed approach. The US Coast Guard's HC-130s do not usually operate with the Fulton gear. Four USAF HC-130Hs were subsequently converted for space capsule recovery as the **JHC-130H** version.

To cope with the increased rescue demands of the Vietnam War an additional 20 HC-130Hs were built but with outer wing pods for inflight-refuelling of helicopters. Designated **HC-130P**, these aircraft worked most successfully with the Sikorsky HH-3E to save many lives. The last rescue Hercules is the **HC-130N** which differs from earlier models in having advanced direction-finding equipment but without the Fulton gear and additional fuel tanks. Fifteen were delivered to the USAF from 1969, and with the earlier types these equip 10 squadrons across the world.

This Lockheed HC-130B serves with the US Coast Guard.

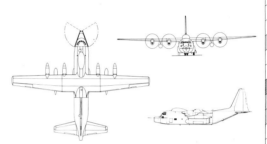

Lockheed HC-130P with Fulton gear (now rarely carried)

This RAF Woodbridge-based HC-130P of the 67th ARRS, US Air Force, is seen refuelling an HH-3 during a deployment to Keflavik, Iceland. The 67th ARRS is responsible for Europe-wide combat rescue.

The US Coast Guard operates a large fleet of HC-130 Hercules for rescue and patrol missions. This HC-130H does not carry the Fulton recovery system, in common with most current examples.

Specification: Lockheed HC-130H Hercules

Origin: USA

Type: rescue and recovery aircraft

Powerplant: four 3362-ekW (4,508-eshp) Allison T56-A-15 turboprop engines

Performance: maximum speed 325 kts (602 km/h; 374 mph) at 30,000 ft (9145 m); initial rate of climb 1,900 ft (579 m) per minute; service ceiling 33,000 ft (10060 m); range with maximum payload and reserve fuel 3792 km (2,356 miles)

Weights: empty 32936 kg (72,611 lb); maximum take-off 70307 kg (155,000 lb)

Dimensions: span 40.41 m (132 ft 7 in); length 30.73 m (100 ft 10 in); height 11.66 m (38 ft 3 in); wing area 162.16 m² (1,745.5 sq ft)

Armament: none

Lockheed KC-130 Hercules

Morocco　Saudi Arabia　Spain　United Kingdom　United States

This KC-130H is operated by Escuadron 312, Spanish air force, from Zaragoza.

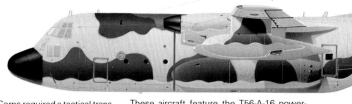

Argentina　Brazil　Indonesia　Israel　Italy

Role
Fighter
Close support
Counter-insurgency
Tactical strike
Strategic bomber
Tactical reconnaissance
Strategic reconnaissance
Maritime patrol
Anti-ship strike
Anti-submarine warfare
Search and rescue
Assault transport
Transport
Liaison
Trainer
Inflight-refuelling tanker
Specialized

Performance
All-weather capability
Rough field capability
STOL capability
VTOL capability
Airspeed 0-250 mph
Airspeed 250 mph-Mach 1
Airspeed Mach 1 plus
Ceiling 0-20,000 ft
Ceiling 20,000-40,000 ft
Ceiling 40,000 ft plus
Range 0-1,000 miles
Range 1,000-3,000 miles
Range 3,000 miles plus

Weapons
Air-to-air missiles
Air-to-surface missiles
Cruise missiles
Cannon
Trainable guns
Naval weapons
Nuclear-capable
Rockets
'Smart' weapon kit
Weapon load 0-4,000 lb
Weapon load 4,000-15,000 lb
Weapon load 15,000 lb plus

Avionics
Electronic Counter Measures
Electronic Support Measures
Search radar
Fire-control radar
Look-down/shoot-down
Terrain-following radar
Forward-looking infra-red
Laser
Television

The US Marine Corps required a tactical transport which could double as an inflight-refuelling tanker using the probe and drogue system. In August 1957 two US Air Force C-130As were borrowed and each fitted with two 1915-litre (506-US gal) tanks in the fuselage and two underwing pods containing the hose equipment. So successful were the trials that 46 **Lockheed KC-130F Hercules** were ordered for delivery from 1960. The KC-130F is based on the C-130B airframe, initially with Allison T56-A-7 engines but later re-engined with the 3661-ekW (4,910-eshp) T56-A-16. An easily removable fuselage tank holding 13,627 litres (3,600 US gal) is fitted, and the two equipment pods enable fuel transfer at the rate of 1136 litres (300 US gal) per minute. As well as the additional fuel, the tanker is able to transfer its own surplus fuel. Originally designated **GV-1**, the first production aircraft flew on 22 January 1960. The type currently equips VMGR-152, -252 and -352 and VR-22 of the US Navy.

To cope with attrition the USMC ordered 14 **KC-130R** tankers based on the C-130H.

These aircraft feature the T56-A-16 powerplant and pylon mounted fuel tanks with an extra 10296 litres (2,720 US gal) of fuel. Fuelling of this variant is by a single point. Initial deliveries were to VMGR-352 at MCAS El Toro, California. Although not in service with US forces, the **KC-130H** (similar in most respects to the KC-130R) has been successfully exported to six countries. The most recent USMC variant is the **KC-130T**, of which at least 11 are on order for VMGR-234. This model has updated avionics, a new search radar and improved navigation systems.

The Falklands war resulted in an urgent RAF demand for increased tanker support. Marshals of Cambridge, the UK support contractor for the Hercules, started work in May 1982 on converting a standard Hercules C.Mk 1 to tanker configuration. Four ex-Andover 4091-litre (900-Imp gal) tanks were fitted in the fuselage and a single Flight Refuelling FR Mk 17B Hose Drum Unit (HDU) attached to the ramp door. First flight was on 7 June 1982, and within three months four aircraft had been converted. Designated **Hercules C.Mk 1K**, six such aircraft are operated by the Lyneham Transport Wing.

Specification: Lockheed KC-130F Hercules
Origin: USA
Type: inflight-refuelling tanker
Powerplant: four 3661-ekW (4,910-eshp) Allison T56-A-16 turboprop engines
Performance: maximum speed 330 kts (612 km/h; 380 mph) at 30,000 ft (9145 m); refuelling speed 308 kts (571 km/h; 355 mph); range at 295 kts (547 km/h; 340 mph) to transfer 14061 kg (31,000 lb) of fuel 1609 km (1,000 miles)
Weights: empty 31434 kg (69,300 lb); maximum take-off 61235 kg (135,000 lb)
Dimensions: span 40.41 m (132 ft 7 in); length 29.79 m (97 ft 9 in); height 11.66 m (38 ft 3 in); wing area 162.16 m² (1,745.5 sq ft)
Armament: none

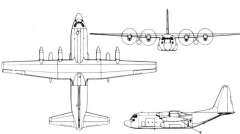

Lockheed KC-130H

This KC-130H was operated by Lockheed-Georgia as a demonstrator, and is seen here drumming up interest from the Colombian air force by refuelling a quartet of its Cessna A-37s.

A prototype AV-8B, representing the future of Marine air power, refuels from a type that forms the backbone of its current fleet, a Lockheed KC-130R of VMGR-352 based at MCAS El Toro.

An early Lockheed L-188 Electra

Lockheed L-188 Electra

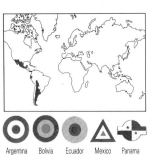

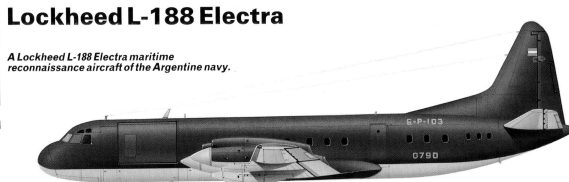

A Lockheed L-188 Electra maritime reconnaissance aircraft of the Argentine navy.

When the Vickers Viscount turboprop airliner began to break into the North American market in the mid-1950s, it not only highlighted to airline operators in that continent the appeal to passengers of turbine-powered aircraft, but also gave an emphatic signal to US manufacturers that it was high time they began to get into the same league. Lockheed took the hint, gaining from American Airlines in June 1955 an initial order for an aircraft which the company had designed to the requirements of this operator for use on domestic routes.

Identified as the **Lockheed L-188 Electra**, the new airliner was a turboprop-powered low-wing monoplane with a circular-section fuselage that provided accommodation for 72 passengers in its initial **L-188A** version, though subsequent revision of interior layout made it possible to accommodate up to 98 passengers in a high-density arrangement. A longer-range version with greater fuel capacity and certificated for operation at a higher gross weight was introduced as the **L-188C**, and a generally similar export version, which differed primarily by having track-mounted

seats, was known as the **L-188B**. The prototype (N1881) was flown for the first time on 6 December 1957 and just over a year later, delayed slightly because of industrial action by airline pilots, the type began domestic service with Eastern Air Lines. Airline and passenger reaction was excellent, and with an order book for more than 140 aircraft Lockheed believed they had a winner.

Unfortunately this was not to be the case. Just over a year after the type's introduction into service three aircraft had been lost, the last two in mid-air disintegrations, and a restriction was imposed which reduced cruising speed from 347 to 256 kts (644-475 km/h; 400-295 mph). By the time the restriction was lifted, on 5 February 1961, passenger confidence in the Electra had gone, and the turboprop airliner as a type had lost favour to newly-introduced aircraft powered by turbojets. In 1962 many airlines began to dispose of their Electras, some of them being converted for use as cargo carriers, and of the total of only 170 built a small number found themselves in military service, used primarily in the utility transport role.

Specification: Lockheed L-188A Electra
Origin: USA
Type: medium-range airliner
Powerplant: four 2796-ekW (3,750-eshp) Allison 501-D13/13A turboprop engines
Performance: maximum speed 389 kts (721 km/h; 448 mph) at 12,000 ft (3660 m); cruising speed 324 kts (600 km/h; 373 mph); initial rate of climb 1,970 ft (600 m) per minute; service ceiling 28,400 ft (8655 m); range with maximum payload 3540 km (2,200 miles)
Weights: empty 26036 kg (57,400 lb); maximum take-off 51256 kg (113,000 lb)
Dimensions: span 30.18 m (99 ft 0 in); length 31.85 m (104 ft 6 in); height 10.00 m (32 ft 10 in); wing area 120.77 m² (1,300.0 sq ft)
Armament: none

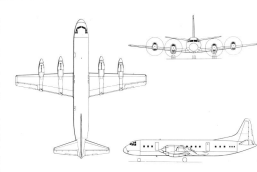

Lockheed L-188 Electra

Argentina procured a handful of Electras after the Falklands war to replace its elderly Neptunes in the maritime reconnaissance and Sigint roles.

Bolivia's Lockheed Electras are used for passenger and freight transport duties, and seem likely to continue in service for some years to come. The Electra's only military users are all found in Latin America.

Lockheed MC-130 Hercules

A Lockheed MC-130H of the Rhein-Main based 7th SOS, US Air Force.

In the late 1970s the USAF began a programme of improving a number of HC-130Es for clandestine work throughout the world. Eventually 14 aircraft were involved and given the designation **Lockheed C-130E-I Hercules**, later changed to **MC-130E**. In the 'Combat Talon' programme the type was equipped for all-weather day/night infiltration and exfiltration of special forces and agents. Additional roles include psychological warfare, resupply, aerial reconnaissance and STAR (Surface To Air Retrievals). The nose suffered yet further indignities with the fitting (to some aircraft) of the Fulton retrieval yoke and also terrain-following radar. Other equipment includes precision ground mapping radar, an inertial navigation system, secure voice UHF/VHF/FM radios, a retractable FLIR pod and an ALQ-87 ECM pod under the port wing. A crew of up to 11 is carried.

From 1979 a number of 'Combat Talon II' aircraft were supplied. These later models are equipped with more advanced avionics in-

cluding the ALR-46 radar-warning receiver and ALE-27 chaff dispenser. Importantly, they are also equipped for inflight-refuelling from the Boeing KC-135 or McDonnell Douglas KC-10. It is understood that some of the earlier MC-130Es are being retrofitted to this higher standard.

The MC-130s are distributed within three operational units. The 1st Special Operations Squadron, 3rd TFW is based at Clark AB, Philippines, whilst the European operator is the 7th SOS, 7575th SOG at Rhein-Main AB, West Germany. In the USA the 8th SOS, 1st SOW at Hurlburt Field, Eglin AFB, Florida has both an operational and training role. The latter unit supplied three aircraft, via Egypt, to fly in 90 special force troops for the abortive Iran rescue attempt in April 1980. The USAF plans to deploy 35 MC-130s by 1992, a reflection perhaps, of the type of limited conflict into which the USA sees itself being drawn in the future.

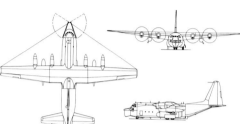

Lockheed MC-130E (Fulton gear not usually carried)

The US Air Force is the only operator of the MC-130, but other users have modified aircraft which are used for clandestine insertion duties. RAF C-130s of No. 47 Squadron's Special Forces Flight are a typical example.

A 'Combat Talon II' MC-130E of the 7th Special Operations Squadron. These aircraft are equipped to fly at low level in all weathers, and for inflight-refuelling.

Specification: Lockheed MC-130E Hercules
Origin: USA
Type: special tactical mission support aircraft
Powerplant: four 3020-ekW (4,050-ehp) Allison T56-A-7 turboprop engines
Performance: maximum speed 318 kts (589 km/h; 366 mph); speed for personnel airdrop 125 kts (232 km/h; 144 mph) at a minimum height of 50 ft (15 m); initial rate of climb 1,600 ft (488 m) per minute; unrefuelled range 3701 km (2,300 miles)
Weights: empty 33063 kg (72,892 lb); maximum take-off 70307 kg (155,000 lb)
Dimensions: span 40.41 m (132 ft 7 in); length 30.73 m (100 ft 10 in); height 11.66 m (38 ft 3 in); wing area 162.16 m² (1,745.5 sq ft)
Armament: none

Role
Fighter
Close support
Counter-insurgency
Tactical strike
Strategic bomber
Tactical reconnaissance
Strategic reconnaissance
Maritime patrol
Anti-ship strike
Anti-submarine warfare
Search and rescue
Assault transport
Transport
Liaison
Trainer
Inflight-refuelling tanker
Specialized

Performance
All-weather capability
Rough field capability
STOL capability
VTOL capability
Airspeed 0-250 mph
Airspeed 250 mph-Mach 1
Airspeed Mach 1 plus
Ceiling 0-20,000 ft
Ceiling 20,000-40,000 ft
Ceiling 40,000ft plus
Range 0-1,000 miles
Range 1,000-3,000 miles
Range 3,000 miles plus

Weapons
Air-to-air missiles
Air-to-surface missiles
Cruise missiles
Cannon
Trainable guns
Naval weapons
Nuclear-capable
Rockets
'Smart' weapon kit
Weapon load 0-4,000 lb
Weapon load 4,000-15,000 lb
Weapon load 15,000 lb plus

Avionics
Electronic Counter Measures
Electronic Support Measures
Search radar
Fire control radar
Look-down/shoot-down
Terrain-following radar
Forward-looking infra-red
Laser
Television

Lockheed Orion AEW & C

By the early 1960s air-defence equipment had so improved that the high-flying attack aircraft was no longer safe. Air forces then turned their attention to low-flying penetration, which delayed detection to the last minute. This new threat then had to be countered and the response was the development of specialized aircraft of the flying radar picket type long used by navies. The size of the radars involved had grown to such an extent that in 1957 Grumman tested the first aerodynamic prototype of the E-1B Tracer with a remarkable 9.14m (30ft) by 6.10m (20ft) 'rotodome' mounted above the fuselage. Other types featuring rotodomes followed, and as radar technology improved the ability to control air defence fighters and other aircraft added to the radar picket's role.

Although many air forces have a requirement for an airborne warning (and ideally control) aircraft, they are needed in relatively small numbers. Aircraft as complex and specialized as the Boeing E-3A Sentry and BAe Nimrod are beyond the pockets (and indeed requirements) of all but a few, so in recent years manufacturers have looked at the possibility of adapting existing types. The attraction to potential purchasers is the wider availability of spares and, if the basic type is already operated, economy of spares stockholdings. A further attraction to air forces operating the original design is the much reduced costs of training. Lockheed has suggested two developments, of the C-130 Hercules and the P-3 Orion, both of which

have obvious attraction. The **Lockheed P-3 AEW & C** flew in aerodynamic prototype form from the company's Palmdale works on 14 June 1984. Rebuilt from an ex-RAAF P-3B and given the civil registration N91LC, the aircraft features a 7.32-m (24-ft) diameter Randtron APA-171 rotodome above the rear fuselage. In due course the General Electric APS-138 radar (as on the Grumman E-2C Hawkeye) and 1553A communications and data handling system will be fitted.

Although it uses the same radar as the smaller E-2C Hawkeye, the Orion AEW&C is a very much more capable aircraft, with greater endurance and range capabilities and with a much larger cabin, which allows a larger number of operators and flight crew to be carried. Two operating crews could be put aboard, dramatically extending sortie endurance.

The same equipment has been proposed for an AEW&C variant of the C-130 Hercules, and this aircraft would offer similar advantages over the smaller Grumman aircraft. Both the Hercules and the Orion are in widespread service over the world, and many existing operators do have a requirement for an AEW aircraft of some sort.

Lockheed claims a 14-hour endurance for the AEW&C Orion, extendable with inflight-refuelling. Several countries have been identified as possible customers, including Australia, Canada, Japan and the US Navy. Deliveries could commence 28 months after the aircraft is put into production.

Specification: Lockheed Orion AEW & C
Origin: USA
Type: airborne early warning and control platform
Powerplant: four 3661-kW (4,910-hp) Allison T56-A-14 turboprop engines
Performance: cruising speed 200 kts (370 km/h; 230 mph) at 30,000 ft (9145 m); endurance 14 hours
Weight: maximum take-off 57833 kg (127,500 lb)
Dimensions: span 30.38 m (99 ft 8 in); length 35.61 m (116 ft 10 in); height 10.27 m (33 ft 8.5 in); wing area 120.77 m² (1,300.0 sq ft)
Armament: none

The prototype Lockheed Orion AEW&C aircraft.

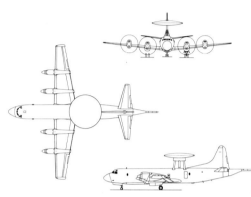

Lockheed Orion AEW&C

The Lockheed Orion AEW&C prototype was converted from an ex-Australian P-3B airframe, and was displayed, albeit without its radar fitted, at the 1985 Paris Air Salon.

At one time, the AEW&C Orion was a contender for the RAF's requirement for an AEW aircraft to replace its ageing Shackletons, in the face of serious problems with the Nimrod AEW.Mk 3.

Lockheed P-3A and P-3B Orion

New Zealand Norway Portugal Spain United States

In August 1957 Type Specification No. 146 was issued by the US Navy, calling for a new anti-submarine aircraft to replace the Lockheed P-2 Neptune. The Lockheed proposal was based on the company's L-188 Electra passenger airliner. In May 1958 Lockheed was awarded a contract largely on the basis of the strength of the aircraft's structure and its size, which was sufficient to house an extensive array of detection systems. Lockheed modified the third Electra airframe (N1883) as the prototype with a tail-mounted magnetic anomaly detector (MAD) boom and a ventral bulge simulating a weapons bay. Following extensive adaptations (including a shortening of the fuselage) the aircraft made a successful maiden flight as the YP3V-1 on 25 November 1959. The navy ordered an initial batch of seven aircraft in October 1960, and the first of these (BuNo 148883) flew in April of the following year. In 1962 the type was redesignated **Lockheed P-3A** and named **Orion**.

The P-3A entered service in the summer of 1962, with Patrol Squadron Eight (VP-8); other units soon followed, and by December 1963 Lockheed had delivered over 50 Orions to eight squadrons. After the production of 109 P-3As, Lockheed incorporated the DELTIC installation in an improvement programme. This doubled sonobuoy information-processing capability and also incorporated redesigned avionics. The first squadron to receive the new **P-3A DELTIC** was

VP-46 at Moffett Field, and within a short time most aircraft had been retrofitted.

In the summer of 1965, after three years experience and with 157 P-3As built, Lockheed started production of a new variant. The **P-3B** was fitted with the more powerful Allison T56-A-14 engine and was heavier than its predecessor, mainly through having provision for the AGM-12 Bullpup ASM, though it maintained basically the same electronics. The P-3B secured the first export orders and became operational with the Royal New Zealand and Norwegian air forces (five aircraft each), and with the RAAF (10 aircraft). From 1977 the USN's P-3Bs have been updated with improved navigation and acoustic-processing equipment and with provision for the AGM-84 Harpoon anti-ship missile. Production of the P-3B ceased in 1969, following the introduction of its successor, the P-3C.

P-3A/Bs remain in service with reserve units having been continuously improved. P-3As were converted to **RP-3A** standard (three aircraft) for oceanographic reconnaissance use by VXN-8, and to **WP-3A** standard (four aircraft) for weather reconnaissance by VW-4. At least five aircraft have been refitted for executive transport use as the **VP-3A**. In 1984 the Lockheed Aircraft Service Company was awarded an initial USN contract for the conversion of 30 aircraft to transport configuration as the **CP-3A**.

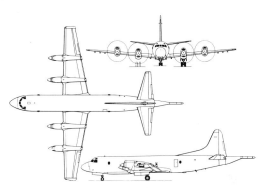

A Lockheed P-3B Orion of the Spanish air force.

Lockheed P-3B Orion

An interesting view of a US Navy P-3B bearing down on a target submarine. Production of the P-3B ended in 1969, and most US Navy aircraft have been exported or converted.

Norwegian Orions wear an overall dark grey colour scheme, with white code letters on each side of the fuselage roundel. This aircraft is a P-3B of 333 Skvadron, based at Andoya.

Specification: Lockheed P-3A Orion
Origin: USA
Type: 10-crew anti-submarine warfare and maritime patrol aircraft
Powerplant: four 3356-kW (4,500-hp) Allison T56-A-10W turboprop engines
Performance: maximum speed 380 kts (703 km/h; 437 mph) at 15,000 ft (4570 m); patrol speed 198 kts (367 km/h; 228 mph); initial rate of climb 2,175 ft (663 m) per minute; service ceiling 28,300 ft (8625 m); maximum mission radius 4075 km (2,532 miles)
Weights: empty 27216 kg (60,000 lb); maximum take-off 57833 kg (127,500 lb)
Dimensions: span 30.38 m (99 ft 8 in); length 35.61 m (116 ft 10 in); height 10.27 m (33 ft 8.5 in); wing area 120.77 m² (1,300.0 sq ft)
Armament: a combination of mines, depth bombs, torpedoes, sonobuoys and rockets can be carried to maximum weights of 3289 kg (7,250 lb) in the lower-fuselage weapons bay and of 7257 kg (16,000 lb) on the 10 underwing stations

Role
Fighter
Close support
Counter-insurgency
Tactical strike
Strategic bomber
Tactical reconnaissance
Strategic reconnaissance
Maritime patrol
Anti-ship strike
Anti-submarine warfare
Search and rescue
Assault transport
Transport
Liaison
Trainer
Inflight-refuelling tanker
Specialized

Performance
All-weather capability
Rough field capability
STOL capability
VTOL capability
Airspeed 0-250 mph
Airspeed 250 mph-Mach 1
Airspeed Mach 1 plus
Ceiling 0-20,000 ft
Ceiling 20,000-40,000 ft
Ceiling 40,000 ft plus
Range 0-1,000 miles
Range 1,000-3,000 miles
Range 3,000 miles plus

Weapons
Air-to-air missiles
Air-to-surface missiles
Cruise missiles
Cannon
Trainable guns
Naval weapons
Nuclear-capable
Rockets
'Smart' weapon kit
Weapon load 0-4,000 lb
Weapon load 4,000-15,000 lb
Weapon load 15,000 lb plus

Avionics
Electronic Counter Measures
Electronic Support Measures
Search radar
Fire control radar
Look-down/shoot-down
Terrain-following radar
Forward-looking infra-red
Laser
Television

Lockheed P-3C Orion

United States

Australia Iran Japan Netherlands

Although the P-3B offered superior power in comparison with the P-3A, there was a need for a more electronically advanced version of the Orion to counter advances in the technology of nuclear submarines. The result was the **Lockheed P-3C Orion**, first flown in September 1968. This much-improved type entered service with VP-56 in 1969. The primary advance was the adoption of the A-NEW system of sensors and control equipment, the heart of which was the UNIVAC ASQ-114 digital computer. This produced more easily interpretable data, allowing the crew more time to perform the task of hunting submarines. Other areas of modification with the P-3C included improved navigation and communications systems.

Since entering service, the P-3C has also been subjected to several important technological updates. The first produced the **P-3C Update I** in 1974 and involved expansion of the computer's memory and some modifications to the navigation system. The **P-3C Update II** programme, undertaken in 1977, involved the introduction of the ARS-3 sonobuoy system enabling the aircraft to locate buoys without having to overfly them and of an infra-red detection system (IRDS) allowing the aircraft to track automatically a detected target by day or night. Against this background of further electronic development,

Update II also conferred on the P-3C the ability to operate with the McDonnell Douglas AGM-84 Harpoon anti-ship missile. The third and most extensive modification, incorporated from 1984 in the **P-3C Update III** programme, involved the installation of the IBM Proteus signal processor which works more efficiently than the previous system. Also included were a new sonobuoy receiver and an improved auxiliary power unit. Now in development is the **P-3C Update IV** programme.

Export successes have been notable for such a complex and expensive aircraft. In 1975 the Imperial Iranian air force acquired six aircraft designated **P-3F** for long-range surface surveillance and anti-submarine warfare duties; these were basic P-3C models equipped for inflight-refuelling (the only P-3s with such a facility). Other operators include Australia, the Netherlands and Japan, making the Orion one of the most widely used aircraft in its field. In addition two P-3Cs were procured as weather reconnaissance **WP-3D** aircraft (N42RF and N43RF) for the National Oceanographic and Atmospheric Administration (NOAA). The 51st P-3C was modified with additional fuel capacity for atmospheric research and magnetic survey, and as the sole **RP-3D** this aircraft is operated by VXN-8 in 'Project Magnet'.

Specification: Lockheed P-3C Orion
Origin: USA
Type: 10-crew anti-submarine warfare and maritime patrol aircraft
Powerplant: four 3661-kW (4,910-hp) Allison T56-A-14 turboprop engines
Performance: maximum speed 411 kts (761 km/h; 473 mph) at 15,000 ft (4570 m); patrol speed 206 kts (381 km/h; 237 mph); initial rate of climb 1,950 ft (594 m) per minute; service ceiling 28,300 ft (8625 m); maximum mission radius 3835 km (2,383 miles)
Weights: empty 27892 kg (61,491 lb); maximum take-off 61235 kg (135,000 lb)
Dimensions: span 30.38 m (99 ft 8 in); length 35.61 m (116 ft 10 in); height 10.27 m (33 ft 8.5 in); wing area 120.77 m² (1,300.0 sq ft)
Armament: one 907-kg (2,000 lb) or three 454-kg (1,000-lb) mines, or eight depth bombs, or torpedoes, or combinations of these weapons in the lower-fuselage weapons bay, plus up to 7257 kg (16,000 lb) of mines, torpedoes, rockets or AGM-84A Harpoon anti-ship missiles on the 10 underwing stations, and 87 sonobuoys launched from tubes in the lower fuselage

A Lockheed P-3C Orion of 51 Kokutai, JMSDF, based at Shimofusa.

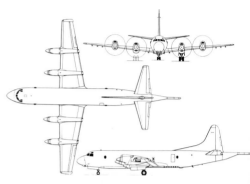

Lockheed P-3C Orion

This is one of two civil-registered WP-3D aircraft operated by the US Department of Commerce, on behalf of the National Oceanographic and Atmospheric Administration for long-range weather reconnaissance.

This Royal Australian Air Force P-3C belongs to No. 10 Squadron, based at Edinburgh. Australia's neighbour, New Zealand, operates the earlier P-3B.

Lockheed S-3 Viking

United States

The growing capability of the submarines in service with the Soviet navy in the 1960s, plus certain domestic factors, highlighted to the US Navy a need for an advanced carrier-borne ASW aircraft. In late 1966 procurement for this VSX requirement began, with Lockheed gaining in August 1969 an initial contract for development of such an aircraft under the designation **Lockheed S-3A**, later named **Viking**.

Lockheed made great efforts to ensure that its design submission, and ultimately the production aircraft, would give the US Navy the aircraft it needed, the company teaming with LTV (Ling-Temco-Vought) to benefit from the latter's experience in ship-based aircraft, and with Univac Federal Systems, specialists in ASW systems. LTV designed and built the engine pods, landing gear, tail unit and wing; Univac produced the complete ASW system; and Lockheed built the fuselage, integrated the systems and carried out final assembly and test. The first of eight pre-production **YS-3A** aircraft (BuNo 157992) made the type's maiden flight on 21 January 1972 and the first batch of production S-3As was authorized in April 1972. Just under two

years later, on 20 February 1974, the S-3A entered service with training squadron VS-41 at NAS North Island, San Diego. VS-21, also based at NAS North Island, was the first operational unit and in July 1975 took the S-3A for its first carrier deployment aboard the USS *John F. Kennedy*. When production ended in mid-1978, a total of 187 S-3As had been built.

In early 1980 demonstration examples of a Carrier Onboard Delivery (COD) **US-3A** and a tanker **KS-3A** were evaluated by the Navy but failed to gain orders, although three of the YS-3As and one-off KS-3A were later converted to US-3A configuration. Also in 1980, Lockheed was awarded a WSIP (Weapon System Improvement Program) contract to give the S-3As expanded ASW capability. This introduced a new generation of avionics and provisions to carry the Harpoon anti-ship missile. The first two WSIP conversions, designated **S-3B**, began service trials in 1985 and two more S-3As are currently undergoing modification; a decision whether to modify the remaining 160 S-3As to S-3B configuration will depend upon the test and evaluation programme now in progress.

A Lockheed S-3 Viking wearing toned-down insignia and the markings of VS-38 the 'Red Griffins'.

Lockheed S-3 Viking

Seen on the flight deck of USS America is this **S-3A Viking of VS-32 'Norsemen', home-based at NAS Cecil Field, Florida, but here forming a component of CVW-1 (Carrier Air Wing One).**

This VS-29 S-3A is landing on USS Kitty Hawk. **VS-29, the 'Vikings', are a Pacific Fleet anti-submarine warfare unit and are home based at NAS North Island, California.**

Specification: Lockheed S-3A Viking
Origin: USA
Type: carrier-based ASW aircraft
Powerplant: two 4207-kg (9,275-lb) thrust General Electric TF34-2 turbofan engines
Performance: maximum speed 450 kts (834 km/h; 518 mph) at 25,000 ft (7620 m); loiter speed 160 kts (296 km/h; 184 mph); initial rate of climb 4,200 ft (1280 m) per minute; service ceiling 35,000 ft (10670 m); combat range more than 3701 km (2,300 miles)
Weights: empty 12088 kg (26,650 lb); maximum take-off 23831 kg (52,539 lb)
Dimensions: span, open 20.93 m (68 ft 8 in); and folded 8.99 m (29 ft 6 in); length 16.26 m (53 ft 4 in) and with tail folded 15.06 m (49 ft 5 in); height 6.93 m (22 ft 9 in) and with tail folded 4.65 m (15 ft 3 in); wing area 55.55 m² (598.0 sq ft)
Armament: internal weapons bay for bombs, depth bombs, destructors, mines or torpedoes, plus two underwing pylons suitable for auxiliary fuel tanks, cluster bombs, flare launchers or rocket pods

Role

Fighter
Close support
Counter-insurgency
Tactical strike
Strategic bomber
Tactical reconnaissance
Strategic reconnaissance
Maritime patrol
Anti-ship strike
Anti-submarine warfare
Search and rescue
Assault transport
Transport
Liaison
Trainer
Inflight-refuelling tanker
Specialized

Performance

All-weather capability
Rough field capability
STOL capability
VTOL capability
Airspeed 0-250 mph
Airspeed 250 mph-Mach 1
Airspeed Mach 1 plus
Ceiling 0-20,000 ft
Ceiling 20,000-40,000 ft
Ceiling 40,000ft plus
Range 0-1,000 miles
Range 1,000-3,000 miles
Range 3,000 miles plus

Weapons

Air-to-air missiles
Air-to-surface missiles
Cruise missiles
Cannon
Trainable guns
Naval weapons
Nuclear-capable
Rockets
'Smart' weapon kit
Weapon load 0-4,000 lb
Weapon load 4,000-15,000 lb
Weapon load 15,000 lb plus

Avionics

Electronic Counter Measures
Electronic Support Measures
Search radar
Fire control radar
Look-down/shoot-down
Terrain-following radar
Forward-looking infra-red
Laser
Television

Lockheed SR-71

United States

Development of the **Lockheed SR-71** was shrouded in secrecy, and much 'information' about this remarkable type is based on assumption and analysis rather than on direct fact. The SR-71 came into service as a result of a decision by the Central Intelligence Agency to acquire an aircraft with both a higher service ceiling and a greater maximum speed than the Lockheed U-2. The new aircraft was to carry out clandestine reconnaissance over the USSR and other sensitive territory, and a contract was awarded to Lockheed in August 1959.

Because of the specific nature of the aircraft's requirements, including a maximum speed of Mach 3 and a ceiling of 85,000ft (25910m), unprecedented problems were encountered during design and construction. These problems emanated from the need to employ refined aerodynamics and construction materials to withstand the inevitable high temperatures. The airframe had to be constructed from titanium, and engineering problems arose with the propulsion and hydraulic systems, which were also constructed on the basis of new materials and techniques. As long range was also required at the high cruise speed, the aircraft has a highly swept delta wing with a camber on the leading edge to induce low drag.

It is believed that approximately 15 aircraft based on the design and designated **A-12** were delivered to the CIA from 1962; they were single-seaters, although one was modified as a trainer and two had an additional seat for a launch officer for the D-21 drone programme. A further three research prototypes (designated **YF-12A**) were built as two-seat interceptors in 1963, with Hughes ASG-18 radar. The A-12s, currently in store at Palmdale, were employed by the USAF for the CIA until the SR-71 (originally designated **RS-71**) came into service from 1964. The SR-71 has a more efficient airframe, greater fuel capacity and a more complex reconnaissance system, but is not fitted with a missile bay.

The first SR-71s were delivered in 1966 to the 4200th SRW, a new unit based at Beale AFB in California, where the special Boeing KC-135Q tankers of the 100th ARW (required for inflight-refuelling with the special JP-7 fuel) were also based. Of the initial batch of 29, two were designated **SR-71B** and fitted with dual pilot controls for use as trainer aircraft; another trainer was produced by converting one YF-12A into an **SR-71C**, and one SR-71A was redesignated YF-12C for NASA research purposes. In June 1966 the 4200th was renumbered the 9th SRW and the SR-71s assigned to the 1st SRS; detachments fly regularly from RAF Mildenhall in the UK and Kadena AB in Okinawa. The 'Blackbird' has established several world speed records (including the fastest flight time from London to New York), and in favourable conditions is capable of reaching a speed of around Mach 3.3.

Specification: Lockheed SR-71A
Origin: USA
Type: strategic reconnaissance aircraft
Powerplant: two 10433-kg (23,000-lb) dry and 14742-kg (32,500-lb) afterburning thrust Pratt & Whitney JT11D-20B (J58) bleed turbojet engines
Performance: maximum speed at 80,000ft (24385m) more than Mach 3 or 1,737 kts (3219km/h; 2,000 mph); ceiling more than 80,000ft (24385m); unrefuelled range at maximum speed 4800 km (2,983 miles)
Weights: empty 27216kg (60,000lb); maximum take-off 77111kg (170,000lb)
Dimensions: span 16.94m (55ft 7in); length 32.74m (107ft 5in); height 5.64m (18ft 6in); wing area 167.22m² (1,800.0 sq ft)
Armament: none

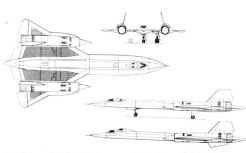

A Lockheed SR-71 of the 9th SRW based at Beale AFB, California.

Lockheed SR-71A (lower side view: SR-71B)

There have been three twin-stick SR-71s. Two were purpose-built SR-71Bs, and one SR-71C, 'The Bastard', was converted from a YF-12A when one of the original trainers was written off.

SR-71 'Blackbirds' fly from two permanent forward-operating bases, with Detachment One, 9th SRW at Kadena AFB, Okinawa, and Detachment Four at RAF Mildenhall, Suffolk. KC-135Q tankers are co-deployed.

Lockheed T-33

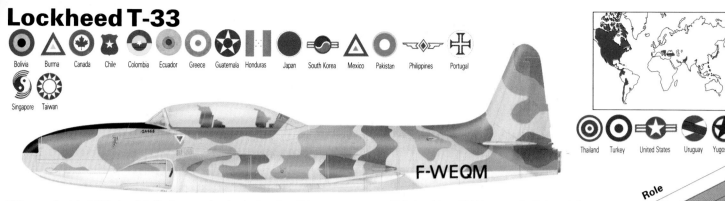

Bolivia · Burma · Canada · Chile · Colombia · Ecuador · Greece · Guatemala · Honduras · Japan · South Korea · Mexico · Pakistan · Philippines · Portugal

Singapore · Taiwan

Thailand · Turkey · United States · Uruguay · Yugoslavia

F-WEQM

With approximately 6,750 aircraft built, the **Lockheed T-33A** is by far the most successful jet trainer yet developed for service anywhere in the world, and it says much for the durability of the 'Tee-bird' that more than 1,000 aircraft remain airworthy around the world today, more than 35 years after the type first flew.

A logical development of the single-seat F-80 (the first jet-powered fighter to become operational with the US Army Air Forces) the T-33A has a lineage made evident by the fact that it actually began life in the late 1940s as the **TF-80C**, being quite simply a stretched tandem two-seater trainer version of the F-80.

Following introduction to service with the US Air Force in the closing stages of the 1940s, the 'Tee-bird' was soon being built in numbers that far outstripped those of the F-80, and it ultimately became the USAF's standard jet trainer type, equipping flying schools at many US air bases for several years in the 1950s. Just under 700 examples of the T-33A were also diverted to the US Navy, by which it initially became known as the **TO-2** although it was soon redesignated **TV-2** (**T-33B** from late 1962).

In addition to being extensively used by the USAF and US Navy, the T-33A also found a ready market overseas, many of the aircraft built being supplied to friendly nations under the Military Assistance Program. Countries which acquired the T-33A in this way include France, Greece, Italy, the Philippines, Portugal, Spain, Taiwan, Thailand, Turkey and West Germany. Licence production was also

undertaken by Canada, which completed 656 **CL-30 Silver Star** aircraft, and by Japan, which assembled 210, many of them still engaged in training duties today.

Although viewed basically as a trainer, Lockheed's jet has performed other roles, a modest number of aircraft being fitted with a camera nose and electronic equipment in the aft cockpit in order to perform reconnaissance functions. Designated **RT-33A**, these single-seaters were produced mainly for MAP, operators including France, Italy, the Netherlands, Pakistan, Thailand and Turkey. A version armed for interdiction and close support was the **AT-33A**, of which numbers are still in service.

Another important role was that of target drone, the US Navy being perhaps the major operator and destroyer of drone-configured 'Tee-birds'. Painted in a garish overall scarlet colour scheme, and often controlled by a **DT-33** director, the **QT-33** took part in numerous weapons test projects, most of the converted aircraft meeting a fiery end over the range areas of the Pacific Missile Test Center and the Naval Weapons Center at Point Mugu and China Lake respectively.

More recently a company known as the Skyfox Corporation has proposed remanufacturing the T-33A as a twin-turbofan advanced trainer, employing externally-mounted Garrett TFE731 engines. Extensive redesign of the fuselage and empennage forms part of the modernization process but thus far the company has found no takers for the **Skyfox**, as the resulting aircraft is known.

Specification: Lockheed T-33A
Origin: USA
Type: two-seat jet trainer
Powerplant: one 2449-kg (5,400-lb) thrust Allison J33-A-35 turbojet engine
Performance: maximum speed 521 kts (966 km/h; 600 mph) at sea level; maximum speed at 25,000 ft (7620 m) 474 kts (879 km/h; 546 mph); initial rate of climb 1484 m (4,870 ft) per minute; service ceiling 48,000 ft (14630 m); endurance 3.12 hours
Weights: empty 3667 kg (8,084 lb); normal take-off 5427 kg (11,965 lb); maximum take-off 6551 kg (14,442 lb)
Dimensions: span 11.85 m (38 ft 10.5 in); length 11.51 m (37 ft 9 in); height 3.56 m (11 ft 8 in); wing area 21.81 m² (234.8 sq ft)
Armament: none

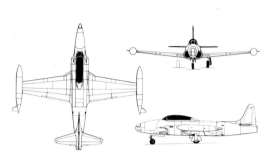

This Lockheed T-33 wears Bolivian air force camouflage and a French ferry registration.

Lockheed T-33 Shooting Star

Many Latin American air arms still use the Lockheed T-33; this one is seen in the markings of the Colombian air force. Some users re-engine their aircraft with Adour turbofans.

This is one of five Canadair CT-133 Silver Stars operated by the 1st Canadian Air Group Target Towing Flight. They are also used for instrument flying training, and general liaison flying.

Role
Fighter
Close support
Counter-insurgency
Tactical strike
Strategic bomber
Tactical reconnaissance
Strategic reconnaissance
Maritime patrol
Anti-ship strike
Anti-submarine warfare
Search and rescue
Assault transport
Transport
Liaison
Trainer
Inflight-refuelling tanker
Specialized

Performance
All-weather capability
Rough field capability
STOL capability
VTOL capability
Airspeed 0-250 mph
Airspeed 250 mph-Mach 1
Airspeed Mach 1 plus
Ceiling 0-20,000 ft
Ceiling 20,000-40,000 ft
Ceiling 40,000 ft plus
Range 0-1,000 miles
Range 1,000-3,000 miles
Range 3,000 miles plus

Weapons
Air-to-air missiles
Air-to-surface missiles
Cruise missiles
Cannon
Trainable guns
Naval weapons
Nuclear-capable
Rockets
'Smart' weapon kit
Weapon load 0-4,000 lb
Weapon load 4,000-15,000 lb
Weapon load 15,000 lb plus

Avionics
Electronic Counter Measures
Electronic Support Measures
Search radar
Fire control radar
Look-down/shoot-down
Terrain-following radar
Forward-looking infra-red
Laser
Television

Lockheed TR-1

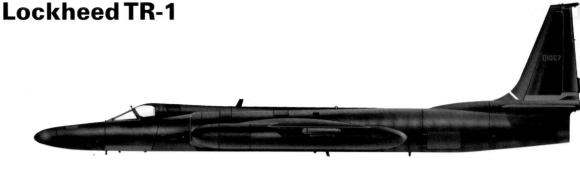

A Lockheed TR-1A of the Alconbury-based 95th RS, 17th RW.

In 1978 the USAF announced a new programme for a tactical reconnaissance aircraft, and in 1979 the U-2R line, which had been dormant for a decade, reopened for production of the **TR-1A**. On 11 May 1981, the first aircraft took to the air. It was the **ER-2**, a demilitarised version for NASA Ames, and was used for earth resources and other high altitude research. Following on 1 August 1981 was the first TR-1A for the USAF.

The TR-1A differs only in secondary systems from the original U-2R, and in primary role. Battlefield surveillance is undertaken with high-resolution radars such as the Hughes ASARS (Advanced Synthetic Aperture Radar System), which allows the TR-1A to patrol for many hours behind friendly lines, the radar searching for enemy tank concentrations and other installations at long oblique ranges. TR-1As retain the strategic reconnaissance capability of the U-2R, and are sometimes seen with large 'farms' of Comint and Elint gathering antennas or windows for optical sensors. The Precision Location Strike System had been developed for use with the TR-1A for locating hostile radar emissions,

but the programme has been cancelled for technical and budgetary problems. It may be replaced by a cheaper and less sophsiticated system.

TR-1As currently serve with two units, the 9th SRW and 17th RW. With the former they serve with the 99th SRS alongside the remaining U-2Rs, and may have replaced lost U-2 airframes. Shortly before the TR-1s first flight, the British government announced that a squadron would be based at RAF Alconbury, and the first aircraft for the 95th RS, 17th RW, arrived in February 1983 for European operations. An original total of 18 was envisaged, but has since been cut to 14 on budgetary grounds.

Training on the type is handled by the 4029th SRTS, 9th SRW 'Dragon Tamers', which operates a pair of **TR-1B**s. This trainer version is not combat-capable, and features a second, raised cockpit replacing the Q-bay. The U-2R/TR-1A has also been apparently evaluated for the AEW role, one U-2R having been seen with a large dorsal radome.

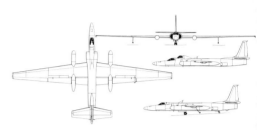

Lockheed TR-1A (upper side view: TR-1B)

This underside view of a TR-1A shows to advantage its long, slender wings and huge 'superpods' containing mission equipment, as well as the sinister matt-black colour scheme.

This 17th RW aircraft has clearly been operating at high altitude, since ice is still visible under its wings as it comes in to land at RAF Alconbury. TR-1s have flown from this base since February 1983.

Specification: Lockheed TR-1A
Origin: USA
Type: single-seat high-altitude reconnaissance aircraft
Powerplant: one 7711-kg (17,000-lb) thrust Pratt & Whitney J75-P-13B turbojet engine
Performance: maximum cruising speed at more than 70,000ft (21336m) 373 kts (692 km/h; 430 mph); service ceiling 80,000ft (24385m); maximum range 10050 km (6,250 miles)
Weights: empty 7030 kg (15,500 lb); maximum take-off 18733 kg (41,300 lb)
Dimensions: span 31.39m (103 ft 0 in); length 19.13m (62 ft 9 in); height 4.88m (16 ft 0 in); wing area 92.9 m² (1,000 sq ft)
Armament: none

Lockheed U-2R

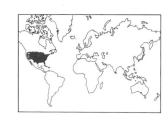

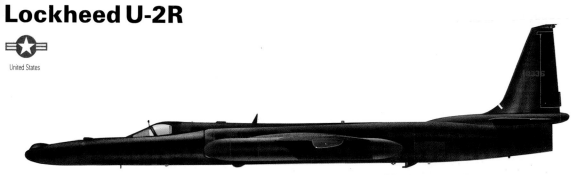

United States

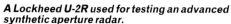

A Lockheed U-2R used for testing an advanced synthetic aperture radar.

Following the explosion of the first Soviet hydrogen bomb in August 1953 and the emergence of the Myasishchyev M-4 'Bison' jet bomber, the USA had an urgent need for a more technically advanced form of espionage. With developments in photographic technology the need could be met by high-level reconnaissance. The **Lockheed U-2** was conceived in the spring of 1954, in response to a call from the USAF and the Central Intelligence Agency (CIA) for an aircraft capable of cruising at extremely high altitudes. Introduced in 1956 the U-2 is essentially a jet-powered glider and fulfilled its role adequately for several years. But by the mid-1960s many had been lost, primarily as the result of flying an aircraft renowned for its poor handling characteristics. Consequently, in August 1966 the CIA and USAF signed a contract with Lockheed for the design and construction of a considerably more advanced variant of the U-2, designated the **U-2R**. The new aircraft was to offer increased range and improved controlability, and to carry a greater payload.

The U-2R was a complete redesign, correcting the original poor engine/airframe match and allowing for greater sensor payload. Handling at low altitude was particularly improved. The incompatibility between the engine and the airframe in the U-2C existed because the airframe was too weak to handle the maximum thrust produced by the engine.

In the U-2R the J75-P-13B and the wing aerofoil section were the only features shared with the earlier design. Apart from a family likeness the U-2R was a new aircraft: wing span was increased by 20 per cent and wing area by 75 per cent, whilst the maximum take-off weight went up by some 77 per cent. Provision was made for two extra-large wing sensor pods, and these distinguish the type in service.

After the first flight on 28 August 1967, six aircraft went to the CIA, the balance going to the 349th SRS, 100th SRW by late 1968. U-2Rs were used widely in South East Asia, flying from U-Tapao RTNAF in Thailand until 1976. The aircraft were also involved in Project 'Senior Book' requiring semi-remotely directed flights around China.

In 1972 the US Navy was loaned two U-2Rs for trials to test the electronics patrol-experiment (EP-X) concept using a new range of sensors for monitoring ship movements. The CIA had earlier, in November 1969, flown a U-2R from the carrier USS *America*. Agency aircraft were detached to the Middle East from 1970 and from 1976 there were permanent detachments of the 99th SRS, 9th SRW at Akrotiri and RAF Mildenhall for signals intelligence gathering (Sigint). Lockheed proposed an unmanned version of the U-2R in response to the ill-fated USAF 'Compass Cope' remotely piloted vehicle (RPV) programme.

Specification: Lockheed U-2R
Origin: USA
Type: single-seat high-altitude reconnaissance aircraft
Powerplant: one 7711-kg (17,000-lb) thrust Pratt & Whitney J75-P-13B turbojet engine
Performance: maximum speed 373 kts (692 km/h; 430 mph); service ceiling 80,000 ft (24385 m); maximum range about 10060 km (6,250 miles)
Weights: empty 6849 kg (15,100 lb); maximum take-off 18597 kg (41,000 lb)
Dimensions: span 31.39 m (103 ft 0 in); length 19.17 m (62 ft 11 in); height 4.88 m (16 ft 0 in); wing area 92.9 m² (1,000 sq ft)
Armament: none

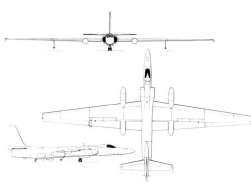

Lockheed U-2R

This U-2R is seen in service with the 9th SRW, based at Beale AFB, California. The U-2R differs from the TR-1 only in its internal equipment fit, and in its primary role of strategic reconnaissance.

This U-2R, while remaining on the strength of the 9th SRW, was used by Lockheed to test ASARS (Advanced Synthetic Aperture Radar System). The U-2R saw war service in Vietnam, and has been used over Central America.

Role
Fighter
Close support
Counter-insurgency
Tactical strike
Strategic bomber
Tactical reconnaissance
Strategic reconnaissance
Maritime patrol
Anti-ship strike
Anti-submarine warfare
Search and rescue
Assault transport
Transport
Liaison
Trainer
Inflight-refuelling tanker
Specialized

Performance
All-weather capability
Rough field capability
STOL capability
VTOL capability
Airspeed 0-250 mph
Airspeed 250 mph-Mach 1
Airspeed Mach 1 plus
Ceiling 0-20,000 ft
Ceiling 20,000-40,000 ft
Ceiling 40,000 ft plus
Range 0-1,000 miles
Range 1,000-3,000 miles
Range 3,000 miles plus

Weapons
Air-to-air missiles
Air-to-surface missiles
Cruise missiles
Cannon
Trainable guns
Naval weapons
Nuclear-capable
Rockets
'Smart' weapon kit
Weapon load 0-4,000 lb
Weapon load 4,000-15,000 lb
Weapon load 15,000 lb plus

Avionics
Electronic Counter Measures
Electronic Support Measures
Search radar
Fire control radar
Look-down/shoot-down
Terrain-following radar
Forward-looking infra-red
Laser
Television

McDonnell Douglas A-4 Skyhawk

A classic aeroplane by any criterion, the relatively small, compact and lightweight **Douglas A-4 Skyhawk** single-seat naval attack bomber has remained in front line service ever since it first joined the US Navy in 1956. What may be termed the first generation of Skyhawks included those versions based on variants up to and including the A-4F. Of low-set delta wing planform, the Skyhawk first flew in prototype form (XA4D-1) on 22 June 1954 with a Wright J65 turbojet (in effect an Armstrong Siddeley Sapphire produced under licence) and featured prominent lateral air inlets on the sides of the fuselage above the wing root leading edges. Considerable wing strength derived from the use of single-piece tip-to-tip spars machined from solid planks; an exceptionally low thickness/chord ratio gave a speed performance well in excess of many contemporary fighters yet, with automatic wing slats, variable-incidence tailplane and long-travel nosewheel landing gear, the Skyhawk remained entirely tractable as a shipborne high-performance aircraft.

After 165 **A4D-1** aircraft had been built, the **A4D-2** (later redesignated the **A-4B**) introduced provision for Martin Bullpup air-to-surface missiles, navigation and bombing computer, powered rudder with unique central 'skin' with external stiffeners, and inflight-refuelling (both as buddy tanker and receiver); 542 were produced for the US Navy and Marines. Of these, 66 were rebuilt

in the late 1960s as the **A-4P** and **A-4Q** for the Argentine air force and navy respectively, being much in evidence during the Falkland Islands campaign of 1982; 40 others were rebuilt as the **A-4S** for the Singapore Air Defence Command with 30-mm guns in place of the US Navy's 20-mm type.

Some 638 A-4C limited all-weather/night attack aircraft started delivery in 1959, introducing improved autopilot, LABS and terrain-avoidance radar, and gave outstanding service during the Vietnam War; few remain in service, although about 77 rebuilt **A-4L** aircraft with J65 engines and dorsal avionic 'humps' are currently in storage. Some 499 **A-4E** aircraft were produced in the early and mid-1960s with a zero/90-kt (167-km/h, 104-mph) ejector seat, five store pylons and J52 turbojet, many of these becoming the first of some 300 Skyhawks of various versions delivered to Israel over the next 10 years, the great majority of which remain in service today. The **A-4F** (of which 147 examples were built) introduced the dorsal avionics hump into the production line, as well as lift dumpers and spoilers, steerable nosewheel, zero/zero seat and extra cockpit armour. A high proportion of these remain in USN and USMC service, while export derivatives included 14 **A-4G** aircraft for the Royal Australian Navy and 10 **A-4K** aircraft for the Royal New Zealand Air Force (the latter with braking parachute).

A McDonnell Douglas A-4C Skyhawk of Grupo 4, Argentine air force.

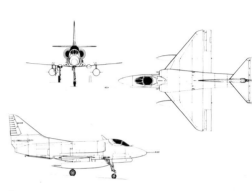

McDonnell Douglas A-4 Skyhawk

The A-4K Skyhawk replaced the Canberra B(I).Mk 12 in RNZAF service and serves with No. 75 Squadron at Ohakea. This aircraft carries a full load of bombs and fuel tanks, and a pair of AIM-9Ds.

The Indonesian air force operates ex-Israeli A-4Es complete with extended IR-suppressing tailpipe and dorsal avionics hump. This aircraft belongs to Skwadron Udara II of No. 300 Wing at Maidun.

Specification: McDonnell Douglas A-4F Skyhawk
Origin: USA
Type: single-seat carrierborne attack fighter-bomber
Powerplant: one 4218-kg (9,300-lb) thrust Pratt & Whitney J52-P-8A turbojet engine
Performance: maximum speed with 1814-kg (4,000-lb) bombload 515 kts (954 km/h; 593 mph) at 34,000 ft (10365 m); initial rate of climb 5,620 ft (1713 m) per minute; maximum unrefuelled range 3307 km (2,055 miles)
Weights: empty equipped 4739 kg (10,448 lb); maximum take-off 12437 kg (27,420 lb)
Dimensions: span 8.38 m (27 ft 6 in); length without refuelling probe 12.27 m (40 ft 3.25 in); height 4.57 m (15 ft 0 in); wing area 24.15 m² (260 sq ft)
Armament: two 20-mm Mk 12 cannon in wing roots; underfuselage mounting for single or multiple store carriers (stressed to 1588 kg; 3,500 lb); and four underwing hardpoints, inboard pair stressed to 1021 kg (2,250 lb) and plumbed for external fuel tanks, outboard pair (dry) stressed to 454 kg (1,000 lb)

McDonnell Douglas A-4 Skyhawk II

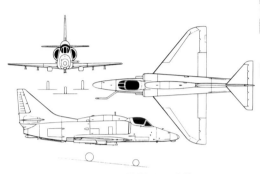

Israel Malaysia United States

Introduction to the Skyhawk of the Pratt & Whitney J52-P-408A turbojet, with its 20 per cent power increase, heralded the beginning of a new generation of the remarkable little attack aircraft, now generally known as the **McDonnell Douglas A-4 Skyhawk II**. Retaining the now-characteristic dorsal avionics hump, the **A-4M** (162 produced for the US Marine Corps during the 1970s, plus four for Kuwait), also introduced doubled ammunition provision, angle-rate bombing system (ARBS), enlarged windscreen, ram-air turbogenerator, cranked inflight-refuelling probe and braking parachute. These Skyhawks entered service with marine attack squadrons and only now are being phased out with the arrival in service of the McDonnell Douglas AV-8B Harrier II; they will then continue to serve alongside the TAV-8B with attack training squadrons. Similar to the A-4M, and built simultaneously, were 117 **A-4N** aircraft for the Israeli air force, which however adopted two 30-mm wing-root cannon and included more advanced avionics, decoy flare dispensers and provision for the carriage of Israeli weapons.

There is no doubt that, other than in an advanced-technology combat environment, the Skyhawk II is still a remarkably potent weapon, capable of delivering a worthwhile warload accurately, and still able to operate from a carrier deck or 1220-m (4,000-ft) runway. Post-delivery modifications have included the addition of radar warning and ECM equipment in the rear fuselage and in a fairing at the top of the fin.

Final new-build Skyhawks in 1979 included a small number of **A-4Y** aircraft for the US Marine Corps which included head-up display and an improved ARBS, and some A-4Ms were scheduled for modification to this standard. In the Far East eight ex-Australian A-4Gs transferred to the RNZAF in 1984-5 were expected, together with New Zealand's own A-4Ks, to undergo an update programme which, depending on costs of an avionic refit, would bring the Skyhawks much closer to the Skyhawk II standard. In the Singapore air force a proof-of-concept proposal has been made to re-engine its A-4S Skyhawks with non-reheated General Electric F404 turbofans, followed by a possible avionics update which will place these aircraft firmly in the 'second generation' of A-4s. The Royal Malaysian air force took delivery of 34 single-seat **A-4PTM** aircraft during 1985 to equip two squadrons, and in the same year the last of about 30 ex-Israeli A-4Es joined the Indonesian Armed Forces – Air Force (TNI-AU) amid reports that these too would be re-engined in due course to A-4M standard.

A McDonnell Douglas A-4N Skyhawk of the Israel Defence Force/Air Force, with extended anti-SAM tailpipe.

McDonnell Douglas A-4M Skyhawk II

These A-4M Skyhawks belong to the El Toro-based VMA-214, 'Black Sheep'. The rear aircraft wears the old-style high-visibility markings.

Malaysia's A-4 Skyhawks are designated A-4 PTM (Peculiar To Malaysia) and are basically surplus A-Cs, Ds and Ls modified to approximately A-4M standard, some with provision for the AGM-65 Maverick missile.

Specification: McDonnell Douglas A-4M Skyhawk II
Origin: USA
Type: single-seat attack fighter-bomber
Powerplant: one 5080-kg (11,200-lb) thrust Pratt & Whitney J52-P-408A turbojet engine
Performance: maximum speed with 1814-kg (4,000-lb) bombload 560 kts (1038 km/h; 645 mph) at 34,000 ft (10365 m); initial rate of climb 8,440 ft (2573 m) per minute; maximum unrefuelled range 3307 km (2,055 miles)
Weights: empty equipped 4747 kg (10,465 lb); maximum take-off 12438 kg (27,420 lb)
Dimensions: span 8.38 m (27 ft 6 in); length without refuelling probe 12.29 m (40 ft 3.75 in); height 4.57 m (15 ft 0 in); wing area 24.15 m² (260 sq ft)
Armament: two 20-mm Mk 12 cannon in wing roots (30-mm DEFA cannon optional in exported versions); underfuselage mounting for single or multiple store carriers (stressed to 1588 kg; 3,500 lb); and four underwing hardpoints, inboard pair stressed to 1021 kg (2,250 lb) and plumbed for external fuel tanks, outboard pair (dry) stressed to 454 kg (1,000 lb)

Role	
Fighter	
Close support	■
Counter-insurgency	
Tactical strike	■
Strategic bomber	
Strategic reconnaissance	
Tactical reconnaissance	
Strategic patrol	
Maritime patrol	
Anti-ship strike	■
Anti-submarine warfare	
Search and rescue	
Assault transport	
Transport	
Liaison	
Trainer	
Inflight-refuelling tanker	
Specialized	

Performance	
All-weather capability	
Rough field capability	
STOL capability	■
VTOL capability	
Airspeed 0-250 mph	
Airspeed 250 mph-Mach 1	■
Airspeed Mach 1 plus	
Ceiling 0-20,000 ft	
Ceiling 20,000-40,000 ft	
Ceiling 40,000ft plus	■
Range 0-1,000 miles	
Range 1,000-3,000 miles	■
Range 3,000 miles plus	

Weapons	
Air-to-air missiles	
Air-to-surface missiles	■
Cruise missiles	
Cannon	■
Trainable guns	
Naval weapons	
Nuclear-capable	
Rockets	■
'Smart' weapon kit	
Weapon load 0-4,000 lb	
Weapon load 4,000-15,000 lb	■
Weapon load 15,000 lb	

Avionics	
Electronic Counter Measures	■
Electronic Support Measures	
Search radar	
Fire control radar	
Look-down/shoot-down	
Terrain-following radar	
Forward-looking infra-red	
Laser	
Television	

McDonnell Douglas C-17

United States

Role

Fighter
Close support
Counter-insurgency
Tactical strike
Strategic bomber
Tactical reconnaissance
Strategic reconnaissance
Maritime patrol
Anti-ship strike
Anti-submarine warfare
Search and rescue
Assault transport
Transport
Liaison
Trainer
Inflight-refuelling tanker
Specialized

Performance

All-weather capability
Rough field capability
STOL capability
VTOL capability
Airspeed 0-250 mph
Airspeed 250 mph-Mach 1
Airspeed Mach 1 plus
Ceiling 0-20,000 ft
Ceiling 20,000-40,000 ft
Ceiling 40,000 ft plus
Range 0-1,000 miles
Range 1,000-3,000 miles
Range 3,000 miles plus

Weapons

Air-to-air missiles
Air-to-surface missiles
Cruise missiles
Cannon
Trainable guns
Naval weapons
Nuclear weapons
Rockets
'Smart' weapon kit
Weapon load 0-4,000 lb
Weapon load 4,000-15,000 lb
Weapon load 15,000 lb plus

Avionics

Electronic Counter Measures
Electronic Support Measures
Search radar
Fire control radar
Look-down/shoot-down
Terrain-following radar
Forward-looking infra-red
Laser
Television

In recognition of a continuing shortfall in its long-range heavy airlift capacity since the late 1970s, the USAF has been examining alternative expedients to correct the situation, including enhancement of existing aircraft capabilities, extension of the Civil Reserve Air Fleet and development of an entirely new long-range cargo aircraft; the last (originally known as the C-X programme) would obviously occupy the longest period of gestation and be the most costly by far. In August 1981 the McDonnell Douglas design tender was accepted but, although a relatively small research and development contract was soon placed, it was not until 1985-6 that funding was sought for full development, the $4 billion cost tag being said to cover the programme to acquire three airframes, one for flight test and two for structural test. Current production plans indicate an intended procurement of 210 aircraft by 1998 at a unit cost of $178 million.

The C-17 as currently proposed is a four-turbofan aircraft with shoulder-mounted swept wing of supercritical section and tip winglets; short-field performance and handling is achieved by leading-edge slats, and flap-blowing over single-hinged double-slotted Fowler flaps using engine exhaust

directed by thrust reversers operable both in flight and on the ground. Raison d'etre of the C-17 is its ability to deliver exceptionally heavy military items (at present only transportable by the Lockheed C-5 Galaxy) into forward airstrips currently accessible only by aircraft such as the Lockheed C-130. To this end two pairs of tandem main landing gear units, each with three wheels, are arranged to retract into large fairings on the sides of the fuselage, giving a runway load classification number of better than 40. Maximum payload, loaded through the rear fuselage up a lowered ramp, includes three of the new infantry AFVs which are also to be air-droppable, and is at present said to be 78109 kg (172,200 lb). Avionics include automatic flight control, four full-colour multi-function displays, twin head-up displays, integrated mission and communication keyboards, and station-keeping equipment. Considerable attention is being paid to damage survivability with redundant load paths designed into the aircraft structure. Representing a capability compromise between the tactical flexibility of the venerable C-130 and the load-carrying ability of the C-5, the C-17 nevertheless remains extremely vulnerable to the criticism of exceptionally high cost.

Specification: McDonnell Douglas C-17
Origin: USA
Type: long-range heavy-lift transport
Powerplant: four 16783-kg (37,000-lb) thrust Pratt & Whitney PW2037 turbofan engines
Performance: (estimated) normal cruising speed at altitude Mach 0.77; maximum cruising speed at low altitude 350 kts (648 km/h; 403 mph); range unrefuelled with 71894-kg (158,500-lb) payload 5005 km (3,110 miles)
Weights: empty equipped 117480 kg (259,000 lb); maximum take-off 258548 kg (570,000 lb)
Dimensions: span 50.29 m (165 ft 0 in); length 53.39 m (175 ft 2 in); height 16.79 m (55 ft 1 in); wing area 353.02 m² (3,800 sq ft)
Armament: none

A McDonnell Douglas C-17 in the markings of Military Airlift Command.

McDonnell Douglas C-17

The C-17 will be able to deliver heavy and bulky items into even the smallest of forward areas. As such it will act largely as a C-130 Hercules replacement.

Production of the McDonnell Douglas C-17 is currently scheduled to total 210 aircraft. The aircraft will be able to carry four UH-60 helicopters, or a pair of AH-64s and three OH-58s.

114

McDonnell Douglas C-9 Nightingale/Skytrain II

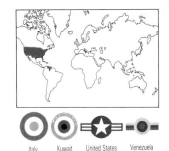

Italy   Kuwait   United States   Venezuela

Experience forthcoming in the early stages of American involvement in the Vietnam War spotlighted the need for a medium-range aeromedical transport capable of accommodating up to 40 litter patients, and as a relatively low-cost expedient an initial order for eight 'off-the-shelf' commercial McDonnell Douglas DC-9 Series 30 twin rear-turbofan airliners was placed, to be set aside for military conversion. Modifications included the provision of a special-care compartment, galleys and toilets fore and aft, and addition of a third access door 3.45 m (11 ft 4 in) wide in the front fuselage with inbuilt hydraulic ramp to facilitate the loading of litters. Accommodation is provided for up to 40 litters and 40 ambulatory patients, two nurses and three aeromedical attendants. The first **McDonnell Douglas C-9A Nightingale** was rolled out on 17 June 1968 and delivered to Scott AFB two months later; subsequent aircraft served with the 375th Aeromedical Airlift Wing of the USAF's MAC, and later with the 55th AAS of the 435th Tactical Airlift Wing. Later orders brought the total deliveries to 21 (in addition to three **VC-9C** executive transports flown by the 89th Military Airlift Group for Headquarters

Command at Pope AFB, Maryland). Two of the early aeromedical aircraft were converted for staff transport work and flown by the 7111th Operations Squadron. An example of the contingency use of the medevac C-9A Nightingale was afforded during the abortive 'Eagle Claw' operation mounted to secure the release of Americans being held hostage in Iran in April 1980 when a C-9A, specially equipped to accommodate a burns treatment unit, was deployed to evacuate the casualties suffered in the collision between a Sikorsky RH-53D helicopter and a Lockheed EC-130E Hercules tanker.

Another version of the DC-9 is the **C-9B Skytrain II**, ordered by the US Navy as a fleet logistic transport. Combining features of both the DC-9 Series 30 and 40, a total of 19 aircraft was delivered for use by navy logistic support squadrons in the USA and two to the US Marine Corps' Station Operations and Engineering Squadron at Cherry Point MCAS, North Carolina. Two similar military aircraft, which retain the DC-9-32CF designation, were delivered to the Kuwaiti air force, being convertible as either passenger or freight transports.

Specification: McDonnell Douglas C-9A Nightingale
Origin: USA
Type: aeromedical airlift transport
Powerplant: two 6577-kg (14,500-lb) thrust Pratt & Whitney JT8D-9 turbofan engines
Performance: maximum cruising speed 491 kts (909 km/h; 565 mph) at 25,000 ft (7620 m); initial rate of climb 6,800 ft (2073 m) per minute; normal range with full accommodation and reserves 2388 km (1,484 miles)
Weights: empty equipped 24011 kg (52,935 lb); maximum take-off 44452 kg (98,000 lb)
Dimensions: span 28.47 m (93 ft 5 in); length 36.36 m (119 ft 3.5 in); height 8.38 m (27 ft 6 in); wing area 92.97 m² (1,000.7 sq ft)
Armament: none

Specification: C-9B Skytrain II
Performance: maximum cruising speed 500 kts (927 km/h; 576 mph); long-range cruising speed 438 kts (811 km/h; 504 mph); range with 4536 kg (10,000 lb) payload, long range cruise speed at 30,000 ft (9145 m) 4704 km (2,923 miles)
Weights: empty, passenger configuration 29612 kg (65,283 lb), cargo configuration 27082 kg (59,706 lb); maximum take-off 49895 kg (110,000 lb)

A McDonnell Douglas C-9B Skytrain II of the US Navy.

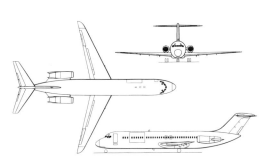

McDonnell Douglas C-9B Skytrain II

The Kuwait air force operates a pair of C-9Ks on VIP and long-range transport duties. They are based in the military area of Kuwait International Airport, and serve alongside a C-130 Hercules.

Two DC-9s serve beside Piaggio PD.808s with the 306 Gruppo, 31 Stormo 'Franco Lucchini', on VIP and transport duties. These fly from Rome's Ciampino airfield.

Role
Fighter
Close support
Counter-insurgency
Tactical strike
Strategic bomber
Tactical reconnaissance
Strategic reconnaissance
Maritime patrol
Anti-ship strike
Anti-submarine warfare
Search and rescue
Assault transport
Transport
Liaison
Trainer
Inflight-refuelling tanker
Specialized

Performance
All-weather capability
Rough field capability
STOL capability
VTOL capability
Airspeed 0-250 mph
Airspeed 250 mph-Mach 1
Airspeed Mach 1 plus
Ceiling 0-20,000 ft
Ceiling 20,000-40,000 ft
Ceiling 40,000 ft plus
Range 0-1,000 miles
Range 1,000-3,000 miles
Range 3,000 miles plus

Weapons
Air-to-air missiles
Air-to-surface missiles
Cruise missiles
Cannon
Trainable guns
Naval weapons
Nuclear-capable
Rockets
'Smart' weapon kit
Weapon load 0-4,000 lb
Weapon load 4,000-15,000 lb
Weapon load 15,000 lb plus

Avionics
Electronic Counter Measures
Electronic Support Measures
Search radar
Fire control radar
Look-down/shoot-down
Terrain-following radar
Forward-looking infra-red
Laser
Television

115

A McDonnell Douglas C-9B Skytrain II of the US Navy

McDonnell Douglas F-4C/D Phantom II

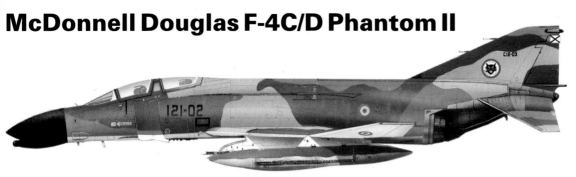

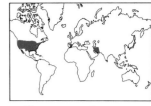

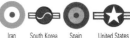

Iran South Korea Spain United States

A measure of the advanced operational concept built into the **McDonnell F-4 Phantom II** may be judged from the fact that though production of the USAF's **F-4C** and **F-4D** ended 20 years ago, some of these fighters were still serving in squadrons of the US Air National Guard and with the air forces of Spain and South Korea (and possible Iran) in the early 1980s. Originally adapted from the US Navy's successful F-4B of the early 1960s as an outcome of a current policy for commonality of equipment among the services, the F-4C (of which 635 production examples were built) was powered by J79-GE-15 turbojets which bestowed a genuine Mach 2 performance at altitude. The F-4Cs equipment fit includes APQ-100 radar, A/A-24G central air data computer, ASN-48 inertial navigator, AJB-7 bombing system and ARW-77 missile system. This version saw considerable action in the early years of the Vietnam War, being joined by the F-4D in 1967. Like their earlier naval counterparts, these Phantoms carried a normal air combat weapon complement of four AIM-7 Sparrow MRAAMs semi-recessed into the fuselage underside and up to four AIM-9 Sidewinder SRAAMs on underwing pylons in addition to external fuel tanks; for deep penetration sorties extensive use was made of inflight-refuelling.

In the F-4D version, which was more suited to the USAF's own operational roles, a part-solid state APQ-109 radar giving air-to-ground ranging replaced the F-4C's APQ-100 radar and optical sight, and the ASN-63 replaced the ASN-48 inertial navigator. Despite these changes, Phantom pilots were critical of the lack of inbuilt gun armament (although a ventral gun pod could be carried at the expense of the centreline drop tank) a deficiency not rectified until the appearance of the F-4E. Despite this and other shortcomings (such as the absence of look-down radar), the Phantom proved a formidable opponent over Vietnam and remained in USAF service until relegated (after life-extension engineering) to the Air National Guard squadrons wherein the F-4Ds remained until the 1980s. The replacement of USAF F-4Cs by F-4Es in Europe provided a ready source for supply of 36 to Spain in 1972, these undergoing thorough refurbishing at the CASA plant at Getafe to reappear with the designation F-4C(S). In the late 1960s Iran, then pursuing considerable modernization of its air force with American assistance, acquired 32 ex-USAF F-4Ds and these equipped two squadrons in 1969; most survivors were probably cannibalized to keep later aircraft airworthy after discontinuation of American support at the end of the 1970s. Eighteen USAF-surplus F-4Ds also equipped a wing of the Republic of Korea Air Force (ROKAF) in 1972, replacing North American F-86s.

A McDonnell Douglas F-4C Phantom of Ala de Caza 12, Spanish air force.

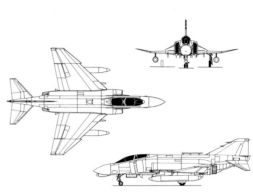

McDonnell Douglas F-4D Phantom

Spain operates the survivors of 40 Phantoms with Escuadrons 121 and 122 from Torrejon, near Madrid. The F-4C is designated C.12 in Spanish air force service.

A small number of F-4Cs remain in service with US Air National Guard Units, but are rapidly being replaced. This aircraft wears the markings of the 182nd TFS, Texas ANG.

Specification: McDonnell Douglas F-4C Phantom II
Origin: USA
Type: two-seat land-based strike fighter
Powerplant: two 7711-kg (17,000-lb) thrust General Electric J79-GE-15 afterburning turbojet engines
Performance: maximum speed Mach 2+ or 1146 kts (2124 km/h; 1,320 mph) at 40,000 ft (12190 m); service ceiling 61,000 ft (18590 m); unrefuelled combat radius 990 km (615 miles)
Weights: empty equipped 13245 kg (29,200 lb); maximum take-off 24766 kg (54,600 lb)
Dimensions: span 11.71 m (38 ft 5 in); length 17.75 m (58 ft 3 in); height 4.95 m (16 ft 3 in); wing area 49.24 m² (530.0 sq ft)
Armament: basic weapon configuration comprises four AIM-7 Sparrow AAMs semi-recessed under fuselage and up to four AIM-9 Sidewinder AAMs on wing pylons in addition to two drop tanks; 20-mm cannon pod or other stores alternative to AIM-7s; maximum bombload of up to 18 340-kg (750-lb) bombs on multiple carriers under fuselage and wings

Role
Fighter
Close support
Counter-insurgency
Tactical strike
Strategic bomber
Tactical reconnaissance
Strategic reconnaissance
Maritime patrol
Anti-ship strike
Anti-submarine warfare
Search and rescue
Assault transport
Transport
Liaison
Trainer
Inflight-refuelling tanker
Specialized

Performance
All-weather capability
Rough field capability
STOL capability
VTOL capability
Airspeed 0-250 mph
Airspeed 250 mph-Mach 1
Airspeed Mach 1 plus
Ceiling 0-20,000 ft
Ceiling 20,000-40,000 ft
Ceiling 40,000ft plus
Range 0-1,000 miles
Range 1,000-3,000 miles
Range 3,000 miles plus

Weapons
Air-to-air missiles
Air-to-surface missiles
Cruise missiles
Cannon
Trainable guns
Naval weapons
Nuclear-capable
Rockets
'Smart' weapon kit
Weapon load 0-4,000 lb
Weapon load 4,000-15,000 lb
Weapon load 15,000 lb plus

Avionics
Electronic Counter Measures
Electronic Support Measures
Search radar
Fire control radar
Look-down/shoot-down
Terrain-following radar
Forward-looking infra-red
Laser
Television

McDonnell Douglas F-4E/F Phantom II

South Korea   Japan   Turkey   United States

Egypt   West Germany   Greece   Iran   Israel

Most widely used of all Phantoms has been the **McDonnell F-4E**, of which 1,329 were produced for the USAF, with delivery to squadrons beginning in 1968. Raison d'etre of this version had been the APQ-109/CORDS (Coherent On Receive Doppler System), but in the event the CORDS element was cancelled in 1968 and the Westinghouse APQ-120 radar was adopted. With a considerably lengthened nose on which the chin-located IR seeker of earlier F-4s was omitted, the F-4E included an integral multi-barrel 20-mm cannon in a long fairing on the centreline. An additional No. 7 fuel cell was included in the rear fuselage to compensate for centre of gravity movement. Martin Baker zero/zero ejector seats were also fitted from the outset and in 1972 (too late to reach operational status over Vietnam) slats were added to the outer wing sections. Avionics updating included the installation in later aircraft of ASX-1 TISEO (Target Identification System, Electro-Optical) and a modified ASG-26 computing sight; a much-enhanced range of weapons became compatible, including the guided bomb family (Mk 84/118 LGB/IR/EO) as well as ALQ-71, -72, -87 and -101 ECM pods.

Numerically, F-4Es continued to dominate the USAF's inventory in all theatres throughout the 1970s despite the arrival in service of McDonnell Douglas F-15s and General Dynamics F-16s. However, such was the aircraft's unquestioned reputation that a considerable export trade flourished, with the largest number (204) being supplied to Israel,

in whose air force the type equipped seven squadrons and took a major part in the 1973 'Yom Kippur' War; much indigenous equipment was added, including the Elta AL/M-2021 multi-mode radar, and it is also said that the Israeli F-4Es were made compatible with the Luz stand-off bomb. Other F-4E user air forces included those of Egypt, Greece, Iran (with eight squadrons), South Korea and Turkey. Australia leased a small number in 1970-2 pending the arrival of General Dynamics F-111s, and Mitsubishi licence-built 140 **F-4EJ** aircraft to equip five squadrons of the JASDF. West Germany also adopted the aircraft as basic strike/fighter equipment, Luftwaffe crews being trained in the USA on F-4Es before the delivery of 175 new-build **F-4F** aircraft during 1975-6 to equip four Jagdgeschwader (interception) and Jagdbombergeschwader (quick reaction strike), replacing Lockheed F-104Gs. Representing the latest aerodynamic standard achieved in production (with slatted wings and other refinements), the F-4F featured simplified APQ-100 radar and reduced fuel capacity, and also lacked the inflight-refuelling facility. Most of the airframe was manufactured in West Germany for final assembly in the USA, and it is assumed that the air defence F-4Fs will remain in service well into the 1990s and be joined by the strike aircraft, which may be re-engineered after replacement by Panavia Tornado IDS aircraft in the near future.

Specification: McDonnell Douglas F-4E Phantom II
Origin: USA
Type: two-seat multi-role strike fighter
Powerplant: two 8119-kg (17,900-lb) thrust General Electric J79-GE-17 afterburning turbojet engines
Performance: maximum speed Mach 2.25 or 1290 kts (2390 km/h; 1,485 mph) at 40,000 ft (12190 m); initial rate of climb 49,800 ft (15179 m) per minute; service ceiling 62,250 ft (18975 m); unrefuelled combat radius 958 km (595 miles)
Weights: empty equipped 13397 kg (29,535 lb); maximum take-off 27964 kg (61,651 lb)
Dimensions: span 11.71 m (38 ft 5 in); length 19.20 m (63 ft 0 in); height 5.03 m (16 ft 6 in); wing area 49.24 m² (530.0 sq ft)
Armament: one M61A1 20-mm six-barrel cannon in nose and four AIM-7 Sparrow MRAAMs semi-recessed into fuselage underside or other weapons up to 1370 kg (3,020 lb) on centreline pylon; four underwing hardpoints stressed to carry a combined load of up to 5888 kg (12,980 lb) of fuel tanks and/or weapons

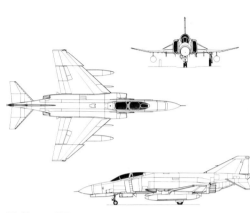

McDonnell Douglas F-4E Phantom II of the US Air Force's 3rd TFW at Clark AB, Philippines.

McDonnell Douglas F-4E Phantom

The Hopsten-based Jagdbombergeschwader 36 operates the F-4F Phantom in the quick-reaction strike role. The aircraft will probably assume an air defence role in the near future.

A pair of 301st Hikotai McDonnell Douglas F-4EJs scramble from Hyakuri. Japan's Phantoms share their air defence task with F-15 Eagles.

McDonnell Douglas F-4G 'Wild Weasel V'

United States

Widespread use by the communist forces in Vietnam of Soviet-supplied SA-2 'Guideline' SAMs was only partly countered by use of such aircraft as the Douglas EB-66 and Grumman EA-6B by the USAF and US Navy respectively, and it was perhaps inevitable that after better success attended development of North American F-100s and Republic F-105s in the radar suppression role the F-4, with its much higher performance and strike capabilities, should come to be introduced for similar tasks. By 1972 about 12 **McDonnell Douglas F-4C 'Wild Weasel IV'** aircraft were in service, employing Westinghouse ECM pods in conjunction with AGM-45 Shrike anti-radiation missiles, such aircraft frequently accompanying routine strike missions by standard F-4Cs.

In due course a much more extensive modification programme was undertaken, a total of 116 **F-4G** aircraft being produced (known initially as **'Advanced Wild Weasel'** or **'Wild Weasel V'**) by modifying F-4Es from production Block 42 onwards when they were returned for life-extension programmes. Changes included deletion of the integral M61A1 cannon and installation of a McDonnell Douglas APR-38 radar warning, homing and missile management system (RHAWS), much of whose component avionics are located in a long cylindrical fairing on top of the aircraft's fin. Associated with

the APR-38 is a Texas Instruments computer whose purpose is to accommodate varying future circumstances without demands for additional electronic hardware in an already densely-packed aircraft (there are no fewer than 52 antennae distributed throughout the airframe). Self-defence weaponry is confined to a pair of Sparrow MRAAMs in the rear fuselage recesses (and perhaps a pair of AIM-9s if pylon stations are available), one of the forward pair normally being occupied by an ECM pod such as ALQ-131. The APR-38 is compatible with the AGM-45 Shrike, AGM-65 Maverick electro-optically guided missile and AGM-88 HARM (High-speed ARM), and features automatic and blind weapon firing. Cockpit displays include annotated threat symbology, while reaction to priority threats is automatically initiated. Most aircraft in service today have been re-equipped with LORAN, while restressing of the fuselage store mounting enables the McDonnell Douglas F-15 type centreline fuel drop tank to be carried: this is cleared to 5g when full, compared with 3g of the F-4's customary tank. The F-4G will most likely remain in front-line service with the USAF for some years and is sure to be the last variant of the classic Phantom in front-line service, following the impending 'Wild Weasel VI' update with APR-47 RHAWS.

Specification: McDonnell Douglas F-4G 'Wild Weasel II'
Origin: USA
Type: two-seat EW/radar suppression/strike aircraft
Powerplant: two 8119-kg (17,900-lb) thrust General Electric J79-GE-17 afterburning turbojet engines
Performance: maximum speed Mach 2.25 or 1290 kts (2390 km/h; 1,485 mph) at 40,000 ft (12190 m); service ceiling 62,250 ft (18975 m); unrefuelled combat radius 958 km (595 miles)
Weights: empty equipped 13300 kg (29,321 lb); maximum take-off 28300 kg (62,390 lb)
Dimensions: span 11.71 m (38 ft 5 in); length 19.20 m (63 ft 0 in); height 5.02 m (16 ft 5.5 in); wing area 49.24 m² (530.0 sq ft)
Armament: provision to mount two AIM-7 Sparrow self-defence MRAAMs in rear fuselage recesses; radar suppression weapons include mix of AGM-45 Shrike, AGM-65 Maverick, or AGM-88 HARM missiles in conjunction with APR-38 RHAWS integral equipment and podded ALQ-119 ECM

A McDonnell Douglas F-4G of the 81st TFS, 52nd TFW based at Spangdahlem, West Germany, and assigned to support NATO's 4th and 2nd ATAFs.

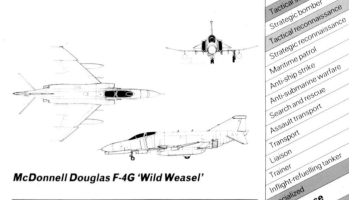

McDonnell Douglas F-4G 'Wild Weasel'

This F-4G 'Wild Weasel' defence suppression Phantom wears the red fin stripe of the 480th TFS, one of three 'Weasel' units based at Spangdahlem.

The F-4G is used for radar suppression duties and is equipped with a comprehensive RHAW system and a variety of anti-radar and other air-to-surface missiles.

Role

- Fighter
- Close support
- Counter-insurgency
- Tactical strike
- Strategic bomber
- Tactical reconnaissance
- Strategic reconnaissance
- Maritime patrol
- Anti-ship strike
- Anti-submarine warfare
- Search and rescue
- Assault transport
- Transport
- Liaison
- Trainer
- Inflight-refuelling tanker
- Specialized

Performance

- All-weather capability
- Rough field capability
- STOL capability
- VTOL capability
- Airspeed 0-250 mph
- Airspeed 250 mph-Mach 1
- Airspeed Mach 1 plus
- Ceiling 0-20,000 ft
- Ceiling 20,000-40,000 ft
- Ceiling 40,000 ft plus
- Range 0-1,000 miles
- Range 1,000-3,000 miles
- Range 3,000 miles plus

Weapons

- Air-to-air missiles
- Air-to-surface missiles
- Cruise missiles
- Cannon
- Trainable guns
- Naval weapons
- Nuclear-capable
- Rockets
- 'Smart' weapon kit
- Weapon load 0-4,000 lb
- Weapon load 4,000-15,000 lb
- Weapon load 15,000 lb plus

Avionics

- Electronic Counter Measures
- Electronic Support Measures
- Search radar
- Fire control radar
- Look-down/shoot-down
- Terrain-following radar
- Forward-looking infra-red
- Laser
- Television

McDonnell Douglas F-4J/N/S Phantom II

United Kingdom   United States

Role
Fighter
Close support
Counter-insurgency
Tactical strike
Strategic bomber
Tactical reconnaissance
Strategic reconnaissance
Maritime patrol
Anti-ship strike
Anti-submarine warfare
Search and rescue
Assault transport
Transport
Liaison
Trainer
Inflight-refuelling tanker
Specialized

Performance
All-weather capability
Rough field capability
STOL capability
VTOL capability
Airspeed 0-250 mph
Airspeed 250 mph-Mach 1
Airspeed Mach 1 plus
Ceiling 0-20,000 ft
Ceiling 20,000-40,000 ft
Ceiling 40,000ft plus
Range 0-1,000 miles
Range 1,000-3,000 miles
Range 3,000 miles plus

Weapons
Air-to-air missiles
Air-to-surface missiles
Cruise missiles
Cannon
Trainable guns
Naval weapons
Nuclear-capable
Rockets
'Smart' weapon kit
Weapon load 0-4,000 lb
Weapon load 4,000-15,000 lb
Weapon load 15,000 lb plus

Avionics
Electronic Counter Measures
Electronic Support Measures
Search radar
Fire control radar
Look-down/shoot-down
Terrain-following radar
Forward-looking infra-red
Laser
Television

Plans to replace the standard naval F-4B in service began in 1963 and the **McDonnell F-4J** reached US Navy squadrons in the Vietnam theatre in 1967. Although still not incorporating inbuilt gun armament (the lack of which constituted one of the main criticisms of the fighter), this version included AWG-10 pulse-Doppler radar with look-down capability, ASW-25 one-way data link for automatic carrier landing, miniaturized communications, navigation and identification gear, and AJB-7 bombing system; airframe improvements included fixed inboard wing leading edges, drooping ailerons, fixed inverted slats on the stabilator and strengthened landing gear. Uprated J79-GE-10s were incorporated to cater for the increased all-up weight and a seventh fuselage fuel tank was added. Production amounted to 637 aircraft.

The introduction of the Grumman F-14A Tomcat into service in the 1970s was so protracted that there remained an urgency to update both the F-4B and F-4J Phantoms, which at the end of the Vietnam War still equipped the vast majority of US Navy fighter squadrons and Marine Corps fighter-attack squadrons, although many of the F-4Bs were still being rebuilt to F-4J standard when undergoing life extension programmes. In 1973, therefore, the **F-4N** arrived in service, this being a version that was confined to rebuilding F-4Js with such equipment updates as provision for Sidewinder Expanded

Acquisition Mode (SEAM), helmet-sight Visual Target Acquisition System (VTAS) and additional structural components to extend service life. Total conversion involved 227 F-4Ns (which included a number of **F-4N(AC)** air combat aircraft for the Marine Corps with manoeuvring wing slats), plus 24 conversions of F-4Bs to **QF-4N**, target drones.

A further Conversion In Lieu of Procurement (CILOP) programme, known as Project 'Bee Line', has resulted in the introduction of some 300 **F-4S** Phantoms, rebuilt from F-4Ns (plus a small number of **QF-4S** drone updates of the QF-4N). Featuring entirely new outer wings with the manoeuvring slats of the Marine Corps' F-4N(AC) version, the F-4S also includes updated avionics, inboard leading-edge flaps, improved airframe corrosion resistance and further enhanced fatigue life for continuation of fleet service to the end of the decade or beyond.

Following the Falkland Islands campaign the UK government negotiated the purchase of 15 F-4Js (as the **F-4J(UK)**) to equip No. 74 Squadron, RAF, as an air defence element in the Falkland Islands but in fact deployed in the UK. These aircraft were drawn from US Navy storage, life-extended and adapted to mount Sky Flash AAMs and SUU-23A centreline gun pod. Unlike other RAF Phantoms, the newly-introduced aircraft retain the J79 turbojets and much other American equipment.

This McDonnell Douglas F-4S wears the insignia of the MCAS Beaufort-based VMFA-333 'Shamrocks'.

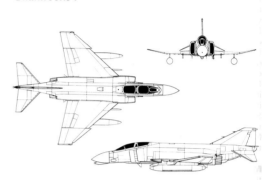

McDonnell Douglas F-4S

Specification: McDonnell Douglas F-4J-33 Phantom II
Origin: USA
Type: two-seat carrier-borne multi-role attack/interceptor fighter
Powerplant: two 8119-kg (17,900-lb) thrust General Electric J79-GE-10 afterburning turbojet engines
Performance: maximum speed Mach 2.23 or 1277 kts (2360 km/h; 1,470 mph) at 40,000 ft (12190 m); service ceiling 61,000 ft (18590 m); unrefuelled intercept (not CAP) combat radius 1001 km (622 miles)
Weights: empty equipped 13566 kg (29,908 lb); maximum take-off 28300 kg (62,390 lb)
Dimensions: span 11.71 m (38 ft 5 in); length 17.78 m (58 ft 4 in); height 5.02 m (16 ft 5.5 in); wing area 49.24 m² (530.0 sq ft)
Armament: basic CAP weapon configuration comprises four AIM-7 Sparrow AAMs semi-recessed under fuselage and up to four AIM-9 Sidewinder AAMs on wing pylons in addition to single centreline gun pod and two wing drop tanks; for interdiction strike sorties air-to-ground missiles or bombs up to approximately 8165 kg (18,000 lb) can be carried in lieu of AAMs and drop tanks

Most recent user of the F-4J is the Royal Air Force, which took delivery of 15 refurbished US Navy aircraft after the Falklands war, designating them F-4J(UK).

The delivery of the F-4J(UK) allowed the reformation of No. 74 'Tiger' Squadron at RAF Wattisham, Suffolk. The aircraft retain a large amount of US Navy equipment.

McDonnell Douglas F-4K/M (Phantom Mks 1 and 2)

United Kingdom

Following discontinuation of the carrierborne Hawker-Siddeley P.1154 for the Royal Navy in 1964, a version of the F-4 for that service was ordered, politically tailored to meet British requirements for maximum use of UK-developed components, including the Rolls-Royce Spey turbofan. In order to cater for the greater mass flow of the British engines extensive changes were necessary in the airframe, including considerably enlarged air inlets. In the event, despite a 16 per cent increase in power (both dry and wet) from the Speys, the British Phantoms were inferior to the current J79-powered F-4Js of the US Navy in speed, climb, range and ceiling, and the installation proved a disappointment.

First flown on 27 June 1966, the **McDonnell F-4K** (**Phantom FG.Mk 1**) for the Royal Navy featured double-hinged folding nose radome, to make the aircraft compatible with the smaller British carriers, inverted stabilator slat and increased nosewheel leg travel to provide optimum wing incidence during carrier catapulting. Changing attitudes towards British naval fixed-wing aircraft operation limited deliveries of the F-4K to 24 for the Royal Navy. Meanwhile the F-4 had also been selected for the RAF (following final cancellation of the P.1154 in February 1965) and the **F-4M**, also Spey-powered, first flew on 28 August 1967. Orders for RAF **Phantom FGR. Mk 2** aircraft totalled 118,

50 per cent of their components being manufactured in the UK. Also developed for the Mk 2 were the BAe Sky Flash MRAAM (developed from the AIM-7 Sparrow), a large EMI multi-sensor reconnaissance pack (carried ventrally), and a completely new Ferranti nav/attack system. Gun armament of both British versions is confined to external pod carriage.

Run-down of the Royal Navy's fighter force resulted in the final 28 F-4Ks being delivered to the RAF, complete with extending nose-wheel leg, slatted stabilator and AWG-11 fire control. The F-4M, on the other hand, features AWG-12 fire control and landing gear similar to that of the F-4C. In due course the surviving F-4Ks, previously flown by the Royal Navy, were also passed to the RAF. Although it was originally planned to phase this heterogeneous collection of Phantoms out of RAF service with the arrival of the Panavia Tornado F. Mk 2/3 in the mid-1980s it is now likely that with life-extension programmes undertaken in the UK the surviving FGR. Mk 2s will remain in service with at least two RAF squadrons until the end of the decade, if not beyond. Despite criticism of the powerplant, the RAF Phantoms have performed well in the RAF both as area-defence interceptors based in the UK and as reconnaissance aircraft in West Germany.

Specification: McDonnell Douglas F-4M Phantom II
Origin: USA (UK)
Type: two-seat multi-role fighter
Powerplant: two 9305-kg (20,515-lb) thrust Rolls-Royce Spey Mk 204 afterburning turbofan engines
Performance: maximum speed Mach 2.1 or 1204 kts (2230 km/h; 1,386 mph) at 36,090 ft (11000 m); initial rate of climb 32,000 ft (9754 m) per minute; combat radius 241 km (150 miles); ferry range 2816 km (1,750 miles)
Weights: empty equipped 14024 kg (30,918 lb); maximum take-off 26308 kg (58,000 lb)
Dimensions: span 11.71 m (38 ft 5 in); length 17.55 m (57 ft 7.07 in); height 4.90 m (16 ft 1 in); wing area 49.24 m² (530.0 sq ft)
Armament: basic weapon configuration comprises four BAe Sky Flash (or Sparrow III) and four AIM-9L Sidewinder AAMs and one SUU-23A gun pod; alternative ground support/attack stores include reconnaissance pack, bombs, rocket-launchers, ECM pods, laser designators, anti-radiation missiles etc

This F-4K Phantom FG.Mk 1 serves with A Squadron, A&AEE at Boscombe Down.

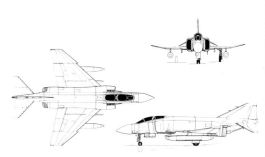

McDonnell Douglas F-4M Phantom FGR.Mk 2

The naval origins of this No. 43 Squadron Phantom FG.Mk 1 quite literally show through, red paint from the No. 892 crest being clearly visible on the fin where the RAF camouflage has worn away.

This black-spined FG.Mk 1 belongs to No. 111 Squadron, based at Leuchars for interception duties alongside the similarly-equipped No. 43 Squadron. Many are ex-Royal Navy aircraft.

Role
- Fighter
- Close support
- Counter-insurgency
- Tactical strike
- Strategic bomber
- Tactical reconnaissance
- Strategic reconnaissance
- Maritime patrol
- Anti-ship strike
- Anti-submarine warfare
- Search and rescue
- Assault transport
- Transport
- Liaison
- Trainer
- Inflight-refuelling tanker
- Specialized

Performance
- All-weather capability
- Rough field capability
- STOL capability
- VTOL capability
- Airspeed 0-250 mph
- Airspeed 250 mph-Mach 1
- Airspeed Mach 1 plus
- Ceiling 0-20,000 ft
- Ceiling 20,000-40,000 ft
- Ceiling 40,000 ft plus
- Range 0-1,000 miles
- Range 1,000-3,000 miles
- Range 3,000 miles plus

Weapons
- Air-to-air missiles
- Air-to-surface missiles
- Cruise missiles
- Cannon
- Trainable guns
- Naval weapons
- Nuclear-capable
- Rockets
- 'Smart' weapon kit
- Weapon load 0-4,000 lb
- Weapon load 4,000-15,000 lb
- Weapon load 15,000 lb plus

Avionics
- Electronic Counter Measures
- Electronic Support Measures
- Search radar
- Fire control radar
- Look-down/shoot-down
- Terrain-following radar
- Forward-looking infra-red
- Laser
- Television

121

McDonnell Douglas RF-4B/C/X Phantom II

West Germany Greece Iran Israel Spain Turkey

United States

Representing a radical breakaway from the basic F-4B/C, a reconnaissance version of the Phantom II was first flown as the **YRF-4C** in demonstration form on 8 August 1963 and, in response to the USAF's Special Operational Requirement 196, entered production the following year as the **McDonnell RF-4C**, being intended to replace the McDonnell RF-101C in service. All the customary missile and bomb delivery systems are deleted and the nose is lengthened to accommodate APQ-99 radar; the ASQ-19 is replaced by ASQ-88B, and other avionics include ASN-56 inertial navigator, APQ-102 SLAR, ASQ-90 data display, ALR-17 ECM receiver, AAS-18 IR detector and APR-25 homing and warning system. A comprehensive range of alternative camera fits is provided for, including high- and low-altitude pan units and forward-facing and oblique cameras in front, centre and rear positions. At the same time a nuclear weapon delivery capability is included (thereby replacing the F-101C in service), single B28, B43 or B57 weapons being carried on the fuselage centreline mounting. For nuclear delivery and reconnaissance sorties ALQ-71, -72 and -87 ECM pods can be carried, although drop tanks usually occupy the wing pylons. RF-4Cs served in Vietnam from 1965 onwards and during the 1970s progressive updates included the introduction of the Westinghouse

ALQ-101 jammer and a range of developed ALQ-series Elint systems.

In due course the US Marine Corps also received a navalized version, the **RF-4B**, and a small number of **RF-4E** aircraft (export RF-4Cs with reduced electronic fit) was supplied to Israel. Total production of the RF-4C amounted to 503 aircraft. In the German Luftwaffe 88 RF-4Es replaced the Lockheed RF-104G in service and the version was also supplied to Australia (on lease during the early 1970s), Iran, Japan (as the **RF-4EJ**), Spain (as the **CR.12**), Greece, Turkey and South Korea.

The reconnaissance Phantom formula was considerably advanced by General Dynamics in the mid-1970s for Israel in a programme codenamed 'Peace Jack', in which three Israeli F-4Es were modified to include a large HIAC-1 high-altitude high-resolution camera in a lengthened nose for long-range oblique photography. Known in turn as **F-4X**, **RF-4X** and **F-4E(S)**, the special aircraft, which included water injection for pre-compressor section cooling and modified engine inlets, was capable of Mach 2.4 cruise at 78,000ft (23775m), permitting high-definition reconnaissance cover of 62160km² (24,000 sq miles) in a four-minute dash at maximum speed and altitude. It is assumed that some, if not all, of these aircraft remain in service today.

Specification: McDonnell Douglas RF-4C Phantom II
Origin: USA
Type: two-seat reconnaissance aircraft
Powerplant: two 7711-kg (17,000-lb) thrust General Electric J79-GE-15 afterburning turbojet engines
Performance: maximum speed Mach 2.21 or 1267 kts (2348 km/h; 1,459 mph) at 40,000 ft (12190m); initial rate of climb 48,000 ft (14630 m) per minute; service ceiling 59,400 ft (18105 m); combat radius 1352 km (840 miles); ferry range 2816 km (1,750 miles)
Weights: empty 12826 kg (28,276 lb); maximum take-off 26308 kg (58,000 lb)
Dimensions: span 11.71 m (38 ft 5 in); length 19.17 m (62 ft 11 in); height 5.03 m (16 ft 6 in); wing area 49.24 m² (530.0 sq ft)
Armament: weapons not normally carried.

This McDonnell Douglas RF-4EJ serves with the 501st Hikotai, JASDF.

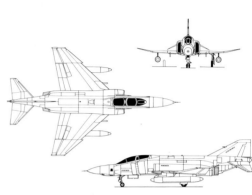

McDonnell Douglas RF-4E

A Luftwaffe RF-4E Phantom of the Leck-based Aufklärungsgeschwader 53 closes in on a USAF KC-135 Stratotanker for an inflight-refuelling. The Luftwaffe received 88 RF-4s.

Eight newly-built RF-4E Phantom IIs were supplied to the Turkish air force and are based at No. 1 Air Base, Eskisehir, with 113 Filo, part of the 1st Tactical Air Force.

An F-15A Eagle with its 4 Sidewinder AAMs

McDonnell Douglas F-15A/C Eagle

Israel   Japan   Saudi Arabia   United States

A McDonnell Douglas F-15C Eagle of the Israeli air force.

Representing a logical progression from the F-4, the **McDonnell Douglas F-15 Eagle** was the outcome of a USAF funding request in 1965 for a new air superiority fighter (at just about the time the US Navy's F-4 was first adopted by the USAF). First flown on 27 July 1972, the **F-15A** emerged as a single-seat twin-turbofan aircraft featuring broad centre and rear fuselage, low aspect ratio fixed-geometry swept wings, tall twin vertical tail surfaces and all-moving horizontal tail surfaces with saw-tooth extended leading edges. Pratt & Whitney F100-PW-100 turbofans with external compression inlets bestow Mach 2.5 performance at high altitude, in turn resulting in extensive use of titanium (more than 20 per cent of airframe weight). Production of the F-15A continued until 1979 with 361 built, including 51 delivered to Israel and 45 to Saudi Arabia.

Principal variant thus far is the **F-15C**, whose first production examples appeared in 1979 and had reached about 400 by the end of 1985. This version, which is now in operational service with USAF tactical fighter wings and fighter interceptor squadrons in the USA (including Alaska), at Kadena (Okinawa), and in Europe, features provision for a pair of conformal fuel tanks (CFTs) which each contain 3228 litres (853 US gal) of usable fuel and which are fitted 'flush' to the sides of the inlet trunks, thus leaving all store hard-

points available for ordnance (or further fuel tanks). Moreover, tangential store mountings have been developed, allowing up to 12 further 454-kg (1,000-lb) stores to be located at the lower shoulders of the CFTs, in all representing an external store load of 10705 kg (23,600 lb). Avionics include Hughes APG-63 X-band pulse-Doppler radar (due to be replaced by APG-70), General Electric automatic analog flight-control system, IBM central computer, Northrop enhanced ALQ-135(V) integral automatic jammer, Magnavox EW warning subsystem and DCC stores management system. Inbuilt armament comprises a single M61A1 six-barrel cannon with 940 rounds in the right-hand wing root, and a normal missile fit is either four AIM-7F/M Sparrow MRAAMs and four AIM-9L/M Sidewinder SRAAMs, or eight AMRAAMs.

In service F-15Cs have replaced all F-15As with regular wings, the redundant aircraft being introduced into the Air National Guard, starting with Louisiana and Georgia squadrons. The F-15C was selected for licence production by Japan, 14 US-built aircraft preceding 88 **F-15J** fighters manufactured by Mitsubishi. A plan to lease F-15As to the RAF to assist in the defence of USAF bases in the UK pending the arrival of Panavia Tornado F. Mk 2/3s in service, though entertained for about three years, did not come to fruition.

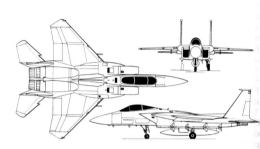

McDonnell Douglas F-15A Eagle

These McDonnell Douglas F-15s of the 32nd TFS are based at Camp New Amsterdam, otherwise known as Soesterberg. The unit reports directly to the Netherlands air force, and is assigned to 2 ATAF.

The 36th TFW at Bitburg consists of three F-15 squadrons; each wears a different coloured fin-band. Here two F-15Cs of the 22nd TFS display their huge dorsal airbrakes on approach.

Specification: McDonnell Douglas F-15C Eagle
Origin: USA
Type: single-seat air superiority fighter with secondary attack role
Powerplant: two 10809-kg (23,830-lb) thrust Pratt & Whitney F100-PW-100 afterburning turbofan engines
Performance: maximum speed more than Mach 2.5 or 1433 kts (2655 km/h; 1,650 mph) at high altitude; service ceiling 60,000 ft (18290 m); maximum unrefuelled ferry range with conformal fuel tanks 5745 km (3,570 miles)
Weights: empty equipped 12973 kg (28,600 lb); maximum take-off 30844 kg (68,000 lb)
Dimensions: span 13.05 m (42 ft 9.75 in); length 19.43 m (63 ft 9 in); height 5.63 m (18 ft 5.5 in); wing area 56.48 m² (608 sq ft)
Armament: air-to-air weaponry comprises one M61A1 20-mm six-barrel cannon and provision for four AIM-9L/M Sidewinders and four AIM-7F Sparrow AAMs or eight AMRAAMs; when configured for the attack role with five weapon stations (including two on CFTs) up to 10705 kg (23,600 lb) of bombs, rockets and other air-to-surface weapons can be carried

Role (sidebar)

- Fighter
- Close support
- Counter-insurgency
- Tactical strike
- Strategic bomber
- Tactical reconnaissance
- Strategic reconnaissance
- Maritime patrol
- Anti-ship strike
- Anti-submarine warfare
- Search and rescue
- Assault transport
- Transport
- Liaison
- Trainer
- Inflight-refuelling tanker
- Specialized

Performance

- All-weather capability
- Rough field capability
- STOL capability
- VTOL capability
- Airspeed 0-250 mph
- Airspeed 250 mph-Mach 1
- Airspeed Mach 1 plus
- Ceiling 0-20,000 ft
- Ceiling 20,000-40,000 ft
- Ceiling 40,000 ft plus
- Range 0-1,000 miles
- Range 1,000-3,000 miles
- Range 3,000 miles plus

Weapons

- Air-to-air missiles
- Air-to-surface missiles
- Cruise missiles
- Cannon
- Trainable guns
- Naval weapons
- Nuclear-capable
- Rockets
- 'Smart' weapon kit
- Weapon load 0-4,000 lb
- Weapon load 4,000-15,000 lb
- Weapon load 15,000 lb plus

Avionics

- Electronic Counter Measures
- Electronic Support Measures
- Search radar
- Fire control radar
- Look-down/shoot-down
- Terrain-following radar
- Forward-looking infra-red
- Laser
- Television

McDonnell Douglas F-15B/D Eagle

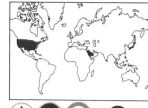

Israel   Japan   Saudi Arabia   United States

Developed more or less simultaneously with the single-seat F-15A Eagle, the first two-seat **McDonnell Douglas F-15B** (originally termed the **TF-15A**) made its maiden flight on 7 July 1973 and started delivery to the USAF on 14 November the following year, first equipping the 58th Tactical Training Wing at Luke AFB. Inclusion of the second cockpit was effected without extensive structural alteration and without overall airframe dimension change, and involved a structural weight penalty of no more than 363 kg (800 lb). All avionic equipment and stores fit are retained, enabling full operational conversion training and check-out to be carried out. F-15Bs figured in the establishment of most F-15A tactical squadrons. Two F-15Bs were included in the export package to Israel in 1977, while the deferred order for F-15s to Saudi Arabia included 15 F-15Bs, eventually delivered in 1982. A total of 58 was completed for the USAF.

As the first F-15Cs appeared in 1979 the two-seat derivative, the **F-15D**, was first flown on 19 June of that year, joining the 18th TFW in December and the 33rd TFW the following March. Like the F-15C single-seater, the two-seater can also accommodate the CFTs as well as the full fuel load, weapon range and ECM fit, and features the entire range of avionics of the single-seater.

Currently being pursued is a programme to arrive at a version of the F-15D to assume the 'Wild Weasel' air-defence suppression tasks currently undertaken by F-4Gs, and early in 1984 a modified F-15D was being evaluated with a chin pack capable of housing a variety of sensors, including APR-38 'Wild Weasel' radar, infra-red search-and-track system and a TV sight; missile fits would include the current ARM and HARM family as well as ECM pods. At the time of writing it is not clear whether or not F-15Ds are a subject of the $86.7 million programme for a Multi-Stage Improvement Program (MSIP) already underway with the single-seat F-15C, which involves a continuing update of all avionics (and, by implication, missiles), but if no two-seat version of the F-15E is forthcoming it seems certain that the F-15D two-seater must be kept abreast of the latest single-seaters. Foreign F-15D two-seaters are currently confined to the Japanese licence-built **F-15DJ**, of which 12 are currently proposed.

Specification: McDonnell Douglas F-15D Eagle
Origin: USA
Type: two-seat air-superiority fighter trainer (with full operational capability)
Powerplant: two 10809-kg (23,830-lb) thrust Pratt & Whitney F100-PW-100 afterburning turbofan engines
Performance: maximum speed Mach 2.5 or 1433 kts (2655 km/h; 1,650 mph) above 40,000 ft (12190 m); service ceiling 60,000 ft (18290 m); maximum unrefuelled range without conformal fuel tanks more than 4631 km (2,878 miles)
Weights: empty equipped 13336 kg (29,400 lb); maximum take-off 30844 kg (68,000 lb)
Dimensions: span 13.05 m (42 ft 9.75 in); length 19.43 m (63 ft 9 in); height 5.63 m (18 ft 5.5 in); wing area 56.48 m² (608 sq ft)
Armament: one M61A1 20-mm six-barrel cannon in starboard wing root; air-to-air missile load comprises four AIM-7F/M Sparrow and four AIM-9L/M Sidewinder AAMs or up to eight AMRAAMs; if fitted with CFTs air-to-surface and ECM stores of up to a total of 10705 kg (23,600 lb) can be carried

This F-15DJ wears the fin badge of the 204 Hikotai, based at Hyakuri air base.

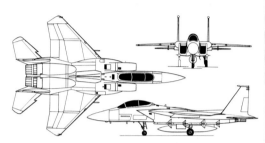

McDonnell Douglas F-15D Eagle

Dog footprints on the fin and a fierce bulldog's-head badge on the engine intake identify this Bitburg-based F-15D as belonging to the 525th TFS, 36th TFW.

The 405th TTW at Luke AFB serves as one of two conversion and refresher training units for the F-15 force. The four squadrons include the 550th TFTS, one of whose aircraft is shown here.

Role
Fighter
Close support
Counter-insurgency
Tactical strike
Strategic bomber
Tactical reconnaissance
Strategic reconnaissance
Maritime patrol
Anti-ship strike
Anti-submarine warfare
Search and rescue
Assault transport
Transport
Liaison
Trainer
Inflight-refuelling tanker
Specialized

Performance
All-weather capability
Rough field capability
STOL capability
VTOL capability
Airspeed 0-250 mph
Airspeed 250 mph-Mach 1
Airspeed Mach 1 plus
Ceiling 0-20,000 ft
Ceiling 20,000-40,000 ft
Ceiling 40,000 ft plus
Range 0-1,000 miles
Range 1,000-3,000 miles
Range 3,000 miles plus

Weapons
Air-to-air missiles
Air-to-surface missiles
Cruise missiles
Cannon
Trainable guns
Naval weapons
Nuclear-capable
Rockets
'Smart' weapon kit
Weapon load 0-4,000 lb
Weapon load 4,000-15,000 lb
Weapon load 15,000 lb plus

Avionics
Electronic Counter Measures
Electronic Support Measures
Search radar
Fire control radar
Look-down/shoot-down
Terrain-following radar
Forward-looking infra-red
Laser
Television

McDonnell Douglas F-15E Eagle

Developed initially under commercial funding, the **McDonnell Douglas F-15E** (originally known as the **Strike Eagle**) is a two-seat dual-role deep interdiction strike aircraft which retains the basic type's proven air-to-air combat capabilities. Using an upgraded F-15B, the prototype was flown in 1982 and following successful competitive evaluation with the General Dynamics F-16XL in 1982-3 the USAF announced its intention to proceed with the F-15E, and manufacture of three prototypes started in 1985. Current plans are for procurement of 392 dual-role Eagles.

Adoption of the two-seat layout for this adverse-weather deep-penetration strike aircraft represented a *volte face* in the USAF, which had tended to the belief that (given adequate avionic sophistication) accurate navigation, and weapon delivery and management were possible by pilot alone. The F-15E's rear seat occupant is provided with four multi-purpose CRT displays for weapon management and selection, and for threat monitoring; the pilot is provided with wide-angle HUD, CRTs and moving map display for navigation, precision radar mapping and automatic terrain following. To accommodate increased avionics one fuselage tank has

been reduced in size, but the F-15E can employ the standard conformal tanks, and an important feature is the widespread inclusion of provision to accommodate physical and performance growth of new equipment without extensive alteration to the aircraft structure. For instance the engine bay has been redesigned so as to accept either the Pratt & Whitney F100 or General Electric F110 turbofans, even when a pair of these or other engines is developed to deliver up to 27215-kg (60,000-lb) thrust. In due course the Hughes APG-70 radar/computer with 1,000K memory and trebled processing speed will also be fitted. Clearance at a maximum take-off weight of 36741kg (81,000lb) will be achieved by local structure strengthening and revised landing gear components. (During early testing an F-15 took-off at 34019kg/75,000lb carrying two full conformal tanks and three 2,309-litre/610-US gal external fuel tanks as well as eight 227-kg/500-lb Mk 82 bombs on CFT tangential racks.) Among the weapon delivery systems that will be compatible with the F-15E will be the LANTIRN illuminator pod with GBU-12, -22 and -24 laser-guided weapons, and the AXQ-14 data link pod with GBU-15 weapon.

Prototype McDonnell Douglas F-15E Strike Eagle interdictor strike aircraft.

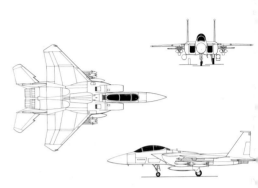

McDonnell Douglas F-15E Strike Eagle

The McDonnell Douglas F-15E Strike Eagle currently wears a sinister two-tone dark green colour scheme, reflecting its low-level interdictor role.

The McDonnell Douglas F-15E Strike Eagle prototype began life in the standard air-superiority grey scheme, and differed from a standard F-15B only in its equipment and armament.

Specification: McDonnell Douglas F-15E Eagle

Origin: USA
Type: two-seat dual-role attack/air-superiority fighter
Powerplant: two 10809-kg (23,830-lb) thrust Pratt & Whitney F100-PW-100 afterburning turbofan engines
Performance: maximum speed more than Mach 2.5 or 1,433 kts (2655 km/h; 1650 mph) above 36,000ft (10970m); service ceiling 60,000 ft (18290m); maximum unrefuelled range with conformal fuel tanks 5745 km (3,570 miles)
Weights: empty equipped 14379 kg (31,700 lb); maximum take-off 36741 kg (81,000lb)
Dimensions: span 13.05m (42 ft 9.75 in); length 19.43m (63 ft 9 in); height 5.63m (18 ft 5.5 in); wing area 56.48m² (608 sq ft)
Armament: one M61A1 Vulcan 20-mm six-barrel cannon in starboard wing root; single centreline store mountings and two underwing pylons for fuel tanks, AIM-7, AIM-9 and/or AIM-120 AAMs; a tangential rack on each CFT allows carriage of six bomb racks; typical loads include 26 Mk 20 Rockeye cluster bombs, six AGM-65 Maverick air-to-surface missiles or nine B61 nuclear weapons

McDonnell Douglas F-18A Hornet

Australia Canada Spain United States

The **McDonnell Douglas F-18A Hornet** was designed to fulfil two distinct roles, and consequently is produced in a form easily adaptable to either of them: fighter escort and light attack. The first of these resulted from the increasing realization in the USA during the early 1970s that there existed the requirement for an aircraft which was inexpensive, straightforward to produce and light in weight, to replace the McDonnell Douglas F-4 Phantom II, and to operate in combination with the more sophisticated, but heavier and more expensive McDonnell Douglas F-15. The light attack requirement derived from the need to replace the Vought A-7 Corsair. For the USN and USMC, the Grumman F-14/F-18 mix was determined, while the USAF adopted the F-15/General Dynamics F-16 combination.

The Hornet was derived from the Northrop YF-17, which had its first flight on 9 June 1974, itself a development of the P.530 Cobra project. In May 1975 it was announced that the new aircraft would be designated F-18A, with McDonnell Douglas the prime contractor and Northrop Corporation undertaking 30 per cent of airframe development and 40 per cent of airframe production work. The prime contractor for the F404 engines was General Electric, while Hughes Aircraft undertook to produce the APG-65 radar. In the develop-

ment of the aircraft from the YF-17 its wing area was increased, a new and more robust landing gear was installed, and it was given a wing fold, a retractable inflight-refuelling probe, provision for AIM-7 Sparrow medium-range missiles, and increased fuel capacity.

Full-scale production of the F-18A began on 22 January 1976 and the maiden flight took place on 18 November 1978. In comparison with its predecessor in the fighter escort role, the Hornet offers a superior rate of acceleration, has a smaller turning radius, offers more accurate detection of enemy aircraft, and is strong enough to withstand the rigour of continued aircraft-carrier take-offs and landings. In its role as a light attack aircraft it is capable of increased speed over targets, and also has an improved thrust-to-weight ratio. Although the aircraft was originally to have been produced to two completely different designs (according to the two different roles), it is built to a single standard and the process of conversion from one role to another is very simple and quick. In addition to those on order for the US Navy, delivery of 138 land-based aircraft to the Canadian Armed Forces began in 1982, acceptance of 75 for the Royal Australian Air Force is under way, and some 72 are being produced for Spain.

This McDonnell Douglas F-18 serves with the Canadian Armed Forces, who designate the type CF-18 and do not officially use the name Hornet.

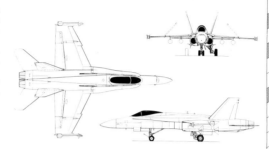

McDonnell Douglas F-18 Hornet

Canada's Europe-based No. 1 CAG has now replaced its ageing CF-104s with CF-18s, giving NATO a much-needed boost in capability. Three squadrons are in service at Baden-Söllingen.

An F-18 of the Lemoore-based VFA-113 'Stingers' lands on USS Constellation. The F-18 has given the US Navy a highly versatile carrierborne fighter and attack aircraft to replace its F-4s and A-7s.

Specification: McDonnell Douglas F-18A Hornet
Origin: USA
Type: single-seat fighter and attack aircraft
Powerplant: two 7257-kg (16,000-lb) thrust General Electric F404-GE-400 low bypass turbofan engines
Performance: maximum speed Mach 1.8+ or more than 1,032 kts (1912 km/h; 1,188 mph) at 40,000 ft (12190 m); combat ceiling approximately 50,000 ft (15240 m); combat radius, fighter escort 740 km (460 miles), attack mission 1065 km (662 miles)
Weights: empty 10455 kg (23,050 lb); maximum take-off 22328 kg (49,224 lb)
Dimensions: span 11.43 m (37 ft 6 in); length 17.07 m (56 ft 0 in); height 4.66 m (15 ft 3.5 in); wing area 37.16 m² (400.0 sq ft)
Armament: one 20-mm M61A1 Vulcan six-barrel rotary cannon, plus nine external weapons stations with a combined capacity of 7711 kg (17,000 lb); air defence weapons include AIM-9 Sidewinder and AIM-7 Sparrow air-to-air missiles

Role
Fighter
Close support
Counter-insurgency
Tactical strike
Strategic bomber
Tactical reconnaissance
Strategic reconnaissance
Maritime patrol
Anti-ship strike
Anti-submarine warfare
Search and rescue
Assault transport
Transport
Liaison
Trainer
Inflight-refuelling tanker
Specialized

Performance
All-weather capability
Rough field capability
STOL capability
VTOL capability
Airspeed 0-250 mph
Airspeed 250 mph-Mach 1
Airspeed Mach 1 plus
Ceiling 0-20,000 ft
Ceiling 20,000-40,000 ft
Ceiling 40,000 ft plus
Range 0-1,000 miles
Range 1,000-3,000 miles
Range 3,000 miles plus

Weapons
Air-to-air missiles
Air-to-surface missiles
Cruise missiles
Cannon
Trainable guns
Naval weapons
Nuclear-capable
Rockets
'Smart' weapon kit
Weapon load 0-4,000 lb
Weapon load 4,000-15,000 lb
Weapon load 15,000 lb plus

Avionics
Electronic Counter Measures
Electronic Support Measures
Search radar
Fire control radar
Look-down/shoot-down
Terrain-following radar
Forward-looking infra-red
Laser
Television

McDonnell Douglas F-18B Hornet

Australia Canada Spain United States

An early production F-18B of the US Navy.

On 18 November 1978 the first Hornet made its maiden flight in St Louis, Missouri as part of a batch of 11 aircraft (BuNos 160775-785) which included two combat-capable two-seat training versions, designated **McDonnell Douglas F-18B Hornet**. By March 1980 all 11 development aircraft had flown, including the two trainer aircraft. The F-18B is produced with the same nav/attack systems and ordnance capability as the single-seat Hornet, and is capable of approximately the same performance, with the exception of its range which is decreased marginally as a result of a 5 per cent reduction in fuel capacity.

The first US Navy Hornet squadron, VFA-125, was commissioned at NAS Lemoore in November 1980, assigned the task of serving as the 'Combat Readiness Training Squadron for Pacific Fleet Units'. As a training unit, VFA-125 employs a 50/50 mix of single-seat and two-seat F-18s. Currently the squadron operates under a dual service command structure with Navy and Marine personnel equally represented. Initially, 32 pilots (16 Navy and 16 Marine Corps) were trained to become instructors. The first set of students began training in the summer of 1982, and VFA-125 now trains up to 70 new pilots per year. Each class lasts six months, during which each student receives over 100 hours flying time. Other squadrons employing the aircraft are VFA-113, VFA-132, VMFA-314, VMFA-323, and VMFA-531.

The US Navy plans to take on a total of 1,370 F-18s before the year 2002, including 129 two-seaters. With the duplication of all instrumentation in the rear cockpit (apart from the head-up display) users no doubt see the advantage of the two-man crewing potential, especially in the attack role. Originally, approximately 8 per cent of all Hornets produced were F-18Bs, but of the 72 aircraft now being delivered to the Spanish air force (initially to No. 151 squadron at Zaragoza) 12 are trainer versions designated EF-18B. The structure of the Canadian Armed Forces' order for 138 aircraft was recently adapted in order to incorporate a greater number of two-seat aircraft: of a total of 138 aircraft the number of two-seat CF-18Bs has increased from 28 to 40. The CAF will have three squadrons (Nos 409, 421 and 439) stationed at Baden-Söllingen in West Germany by 1987, two (425 and 433) at home in Bagotville, and a further two (416 and 441) at Cold Lake, where No. 410 Squadron is already operating.

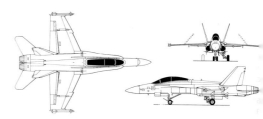

McDonnell Douglas F-18B Hornet

This view of the first EF-18B Hornet at its roll-out ceremony shows to good effect the huge leading-edge strakes that give the Hornet its outstanding handling at high AOA.

The first of 75 Hornets ordered by the Royal Australian Air Force was this F-18B. Three squadrons are to form, and will replace the ageing fleet of Dassault-Breguet Mirage IIIOs.

Specification: McDonnell Douglas F-18B Hornet
Origin: USA
Type: two-seat combat capable conversion trainer
Powerplant: two 7257-kg (16,000-lb) thrust General Electric F404-GE-400 low bypass turbofan engines
Performance: maximum level speed at 40,000 ft (12190 m) Mach 1.8 or 1032 kts (1912 km/h; 1,188 mph); sustained manoeuvre ceiling more than 49,000 ft (14935 m); attack combat radius 1020 km (634 miles); ferry range 3520 km (2,187 miles)
Weights: fighter mission take-off 15234 kg (33,585 lb); attack mission take-off 21319 kg (47,000 lb)
Dimensions: span 11.43 m (37 ft 6 in); length 17.07 m (56 ft 0 in); height 4.66 m (15 ft 3.5 in); wing area 37.16 m² (400.0 sq ft)
Armament: one 20-mm M61A1 Vulcan six-barrel rotary cannon, plus nine external weapons stations with a combined capacity of 7711 kg (17,000 lb); attack weapons include conventional bombs, AGM-65 Maverick, AGM-88A HARM and AGM-62 Walleye air-to-surface missiles, and Mk 20 Rockeye cluster bombs

Role
- Fighter
- Close support
- Counter-insurgency
- Tactical strike
- Strategic bomber
- Tactical reconnaissance
- Strategic reconnaissance
- Maritime patrol
- Anti-ship strike
- Anti-submarine warfare
- Search and rescue
- Assault transport
- Transport
- Liaison
- Trainer
- Inflight-refuelling tanker
- Specialized

Performance
- All-weather capability
- Rough field capability
- STOL capability
- VTOL capability
- Airspeed 0-250 mph
- Airspeed 250 mph-Mach 1
- Airspeed Mach 1 plus
- Ceiling 0-20,000 ft
- Ceiling 20,000-40,000 ft
- Ceiling 40,000 ft plus
- Range 0-1,000 miles
- Range 1,000-3,000 miles
- Range 3,000 miles plus

Weapons
- Air-to-air missiles
- Air-to-surface missiles
- Cruise missiles
- Cannon
- Trainable guns
- Naval weapons
- Nuclear-capable
- Rockets
- 'Smart' weapon kit
- Weapon load 0-4,000 lb
- Weapon load 4,000-15,000 lb
- Weapon load 15,000 lb plus

Avionics
- Electronic Counter Measures
- Electronic Support Measures
- Search radar
- Fire control radar
- Look-down/shoot-down
- Terrain-following radar
- Forward-looking infra-red
- Laser
- Television

McDonnell Douglas Helicopter (Hughes) AH-64

United States

Formulated in the early 1970s, the US Army's requirement for an advanced attack helicopter (AAH) visualized an aircraft operating in and fighting from a front-line environment, and suitable for a day/night/adverse weather anti-armour role. US manufacturers Bell and Hughes were selected to build competing prototypes, the YAH-63 and **YAH-64** respectively, but it was the Hughes submission that on 10 December 1976 was declared winner of the first stage. Six more aircraft were built for continuing development during the second phase of the programme, concerned primarily with evaluation of the avionics, electro-optical and fire-control systems. It was not until 26 March 1982 that final production approval was given with the issue of a US Army contract for an initial batch of 11 **Hughes AH-64A** helicopters, to which the name **Apache** had been given almost a year earlier. Total planned procurement was 536, a figure which rising costs later cut back to 446, but since then growing confidence in the Apache's capability has brought further revisions and the US Army now hopes to procure 675 by the end of 1988.

In formulating its **Model 77** design for the US Army's AAH requirement, Hughes began with a fuselage structure to survive fire from 12.7-mm (0.5-in) machine-guns and 23-mm cannon. The fuselage is carried on fixed tailwheel landing gear, the main units of which fold to reduce height for storage/

transport, and has seats in tandem for the co-pilot/gunner (forward) and pilot, the latter with a raised (by 48.3cm/19in) seat. There is extensive armour protection, and the crew's seats, adjacent fuselage structure and landing gear are designed to give the crew a 95 per cent chance of surviving a ground impact of up to 12.8m (42ft) per second. The main rotor has four wide-chord blades with swept tips, and the blades can be folded or easily removed for transport; the tail rotor (port) is unusual, its four blades being located at an optimum quiet setting of about 55°/125° to each other. The two turboshaft engines are mounted one each side of the fuselage, above removable stub-wings that each have two hardpoints beneath them for weapons or auxiliary fuel. Beneath the fuselage, forward of the mainwheel legs, is mounted a McDonnell Douglas (Hughes) M230 30-mm Chain Gun. Avionics include the specially developed PNVS and TADS, in independent nose-mounted turrets. The Pilot's Night-Vision System incorporates FLIR to give night vision, while the Target-Acquisition and Designation System combines TV camera, laser spot tracker and laser designator/rangefinder. Together with an inertial attitude/heading reference system, Doppler radar and other advanced features, the crew can fly nap-of-the-Earth sorties with confidence by day or night and in all weather conditions.

Specification: McDonnell Douglas (Hughes) AH-64A Apache
Origin: USA
Type: attack helicopter
Powerplant: two 1265-kW (1,696-shp) General Electric T700-GE-701 turboshaft engines, derated for normal operations
Performance: (at mission gross weight) maximum speed 160 kts (296 km/h; 184mph); initial vertical climb rate 2,500 ft (762 m) per minute; service ceiling 21,000 ft (6400 m); maximum range with internal fuel 483 km (300 miles)
Weights: empty 4881 kg (10,760 lb); primary mission take-off 6552 kg (14,445 lb); maximum take-off 9525 kg (21,000 lb)
Dimensions: main rotor diameter 14.63 m (48 ft 0 in); length, rotors turning 17.76 m (58 ft 3.1 in); height overall 5.12 m (16 ft 9.5 in); main rotor disc area 168.11 m² (1,809.56 sq ft)
Armament: one M230 30-mm Chain gun with up to 1,200 rounds, plus four underwing pylons for up to 16 Hellfire anti-tank missiles, or 76 2.75-in (69.85-mm) rockets, or combinations of both

A McDonnell Douglas Helicopter (Hughes) AH-64 Apache of the US Army.

McDonnell Douglas Helicopter (Hughes) AH-64 Apache

A prototype AH-64 Apache carries clusters of four Rockwell Hellfire anti-tank missiles under each of its stub wings, with rocket pods at the tips. A 30-mm Chain Gun is located under the nose.

The AH-64 is now entering service in large numbers, but has had a troubled gestation, with groundings and restrictions affecting the whole fleet on several occasions.

Role	
Fighter	
Close support	■
Counter-insurgency	
Tactical strike	
Strategic bomber	
Tactical reconnaissance	
Strategic reconnaissance	
Maritime patrol	
Anti-ship strike	
Anti-submarine warfare	
Search and rescue	
Assault transport	
Transport	
Liaison	
Trainer	
Inflight-refuelling tanker	
Specialized	

Performance	
All-weather capability	■
Rough field capability	■
STOL capability	
VTOL capability	■
Airspeed 0-250 mph	■
Airspeed 250 mph-Mach 1	
Airspeed Mach 1 plus	
Ceiling 0-20,000 ft	■
Ceiling 20,000-40,000 ft	
Ceiling 40,000ft plus	
Range 0-1,000 miles	■
Range 1,000-3,000 miles	
Range 3,000 miles plus	

Weapons	
Air-to-air missiles	
Air-to-surface missiles	■
Cruise missiles	
Cannon	■
Trainable guns	■
Naval weapons	
Nuclear-capable	
Rockets	■
'Smart' weapon kit	
Weapon load 0-4,000 lb	■
Weapon load 4,000-15,000 lb	
Weapon load 15,000 lb plus	

Avionics	
Electronic Counter Measures	
Electronic Support Measures	
Search radar	
Fire control radar	
Look-down/shoot-down	
Terrain-following radar	
Forward-looking infra-red	■
Laser	■
Television	■

McDonnell Douglas Helicopter (Hughes) OH-6A

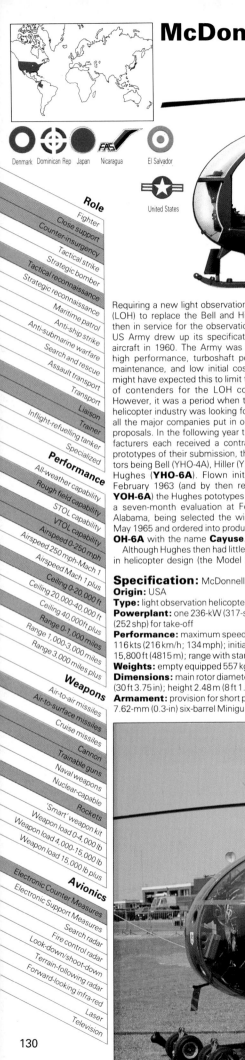

Requiring a new light observation helicopter (LOH) to replace the Bell and Hiller aircraft then in service for the observation role, the US Army drew up its specification for the aircraft in 1960. The Army was looking for high performance, turboshaft power, easy maintenance, and low initial cost, and one might have expected this to limit the number of contenders for the LOH competition. However, it was a period when the nation's helicopter industry was looking for work and all the major companies put in one or more proposals. In the following year three manufacturers each received a contract for five prototypes of their submission, the competitors being Bell (YHO-4A), Hiller (YHO-5A) and Hughes (**YHO-6A**). Flown initially on 27 February 1963 (and by then redesignated **YOH-6A**) the Hughes pototypes took part in a seven-month evaluation at Fort Rucker, Alabama, being selected the winner on 26 May 1965 and ordered into production as the **OH-6A** with the name **Cayuse**.

Although Hughes then had little experience in helicopter design (the Model 269 was at that time in the early production stage) the LOH submission, company designation **Hughes Model 369**, introduced an innovative four-blade rotor offering good control and manoeuvre characteristics. The use of four blades (instead of two) meant that individual blade loading was lower and that a power-boosted (and thus complex) control system was not needed.

Initial production delivery of OH-6As to the US Army began in September 1966 and the new type's performance and reliability in combat in Vietnam left little doubt that the anticipated procurement of some 4,000 would follow. However, the war in Vietnam created enormous demands for aircraft, resulting in material shortages and rising costs, and when Hughes began to push up prices and fall behind on deliveries the Army decided to re-open the LOH competition in late 1967 (won by Bell Helicopters) after contracting for 1,434 OH-6As, all of them delivered by the end of 1970. Some 350 remain in service in 1986 with the US Army National Guard.

Specification: McDonnell Douglas (Hughes) OH-6A Cayuse
Origin: USA
Type: light observation helicopter
Powerplant: one 236-kW (317-shp) Allison T63-A-5A turboshaft engine derated to 188 kW (252 shp) for take-off
Performance: maximum speed 130 kts (241 km/h; 150 mph) at sea level; cruising speed 116 kts (216 km/h; 134 mph); initial climb rate 1,840 ft (561 m) per minute; service ceiling 15,800 ft (4815 m); range with standard fuel 612 km (380 miles)
Weights: empty equipped 557 kg (1,229 lb); maximum take-off 1225 kg (2,700 lb)
Dimensions: main rotor diameter 8.03 m (26 ft 4 in); length, rotors turning 9.24 m (30 ft 3.75 in); height 2.48 m (8 ft 1.5 in); main rotor disc area 50.60 m² (544.63 sq ft)
Armament: provision for short pylon on the port side of the fuselage to mount an XM27 7.62-mm (0.3-in) six-barrel Minigun or an XM75 grenade-launcher

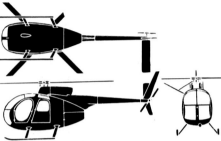

A McDonnell Douglas Helicopter (Hughes) OH-6A Cayuse of the US Army.

McDonnell Douglas Helicopter (Hughes) OH-6A Cayuse

This OH-6A was modified by the manufacturers to serve as a NOTARR (NO TAil RotoR) testbed under a DARPA (Defence Advanced Research Project Agency) contract.

The Danish army operates about a dozen Hughes Model 369s from Vandel in central Jutland. These aircraft are mainly used for observation and reconnaissance duties.

McDonnell Douglas KC-10A Extender

United States

Outcome of a US Air Force requirement, recognized during the mid-1970s, for an advanced tanker/cargo aircraft (ATCA), the McDonnell Douglas DC-10-30 three-turbofan airliner was selected in December 1977 for development to perform this role, designated **McDonnell Douglas KC-10** and later named **Extender**. Following initial research, development and tooling contracts, orders for a total of 16 production **KC-10A** aircraft had been placed by January 1982, with future planning announced to increase the fleet of these tankers to 60 by the end of 1987, subject to annual congressional approval.

Modification of the basic commercial DC-10-30CF to the military configuration was extensive, comprising in the main of the inclusion of seven bladder fuel cells in the lower fuselage compartments (containing a total of 53446 kg/117,829 lb of fuel), provision of an inflight-refuelling boom under the rear fuselage, a boom operator's station, and inclusion of various alternative seating layouts in the forward section of the main cabin. An advanced boom operating system, employing a digital fly-by-wire control procedure, was provided by Sperry Flight Systems, and an alternative hose/reel probe-and-drogue installation was also incorporated for use by US Navy and Marine Corps aircraft. A refuelling receptacle enables the KC-10A itself to be refuelled in flight, but even without this facility the total fuel load capable of being carried, including the tanker's own fuel system, amounts to 108062 kg (238,236 lb), any of which can be used either to extend the tanker's range or replenish other aircraft in flight. In practice this enables the KC-10A to pass 90718 kg (200,000 lb) of fuel to other aircraft 3540 km (2,200 miles) from its home base and then return to that base. Thus it would require just 17 KC-10As to support an entire fighter squadron on a nonstop flight from the USA to the Middle East, at the same time transporting all ground personnel and equipment simultaneously. The task would otherwise require the deployment of 40 Boeing KC-135s. Avionics now provided include a beacon transponder and a radar beacon mode, enabling the KC-10A to act as a pathfinder for such a long-range deployment of fighter aircraft.

First flight by a KC-10A was made on 12 July 1980, and by the end of 1985 Extenders were in service with the 22nd ARW at March AFB, California, the 2nd BW at Barksdale AFB, Louisiana, and the 68th ARG at Seymour Johnson AFB, North Carolina, with Air Force Reserve (Associate) Squadron crews sharing the aircraft of the active duty squadrons.

Specification: McDonnell Douglas KC-10A Extender
Origin: USA
Type: advanced tanker/cargo aircraft
Powerplant: three 23814-kg (52,500-lb) thrust General Electric CF6-50C2 turbofan engines
Performance: maximum speed at 25,000 ft (7620 m) 530 kts (982 km/h; 610 mph); maximum cruising speed 490 kts (908 km/h; 564 mph) at 30,000 ft (9145 m); maximum rate of climb at sea level 2,680 ft (817 m) per minute; unrefuelled range with maximum cargo 7033 km (4,370 miles)
Weights: empty equipped, as tanker 109328 kg (241,027 lb); maximum take-off 267620 kg (590,000 lb)
Dimensions: span 50.40 m (165 ft 4.4 in); length 55.35 m (181 ft 7 in); height 17.70 m (58 ft 1 in); wing area 367.7 m² (3,958 sq ft)
Armament: none

McDonnell Douglas KC-10A, Strategic Air Command, US Air Force.

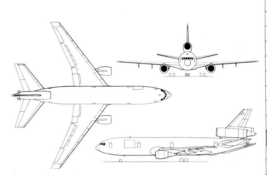

McDonnell Douglas KC-10A Extender

As well as boom capability, the KC-10A has a hose and drogue for probe-equipped receivers. Here an AV-8B prepares to take on fuel.

Definitive colour scheme for the KC-10A is this charcoal grey with light grey undersides. Note the central main wheel inherited from the DC-10 Series 30.

Role
Fighter
Close support
Counter-insurgency
Tactical strike
Strategic bomber
Tactical reconnaissance
Strategic reconnaissance
Maritime patrol
Anti-ship strike
Anti-submarine warfare
Search and rescue
Assault transport
Transport
Liaison
Trainer
Inflight-refuelling tanker
Specialized

Performance
All-weather capability
Rough field capability
STOL capability
VTOL capability
Airspeed 0-250 mph
Airspeed 250 mph-Mach 1
Airspeed Mach 1 plus
Ceiling 0-20,000 ft
Ceiling 20,000-40,000 ft
Ceiling 40,000ft plus
Range 0-1,000 miles
Range 1,000-3,000 miles
Range 3,000 miles plus

Weapons
Air-to-air missiles
Air-to-surface missiles
Cruise missiles
Cannon
Trainable guns
Naval weapons
Nuclear-capable
Rockets
'Smart' weapon kit
Weapon load 0-4,000 lb
Weapon load 4,000-15,000 lb
Weapon load 15,000 lb plus

Avionics
Electronic Counter Measures
Electronic Support Measures
Search radar
Fire control radar
Look-down/shoot-down
Terrain-following radar
Forward-looking infra-red
Laser
Television

United States

Role

Fighter
Close support
Counter-insurgency
Tactical strike
Strategic bomber
Tactical reconnaissance
Strategic reconnaissance
Maritime patrol
Anti-ship strike
Anti-submarine warfare
Search and rescue
Assault transport
Transport
Liaison
Trainer
Inflight-refuelling tanker
Specialized

Performance

All-weather capability
Rough field capability
STOL capability
VTOL capability
Airspeed 0-250 mph
Airspeed 250 mph-Mach 1
Airspeed Mach 1 plus
Ceiling 0-20,000 ft
Ceiling 20,000-40,000 ft
Ceiling 40,000 ft plus
Range 0-1,000 miles
Range 1,000-3,000 miles
Range 3,000 miles plus

Weapons

Air-to-air missiles
Air-to-surface missiles
Cruise missiles
Cannon
Trainable guns
Naval weapons
Nuclear-capable
Rockets
'Smart' weapon kit
Weapon load 0-4,000 lb
Weapon load 4,000-15,000 lb
Weapon load 15,000 lb plus

Avionics

Electronic Counter Measures
Electronic Support Measures
Search radar
Fire control radar
Look-down/shoot-down
Terrain-following radar
Forward-looking infra-red
Laser
Television

After both unsuccessfully pursuing their own lines of development to create a successor to the AV-8A and Harrier, McDonnell Douglas and British Aerospace decided to collaborate on the joint **McDonnell Douglas/BAe Harrier II** programme for the US Marine Corps (**AV-8B**) and the RAF (Harrier GR.Mk5). The first step in the construction of the American model was the modification by McDonnell Douglas of two AV-8As as **YAV-8B** prototypes; the first flight of aircraft 158394 occurred on 9 November 1978. Four full-scale development AV-8Bs, each fitted with the F402-RR-404A (Pegasus 11 Mk 103) engine were ordered in April 1979, and the first (161396) flew on 5 November 1981.

The planned USMC programme calls for production of 300 AV-8Bs and 28 two-seat TAV-3B trainers, to replace three squadrons of AV-8As and five squadrons of McDonnell Douglas A-4 Skyhawk attack aircraft. The AV-8B was designed specifically to meet the requirements of the Marine Corps ground commander: an aircraft based as close as possible to the scene of action and with the ability to operate from a variety of assault ships or other bases. High flight rates from forward bases would mean more aircraft time on target and significant fuel savings. Although the AV-8A has pioneered the idea of instant close support, the most significant advantage of the new model is that is it able to operate with the payload and range of most conventional strike aircraft, abilities always beyond the scope of the AV-8A.

These improvements were made possible primarily by complete redesign of the wing, which is now constructed entirely of advanced carbonfibre epoxy composite material. The AV-8B is the first aircraft to fly with a wing made entirely of the material, which is not only particularly strong and light but also resists corrosion and fatigue better than metal. Other major improvements include improved engine air inlets, a revised cockpit with better fields of view, improved avionics, lift improvement devices (LIDs) that increase the aircraft's vertical take-off and landing capability, and modifications to the wing's leading edges for better manoeuvrability. McDonnell Douglas manufactures the forward fuselage and wings whilst BAe builds the centre and rear sections including the fin, rudder, and tailplane.

The first operational AV-8B squadron, VMA-331, was commissioned at MCAS Cherry Point, North Carolina in January 1985. Full operational readiness was scheduled for mid-1986, for 20 AV-8Bs. As yet the only export customer for the Harrier II is the Spanish government, which requires 12 aircraft, designated EAV-8B and due for delivery in 1987.

Specification: McDonnell Douglas/BAe AV-8B
Origin: USA/UK
Type: single-seat STOVL close support aircraft
Powerplant: one 9775-kg (21,550-lb) thrust Rolls Royce F402-RR-406 (Pegasus 11-21) vectored-thrust turbofan engine
Performance: maximum speed at sea level Mach 0.85 or 562 kts (1041 km/h; 647 mph), or at altitude Mach 0.91 or 521 kts (966 km/h; 600 mph); initial climb rate 14,715 ft (4485 m) per minute; service ceiling more than 50,000 ft (15240 m); combat radius 277 km (172 miles) with 2722-kg (6,000-lb) bombload
Weights: empty 5936 kg (13,086 lb); maximum take-off 13494 kg (29,750 lb)
Dimensions: span 9.25 m (30 ft 4 in); length 14.12 m (46 ft 4 in); height 3.55 m (11 ft 7.75 in); wing area 21.37 m² (230.0 sq ft)
Armament: one 25-mm cannon based on the General Electric GAU-12/U with 300 rounds mounted under the fuselage, plus six underwing weapons stations to carry up to 3175 kg (7,000 lb) of weapons (for a vertical take-off) including Paveway II 'smart' bombs, AGM-62 Walleye and AGM-65 Maverick ASMs, bombs, dispensers and rocket launchers; for a short take-off the weapon load can be as high as 7711 kg (17,000 lb)

McDonnell Douglas AV-8B in USMC green/grey camouflage.

McDonnell Douglas/BAe AV-8B Harrier II

An early AV-8B is seen on weapons evaluation tests, carrying seven Mk 82 'slick' bombs on wing and fuselage pylons. The weapons are inert.

VMAT-203 was the first recipient of the AV-8B, although not front-line. Weapon pylons, undercarriage and airbrakes are all shown to advantage by this hovering aircraft.

McDonnell Douglas/BAe TAV-8B Harrier II

McDonnell Douglas/BAe TAV-8B of the US Marine Corps.

On 24 August 1981 the decision was finally taken to commit the Harrier II to production. At this time the initial indicated requirements for the aircraft were 60 for the RAF and 257 for the USMC. The USMC requirement has since risen to 328, 28 of which are to be two-seat trainer aircraft, designated **McDonnell Douglas/BAe TAV-8B Harrier II**. The first of these aircraft to be ordered was one of a batch of 27 (the rest of which were AV-8Bs) in 1984, and the first flight of the TAV-8B was scheduled for late 1986.

There was originally some possibility that the earlier trainer model, the TAV-8A, would be retained in preference to the expensive development of the new aircraft. These plans were eventually dropped because the AV-8B has sufficiently different handling, avionics, and cockpit layout from its predecessor to make the original trainer version inappropriate. The US General Accounting Office suggests that use of the new aircraft will reduce conversion time from 91 to around 79 days, and will also ease the conversion from

trainer to combat aircraft since the student will be more familiar with the cockpit and handling of the new aircraft.

The TAV-8B's forward fuselage is 1.22 m (4.0 ft) longer than that of the AV-8B to accommodate the extra seat, and the vertical tail has been enlarged as a compensatory measure. Although the empty weight of the aircraft is 601 kg (1,325 lb) greater than that of the AV-8B, McDonnell Douglas maintains that the TAV-8B will still be convertible into a two-seat light attack aircraft.

The main subcontractor is British Aerospace, and the aircraft will have the same engine as the AV-8B. For weapons training it will carry Mk 76 practice bombs, LAU-68 rocket launchers or 1136-litre (300-US gal) external fuel tanks. The USMC planned to begin training in late 1986 at MCAS Cherry Point, North Carolina, and expects to train about 120 pilots each year. There is apparently no intention of developing a two-seater version of the Harrier GR.Mk 5, and RAF pilots will be trained as at present on the Harrier T. Mk 4.

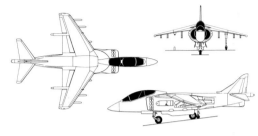

McDonnell Douglas/BAe TAV-8B

The large humped cockpit is readily apparent in this view. Although its main use will be conversion training, the TAV-8B is capable of combat operations.

The prototype TAV-8B seen on a test flight, complete with air data sensors mounted on the nose probe. The RAF has no plans yet to procure the advanced trainer.

Specification: McDonnell Douglas/BAe TAV-8B

Origin: USA/UK
Type: two-seat STOVL trainer aircraft
Powerplant: one 9775-kg (21,550-lb) thrust Rolls Royce F402-RR-406 (Pegasus 11-21) vectored-thrust turbofan engine
Performance: maximum speed at sea level Mach 0.85 or 562 kts (1041 km/h; 647 mph), or at altitude Mach 0.91 or 521 kts (966 km/h; 600 mph); maximum operational radius with no loiter 890 km (553 miles)
Weights: empty 6384 kg (14,075 lb)
Dimensions: span 9.25 m (30 ft 4 in); length 15.37 m (50 ft 5 in); height 4.09 m (13 ft 5 in); wing area 21.37 m² (230.0 sq ft)
Armament: one 25-mm cannon based on the General Electric GAU-12/U with 300 rounds, plus underwing weapons stations to carry the AV-8B's usual weaponry and facility for lift-improvement device when gun pods are not fitted.

McDonnell Douglas/Boeing F-4 Enhanced Phantom

With current forecasts of as many as 2,000 F-4 Phantom IIs (many with considerable unexpired life remaining) surviving at the end of the century, several proposals have been put forward to enhance their performance and efficiency, enabling them to remain compatible with modern operational environments up to and beyond that date. Of these, a proposal by Boeing Military Aircraft Company was announced in January 1984 and 17 months later gained approval from the US government for the preparation of a feasibility demonstration example. Basis of this proposal was the substitution of the standard (but now 30-year-old) General Electric J79 turbojets by Pratt & Whitney PW1120 turbofans, each providing some 15 per cent greater thrust than the turbojet. Interest was also expressed by Israel in the proposal (which nation alone still possesses about 200 F-4s of several versions), and a single demonstration aircraft, with one of the J79s replaced by a PW1120, was completed in 1985 for the Israeli air force.

However, the Boeing proposal goes much further than simply replacing the engines, and the American demonstrator will probably also feature a large conformal belly fuel tank which extends aft from the F-4E's nose gun fairing to the engine exhaust nozzles. Stressed to the aircraft's limit this tank accommodates 4164 litres (1,100 US gal) of fuel in the centre section and internal chaff/flare dispensers in the rear, and also incorporates doors to permit retraction of the nose landing gear through the forward section. Two new-generation MRAAMs will be mounted at shoulder positions on the conformal tank. It is also proposed to offer updated avionics, a representative fit including the Hughes APG-65 multi-mode radar, GEC Avionics head-up display and air data computer, Honeywell 423 ring laser gyro inertial navigator, and Sperry multi-mode display system. At the same time an airframe life-extension programme would be undertaken to increase the aircraft's life by up to 3,000 hours. Provision of this extensive update is being offered to customers with their own collaboration in their own countries.

Specification: McDonnell Douglas/Boeing F-4 Enhanced Phantom
Origin: USA/Israel
Type: two-seat multi-role fighter
Powerplant: two 9344-kg (20,600-lb) thrust Pratt & Whitney PW1120 afterburning turbofan engines
Performance: (estimated) maximum speed Mach 2.3 or 1318 kts (2443 km/h; 1,518 mph) at 40,000 ft (12190 m); initial rate of climb 47,570 ft (14500 m) per minute; service ceiling 63,000 ft (19200 m); unrefuelled combat radius 1262 km (784 miles)
Weights: (estimated) empty equipped 12712 kg (28,026 lb); maximum take-off 28123 kg (62,000 lb)
Dimensions: span 11.71 m (38 ft 5 in); length with APG-65 nose radar 19.85 m (65 ft 1.5 in); wing area 49.24 m² (530.0 sq ft)
Armament: (as currently proposed) one M61A1 Vulcan 20-mm six-barrel cannon under nose, four Hughes AIM-120A AMRAAMs and four ASRAAMs; ordnance load capability increased by 1927 kg (4,248 lb) over that of F-4E

An artist's impression of how the Enhanced Phantom might look in USAF service.

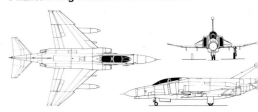

McDonnell Douglas/Boeing F-4 Enhanced Phantom

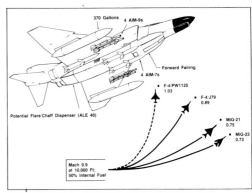

These two diagrams show the conformal fuel tanks and chaff dispensers of the Enhanced Phantom (upper) and the thrust-to-weight ratio compared with other contemporary fighters.

This illustration gives a good idea of the origin of the Enhanced Phantom's avionics.

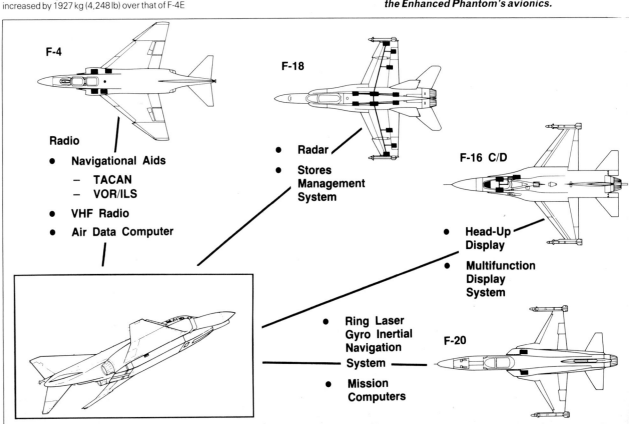

134

North American F-86 Sabre

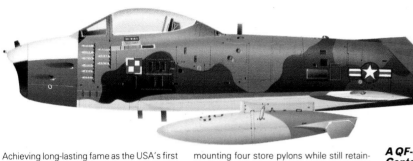

Argentina Bolivia Honduras Tunisia United States

Achieving long-lasting fame as the USA's first transonic fighter and the only aircraft in the UN inventory during the Korean War capable of matching the communists' Mikoyan-Gurevich MiG-15 jet fighter, the **North American F-86 Sabre** has survived in diminishing numbers with the world's air forces throughout the past 30 years. From a total of more than 5,000 built in the USA fewer than 300 serve with the air forces of Bolivia, Japan, Pakistan, Philippines, Portugal, South Africa, South Korea, Tunisia and Venezuela, almost all of them in various training roles. First flown as the **XP-86** on 1 October 1947, the Sabre entered USAF service as the **F-86A** in 1949 powered by a 2200-kg (4,850-lb) thrust General Electric J47-GE-1 turbojet. Incorporating modest sweepback on all flying surfaces, the Sabre is a low-wing monoplane with tricycle landing gear, and its nose air inlet supplies air to the midships-mounted engine which exhausts through a long tailpipe to the extreme tail. Early experience over Korea led progressively to the **F-86E** and **F-86F**, of which the latter proved by far the most effective in combat, as well as surviving most widely today. Powered by a 2681-kg (5,910-lb) J47-GE-27 engine, the F-86F introduced a slatted wing capable of

mounting four store pylons while still retaining the gun armament of six 12.7-mm (0.5-in) machine-guns. Too late to see service in Korea, the **F-86H** fighter-bomber (477 built) featured a much-welcomed change to four 20-mm cannon, improved wing design and a nuclear capability (first introduced in the F-86F-35). It was only in the early 1980s that Japan's large number of F-86Fs (used for fighter training) underwent a rapid rundown as the indigenous Mitsubishi F-1 entered service.

The other version of the F-86 to have survived is the **F-86D** (and the associated but simplified **F-86K**). This all-weather fighter entered service with the USAF in 1953 with an E-4 fire-control system in a large nose radome over a chin engine air inlet; gun armament was deleted in favour of 69.85-mm (2.75-in) Mighty Mouse folding-fin unguided rockets, 24 of which were fired from a retractable mounting under the fighter's nose. About a dozen F-86Ds are believed to remain in service in South Korea, and a similar number of the F-86K (with simplified MG-4 fire-control system and reversion to four 20-mm guns) served with Grupo 12 of Venezuela's FAV in the early 1980s.

A QF-86H target drone of the Naval Weapons Center, China Lake. This aircraft is almost certainly an ex-ANG example.

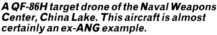

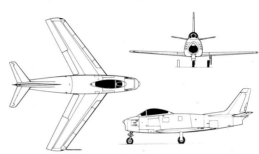

North American F-86E Sabre

This former Japanese F-86F is seen as an NWC QF-86F unmanned target drone. Some of these aircraft lead surprisingly long lives, completing many unmanned missions.

A few Latin American air arms, including the Bolivian and Honduran (seen here) air forces, operate the F-86 in its original fighter role, although their days are numbered.

Specification: North American F-86H-10 Sabre

Origin: USA
Type: single-seat fighter/fighter-bomber
Powerplant: one 4046-kg (8,920-lb) thrust General Electric J73-GE-3E turbojet engine
Performance: maximum speed, clean Mach 0.91 or 601 kts (1113 km/h; 692 mph) at sea level or 536 kts (993 km/h; 617 mph) at 35,000 ft (10670 m); initial climb rate 12,900 ft (3932 m) per minute; service ceiling 50,800 ft (15485 m); combat radius on internal fuel 835 km (519 miles)
Weights: empty equipped 6276 kg (13,836 lb); maximum take-off 10024 kg (22,100 lb)
Dimensions: span 11.93 m (39 ft 1.5 in); length 11.84 m (38 ft 10 in); height 4.57 m (15 ft 0 in); wing area 29.11 m² (313.4 sq ft)
Armament: four 20-mm T160 cannon with 600 rounds, plus four wing hardpoints capable of carrying two 454-kg (1,000-lb) bombs and two 757-litre (200-US gal) drop tanks; the F-86H-10 was nuclear-capable, being equipped to mount one 544-kg (1,200-lb) nuclear store under port wing

North American F-100 Super Sabre

Taiwan   Turkey   United States

Although only now approaching extinction as a combat aircraft, the **North American F-100 Super Sabre** entered the design stage as long ago as 1951 and made its maiden flight on 25 May 1953, just weeks before the end of the Korean War. Originating as a private venture, the aircraft was eagerly accepted by the USAF and entered service as the **F-100A** interceptor in the following year. Employing a low-set 45° swept wing of 7 per cent thickness-chord the Super Sabre was the USAF's first level-flight supersonic fighter, being powered by an afterburning Pratt & Whitney J57 turbojet with nose inlet; flying controls included single-piece flying tail and automatic wing slats, though no landing flaps were included. Armament of the early aircraft was confined to four Pontiac-built M39E 20-mm guns with an APX-6 radar gunsight. Total production of the F-100A amounted to no more than 203 aircraft, of which 80 were modified to F-100D standard (see below) and supplied to Taiwan in 1960 (followed by 10 more in 1970). USAF service life of the F-100A was short, although some examples were modified for reconnaissance as the **RF-100A** and saw limited use in Vietnam. The first dual-role strike/interceptor version was to be the **F-100C**, which was also the first to include an inflight-refuelling probe; it featured eight external store

stations, increased internal fuel capacity and an APG-30 radar gunsight. Once again service of the F-100C, of which 476 were built, was short in the USAF, but more than 200 surplus aircraft were supplied to Turkey, starting in 1958.

The main production version was the **F-100D** which was not only nuclear capable but was equipped to mount AIM-9B Sidewinders or AGM-12A Bullpup ASMs on the inboard wing pylons. Starting delivery in 1956 the **F-100D**, of which 1,274 examples were produced in only two years, was not finally phased out of USAF service until 1972. Deliveries of this version to NATO air forces included a large number to France (before that nation's departure from the organization), a further batch to Turkey and 24 to Denmark. A two-seat version, the **F-100F**, was also produced (339 built and delivered from 1957), this variant in particular giving excellent service with the USAF in Vietnam as forward air control aircraft. Today no F-100s survive in the USAF, or in Danish and French service, and it is believed that re-equipping of the five squadrons that were still serving in the early 1980s in Turkey has been completed. Only Taiwan is thought to operate some F-100Ds and a few F-100F two-seaters within its first-line strength.

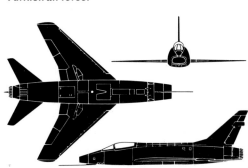

A North American F-100 Super Sabre of the Turkish air force.

North American F-100D Super Sabre

Specification: North American F-100D Super Sabre
Origin: USA
Type: single-seat fighter-bomber
Powerplant: one 7711-kg (17,000-lb) afterburning thrust Pratt & Whitney J57-P-21A turbojet engine
Performance: maximum speed Mach 1.3 or 750 kts (1390 km/h; 864mph) at 35,000 ft (10670m); initial climb rate 16,000 ft (4875m) per minute; service ceiling 46,000 ft (14020m); range on internal fuel 966 km (600 miles)
Weights: empty equipped 9525 kg (21,000 lb); maximum take-off 15800 kg (34,832 lb)
Dimensions: span 11.82 m (38 ft 9.5 in); length excluding nose boom 14.36 m (47 ft 1.25 in); height 4.95 m (16 ft 3 in); wing area 35.77 m² (385.0 sq ft)
Armament: four T160 20-mm cannon, plus four underwing hardpoints capable of carrying up to 3402 kg (7,500 lb) of ordnance or drop tanks; in US service the variant was nuclear capable, being equipped with LABS for toss delivery

Taiwan still operates a small number of F-100Ds and F-100F two-seaters, but has retired its ageing F-100As, like this aircraft, seen in the Chung Cheng museum.

This well-worn QF-100D is owned and operated by Flight Systems Incorporated from Mojave, in support of the QF-100 fleet operated by the USAF from Tyndall AFB, Florida.

North American T-28 Trojan

Honduras Kampuchea South Korea Laos Mexico Philippines Taiwan Uruguay

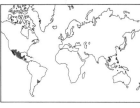

First flown on 24 September 1949, the **North American T-28** was conceived to fill the gap left by the T-6 Texan in the USAF's Air Training Command as a combined basic and primary trainer. Superficially the new aircraft perpetuated the configuration of the Texan, being a low-wing all-metal monoplane with tandem cockpits for instructor and student pilot. New, however, was the tricycle landing gear with steerable nosewheel, while power was provided (in the **T-28A**) by a 597-kW (800-hp) Wright R-1300-1A radial driving a two-blade variable-pitch propeller. A total of 1,194 T-28As was produced and this version remained in USAF service until 1956. This initial type was followed by 489 **T-28B Trojan** aircraft powered by the 1063-kW (1,425-hp) Wright R-1820 engine driving a three-blade propeller, and by 299 **T-28C** aircraft with deck hook and strengthened airframe to withstand carrier landings, both these version serving with the US Navy and Marine Corps until the 1970s.

Many T-28As were, however, extensively re-engineered to become **T-28D** aircraft with R-1820 engines, three-blade propellers, armour protection for the crew and six underwing stores hardpoints. This updating programme was undertaken at the beginning

of American involvement in Vietnam in the early 1960s to provide a light attack aircraft, and was effected by removal of aircraft from storage. In this role the T-28Ds served with US air commando squadrons, being fitted to carry podded 12.7-mm (0.5-in) guns, 227-kg (500-lb) bombs, rockets and napalm weapons. Their employment was not considered entirely satisfactory and about 100 aircraft were turned over to the air forces of South Vietnam and the Philippines; in the latter two T-28D-equipped squadrons were still operational for COIN duties in the early 1980s.

France had acquired about 245 surplus T-28As during 1960-1 and these, under the name **Fennec**, saw widespread service in Algeria in the light attack role; later, as the type was withdrawn from service, surplus Fennecs were sold to Morocco, Honduras and, modified with deck hook, to the Argentine navy. Ex-USAF T-28As were also sold to Mexico whose air force until recently still operated four ground-attack/training squadrons equipped with the type. The T-28D remains the most widely-used variant, and serves in training and counter-insurgency squadrons with the air forces of Taiwan, Thailand, the Philippines, the Dominican Republic, Nicaragua, Ethiopia and Zaire.

Specification: North American T-28B Trojan
Origin: USA
Type: two-seat basic trainer (with COIN/battlefield support applications)
Powerplant: one 1063-kW (1,425-hp) Wright Cyclone R-1820-86 14-cylinder air-cooled radial piston engine
Performance: maximum speed 298kts (552 km/h; 343 mph) at 10,000 ft (3050 m); initial rate of climb 3,540 ft (1079 m) per minute; service ceiling 35,500 ft (10820 m); range 1706 km (1,060 miles)
Weights: empty equipped 2914 kg (6,424 lb); maximum take-off 3856 kg (8,500 lb)
Dimensions: span 12.22 m (40 ft 1 in); length 10.06 m (33 ft 0 in); height 3.86 m (12 ft 8 in); wing area 24.90 m² (268.0 sq ft)
Armament: none; the T-28D features six underwing hardpoints for a variety of light stores including Minigun pods, rocket-launchers and light bombs up to total of 544 kg (1,200 lb)

A North American T-28 Trojan of the Chinese Nationalist air force.

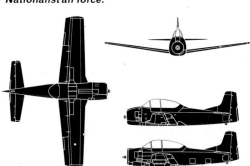

North American T-28A Trojan (lower side view: T-28D)

This ageing T-28D Trojan is one of about 30 survivors remaining in service with the Lao People's Liberation Army Air Force. They are operational in the close support role.

This is one of the eight ex-Moroccan air force T-28A Fennecs supplied to the Fuerza Aérea Hondurena. One has been written off, but the other seven remain in use.

Role

Fighter
Close support
Counter-insurgency
Tactical strike
Strategic bomber
Tactical reconnaissance
Strategic reconnaissance
Maritime patrol
Anti-ship strike
Anti-submarine warfare
Search and rescue
Assault transport
Transport
Liaison
Trainer
Inflight-refuelling tanker
Specialized

Performance

All-weather capability
Rough field capability
STOL capability
VTOL capability
Airspeed 0-250 mph
Airspeed 250 mph-Mach 1
Airspeed Mach 1 plus
Ceiling 0-20,000 ft
Ceiling 20,000-40,000 ft
Ceiling 40,000 ft plus
Range 0-1,000 miles
Range 1,000-3,000 miles
Range 3,000 miles plus

Weapons

Air-to-air missiles
Air-to-surface missiles
Cruise missiles
Cannon
Trainable guns
Naval weapons
Nuclear-capable
Rockets
'Smart' weapon kit
Weapon load 0-4,000 lb
Weapon load 4,000-15,000 lb
Weapon load 15,000 lb plus

Avionics

Electronic Counter Measures
Electronic Support Measures
Search radar
Fire control radar
Look-down/shoot-down
Terrain-following radar
Forward-looking infra-red
Laser
Television

F-5Es of 527th AS from RAF Alconbury

Northrop F-5E Tiger II

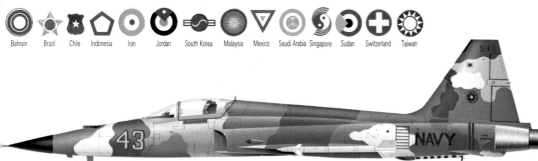

Bahrain · Brazil · Chile · Indonesia · Iran · Jordan · South Korea · Malaysia · Mexico · Saudi Arabia · Singapore · Sudan · Switzerland · Taiwan

Thailand · Tunisia · United States · Vietnam · Yemen

In November 1970 the US government chose the **Northrop F-5E Tiger II** as winner of its International Fighter Aircraft (IFA) competition to replace the outdated F-5A; contenders for the new type had included the Lockheed CL-1200 Lancer, Vought V-1000 and a stripped-down variant of the McDonnell Douglas F-4 Phantom II. A combination of increased engine power and a two-position extending nosewheel unit gave the F-5E an improvement of some 30 per cent in take-off performance over earlier versions, while the provision of arrester gear permitted operation from very short runways. The fuselage of the Tiger II is widened, which increases the wing span of the aircraft, and the wing loading on the F-5E is thus maintained at approximately the same value as that of the F-5A.

First flight of a production F-5E took place on 11 August 1972, and first deliveries were made on 4 April 1973 to the USAF's 425th Tactical Fighter Training Squadron. In the design and construction of the aircraft there was considerable emphasis on aerial agility rather than on high speed, particularly through the use of manoeuvring flaps. Powered by two General Electric J85-GE-21 turbojet engines, the Tiger II nonetheless has

very useful performance in terms of speed, rate of climb and ceiling. As well as serving in the tactical fighter role with many countries in the US political orbit, the F-5E also operates in the 'aggressor' role at US combat training stations based in the USA, UK and Philippines. The 64th and 65th Aggressor Squadrons operate at Nellis AFB in the USA as part of the 57th Fighter Weapons Wing, and the 527th AS operates at RAF Alconbury in the UK, flying training missions for NATO. The Philippines-based squadron, the 26th AS, is stationed at Clark AFB and performs training missions for Far East squadrons.

A two-seat trainer version of the F-5E is also produced with the designation **F-5F**, and this is also capable of carrying out combat duties. It has a fuselage lengthened by 1.02 m (3 ft 4 in) and its development was approved by the USAF in early 1974, the first flight taking place on 25 September 1974. Deliveries of 118 aircraft began in the summer of 1976. Export orders for the F-5E are numerous. The variant delivered to the Brazilian air force has a large dorsal fin to accommodate an ADF antenna, and those delivered to the Royal Saudi air force have a Litton LN-33 INS and inflight refuelling capability.

Specification: Northrop F-5E Tiger II
Origin: USA
Type: single-seat light tactical fighter
Powerplant: two 2268-kg (5,000-lb) General Electric J85-GE-21B turbojet engines
Performance: maximum speed at 36,000 ft (10975 m) Mach 1.64 or 940 kts (1741 km/h; 1,082 mph); initial climb rate 34,500 ft (10516 m) per minute; service ceiling 51,800 ft (15790 m); combat radius with maximum load 306 km (190 miles); ferry range 3724 km (2,314 miles)
Weights: empty 4410 kg (9,723 lb); maximum take-off 11214 kg (24,722 lb)
Dimensions: span 8.13 m (26 ft 8 in); length 14.45 m (47 ft 4.75 in); height 4.07 m (13 ft 4.25 in); wing area 17.28 m² (186.0 sq ft)
Armament: two AIM-9 Sidewinders on wingtip launchers, two 20-mm cannon with 280 rounds per gun in the nose and five hardpoints (one under the fuselage and four under the wings) for a maximum disposable load of 3175 kg (7,000 lb) of bombs, missiles, rocket-launcher pods, drop tanks and other stores.

This F-5E serves with the US Navy Fighter Weapons School at NAS Miramar, providing adversary aircraft for the 'Top Gun' programme.

Northrop F-5E Tiger II

A Force Aérienne de la Republique de Tunisie Northrop F-5F Tiger II is seen on its delivery flight, staging through RAF Alconbury, carrying a long range ferry tank.

This F-5E of No. 14 Skwadron, 300 Wing, Tentara Nasional Indonesia-Angkatan Udara (Indonesian air force) is based at Meidun and operates primarily in the air defence role.

Role
Fighter
Close support
Counter-insurgency
Tactical strike
Strategic bomber
Tactical reconnaissance
Strategic reconnaissance
Maritime patrol
Anti-ship strike
Anti-submarine warfare
Search and rescue
Assault transport
Transport
Liaison
Trainer
Inflight-refuelling tanker
Specialized

Performance
All-weather capability
Rough field capability
STOL capability
VTOL capability
Airspeed 0-250 mph
Airspeed 250 mph-Mach 1
Airspeed Mach 1 plus
Ceiling 0-20,000 ft
Ceiling 20,000-40,000 ft
Ceiling 40,000ft plus
Range 0-1,000 miles
Range 1,000-3,000 miles
Range 3,000 miles plus

Weapons
Air-to-air missiles
Air-to-surface missiles
Cruise missiles
Cannon
Trainable guns
Naval weapons
Nuclear-capable
Rockets
'Smart' weapon kit
Weapon load 0-4,000 lb
Weapon load 4,000-15,000 lb
Weapon load 15,000 lb plus

Avionics
Electronic Counter Measures
Electronic Support Measures
Search radar
Fire control radar
Look-down/shoot-down radar
Terrain-following radar
Forward-looking infra-red
Laser
Television

Northrop T-38 Talon

10868

Role
Fighter
Close support
Counter-insurgency
Tactical strike
Strategic bomber
Tactical reconnaissance
Strategic reconnaissance
Maritime patrol
Anti-ship strike
Anti-submarine warfare
Search and rescue
Assault transport
Transport
Liaison
Trainer
Inflight-refuelling tanker
Specialized

Performance
All-weather capability
Rough field capability
STOL capability
VTOL capability
Airspeed 0-250 mph
Airspeed 250 mph-Mach 1
Airspeed Mach 1 plus
Ceiling 0-20,000 ft
Ceiling 20,000-40,000 ft
Ceiling 40,000 ft plus
Range 0-1,000 miles
Range 1,000-3,000 miles
Range 3,000 miles plus

Weapons
Air-to-air missiles
Air-to-surface missiles
Cruise missiles
Cannon
Trainable guns
Naval weapons
Nuclear-capable
Rockets
'Smart' weapon kit
Weapon load 0-4,000 lb
Weapon load 4,000-15,000 lb
Weapon load 15,000 lb plus

Avionics
Electronic Counter Measures
Electronic Support Measures
Search radar
Fire control radar
Look-down/shoot-down
Terrain-following radar
Forward-looking infra-red
Laser
Television

Initial development of the **Northrop T-38 Talon** resulted from studies carried out by the company which showed that the most significant cost factors in the life of an aircraft were those of maintenance and operation rather than those associated with research, development and production. The original outcome of these studies was the completion of designs, by Northrop, for a tactical fighter-bomber designated N-156F (developed as the F-5) and a two-seat trainer version designated **N-156T**. Development of these types was continued as a private venture until the USAF issued a General Operational Requirement for a supersonic basic trainer support system. Northrop met this requirement with a variant of the N-156T design, and was awarded a contract in 1956. During the next two years production of the trainer aircraft, designated **T-38A**, took precedence over that of the fighter.

The T-38 first flew on 10 April 1959, powered by two non-afterburning General Electric YJ85-GE-5 engines each rated at 953-kg (2,100-lb) thrust, and a second aircraft was

flown on 12 June 1959. The first production aircraft was flown in January 1960, powered by two afterburning engines each giving a thrust of 1633 kg (3,600 lb); later production aircraft used the 1746-kg (3,850-lb) afterburning thrust J85-GE-5. The first supersonic aircraft designed from the outset specifically to fulfil the training role, the Talon entered service on 17 March 1961 with the USAF's Air Training Command Instructors School at Randolph AFB as a successor to the subsonic Lockheed T-33A; the first group of students began basic training in the aircraft in September 1961.

Excluding prototype and pre-production aircraft, 1,139 Talons were produced, and although the aircraft served primarily with the USAF, the type was exported to West Germany, among other countries. A number of performance records set by the T-38 reflects the high quality of its design, and the aircraft (together with its combat counterpart, the F-5 series) will remain operational for many years to come.

Specification: Northrop T-38A Talon
Origin: USA
Type: two-seat supersonic basic trainer aircraft
Powerplant: two 1746-kg (3,850-lb) General Electric J85-GE-5 turbojet engines
Performance: maximum speed at 36,000 ft (10975 m) Mach 1.3 or 745 kts (1381 km/h; 858 mph); initial climb rate 33,600 ft (10241 m) per minute; service ceiling 53,600 ft (16340 m); range with maximum fuel 1759 km (1,093 miles)
Weights: empty 3254 kg (7,174 lb); maximum take-off 5361 kg (11,820 lb)
Dimensions: span 7.70 m (25 ft 3 in); length 14.14 m (46 ft 4.5 in); height 3.92 m (12 ft 10.5 in); wing area 15.79 m² (170.0 sq ft)
Armament: none

A Northrop T-38 Talon of the Força Aérea Portuguesa.

Northrop T-38 Talon

23639

This Talon serves with the Air Force Flight Test Center, for a variety of duties. The Talons sometimes act as chase aircraft, and are used by Shuttle pilots for training purposes.

In Turkish air force service, the T-38 Talon serves with the Izmir-Cigli based 121 Filo for advanced pilot training. About 30 were delivered, and most remain in use.

Piper PA-23 Apache and Aztec

A Piper PA-23-250E Aztec of the Spanish air force.

Under the designation **Piper PA-23**, the company during the spring of 1952 flew the first example of a new twin-engined four-seat cabin monoplane to which it gave the name Twin Stinson. Of all-metal construction and of low-wing configuration, this somewhat portly little aircraft was at first distinguished by having (set high on the fuselage) a tailplane which incorporated twin endplate fins and rudders. Flight testing proved this last feature to be unsatisfactory, and when the type entered production in early 1954 it had acquired a conventional tail unit with single fin and rudder. The aircraft was marketed originally as the **PA-23 Apache**, a title soon changed to **PA-23 Apache 150** in indication of the horsepower of the two Avco Lycoming O-320 engines that powered it.

When production switched to the four/five-seat **PA-23 Apache 160** in 1958 (the changed designation confirming the power of its Lycoming O-320-B engines), a total of 1,231 of the original version had been built. Construction of 816 Apache 160s was followed by that of 119 **PA-23 Apache 235** aircraft with swept tail surfaces and 175-kW (235-hp) Lycoming O-540-B1A5 engines. Inevitably the moment came when interest in the Apache began to dwindle and production ended in 1965 after a total of 2,166 of all versions had been built.

As soon as sales of the Apache began to show a steady fall the company had introduced in late 1959 a more developed version, designated **PA-23-250 Aztec**, with true five-seat accommodation and 186-kW (250-hp) engines. At that time the US Navy was looking for an 'off-the-shelf' utility transport and, in February 1960, contracted for the supply of 20 under the designation **UO-1**; in 1962 under the tri-service unification of designations they became instead **U-11A**. Those in navy service differed from production for civil use by introducing propeller anti-icing, improved communications equipment and an oxygen supply. Piper's development, production and sale of the Aztec continued until early 1982, by which time the current versions, both of six-seat capacity, were the **PA-23-250 Aztec F** and **PA-23T-250 Turbo Aztec F**, the latter with a turbocharged engine. Over the years, since its introduction in 1959, several governments and air arms have acquired small numbers of the Aztec for use in military roles.

Specification: Piper PA-23-250 Aztec (U-11A)
Origin: USA
Type: utility transport
Powerplant: two 186-kW (250-hp) Avco Lycoming O-540-A1A flat-six piston engines
Performance: maximum speed 187 kts (346 km/h; 215 mph); cruising speed 174 kts (322 km/h; 200 mph) at 9,000 ft (2745 m); initial climb rate 1,650 ft (503 m) per minute; service ceiling 22,500 ft (6860 m); maximum range 1931 km (1,200 miles)
Weights: empty 1259 kg (2,775 lb); maximum take-off 2177 kg (4,800 lb)
Dimensions: span 11.28 m (37 ft 0 in); length 8.41 m (27 ft 7 in); height 3.14 m (10 ft 3.5 in); wing area 19.23 m² (207.0 sq ft)
Armament: none

Piper PA-28 Aztec-D

Despite phenomenal success in the civil field, the PA-23 Aztec has not caught on with military customers. Most are used on liaison duties.

This is one of two Piper PA-23-250 Aztecs delivered to the Republic of Uganda's air force. They may remain in service for liaison and training duties.

Costa Rica
Madagascar
Mexico Spain Uganda United States Uruguay

Role
Fighter
Close support
Counter-insurgency
Tactical strike
Strategic bomber
Tactical reconnaissance
Strategic reconnaissance
Maritime patrol
Anti-ship strike
Anti-submarine warfare
Search and rescue
Assault transport
Transport
Liaison
Trainer
Inflight-refuelling tanker
Specialized

Performance
All-weather capability
Rough field capability
STOL capability
VTOL capability
Airspeed 0-250 mph
Airspeed 250 mph-Mach 1
Airspeed Mach 1 plus
Ceiling 0-20,000 ft
Ceiling 20,000-40,000 ft
Ceiling 40,000 ft plus
Range 0-1,000 miles
Range 1,000-3,000 miles
Range 3,000 miles plus

Weapons
Air-to-air missiles
Air-to-surface missiles
Cruise missiles
Cannon
Trainable guns
Naval weapons
Nuclear-capable
Rockets
'Smart' weapon kit
Weapon load 0-4,000 lb
Weapon load 4,000-15,000 lb
Weapon load 15,000 lb plus

Avionics
Electronic Counter Measures
Electronic Support Measures
Search radar
Fire control radar
Look-down/shoot-down
Terrain-following radar
Forward-looking infra-red
Laser
Television

A B-1B in its low-visibility colour scheme

Rockwell International B-1B

United States

To provide an important component of the United States' 'triad' defence system, studies initiated in 1962 led, in 1965, to the USAF's Advanced Manned Strategic Aircraft (AMSA) requirement for a low-altitude penetration bomber. Following the usual USAF procurement policy, the company then known as North American Rockwell was selected as prime contractor for a new bomber, to be designated **B-1**, as was General Electric for the F101 turbofan engines to power it. Both companies were awarded contracts on 5 June 1970 for the prototypes of a planned 244 aircraft, all of them scheduled for delivery by 1981. The programme was duly initiated, the first B-1 prototype (74-158) making its maiden flight on 23 December 1974, but was brought to a halt when, on 30 June 1977, President Carter announced that the B-1 would be cancelled and financial priority given instead to cruise missiles.

USAF and DoD studies of a manned aircraft to serve as a cruise missile carrier led to selection of a derivative of the B-1 for this role. The type was also to have a multi-mission capability, and in October 1981 President Reagan announced that the USAF would receive 100 of the derived **B-1B** aircraft. Contracts for prototype aircraft and engines were finalized on 20 January 1982.

The resulting B-1B has a low-set variable-geometry wing blended into the fuselage structure. Construction is largely of aluminium alloys and titanium, hardened to survive nuclear blast and overpressure, and by the incorporation of 'low observable' technology features has a radar cross-section only one per cent that of a Boeing B-52. Its operational capability will rely upon advanced avionics, including radar and navigation equipment developed for the latest-generation fighter aircraft, plus the offensive avionics developed for the original B-1 and both the B-52G and B-52H. The B-1B's avionics fit includes an AFSATCOM communications link, Doppler radar altimeter, forward-looking and terrain-following radars, INS, and defensive avionics based on the ALQ-161 ECM system with wider frequency coverage, expendable decoys and tail-warning radar. The first production B-1B was flown on 18 October 1984 and the initial USAF delivery, to Dyess AFB, Texas, was made on 29 June 1985. Deliveries to Dyess now approach the 15 aircraft with which the 337th Bombardment Squadron of the 96th Bombardment Wing was scheduled to attain IOC in October 1986. The remaining B-1B bases are to be Ellsworth AFB, South Dakota; Grand Forks AFB, North Dakota; and McConnell AFB, Kansas, with all deliveries to be completed in 1988.

A Rockwell B-1B of Strategic Air Command, US Air Force.

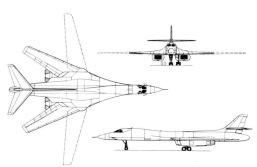

Rockwell International B-1B

A Rockwell B-1B of the 96th Bombardment Wing, first unit to receive this awesome new bomber to replace its lumbering B-52s. Serviceability problems and fuel leaks have plagued the 96th.

When serviceability problems and avionics shortcomings have been solved the B-1B will be a worthy successor to the B-52. The aircraft is capable of extremely high speed at ultra low level.

Specification: Rockwell International B-1B
Origin: USA
Type: long-range multi-role strategic bomber
Powerplant: four General Electric F101-GE-102 augmented turbofan engines, each developing some 13608-kg (30,000-lb) thrust
Performance: (design) maximum speed Mach 1.25 at optimum altitude; penetration speed more than 521 kts (966 km/h; 600 mph) at about 200 ft (60 m); maximum unrefuelled range about 12000 km (7,455 miles)
Weights: empty equipped 87090 kg (192,000 lb); maximum take-off 216364 kg (477,000 lb)
Dimensions: span, wings spread 41.67 m (136 ft 8.5 in) and swept 23.84 m (78 ft 2.5 in); length 44.81 m (147 ft 0 in); height 10.36 m (34 ft 0 in); wing area about 181.15 m² (1,950.0 sq ft)
Armament: three internal bays for up to 34019 kg (75,000 lb) of weapons, plus eight underfuselage stations with a capacity of 26762 kg (59,000 lb); weapons can include AGM-69 SRAMs, AGM-86B ALCMs, B-28, B-43, B-61 or B-83 nuclear bombs, and Mk 82 or Mk 84 conventional bombs

Role
Fighter
Close support
Counter-insurgency
Tactical strike
Strategic bomber
Tactical reconnaissance
Strategic reconnaissance
Maritime patrol
Anti-ship strike
Anti-submarine warfare
Search and rescue
Assault transport
Transport
Liaison
Trainer
Inflight-refuelling tanker
Specialized

Performance
All-weather capability
Rough field capability
STOL capability
VTOL capability
Airspeed 0-250 mph
Airspeed 250 mph-Mach 1
Airspeed Mach 1 plus
Ceiling 0-20,000 ft
Ceiling 20,000-40,000 ft
Ceiling 40,000 ft plus
Range 0-1,000 miles
Range 1,000-3,000 miles
Range 3,000 miles plus

Weapons
Air-to-air missiles
Air-to-surface missiles
Cruise missiles
Cannon
Trainable guns
Naval weapons
Nuclear-capable
Rockets
'Smart' weapon kit
Weapon load 0-4,000 lb
Weapon load 4,000-15,000 lb
Weapon load 15,000 lb plus

Avionics
Electronic Counter Measures
Electronic Support Measures
Search radar
Fire control radar
Look-down/shoot-down
Terrain-following radar
Forward-looking infra-red
Laser
Television

Rockwell International OV-10 Bronco

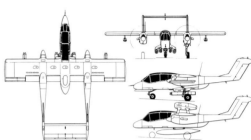

West Germany | Indonesia | Morocco | Thailand | United States | Venezuela

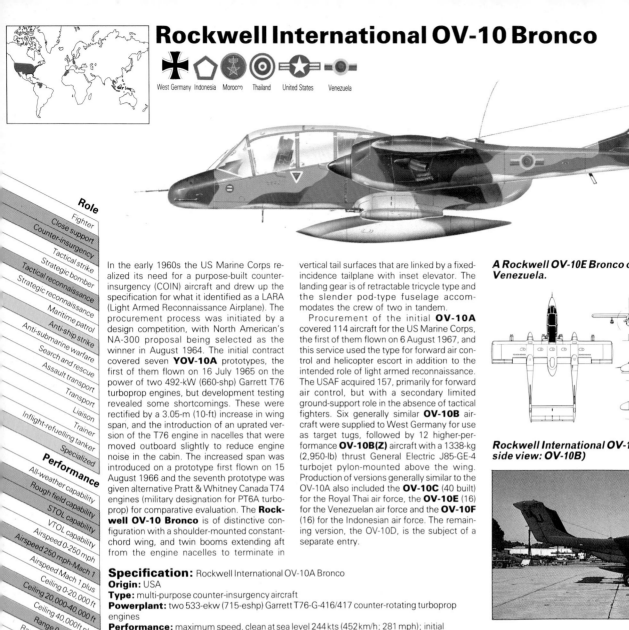

In the early 1960s the US Marine Corps realized its need for a purpose-built counter-insurgency (COIN) aircraft and drew up the specification for what it identified as a LARA (Light Armed Reconnaissance Airplane). The procurement process was initiated by a design competition, with North American's NA-300 proposal being selected as the winner in August 1964. The initial contract covered seven **YOV-10A** prototypes, the first of them flown on 16 July 1965 on the power of two 492-kW (660-shp) Garrett T76 turboprop engines, but development testing revealed some shortcomings. These were rectified by a 3.05-m (10-ft) increase in wing span, and the introduction of an uprated version of the T76 engine in nacelles that were moved outboard slightly to reduce engine noise in the cabin. The increased span was introduced on a prototype first flown on 15 August 1966 and the seventh prototype was given alternative Pratt & Whitney Canada T74 engines (military designation for PT6A turboprop) for comparative evaluation. The **Rockwell OV-10 Bronco** is of distinctive configuration with a shoulder-mounted constant-chord wing, and twin booms extending aft from the engine nacelles to terminate in

vertical tail surfaces that are linked by a fixed-incidence tailplane with inset elevator. The landing gear is of retractable tricycle type and the slender pod-type fuselage accommodates the crew of two in tandem.

Procurement of the initial **OV-10A** covered 114 aircraft for the US Marine Corps, the first of them flown on 6 August 1967, and this service used the type for forward air control and helicopter escort in addition to the intended role of light armed reconnaissance. The USAF acquired 157, primarily for forward air control, but with a secondary limited ground-support role in the absence of tactical fighters. Six generally similar **OV-10B** aircraft were supplied to West Germany for use as target tugs, followed by 12 higher-performance **OV-10B(Z)** aircraft with a 1338-kg (2,950-lb) thrust General Electric J85-GE-4 turbojet pylon-mounted above the wing. Production of versions generally similar to the OV-10A also included the **OV-10C** (40 built) for the Royal Thai air force, the **OV-10E** (16) for the Venezuelan air force and the **OV-10F** (16) for the Indonesian air force. The remaining version, the OV-10D, is the subject of a separate entry.

A Rockwell OV-10E Bronco of the Fuerza Aérea Venezuela.

Rockwell International OV-10A Bronco (lower side view: OV-10B)

Specification: Rockwell International OV-10A Bronco
Origin: USA
Type: multi-purpose counter-insurgency aircraft
Powerplant: two 533-ekw (715-eshp) Garrett T76-G-416/417 counter-rotating turboprop engines
Performance: maximum speed, clean at sea level 244 kts (452 km/h; 281 mph); initial climb rate 2,600 ft (792 m) per minute; service ceiling 24,000 ft (7315 m); combat radius with maximum weapon load and no loiter 367 nm (228 miles)
Weights: empty 3127 kg (6,893 lb); maximum take-off 6552 kg (14,444 lb)
Dimensions: span 12.19 m (40 ft 0 in); length 12.67 m (41 ft 7 in); height 4.62 m (15 ft 2 in); wing area 27.03 m² (291.0 sq ft)
Armament: one underfuselage station, plus four weapon attachment points on short sponsons for a combined weapon load of 1633 kg (3,600 lb) suitable for a wide range of bombs, rockets, machine-gun and cannon pods, flares and smoke tanks; each sponson also houses two 7.62-mm (0.3-in) M60C machine-guns, each with 500 rounds

This US Marine Corps OV-10A belongs to Marine Observation Squadron (VMO-) 2, the Atlanta-based reserve squadron. The Bronco's main roles are FAC and COIN.

This OV-10A Bronco is seen in the markings of the 601st Tactical Control Wing, based at Sembach in West Germany. The wing's Broncos have been passed on to the George-based 27th TASS.

Role
Fighter
Close support
Counter-insurgency
Tactical strike
Strategic bomber
Tactical reconnaissance
Strategic reconnaissance
Maritime patrol
Anti-ship strike
Anti-submarine warfare
Search and rescue
Assault transport
Transport
Liaison
Trainer
Inflight-refuelling tanker
Specialized

Performance
All-weather capability
Rough field capability
STOL capability
VTOL capability
Airspeed 0-250 mph
Airspeed 250 mph-Mach 1
Airspeed Mach 1 plus
Ceiling 0-20,000 ft
Ceiling 20,000-40,000 ft
Ceiling 40,000 ft plus
Range 0-1,000 miles
Range 1,000-3,000 miles
Range 3,000 miles plus

Weapons
Air-to-air missiles
Air-to-surface missiles
Cruise missiles
Cannon
Trainable guns
Naval weapons
Nuclear-capable
Rockets
'Smart' weapon kit
Weapon load 0-4,000 lb
Weapon load 4,000-15,000 lb
Weapon load 15,000 lb plus

Avionics
Electronic Counter Measures
Electronic Support Measures
Search radar
Fire control radar
Look-down/shoot-down
Terrain-following radar
Forward-looking infra-red
Laser
Television

Rockwell International OV-10D Bronco

United States

From early 1961 the US was busy advising the Republic of Vietnam how best to resist the incursions of communist guerrillas from North Vietnam. This became more urgent in late 1963 when infiltration into South Vietnam was stepped up. At this time the US Navy began procurement of the Light Armed Reconnaissance Airplane that led to the OV-10 designed for counter-insurgency operations. When the OV-10As began operating in South Vietnam it was already clear that a prime task for aircraft in this theatre was to reduce the infiltration into South Vietnam of men and supplies down the Ho Chi Minh Trail. It was a difficult task at the best of times, and nearly impossible during the hours of darkness.

The OV-10, suitably equipped, seemed ideal to fulfil a night forward air control and strike designation role, and in the early 1970s 15 OV-10As were modified under the USAF's 'Pave Nail' programme. Specialized equipment given to these aircraft included a combined laser rangefinder/target illuminator, a Loran receiver and a Loran co-ordinate converter. After the withdrawal from Vietnam these 'Pave Nail' OV-10s reverted to standard configuration. The US Navy had been slightly ahead of the USAF in considering the OV-10A for such a task, and in 1970 two Navy OV-10As were converted as **Rockwell YOV-10D Night Observation/Gunship System** prototypes. They were equipped with an undernose turret for installation of FLIR and a laser target designator, a rear underfuselage turret to mount a 20-mm cannon, and two underwing pylons carrying extra stores. By the time that evaluation was complete the USA had withdrawn its forces from Vietnam, but in 1974 the US Navy contracted Rockwell to establish and test an **OV-10D** production configuration. This resulted in 17 of the US Marine Corps' OV-10As being converted as OV-10Ds for a NOS (Night Observation Surveillance) role, all of them being redelivered to the USMC during 1979-80. They are equipped with an AAS-37 pod which incorporates a FLIR sensor, laser target designator and automatic video tracker, and can be armed with an M197 20-mm three-barrel cannon with 1,500 rounds of ammunition (in place of the OV-10A's conventional armament) which can be directed by the AAS-37 system. These OV-10Ds also have uprated engines, and additional underwing pylons suitable for weapons or auxiliary fuel. It has been rumoured that Rockwell's production line may be reopened to build 24 OV-10D NOS aircraft for South Korea.

A Rockwell International OV-10D of the US Marine Corps.

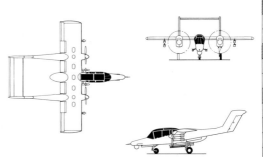

Rockwell International OV-10D NOGS

This OV-10D Bronco serves with VMO-1, based at New River Marine Corps Air Station, North Carolina, for night observation and surveillance duties.

The Rockwell International YOV-10D NOGS (Night Observation/Gunship System) prototype, complete with FLIR, laser designator and video tracker. A gun turret can be installed under the belly.

Specification: Rockwell International OV-10D
Origin: USA
Type: night surveillance aircraft
Powerplant: two 776-ekw (1,040-eshp) Garrett T76-G-420/421 counter-rotating turboprop engines
Performance: maximum speed, clean at sea level 250 kts (463 km/h; 288 mph); initial climb rate 3,020 ft (920 m) per minute; service ceiling 30,000 ft (9145 m); combat radius with maximum weapons and no loiter 367 km (228 miles)
Weights: empty 3127 kg (6,893 lb); maximum take-off 6552 kg (14,444 lb)
Dimensions: span 12.19 m (40 ft 0 in); length 13.41 m (44 ft 0 in); height 4.62 m (15 ft 2 in); wing area 27.03 m² (291.0 sq ft)
Armament: generally as for OV-10 Bronco, plus two underwing pylons with combined capacity of 544 kg (1,200 lb) and suitable for the carriage of cluster bombs, flares, laser guided bombs and rocket pods; an M197 20-mm cannon with 1,500 rounds can be installed on the centreline underfuselage station if no weapons are carried on the sponsons

Rockwell International T-2 Buckeye

Greece   United States   Venezuela

Role

Fighter
Close support
Counter-insurgency
Tactical strike
Strategic bomber
Tactical reconnaissance
Strategic reconnaissance
Maritime patrol
Anti-ship strike
Anti-submarine warfare
Search and rescue
Assault transport
Transport
Liaison
Trainer
Inflight-refuelling tanker
Specialized

Performance

All-weather capability
Rough field capability
STOL capability
VTOL capability
Airspeed 0-250 mph
Airspeed 250 mph-Mach 1
Airspeed Mach 1 plus
Ceiling 0-20,000 ft
Ceiling 20,000-40,000 ft
Ceiling 40,000ft plus
Range 0-1,000 miles
Range 1,000-3,000 miles
Range 3,000 miles plus

Weapons

Air-to-air missiles
Air-to-surface missiles
Cruise missiles
Cannon
Trainable guns
Naval weapons
Nuclear-capable
Rockets
'Smart' weapon kit
Weapon load 0-4,000 lb
Weapon load 4,000-15,000 lb
Weapon load 15,000 lb plus

Avionics

Electronic Counter Measures
Electronic Support Measures
Search radar
Fire control radar
Look-down/shoot-down
Terrain-following radar
Forward-looking infra-red
Laser
Television

In 1956 the US Navy identified the requirement for a jet trainer that would be suitable to take the pupil, after his completion of the ab initio phase, through all the more advanced stages, including bombing, gunnery and fighter tactics to the point of carrier qualification. Competitive procurement was contested by a number of US manufacturers but North American Aviation, which incorporated in its NA-249 design proposal proven features from in-production aircraft (the FJ-1 Fury and T-28 Trojan), was selected and contracted in late 1946 to build six pre-production **YT2J-1** aircraft for evaluation; there was no prototype as such.

The first of the pre-production aircraft, flown initially on 31 January 1958, was a mid-wing monoplane with retractable tricycle landing gear, accommodating pupil and instructor in tandem on LS-1 ejector seats; the instructor's seat, at the rear, was raised to provide a good view forward. The design provided robust landing gear, powered controls, large trailing-edge flaps, an airbrake on each side of the fuselage and a retractable sting-type arrester hook, all of them hydraulically actuated. Power for the YT2J-1 and initial production **T2J-1** (**T-2A** from 1962) was one 1542-kg (3,400-lb) thrust Westinghouse J34-WE-48 turbojet within the fuse-

lage. Named **Buckeye** before entering service in July 1959, the T2J-1 initially equipped BTG-7, later renamed VT-7, based at NAS Meridian. T2J-1 (T-2A) production totalled 201 aircraft.

On 30 August 1962 the first of two **YT2J-2** test aircraft (conversions from T2J-1s) was flown with two 1361-kg (3,000-lb) thrust Pratt & Whitney J60-P-6 turbojets. This version was selected to supersede the T-2A, the first of 97 production **T-2B** aircraft being flown on 21 May 1965 and entering service with Training Squadron VT-4 at NAS Pensacola in December 1965. Following evaluation of a T-2B converted to **YT-2C** configuration with two General Electric J85-GE-4 engines, 231 aircraft designated **T-2C** were built for the US Navy Air Training Command, the first production example being flown initially on 10 December 1968. At a later date small numbers of T-2B and T-2C aircraft were converted as drone directors under the respective designations **DT-2B** and **DT-2C**. In 1982 17 US Navy T-2Bs were removed from storage and refurbished, 15 of them later entering service to supplement the T-2Cs which currently remain in service. The US Navy also procured, on behalf of the Venezuelan and Greek air forces respectively, 24 **T-2D** and 40 **T-2E** aircraft basically similar to the T-2C.

Specification: Rockwell International T-2C Buckeye
Origin: USA
Type: general-purpose jet trainer
Powerplant: two 1338-kg (2,950-lb) thrust General Electric J85-GE-4 turbojet engines
Performance: maximum speed 460 kts (852 km/h; 530mph) at 25,000 ft (7620 m); initial climb rate 5,900 ft (1798 m) per minute; service ceiling 45,500 ft (13870 m); maximum range 1722 km (1,070 miles)
Weights: empty 3681 kg (8,115 lb); maximum take-off 5983 kg (13,190 lb)
Dimensions: span over wingtip tanks 11.62 m (38 ft 1.5 in); length 11.67 m (38 ft 3.5 in); height 4.51 m (14 ft 9.5 in); wing area 23.69 m² (255.0 sq ft)
Armament: can have up to four underwing stations with a maximum capacity of 1588 kg (3,500 lb) comprising gun or rocket pods and practice bombs

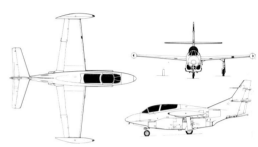

This shark-mouthed T-2 Buckeye serves with VT-23, Training Wing 2, US Navy.

Rockwell International T-2 Buckeye

A formation of Hellenic air force T-2E Buckeyes. Greece has two Buckeye squadrons, 362 and 363 Miras, both based at Kalamata with Air Training Command.

The Venezuelan air force operates the survivors of 24 T-2D Buckeyes for advanced training duties with Grupo de Entrenamiento, Aéreo Escuela de Aviacion Militar at Palo Negro, Maracay.

Sikorsky S-61 (SH-3/VH-3 Sea King)

Argentina Brazil Canada

Denmark Japan Malaysia Spain United States

US Navy experience with the Sikorsky S-58 (USN designation HSS-1 Seabat) highlighted the shortcomings of hunter/killer pairs of helicopters used in the ASW role. On 24 December 1957 a contract was finalized with Sikorsky Aircraft for the development of a helicopter to combine the hunter and killer roles, the resulting **Sikorsky S-61** prototype (USN designation **XHSS-2**) recording the type's maiden flight on 11 March 1959. Ten **YHSS-2** pre-production aircraft were built, seven of them being used for service trials, leading to initial deliveries of production **HSS-2 Sea King** helicopters in September 1961 to Navy squadrons VHS-10 and VHS-3, based respectively at Ream Field, California, and Norfolk, Virginia.

Features of this new, large helicopter included five-blade main and six-blade tail rotors, two 932-kW (1,250-shp) General Electric T58-GE-8B turboshafts mounted above the cabin and adjacent to the main rotor shaft, a rugged fuselage structure incorporating a watertight hull, and stabilizing floats on each side of the fuselage into which the main units of the tailwheel landing gear could retract, thus giving the Sea King true amphibious capability.

In September 1962 the HSS-2 was redesignated **SH-3A**. Operated by a crew of four (pilot, co-pilot and two sonar operators) it was equipped for the ASW role with Bendix AQS-10 or AQS-13 sonar and had a system to hold

automatic hover in conjunction with APN-130 Doppler and a radar altimeter; for true all-weather capability an auto-stabilization system was provided. A total of 245 SH-3As was produced for the Navy, and after token deliveries the type was built by Mitsubishi in Japan as the HSS-2 for the JMSDF and by United Aircraft Corporation in Canada for the CAF, which designated the helicopter **CH-124**. The following **Sikorsky SH-3D** (72 built) had more powerful turboshafts, increased fuel capacity and improved sonar, and this was the last new-build SH-3 variant. Subsequent SH-3A conversions include nine for mine countermeasures use with the US Navy, redesignated **RH-3A**; 105 conversions of SH-3A/SH-3D for a utility role under the designation **SH-3G**; and 112 SH-3A/SH-3D and SH-3G conversions to an **SH-3H** improved ASW configuration. This last variant, based on the SH-3D, has advanced radar and MAD gear plus updated avionics. Ten SH-3As with VIP interiors were operated jointly by the US Army and Marine Corps under the designation **VH-3A** for VIP transport and based with the Executive Flight Detachment at Andrews AFB, Washington; they were replaced subsequently by 11 **VH-3D** aircraft based on the improved SH-3D. Sikorsky export versions based on the SH-3A/SH-3D include the **S-61A**, the **S-61A-4 Nuri** for the Royal Malaysian air force and the **S-61D-4** for the Argentine navy.

A Sikorsky S-61A-4 of the Malaysian air force.

Sikorsky SH-3H Sea King

The SH-3A is known as the CH-124 in Canadian service and serves with the Shearwater-based 423 and 443 Squadrons on anti-submarine and search and rescue duties.

This SH-3H belongs to HS-11, 'Sea Seekers', and is seen on board the USS America shortly before the squadron's participation in Operation Eldorado Canyon.

Specification: Sikorsky SH-3D
Origin: USA
Type: amphibious all-weather ASW helicopter
Powerplant: two 1044-kW (1,400-shp) General Electric T58-GE-10 turboshaft engines
Performance: maximum speed 144 kts (267 km/h; 166 mph); economic cruising speed 118 kts (219 km/h; 136 mph); initial climb rate 2,200 ft (671 m) per minute; service ceiling 14,700 ft (4480 m); range with maximum fuel and 10 per cent reserves 1006 km (625 miles)
Weights: empty 5382 kg (11,865 lb); maximum take-off 9752 kg (21,500 lb)
Dimensions: main rotor diameter 18.90 m (62 ft 0 in); length, rotors turning 22.15 m (72 ft 8 in); height 4.72 m (15 ft 6 in); main rotor disc area 280.47 m² (3,019.08 sq ft)
Armament: provision to carry 381 kg (840 lb) of depth bombs, homing torpedoes or other stores

Role

Fighter
Close support
Counter-insurgency
Tactical strike
Strategic bomber
Tactical reconnaissance
Strategic reconnaissance
Maritime patrol
Anti-ship strike
Anti-submarine warfare
Search and rescue
Assault transport
Transport
Liaison
Trainer
Inflight-refuelling tanker
Specialized

Performance

All-weather capability
Rough field capability
STOL capability
VTOL capability
Airspeed 0-250 mph
Airspeed 250 mph-Mach 1
Airspeed Mach 1 plus
Ceiling 0-20,000 ft
Ceiling 20,000-40,000 ft
Ceiling 40,000 ft plus
Range 0-1,000 miles
Range 1,000-3,000 miles
Range 3,000 miles plus

Weapons

Air-to-air missiles
Air-to-surface missiles
Cruise missiles
Cannon
Trainable guns
Naval weapons
Nuclear-capable
Rockets
'Smart' weapon kit
Weapon load 0-4,000 lb
Weapon load 4,000-15,000 lb
Weapon load 15,000 lb plus

Avionics

Electronic Counter Measures
Electronic Support Measures
Search radar
Fire control radar
Look-down/shoot-down
Terrain-following radar
Forward-looking infra-red
Laser
Television

Sikorsky S-61R (CH-3/HH-3)

United States

The first HH-3 designation was that applied to a search-and-rescue version of the SH-3A for US Navy service in combat areas. The first conversion from SH-3A to **HH-3A** configuration was completed by Sikorsky, the Navy's repair and overhaul base at Quonset Point, Rhode Island, then making 11 more conversions from kits supplied by Sikorsky. These added to the basic SH-3A two 7.62-mm (0.3-in) barbettes in each sponson, a fast refuelling and fuel jettison system, and provision for auxiliary fuel tanks, armour protection for the crew, a high-speed rescue hoist, a revised avionics package, and 1019-kW (1,350-shp) General Electric T58-GE-8F turboshafts.

US Air Force interest in the S-61 for use in a transport role resulted in six SH-3As being loaned by the US Navy, under the designation **CH-3B**, primarily for missile site support and drone recovery duties. These were used pending initial USAF procurement of a long-range transport version. Specific USAF requirements meant these transports incorporated some important changes (resulting in the revised company designation **Sikorsky S-61R**), including advanced main and tail rotors; retractable tricycle landing gear, the main units housed in sponsons when retracted; an internal cargo handling winch with a capacity of 907 kg (2,000 lb); and a hydraulic-ally-actuated tail loading ramp to give direct access for vehicles. These entered service under the designation **CH-3C**, the first being delivered on 30 December 1963. A total of 41 was built with 981-kW (1,300-shp) T58-GE-1 engines before production switched to 42 **CH-3E** helicopters with uprated T58-GE-5 turboshafts, the 41 earlier aircraft later being converted to CH-3E standard. Both variants gave valuable service, and were able to carry up to 25 fully equipped troops, or 15 stretchers, or 2268 kg (5,000 lb) of cargo.

The final USAF variant was the **HH-3E**, an armed rescue version of the CH-3E for service with the Aerospace Rescue and Recovery Service. About 50 were completed as a mix of newly-built aircraft and conversions from CH-3Es. These had additional armour, a high-speed rescue hoist, self-sealing fuel tanks and a retractable inflight-refuelling probe. The HH-3E gave valuable service in Vietnam where, with the nickname **Jolly Green Giant**, its long-range rescue operations into enemy airspace have become part of USAF legend. In 1968 the US Coast Guard received the first of 40 **HH-3F Pelican** rescue aircraft, and these were similar to the HH-3E but without armament, armour or self-sealing tanks.

An **HH-3E** of the 305th ARRS, Air Force Reserve, based at Selfridge ANGB.

Sikorsky CH-3D

The HH-3 forms the backbone of the US Coast Guard helicopter fleet, having sufficient range, endurance and payload to be a very useful search and rescue tool.

This HH-3E serves with Detachment 14 of the 67th ARRS at Keflavik, Iceland. The squadron's various detachments provide SAR and combat rescue cover for the USAF in Europe.

Specification: Sikorsky CH-3E

Origin: USA
Type: amphibious transport helicopter
Powerplant: two 1132-kW (1,500-shp) General Electric T58-GE-5 turboshaft engines
Performance: maximum speed 141 kts (261 km/h; 162 mph) at sea level; economic cruising speed 125 kts (232 km/h; 144 mph); initial climb rate 1,310 ft (399 m) per minute; service ceiling 11,100 ft (3385 m); range with maximum fuel and 10 per cent reserves 748 km (465 miles)
Weights: empty 6012 kg (13,255 lb); maximum take-off 10002 kg (22,050 lb)
Dimensions: main rotor diameter 18.90 m (62 ft 0 in); length, rotors turning 22.25 m (73 ft 0 in); height 4.90 m (16 ft 1 in); main rotor disc area 280.47 m² (3,019.08 sq ft)
Armament: pod-mounted turret at each sponson, each housing a six-barrel 7.62-mm (0.3-in) General Electric Minigun and 8,000 rounds of ammunition

Sikorsky S-62 (HH-52A)

Japan Taiwan Thailand United States

Believing there was a market for an amphibious transport helicopter of smaller capacity than the S-61, the company began design of its **Sikorsky S-62** in 1957; a basic feature was incorporation of the rotor, transmission and some other systems from the already well-proven S-55. Completely new, however, was the all-metal fuselage, for it had been decided to avoid the easy option of a conventional structure with flotation gear added for overwater flights. Thus the lower fuselage was a watertight boat hull, of adequate strength to allow landings on water or snow. Stability on the water was provided by two outrigger floats, positioned well forward and away from the fuselage, and these proved adequate to allow the S-62 to be operated safely in wave heights of up to 3.05 m (10 ft 0 in).

Another new and important feature was the introduction of a 932-kW (1,250-shp) turboshaft engine mounted above the fuselage. Derated to 544 kW (730 shp), this was able to maintain its output to the S-62's maximum altitude. Given the lower weight of

this powerplant by comparison with the S-55's radial piston engine, the S-62 was able to lift a far heavier payload than the S-55 under all conditions. The first of two prototypes (N880) was flown on 22 May 1958.

In late 1961 the US Navy began service trials of a modified S-62A, leading to procurement for the US Coast Guard of a SAR variant under the initial designation **HU2S-1G**, later **HH-52A**. This model had a rescue hoist of 272-kg (600-lb) capacity, and a platform that folded down from the cabin door to help in an on-water rescue; the Coast Guard eventually received 99 to replace the HH-34F in the SAR role. Other variants included the commercial **S-62B**, similar to the S-62A but With a reduced-diameter version of the main rotor system of the S-58, and the commercial and export military **S-62C** which was basically similar to the HH-52A. However, sales were very limited and apart from those for the US Coast Guard, and a small number built under licence by Mitsubishi in Japan, the S-62 was a disappointing production exercise for Sikorsky.

Specification: Sikorsky HH-52A
Origin: USA
Type: amphibious SAR helicopter
Powerplant: one 932-kW (1,250-shp) General Electric T58-GE-8 turboshaft engine
Performance: maximum speed 95 kts (175 km/h; 109 mph) at sea level; maximum cruising speed 85 kts (158 km/h; 98 mph); initial climb rate 1,070 ft (326 m) per minute; service ceiling 11,200 ft (3415 m); range with maximum fuel and 10 per cent reserves 763 km (474 miles)
Weights: empty 2224 kg (4,903 lb); maximum take-off 3674 kg (8,100 lb)
Dimensions: main rotor diameter 16.15 m (53 ft 0 in); fuselage length 13.58 m (44 ft 6.5 in); height 4.33 m (14 ft 2.5 in); main rotor disc area 204.96 m² (2,206.19 sq ft)
Armament: none

A Sikorsky HH-52A of the United States Coast Guard.

Sikorsky S-62/HH-52A

This Los Angeles based US Coast Guard HH-52A shot to stardom in the film 'Airport 77', before returning to more mundane rescue duties. The aircraft was not procured in large numbers.

One of nine Mitsubishi Sikorsky S 62Js delivered to the Japanese Maritime Self Defence Force, where they serve with the rescue flights at Atsugi, Kanoya and Tokushima.

Role
Fighter
Close support
Counter-insurgency
Tactical strike
Strategic bomber
Tactical reconnaissance
Strategic reconnaissance
Maritime patrol
Anti-ship strike
Anti-submarine warfare
Search and rescue
Assault transport
Transport
Liaison
Trainer
Inflight-refuelling tanker
Specialized

Performance
All-weather capability
Rough field capability
STOL capability
VTOL capability
Airspeed 0-250 mph
Airspeed 250 mph-Mach 1
Airspeed Mach 1 plus
Ceiling 0-20,000 ft
Ceiling 20,000-40,000 ft
Ceiling 40,000 ft plus
Range 0-1,000 miles
Range 1,000-3,000 miles
Range 3,000 miles plus

Weapons
Air-to-air missiles
Air-to-surface missiles
Cruise missiles
Cannon
Trainable guns
Naval weapons
Nuclear-capable
Rockets
'Smart' weapon kit
Weapon load 0-4,000 lb
Weapon load 4,000-15,000 lb
Weapon load 15,000 lb plus

Avionics
Electronic Counter Measures
Electronic Support Measures
Search radar
Fire control radar
Look-down/shoot-down
Terrain-following radar
Forward-looking infra-red
Laser
Television

Sikorsky S-64 Skycrane (CH-54 Tarhe)

Development by Sikorsky of a flying-crane helicopter, intended to lift heavy slung loads rather than carry them internally, began in 1958 when an aircraft designated S-60 was developed from the S-56 transport helicopter. The S-60 (N807) was first flown on 25 March 1959 and used for test, evaluation and development before it crashed in 1961. By then the company had completed the design of and started to build an enlarged **Sikorsky S-64** which it later named **Skycrane**.

First flown on 9 May 1962, the **S-64A** prototype (N325Y) had a pod-and-boom fuselage structure, the comparatively small pod incorporating the nosewheel of the landing gear and seating a pilot and co-pilot forward, a third (rearward-facing) seat with flying controls being provided to allow a pilot to take full control during loading/unloading operations. The long and strong boom served to mount all other features of the S-64: its two turboshaft engines forward of the six-blade main rotor, two outriggers for the main units of the fixed tricycle landing gear (giving a wheel track of 6.02 m/19 ft 9 in to clear wide loads), a removable hoist of 9072-kg (20,000-lb) capacity, and a pylon for the four-blade tail rotor (port) and horizontal stabilizer (starboard). Attachments were provided on the landing gear outriggers and fuselage boom to mount

bulky loads, including specially developed pods or vans to house, for example, 67 troops, or 48 stretchers, or a field hospital unit, or 10383 kg (22,890 lb) of cargo.

Following evaluation of the first of the three prototypes, the US Army ordered six S-64As, designating them **CH-54A** and naming them **Tarhe**. Five were delivered during 1964-5, equipping initially the 478th Aviation Company of the US Army's 1st Cavalry Division in Vietnam, where they quickly proved to be immensely valuable. They were soon airlifting such items as bulldozers and road graders weighing up to 9072 kg (20,000 lb), retrieving damaged aircraft from enemy territory and, in one instance, lifting its crew of three and 87 troops in a detachable van. Additional orders soon followed and CH-54A procurement totalled 54, being followd by 37 **CH-54B** helicopters which differed by having structural strengthening, 3579-kW (4,800-shp) Pratt & Whitney T73-P-700 turboshaft engines, heavy-lift rotor blades, twin wheels on the main gear units, an improved automatic flight control system, and detail improvements.

In addition to its manufacture of CH-54A/B aircraft for the US Army, Sikorsky also built small numbers for commercial use.

Specification: Sikorsky CH-54A
Origin: USA
Type: flying-crane helicopter
Powerplant: two 3356-kW (4,500-shp) Pratt & Whitney T73-P-1 turboshaft engines
Performance: maximum speed 109 kts (203 km/h; 126 mph) at sea level; maximum cruising speed 91 kts (169 km/h; 105 mph); initial climb rate 1,330 ft (405 m) per minute; service ceiling 9,000 ft (2745 m); range with maximum fuel and 10 per cent reserves 370 km (230 miles)
Weights: empty 8724 kg (19,234 lb); maximum take-off 19051 kg (42,000 lb)
Dimensions: main rotor diameter 21.95 m (72 ft 0 in); length, rotors turning 26.97 m (88 ft 6 in); height 7.75 m (25 ft 5 in); main rotor disc area 378.24 m² (4,071.5 sq ft)
Armament: none

A Sikorsky CH-54B Tarhe of the US Army.

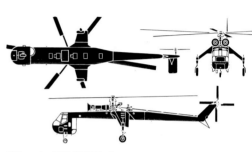

Sikorsky CH-54A Tarhe

The CH-54 Tarhe has built up an impressive record as a flying crane and saw active service during the Vietnam war. The helicopter has now been withdrawn to second-line units.

In its day the Tarhe was a powerful flying crane, but now that the CH-47D version of the Chinook can lift heavier weights the Tarhe has been relegated to ANG units.

Sikorsky S-65 (CH-53 Sea Stallion)

West Germany   Israel   United States

Sikorsky started design and development of large transport helicopters at the beginning of the 1950s, and its S-56 which saw service with the US Army, Navy and Marine Corps from 1955 was, for almost a decade, the largest helicopter flying outside the USSR. In the late 1950s the company began work on large flying-crane helicopters and then drew up its proposals to meet a US Marine Corps requirement for a ship-based heavy assault transport. Identified as the **Sikorsky S-65A**, this was selected by the USMC in August 1962 to fill this role, being allocated the service designation **CH-53A** and named **Sea Stallion**.

The S-65A was something of a hybrid, with features of the S-64 Skycrane developed at about the same time and a watertight hull that benefited from experience with the S-61 family. The S-65 was much larger than the latter, however, with sufficient volume in a fuselage structure which equated with that of a conventional fixed-wing aircraft to accommodate a crew of three and up to 38 equipped troops. Alternative loads included 24 stretchers, or some 3629 kg (8,000 lb) of cargo or, via a rear door/ramp, such military loads as a 1.5-ton truck and its trailer, a 105-mm (4.13-in) howitzer, a HAWK SAM system or an Honest John SSM on its trailer. Alternatively, an external slung load of 5897 kg (13,000 lb) could be carried. The configuration includes

six-blade main and four-blade tail rotors, stabilizing sponsons on each side of the fuselage for on-water operations and into which the main units of the tricycle landing gear retract, and twin-turbine powerplant mounted above the cabin. In the initial CH-53A, first flown on 14 October 1964 and entering service in mid-1966, the powerplant consisted of two 2125-kW (2,850-shp) General Electric T64-GE-6 turboshafts, but the alternative T64-GE-1 of 2297 kW (3,080 shp) or T64-GE-16 (mod) of 2561 kW (3,435 shp) could be installed without modification.

An improved version designated **CH-53D** was introduced on the production line late in 1968, with initial deliveries made on 3 March 1969. The major changes involved were internal revisions to make it possible to seat up to 55 troops, the installation of either 2755-kW (3,695-shp) T64-GE-412 or 2927-kW (3,925-shp) T64-GE-413 turboshafts, and the incorporation of automatic folding of the main and tail rotors to simplify stowage on board aircraft-carriers. Production for the USMC ended in January 1972 after 139 CH-53A and 126 CH-53D Sea Stallions had been completed. Two **CH-53G** helicopters, of a type basically similar to the CH-53D, were built as sample aircraft for West Germany, where VFW-Fokker assembled under licence an additional 110.

Specification: Sikorsky CH-53D Sea Stallion

Origin: USA
Type: assault transport helicopter
Powerplant: two 2927-kW (3,925-shp) General Electric T64-GE-413 turboshaft engines
Performance: maximum speed 170 kts (315 km/h; 196 mph) at sea level; cruising speed 150 kts (278 km/h; 173 mph); initial climb rate 2,180 ft (664 m) per minute; service ceiling 21,000 ft (6400 m); range with maximum standard fuel and 10 per cent reserves 414 km (257 miles)
Weights: empty 10653 kg (23,485 lb); mission take-off 16511 kg (36,400 lb); maximum take-off 19051 kg (42,000 lb)
Dimensions: main rotor diameter 22.02 m (72 ft 3 in); length, rotors turning 26.90 m (88 ft 3 in); height 7.59 m (24 ft 11 in); main rotor disc area 380.87 m² (4,099.8 sq ft)
Armament: none

A CH-53G of West German army aviation (Heeresflieger).

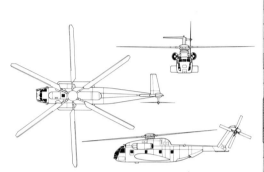

Sikorsky CH-53 Sea Stallion

This elderly CH-53A serves with the shore-based heavy transport squadron HMT-301 at MCAS Tustin, California, a composite unit which also operates the CH-46E, and the CH-53E.

Over 100 CH-53Gs were delivered to the Heeresflieger, and most remain in front-line service. The CH-53G is essentially similar to the CH-53D.

Sikorsky S-65 (CH-53E/MH-53E)

Although both the US Navy and Marine Corps had gained good service in heavy transport and minesweeping roles from the Sikorsky CH-53D and RH-53D, it was clear by the early 1970s that an even more capable helicopter could be built to fulfil such tasks. In 1973 the Sikorsky S-65 was selected for development, and in May of that year the construction of two **YCH-53E** prototypes was initiated, the first of them flying on 1 March 1974. The first of two pre-production aircraft flew on 13 December 1980, and initial production deliveries of the **Sikorsky CH-53E Super Stallion** to Marine Corps squadron HMH-464, at New River, North Carolina, began on 16 June 1981. The US Navy plans to procure ultimately at least 300 of these helicopters, and about 100 had been delivered in mid-1986. By comparison with the CH-53D, the new helicopter has a lengthened fuselage, three turboshaft engines, an increased diameter seven-blade main rotor and an uprated transmission, giving double the lift capability of the twin-turbine H-53s with only 50 per cent more engine power. With a single-point cargo hook rated at 16329 kg (36,000 lb), the CH-53E is suitable for combat tasks such as lifting battle-damaged aircraft from carrier decks, or the support of mobile construction battalions, and for vertical onboard delivery has

an internal cargo load of 13608 kg (30,000 lb).

Further capability enhancement for the mine countermeasures helicopter was explored first with a prototype, initially designated **CH/MH-53E**, which was a conversion from a pre-production CH-53E and flown for the first time on 23 December 1981. Early evaluation by the US Navy resulted in the construction of a pre-production aircraft, then designated **MH-53E** and named **Sea Dragon**, which was flown on 1 September 1983. Since then the Navy has stated its requirement for at least 57 of these aircraft and the first production example was scheduled for delivery during 1986. The MH-53E is easily identified externally by its enlarged sponsons containing additional fuel and allowing the helicopter to operate for up to six hours on station; it is also equipped with an inflight-refuelling probe and, at the hover, can refuel by hose from a surface vessel. Extended capability is provided by duplicated digital automatic flight-control systems and automatic tow couplers which allow automatic approach to and departure from the hover. Export versions of the CH-53E and MH-53E are being offered by Sikorsky under the respective designations **S-80E** and **S-80M**.

Specification: Sikorsky CH-53E Super Stallion
Origin: USA
Type: heavy-duty multi-role helicopter
Powerplant: three 3266-kW (4,380-shp) General Electric T64-GE-416 turboshaft engines
Performance: maximum speed 170 kts (315 km/h; 196 mph) at sea level; cruising speed at sea level 150 kts (278 km/h; 173 mph); initial climb rate 2,500 ft (762 m) per minute; service ceiling 18,500 ft (5640 m); unrefuelled self-ferry range 2076 km (1,290 miles)
Weights: empty 15071 kg (33,226 lb); maximum take-off, internal payload 31638 kg (69,750 lb) and external payload 33339 kg (73,500 lb)
Dimensions: main rotor diameter 24.08 m (79 ft 0 in); length, rotors turning 30.19 m (99 ft 0.5 in); height, tail rotor turning 8.66 m (28 ft 5 in); main rotor disc area 455.37 m² (4,901.68 sq ft)
Armament: none, but there are suggestions that AIM-9 Sidewinders might be provided to give a self-defence capability

A Sikorsky MH-53E Sea Dragon of the US Navy.

Sikorsky CH-53E Sea Stallion Super

Two CH-53E Super Stallions of the US Marine Corps, refuelling from a KC-130T Hercules. The CH-53E differs from earlier variants in having three engines and an uprated transmission.

This CH-53E Super Stallion serves with the US Navy's VC-5, 'Workhorse of the Fleet', a composite evaluation and general duties squadron which operates from Cubi Point, Philippines.

A CH-53E Super Stallion of the US Navy

Sikorsky S-65 (HH-53)

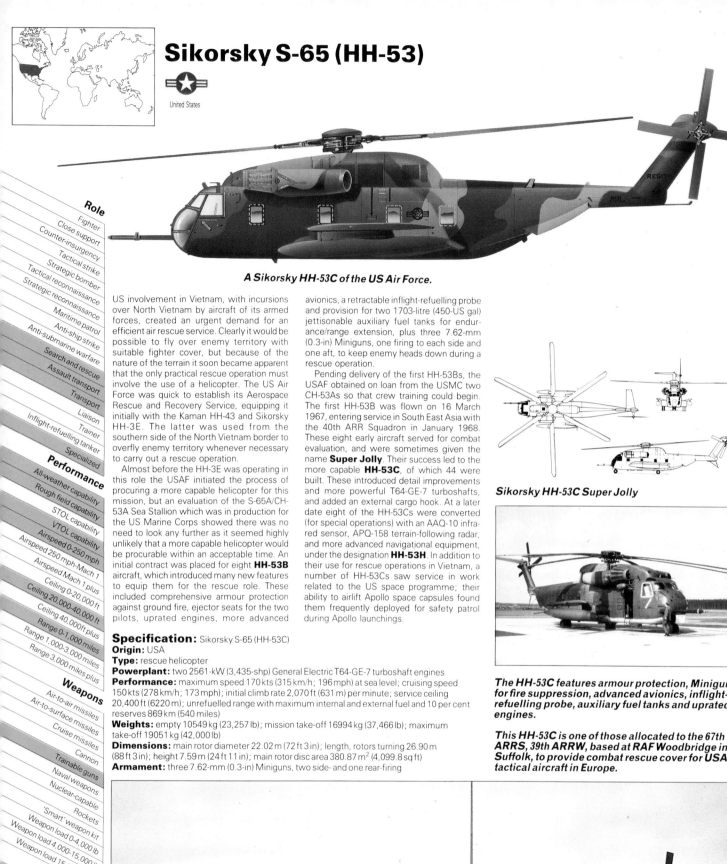

A Sikorsky HH-53C of the US Air Force.

US involvement in Vietnam, with incursions over North Vietnam by aircraft of its armed forces, created an urgent demand for an efficient air rescue service. Clearly it would be possible to fly over enemy territory with suitable fighter cover, but because of the nature of the terrain it soon became apparent that the only practical rescue operation must involve the use of a helicopter. The US Air Force was quick to establish its Aerospace Rescue and Recovery Service, equipping it initially with the Kaman HH-43 and Sikorsky HH-3E. The latter was used from the southern side of the North Vietnam border to overfly enemy territory whenever necessary to carry out a rescue operation.

Almost before the HH-3E was operating in this role the USAF initiated the process of procuring a more capable helicopter for this mission, but an evaluation of the S-65A/CH-53A Sea Stallion which was in production for the US Marine Corps showed there was no need to look any further as it seemed highly unlikely that a more capable helicopter would be procurable within an acceptable time. An initial contract was placed for eight **HH-53B** aircraft, which introduced many new features to equip them for the rescue role. These included comprehensive armour protection against ground fire, ejector seats for the two pilots, uprated engines, more advanced

avionics, a retractable inflight-refuelling probe and provision for two 1703-litre (450-US gal) jettisonable auxiliary fuel tanks for endurance/range extension, plus three 7.62-mm (0.3-in) Miniguns, one firing to each side and one aft, to keep enemy heads down during a rescue operation.

Pending delivery of the first HH-53Bs, the USAF obtained on loan from the USMC two CH-53As so that crew training could begin. The first HH-53B was flown on 16 March 1967, entering service in South East Asia with the 40th ARR Squadron in January 1968. These eight early aircraft served for combat evaluation, and were sometimes given the name **Super Jolly**. Their success led to the more capable **HH-53C**, of which 44 were built. These introduced detail improvements and more powerful T64-GE-7 turboshafts, and added an external cargo hook. At a later date eight of the HH-53Cs were converted (for special operations) with an AAQ-10 infrared sensor, APQ-158 terrain-following radar, and more advanced navigational equipment, under the designation **HH-53H**. In addition to their use for rescue operations in Vietnam, a number of HH-53Cs saw service in work related to the US space programme; their ability to airlift Apollo space capsules found them frequently deployed for safety patrol during Apollo launchings.

Specification: Sikorsky S-65 (HH-53C)
Origin: USA
Type: rescue helicopter
Powerplant: two 2561-kW (3,435-shp) General Electric T64-GE-7 turboshaft engines
Performance: maximum speed 170 kts (315 km/h; 196 mph) at sea level; cruising speed 150 kts (278 km/h; 173 mph); initial climb rate 2,070 ft (631 m) per minute; service ceiling 20,400 ft (6220 m); unrefuelled range with maximum internal and external fuel and 10 per cent reserves 869 km (540 miles)
Weights: empty 10549 kg (23,257 lb); mission take-off 16994 kg (37,466 lb); maximum take-off 19051 kg (42,000 lb)
Dimensions: main rotor diameter 22.02 m (72 ft 3 in); length, rotors turning 26.90 m (88 ft 3 in); height 7.59 m (24 ft 11 in); main rotor disc area 380.87 m² (4,099.8 sq ft)
Armament: three 7.62-mm (0.3-in) Miniguns, two side- and one rear-firing

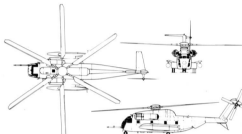

Sikorsky HH-53C Super Jolly

The HH-53C features armour protection, Miniguns for fire suppression, advanced avionics, inflight-refuelling probe, auxiliary fuel tanks and uprated engines.

This HH-53C is one of those allocated to the 67th ARRS, 39th ARRW, based at RAF Woodbridge in Suffolk, to provide combat rescue cover for USAF tactical aircraft in Europe.

Sikorsky S-65 (RH-53)

Iran   United States

The growing range and heavy-lift capability of helicopters led to their evaluation for one of the most difficult naval operations, the sweeping of enemy mines. It was realized that with an aircraft operating at a height well above the surface to tow sweep gear or mine detectors, there was little chance of the helicopter being endangered by the detonation of a mine, making it a most attractive towing vehicle for use in this role.

Bearing in mind such a potential use for its CH-53As, the US Marine Corps ensured that of the 139 of this version procured, all but the first 32 were equipped with suitable hardpoints to enable minesweeping gear to be towed. Evaluation by the US Navy of the capability of the CH-53A when deployed for minesweeping led in 1971 to the transfer from the USMC to the USN of 15 CH-53As with hardpoints. Since these were intended specifically for a minesweeping role, a task requiring good heavy-lift capability, they were first re-engined with 2927-kW (3,925-shp) T64-GE-413 turboshafts, then becoming redesignated **RH-53A**, and were used to equip the USN's first helicopter mine countermeasures squadron, HM-12.

US Navy experience with the RH-53A resulted in the procurement of a version of the S-65 optimized for the minesweeping task,

Sikorsky receiving a contract for 30 under the service designation **RH-53D**. Based upon the improved CH-53D, they were given structural strengthening for the towing task and reinforced landing gear for operation at a higher gross weight. Powered initially by T64-GE-413 turboshafts, they were later retro-fitted with T64-GE-415s, each developing a maximum 3266 kW (4,380 shp). To provide worthwhile mission endurance, a 1893-litre (500-US gal) fuel tank was mounted on each sponson, and a nose-mounted inflight-refuelling probe installed. Special equipment included interconnection to the AFCS to give automatic tow cable yaw angle retention, with an automatic cable release should pre-set limits of tow cable tension and yaw angle be exceeded. First flown on 27 October 1972, and entering service with Navy squadron HM-12 in September 1973, the RH-53D is suitable for sweeping acoustic, magnetic and mechanical mines. When required to deploy sweep gear too large to be carried internally, it uses its tow hook to pick up equipment first streamed behind a surface vessel. In addition to the contract for 30 RH-53Ds for its own use, the US Navy also procured six additional examples which were supplied for service with Iran's naval air arm.

Specification: Sikorsky RH-53D
Origin: USA
Type: minesweeping and multi-role helicopter
Powerplant: two 3266-kW (4,380-shp) General Electric T64-GE-415 turboshaft engines
Performance: unrefuelled endurance over 4 hours
Weights: normal take-off 19051 kg (42,000 lb); maximum take-off 22680 kg (50,000 lb)
Dimensions: main rotor diameter 22.02 m (72 ft 3 in); length, rotors turning 26.90 m (88 ft 3 in); height 7.59 m (24 ft 11 in); main rotor disc area 380.87 m² (4,099.8 sq ft)
Armament: provision for two 12.7-mm (0.5-in) machine-guns for use in detonating surfaced mines

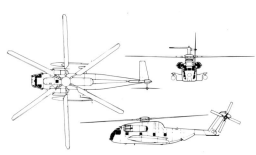

A Sikorsky RH-53D of Helicopter Mine Countermeasures Squadron 12 (HM-12), US Navy.

Sikorsky S-65/RH-53D

The RH-53D was the helicopter used in the abortive Operation 'Eagle Claw', the ill-fated mission to rescue the American hostages held in Tehran during April 1980.

This RH-53D wears an orthodox sea grey colour scheme and serves with the US Navy's HM-12 'Sea Dragons', the Norfolk-based mine countermeasures unit.

Role
Fighter
Close support
Counter-insurgency
Tactical strike
Strategic bomber
Tactical reconnaissance
Strategic reconnaissance
Maritime patrol
Anti-ship strike
Anti-submarine warfare
Search and rescue
Assault transport
Transport
Liaison
Trainer
Inflight-refuelling tanker
Specialized

Performance
All-weather capability
Rough field capability
STOL capability
VTOL capability
Airspeed 0-250 mph
Airspeed 250 mph-Mach 1
Airspeed Mach 1 plus
Ceiling 0-20,000 ft
Ceiling 20,000-40,000 ft
Ceiling 40,000ft plus
Range 0-1,000 miles
Range 1,000-3,000 miles
Range 3,000 miles plus

Weapons
Air-to-air missiles
Air-to-surface missiles
Cruise missiles
Cannon
Trainable guns
Naval weapons
Nuclear-capable
Rockets
'Smart' weapon kit
Weapon load 0-4,000 lb
Weapon load 4,000-15,000 lb
Weapon load 15,000 lb plus

Avionics
Electronic Counter Measures
Electronic Support Measures
Search radar
Fire control radar
Look-down/shoot-down
Terrain-following radar
Forward-looking infra-red
Laser
Television

Sikorsky S-70 (EH-60, HH-60 and UH-60)

China   Philippines   I Taiwan   United States

Role
Fighter
Close support
Counter-insurgency
Tactical strike
Strategic bomber
Tactical reconnaissance
Strategic reconnaissance
Maritime patrol
Anti-ship strike
Anti-submarine warfare
Search and rescue
Assault transport
Transport
Liaison
Trainer
Inflight-refuelling tanker
Specialized

Performance
All-weather capability
Rough field capability
STOL capability
VTOL capability
Airspeed 0-250 mph
Airspeed 250 mph-Mach 1
Airspeed Mach 1 plus
Ceiling 0-20,000 ft
Ceiling 20,000-40,000 ft
Ceiling 40,000ft plus
Range 0-1,000 miles
Range 1,000-3,000 miles
Range 3,000 miles plus

Weapons
Air-to-air missiles
Air-to-surface missiles
Cruise missiles
Cannon
Trainable guns
Naval weapons
Nuclear-capable
Rockets
'Smart' weapon kit
Weapon load 0-4,000 lb
Weapon load 4,000-15,000 lb
Weapon load 15,000 lb plus

Avionics
Electronic Counter Measures
Electronic Support Measures
Search radar
Fire control radar
Look-down/shoot-down
Terrain-following radar
Forward-looking infra-red
Laser
Television

The US Army's need for a Utility Tactical Transport Aircraft System (UTTAS) led, in late August 1972, to Boeing Vertol and Sikorsky being selected to build competing prototypes of their design proposals. The first of three **Sikorsky S-70** flying prototypes was flown on 17 October 1974, these having the service designation **YUH-60A**. Technical evaluation and seven months of competitive flight test against Boeing Vertol's YUH-61A saw Sikorsky's design selected for production as the **UH-60A** with the name **Black Hawk**. The Army plans to procure a possible total of up to 1,715 by the 1990s, and following the first flight of a production aircraft during October 1978 almost 700 are now in service.

Intended as the US Army's primary combat assault helicopter, carrying 11 equipped troops and a crew of three, the UH-60A has a cabin which is suitable also for medevac, reconnaissance or troop resupply missions. Its external cargo hook has a capacity of up to 3629 kg (8,000 lb). One UTTAS requirement was that it could be easily airlifted: with the use of kits designed by Sikorsky, the USAF's Lockheed C-130, C-141 and C-5 can carry respectively one, two and six. Battlefield survivability features of the UH-60A include main rotor blades tolerant to 23-mm gunfire, transmission system operable for up to 30 minutes following total oil loss, twin turbines, crashworthy bulletproof fuel cells, and armour-protected seats for pilot and co-pilot.

An external stores support system (ESSS), with conversion kits delivered from early 1986, allows the carriage on four pylons of auxiliary fuel, stores or weapons.

Following preparation of a **YEH-60A** prototype during 1981, flown for the first time on 24 September 1981 and equipped with 'Quick Fix IIB' ECM to intercept, monitor and jam enemy communications, the conversion of 40 UH-60As to **EH-60A** ECM/ESM configuration began following the award of a contract to Tracor Aerospace Group, which is responsible for production and installation of the ECM/ESM equipment. The US Army plans to procure up to 132 EH-60As under its SEMA (Special Electronic Mission Aircraft) programme. An **EH-60B** variant for the Army's SOTAS (Stand-Off Target Acquisition System) programme was abandoned in late 1981.

Under development for the US Air Force is a day/night combat rescue version which has the designation **HH-60A Night Hawk**. Able to carry a crew of two and 10 passengers, or four stretchers and three seated casualties, the HH-60A has equipment that includes a rescue hoist, external auxiliary fuel and inflight-refuelling capability for adequate mission radius, advanced avionics for accurate navigation, and defensive equipment. The USAF hopes to acquire 90 for delivery from 1988.

Specification: Sikorsky UH-60A
Origin: USA
Type: combat assault transport helicopter
Powerplant: two 1163-kW (1,560-shp) General Electric T700-GE-700 turboshaft engines
Performance: maximum speed 160 kts (296 km/h; 184 mph) at sea level; maximum cruising speed at 4,000 ft (1220 m) 145 kts (269 km/h; 167 mph); initial vertical climb rate more than 450 ft (137 m) per minute; service ceiling 19,000 ft (5790 m); range with maximum internal and external fuel 2221 km (1,380 miles)
Weights: empty 4819 kg (10,624 lb); mission take-off 7375 kg (16,260 lb); maximum take-off 9185 kg (20,250 lb)
Dimensions: main rotor diameter 16.36 m (53 ft 8 in); length, rotors turning 19.76 m (64 ft 10 in); height, rotors turning 5.13 m (16 ft 10 in); main rotor disc area 210.14 m^2 (2,262.04 sq ft)
Armament: one or two side-firing 7.62-mm (0.3-in) M60 machine-guns in cabin, plus Hellfire ASMs, rockets, mine dispensers, jamming flares and chaff dispensers on pylons

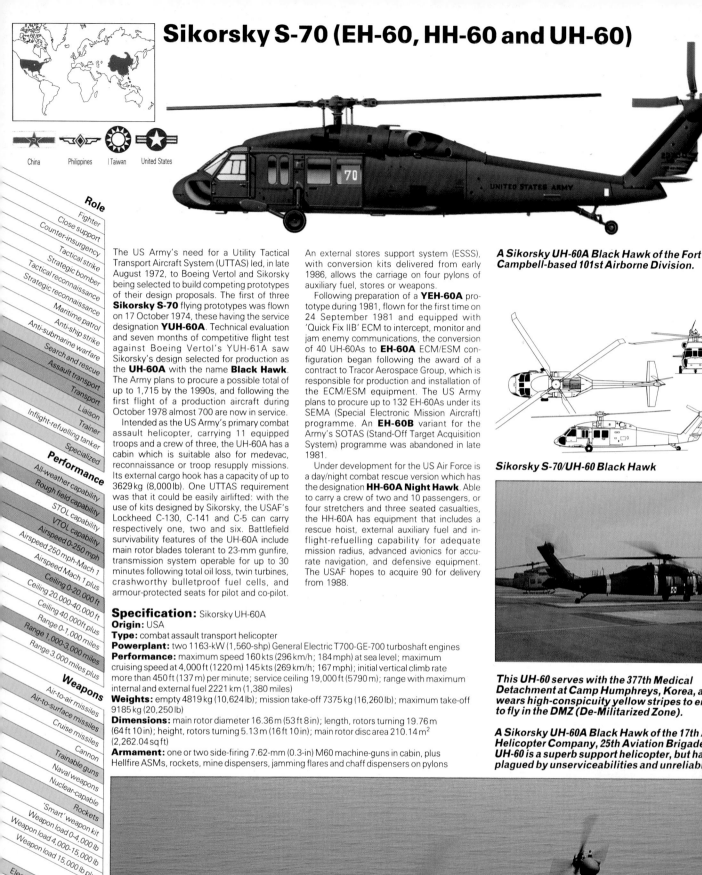

A Sikorsky UH-60A Black Hawk of the Fort Campbell-based 101st Airborne Division.

Sikorsky S-70/UH-60 Black Hawk

This UH-60 serves with the 377th Medical Detachment at Camp Humphreys, Korea, and wears high-conspicuity yellow stripes to enable it to fly in the DMZ (De-Militarized Zone).

A Sikorsky UH-60A Black Hawk of the 17th Army Helicopter Company, 25th Aviation Brigade. The UH-60 is a superb support helicopter, but has been plagued by unserviceabilities and unreliability.

Sikorsky S-70B (SH-60B)

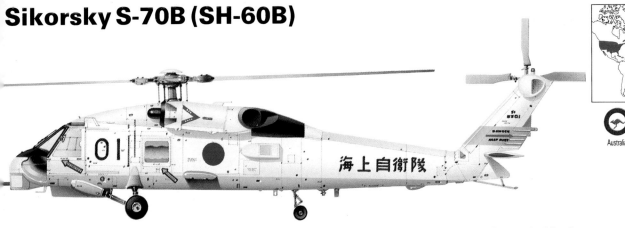

Australia Japan Spain United States

The undoubted success of the US Navy's LAMPS (Light Airborne Multi-Purpose System) aircraft in the ASW/ASST/SAR roles spurred the development of more capable systems. However, the Kaman SH-2F LAMPS Mk I helicopter was considered to be unsuitable to carry more advanced equipment and a LAMPS Mk II system was abandoned pending the availability of a more suitable carrier. In 1977, about a year after the Sikorsky S-70A had been selected by the US Army to meet its UTTAS requirement, the US Navy conducted a similar fly-off and techncial evaluation of a developed version of the Boeing Vertol YUH-61A and Sikorsky YUH-60A, selecting the Sikorsky airframe for integration of the LAMPS Mk III system. This last had been under development by IBM Federal Systems Division since 1974, a three-year period which perhaps emphasized better than anything the complexity and, consequently, the cost and capability of this advanced system.

US Navy adoption of the **Sikorsky S-70B** airframe as the **SH-60B Seahawk** LAMPS Mk III carrier resulted in the construction of five **YSH-60B** prototypes, the first of them flying initially on 12 December 1979. Almost two and a half years of development and operational tests followed before the initial production contract was authorized, the first production aircraft flying on 11 February

1983. HSL-41, based at North Island, San Diego, was the first USN squadron to be equipped, gaining initial operational capability in 1984.

The SH-60B differs in several ways from the US Army's UH-60A, including the introduction of more powerful and navalized engines, automatic main rotor folding, a rotor brake, tail pylon folding, buoyancy features incorporated in the airframe structure, simplified landing gear, a sliding cabin door, provision of a sensor operator's station, rescue hoist, and pilot/co-pilot seats without armour. Optimum mission capability is provided by such features as increased fuel and hovering inflight-refuelling capability, cargo hook, RAST (Recovery, Assist, Secure and Traversing) gear to help land and hangar the helicopter in rough sea conditions, search radar, a pylon (starboard) for MAD gear, a pylon on each side for torpedoes or auxiliary fuel tanks, a sonobuoy launcher, and chin-mounted pods for ESM equipment. Secure communications are provided, plus a data-link between the helicopter and its mother ship, and the LAMPS Mk III system provides comprehensive avionics for the expected roles. The US Navy hopes to procure a total of 204 SH-60Bs, plus an unspecified number of an **SH-60F** version under development to defend the inner zone of a carrier battle group from submarine attack.

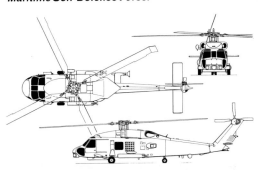

A Sikorsky XSH-60J Seahawk of the Japan Maritime Self-Defence Force.

Sikorsky S-70B/SH-60B Seahawk

An SH-60B Seahawk of VX-1, a Patuxent River-based evaluation and experimental unit. The Seahawk will replace the Kaman SH-2F SeaSprite as the US Navy LAMPS platform.

NAS North Island is a major US Navy air base in California, with a large number of resident units, including two SH-60B squadrons, HSL-43 'Battle Cats' and HSL-41.

Specification: Sikorsky SH-60B
Origin: USA
Type: ASW/ASST/SAR helicopter
Powerplant: two 1260-kW (1,690-shp) General Electric T700-GE-401 engines
Performance: maximum speed in tropical day conditions at 5,000ft (1525m) 126kts (233km/h; 145mph); initial vertical climb rate 700ft (213m) per minute
Weights: (estimated, ASW role) empty 6191kg (13,648lb); mission take-off 9183kg (20,244lb)
Dimensions: main rotor diameter 16.36m (53ft 8in); length, rotors turning 19.76m (64ft 10in); height, rotors turning 5.18m (17ft 0in); main rotor disc area 210.14m² (2,262.04sqft)
Armament: can include two Mk 46 torpedoes

Role	
Fighter	
Close support	
Counter-insurgency	
Tactical strike	
Strategic bomber	
Tactical reconnaissance	
Strategic reconnaissance	
Maritime patrol	■
Anti-ship strike	■
Anti-submarine warfare	■
Search and rescue	■
Assault transport	
Transport	
Liaison	
Trainer	
Inflight-refuelling tanker	
Specialized	

Performance	
All-weather capability	■
Rough field capability	
STOL capability	
VTOL capability	■
Airspeed 0-250 mph	■
Airspeed 250 mph-Mach 1	
Airspeed Mach 1 plus	
Ceiling 0-20,000 ft	■
Ceiling 20,000-40,000 ft	
Ceiling 40,000ft plus	
Range 0-1,000 miles	■
Range 1,000-3,000 miles	
Range 3,000 miles plus	

Weapons	
Air-to-air missiles	
Air-to-surface missiles	
Cruise missiles	
Cannon	
Trainable guns	
Naval weapons	■
Nuclear-capable	
Rockets	
'Smart' weapon kit	
Weapon load 0-4,000 lb	■
Weapon load 4,000-15,000 lb	
Weapon load 15,000 lb plus	

Avionics	
Electronic Counter Measures	■
Electronic Support Measures	■
Search radar	■
Fire control radar	
Look-down/shoot-down	
Terrain-following radar	
Forward-looking infra-red	
Laser	
Television	

An A-7D of 354th TFW before conversion to the A-10A

Vought A-7A, B, C, E and L Corsair II

United States

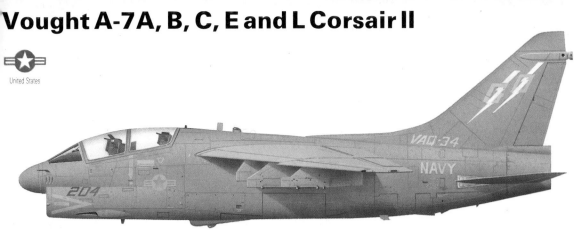

The Vought A-7 Corsair II was designed to replace the McDonnell Douglas A-4 Skyhawk, the US Navy's standard carrierborne light attack aircraft during the late 1950s and early 1960s. The A-4, affectionately known as the 'Scooter', was fast and agile but lacked range and load-carrying capability. On 11 February 1964 it was announced that Vought had won the competition to produce a low-cost replacement, which was to have a longer range and greater payload. Whereas the A-4 had been optimized for the delivery of a single nuclear weapon, its replacement was to be the first post-war aircraft to be developed for close air support and battlefield attack targets.

America's involvement in the Vietnam war highlighted the shortcomings of the A-4, and every effort was made to get the new aircraft into service as soon as possible. It was decided at a very early stage that the new aircraft should be an adaptation of an existing design, and that it should use an existing engine. Vought's submission was based on the successful F-8 Crusader supersonic fighter, but using the Pratt & Whitney TF30 turbofan of the ill-starred F-111B.

Whereas the slim and shapely Crusader was highly supersonic, the new A-7 had a shorter, fatter fuselage, a shortened fin and a blunt nose, and was designed from the outset to be subsonic, with long range and endurance being more important priorities

than high speed. A prototype was quickly constructed, and made its maiden flight on 27 September 1965.

One hundred and ninety-nine of the initial production variant, the **A-7A**, were eventually ordered by the US Navy, the first entering service with VA-174 'Hell Razors' on 14 October 1966. Steam ingestion problems restricted the A-7A's catapult launch weight to 17236kg (38,000 lb), but this problem was remedied in the **A-7B**, powered by the more powerful TF-30-P-8 turbofan. One hundred and ninety-six A-7Bs were built, 24 later being converted to two-seaters with the designation **TA-7C**.

The 67 **A-7C**s built were an interim variant with a new head-up display, updated bombing system and a single M61A1 Vulcan cannon with 1,000 rounds of ammunition replacing the twin Mk 12 20-mm cannon with their 680 rounds. Thirty-six were later converted to TA-7Cs. Forty-nine TA-7Cs are being rebuilt with TF41 engines, new ejection seats and automatic manoeuvring flaps.

Six of these will be the aircraft reassigned to VAQ-34 for electronic warfare duties and redesignated **EA-7L** during March 1983. The final US Navy Corsair variant was the **A-7E**, basically an A-7C with the TF41-A-2 turbofan, a development of the Rolls-Royce Spey. These modifications were similar to those specified by the US Air Force for its A-7s. Five hundred and thirty-five were built.

A Vought EA-7L Corsair II ECM aircraft of VAQ-34.

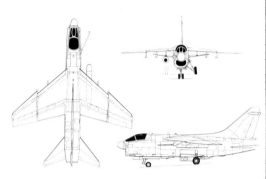

Vought A-7E Corsair II

Although many Corsair units have already re-equipped with the more versatile and more modern McDonnell Douglas F-18 Hornet, the A-7E will be in service for some years.

Many surviving US Navy A-7E Corsair IIs have been re-equipped with FLIR pods for all-weather attack duties, and some will remain in front line service until the end of the decade.

Specification: Vought A-7E Corsair II
Origin: USA
Type: single-seat tactical fighter
Powerplant: one 6804-kg (15,000-lb) thrust Allison TF41-A-2 turbofan engine
Performance: maximum speed 600 kts (1112 km/h; 691 mph) at sea level; maximum speed at 5,000 ft (1525 m) with a 2722-kg (6,000 lb) bombload 561 kts (1040 km/h; 646 mph); service ceiling 51,000 ft (15545 m); ferry range on internal fuel 3669 km (2,280 miles)
Weights: empty 8676 kg (19,127 lb); maximum take-off 19051 kg (42,000 lb)
Dimensions: span 11.81 m (38 ft 9 in); length 14.06 m (46 ft 1.5 in) height 4.90 m (16 ft 0.75 in); wing area 34.84 m² (375.0 sq ft)
Armament: one M61A1 20-mm cannon with 1,000 rounds in the port lower fuselage, plus more than 6804 kg (15,000 lb) of stores on eight weapon stations.

Role	
Fighter	
Close support	
Counter-insurgency	
Tactical strike	
Strategic bomber	
Tactical reconnaissance	
Strategic reconnaissance	
Maritime patrol	
Anti-ship strike	
Anti-submarine warfare	
Search and rescue	
Assault transport	
Transport	
Liaison	
Trainer	
Inflight-refuelling tanker	
Specialized	
Performance	
All-weather capability	
Rough field capability	
STOL capability	
VTOL capability	
Airspeed 0-250 mph	
Airspeed 250 mph-Mach 1	
Airspeed Mach 1 plus	
Ceiling 0-20,000 ft	
Ceiling 20,000-40,000 ft	
Ceiling 40,000ft plus	
Range 0-1,000 miles	
Range 1,000-3,000 miles	
Range 3,000 miles plus	
Weapons	
Air-to-air missiles	
Air-to-surface missiles	
Cruise missiles	
Cannon	
Trainable guns	
Naval weapons	
Nuclear-capable	
Rockets	
'Smart' weapon kit	
Weapon load 0-4,000 lb	
Weapon load 4,000-15,000 lb	
Weapon load 15,000 lb plus	
Avionics	
Electronic Counter Measures	
Electronic Support Measures	
Search radar	
Fire control radar	
Look-down/shoot-down	
Terrain-following radar	
Forward-looking infra-red	
Laser	
Television	

Vought A-7D and K

United States

Although originally designed as a strike fighter for the US Navy, the Corsair soon began to attract interest from the US Air Force, who saw the aircraft as an ideal replacement for the F-100 Super Sabre and F-105 Thunderchief in the tactical strike role. Although attempts to write a common USN/USAF specification for a new attack aircraft failed, USAF interest in the A-7 Corsair was always strong, and grew steadily. A request to buy A-7s was included in the FY 1967 budget.

To meet USAF requirements a new variant, the **A-7D**, was developed. Although the first two **YA-7D** prototypes were initially powered by the standard TF-30-P-6 of the A-7B and A-7C, the other three prototypes, and all production USAF aircraft were powered by the Allison TF41-A-2 turbofan, developed from the Rolls-Royce Spey.

Other changes incorporated in the USAF aircraft included an updated and refined nav/attack system, a new head-up display, and new internal cannon armament. The twin Mk 12 20-mm cannon, with their 680 rounds of ammunition, were replaced by a single M61A1 Vulcan with 1,000 rounds. The pilot can select several different rates of fire between 4,000 to 6,000 rounds per minute.

The first YA-7D made its maiden flight on 6 April 1968, and the third TF41-A-2 powered YA-7D followed on 26 September. The first 16 A-7Ds were delivered with a US Navy style retractable inflight-refuelling probe, but later aircraft had a standard USAF refuelling receptacle on the fuselage spine. 459 A-7Ds

were built, one being converted to two-seat configuration to serve as the A-87K prototype.

Initial service deliveries were made in December 1969, to the 4525th Fighter Weapons Wing at Luke AFB, and the type was soon in service in South East Asia. By the mid-1970s the US Air Force was examining its requirements for a new attack aircraft optimized for dealing with the Soviet armoured threats. Tests were carried out with an A-7D armed with two podded underwing GAU-8/A 30 cannon, but this solution was rejected in favour of procurement of the Fairchild A-10A Thunderbolt II, which began to replace the A-7 in front line squadrons during the early 1980s.

The A-7D's career is far from over, however, since it continues to serve with the Nellis-based 4450th Tactical Training Group, and with 14 squadrons of the Air National Guard. The first ANG squadron re-equipped with the A-7 during October 1975, and a 15th unit may convert from the A-37.

All surviving A-7Ds were retro-fitted with Automatic Manoeuvring Flaps from 1977, these being fitted to the last two production aircraft 'on the line'. Thirty two-seat **A-7K**s were built, the last being delivered in September 1984. None served with the active duty air force. Forty-eight A-7Ds and six A-7Ks are currently being fitted with Low Altitude Night Attack (LANA) pods, containing a FLIR. The name Corsair II has never been formally adopted by the US Air Force.

Specification: Vought A-7D
Origin: USA
Type: single-seat tactical fighter
Powerplant: one 6577 kg (14,500-lb) Allison T41-A-1 non afterburning turbofan engine
Performance: maximum speed 600 kts (1112 km/h; 691 mph) at sea level; maximum speed at 5,000 ft (1525 m) with a 2722-kg (6,000 lb) bombload 561 kts (1040 km/h; 646 mph); service ceiling 51,000 ft (15545 m); ferry range on internal fuel 3669 km (2,280 miles)
Weights: empty 8676 kg (19,127 lb); maximum take-off 19051 kg (42,000 lb)
Dimensions: span 11.81 m (38 ft 9 in); length 14.06 m (46 ft 1.5 in) height 4.90 m (16 ft 0.75 in); wing area 34.84 m² (375.0 sq ft)
Armament: one M61A1 20-mm Vulcan cannon with 1,000 rounds in the port lower fuselage, plus more than 6804 kg (15,000 lb) of stores on eight weapons stations.

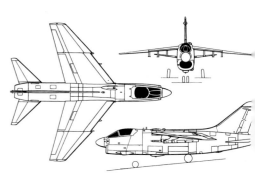

An A-7K of the 125th Tactical Fighter Squadron, Oklahoma Air National Guard.

Vought A-7D

This A-7D of the 175th TFS, South Dakota Air National Guard, was pictured during the 'Coronet Buffalo' deployment to RAF Waddington, from Joe Foss Field, Sioux Falls.

This A-7K wears the 'HA' tailcode and yellow fin stripe of the 174th TFS, Idaho Air National Guard, based at Sioux City Municipal Airport. A small bat emblem decorates the fin stripe.